THE GREAT AMERICAN COOKIE COOKBOOK

Publications International, Ltd.

Favorite Brand Name Recipes at www.fbnr.com

Pictured on the front cover *(clockwise from top right):* Irresistible Peanut Butter Cookie *(page 32)*, Peanut Butter Jumbo *(page 36)*, Viennese Hazelnut Butter Thin *(page 394)*, Dreamy Chocolate Chip Cookie *(page 310)* and Linzer Sandwich Cookie *(page 232)*.

Pictured on the back cover *(clockwise from top right):* Orange Pecan Gem *(page 34)*, Lemon Cookie *(page 80)*, Marshmallow Sandwich Cookie *(page 324)*, Swiss Mocha Treat *(page 332)* and Double-Dipped Chocolate Peanut Butter Cookie *(page 503)*.

ISBN: 0-7853-5086-1

Library of Congress Control Number: 2001087267

Manufactured in China.

8 7 6 5 4 3 2 1

Microwave Cooking: Microwave ovens vary in wattage. Use the cooking times as guidelines and check for doneness before adding more time.

Preparation/Cooking Times: Preparation times are based on the approximate amount of time required to assemble the recipe before cooking, baking, chilling or serving. These times include preparation steps such as measuring, chopping and mixing. The fact that some preparations and cooking can be done simultaneously is taken into account. Preparation of optional ingredients and serving suggestions is not included.

CONTENTS

All About Cookies	4
Drop by the Cookie Jar	10
Ship-Shape Cookies	58
Wonderful Bar Cookies	100
Brownies & Blondies Galore	142
Slice 'n' Bake Beauties	188
Charming Cookie Cutouts	224
No-Bake Sensations	268
Outrageous Chocolate	298
Wildly Delicious Fruit & Nuts	344
Around the World	384
Kooky Kiddie Cookies	420
Celebration Cookies	462
The Holiday Cookie Plate	506
Just the Basics	552
Acknowledgments	558
Index	559

ALL ABOUT COOKIES

YOU SAY KOEKJE—I SAY COOKIE

The word "cookie" comes from the Dutch word "koekje," meaning "little cake." The Dutch brought these little cakes to their first settlements in America, and the sweet treats have been popular ever since. With so many flavors, shapes and sizes to choose from, cookies have earned their place as America's favorite snack.

THE WAY THE COOKIE CRUMBLES

Cookies can be divided into five basic types: bar, drop, refrigerator, rolled and shaped. These types are determined by the consistency of the dough and how it is formed into cookies.

Bar Cookies: Bar cookies and brownies are some of the easiest cookies to make—simply mix the batter, spread it in the pan and bake. These cookies are also quick to prepare, since they bake all at once rather than in batches. In general, bar cookies are done baking when a toothpick inserted into the center comes out clean and dry.

Drop Cookies: These cookies are named for the way in which they are formed on the cookie sheet. The soft dough mounds when dropped from a spoon and then flattens slightly during baking. Drop cookies are done baking when their tops and edges are lightly browned, and a slight imprint remains after touching the surface.

Refrigerator Cookies: Refrigerator, or slice-and-bake doughs are perfect for making in advance. Tightly wrapped rolls of dough can be stored in the refrigerator for one week or frozen for six weeks. That way they're ready to be sliced and baked at a moment's notice. They are done baking when the edges are firm and the bottoms are lightly browned.

Rolled Cookies: Rolled, or cutout cookies are made from stiff doughs that are usually chilled, rolled out and then cut into fancy shapes with floured cookie cutters, a knife, or a pastry wheel. Rolled cookies are done baking when the edges are firm and the bottoms are lightly browned.

Shaped Cookies: Shaped cookies are made from dough that is easily formed into balls, logs or crescents with your hands. It can also be forced through a cookie press or pastry bag, or baked in cookie molds. These cookies are done baking when the edges are lightly browned.

GET BACK TO BASICS

Great cookies start with good baking habits. Keep the following basic techniques in mind when you're baking cookies.

- Read the entire recipe before beginning to make sure you have all the necessary ingredients, baking utensils and supplies.

- For the best results, use the ingredients called for in the recipe. Butter, margarine and shortening are not always interchangeable.

- Follow the recipe directions and baking times exactly. Check for doneness using the test given in the recipe. Most cookies bake quickly, so check them at the minimum baking time, then watch carefully to make sure they don't burn. It is generally better to slightly underbake, rather than to overbake, cookies.

- Remove butter, margarine and cream cheese from the refrigerator to soften, if necessary.

- Toast and chop nuts, peel and slice fruit, and melt chocolate before preparing the cookie dough.

- Measure all the ingredients accurately and assemble them in the order they are called for in the recipe.

- Adjust the oven racks and preheat the oven. Check the oven temperature for accuracy with an oven thermometer.

- Space unbaked cookies about 2 inches apart on the cookie sheets to allow for spreading, unless the recipe directs otherwise.

MEASURE FOR MEASURE

Dry Ingredients: Always use standardized measuring spoons and cups. Fill the appropriate measuring spoon or cup to overflowing and level it off with a metal spatula or the flat edge of a knife. When measuring flour, lightly spoon it into the measuring cup and then level it off. Do not tap or bang the measuring cup, since this will pack the flour. If a recipe calls for "sifted flour," sift the flour before it is measured. If a recipe calls for "flour, sifted," measure the flour first, and then sift.

Liquid Ingredients: Use a standardized glass or plastic measuring cup with a pouring spout and calibrations marked on the side. Place the cup on a flat surface, fill to the desired mark, and check the measurement at eye level. To make sure sticky liquids such as honey and molasses won't cling to the measuring cup, grease the cup or spray it with nonstick cooking spray first.

COOKIE DOUGH FACTS

- Cookies that are uniform in size and shape will finish baking at the same time. To easily shape drop cookies into a uniform size, use an ice cream scoop with a release bar. The bar usually has a number on it indicating the number of scoops that can be made from one quart of ice cream. The handiest size for cookies is a #50 or #40 scoop. These will make 2- or 3-inch cookies, respectively.

- Always shape dough for refrigerator cookies into rolls before chilling. Shaping is easier if you first place the dough on a piece of waxed paper or plastic wrap. If desired, you can gently press chopped nuts, flaked coconut or colored sugar into the rolls. Before chilling, wrap the rolls securely in plastic wrap so that air cannot penetrate to the dough and cause it to dry out.

- Use gentle pressure and a back-and-forth sawing motion when slicing refrigerator cookie dough, so that the cookies will have a nice round shape. Rotating the roll while slicing also prevents one side from getting flat.

- For easier handling, chill cookie dough for cutouts before rolling. Remove only enough dough from the refrigerator to work with at one time. Save any trimmings and reroll them all at once to prevent the dough from becoming tough.

- Unbaked cookie dough can be refrigerated for up to two weeks or frozen for up to six weeks. Rolls of dough should be wrapped tightly in plastic wrap; other doughs should be stored in airtight containers. Label the dough with baking information for convenience.

COOKIE SHEET SAVVY

Not all cookie sheets are created equal. Here are a few guidelines for using cookie sheets and pans.

- The best cookie sheets to use are those with little or no sides. They allow the heat to circulate easily during baking and promote even browning.

- Use shiny cookie sheets for the best cookie baking results. Dark cookie sheets will cause the bottoms of the cookies to be dark.

- When making bar cookies or brownies, use the pan size specified in the recipe, and prepare the pans according to the recipe directions.

- Grease the cookie sheets only if directed to do so in the recipe. When a recipe does call for greasing, use shortening or nonstick cooking spray for best results.

- Lining cookie sheets with parchment paper is an alternative to greasing. It eliminates cleanup and allows the cookies to bake more evenly and cool right on the paper, instead of on wire racks.

- For even baking and browning, place only one cookie sheet at a time in the center of the oven. If the heat distribution in your oven is uneven, turn the cookie sheet halfway through the baking time. Also, if you do use more than one sheet at a time, rotate the cookie sheets from top to bottom halfway through the baking time.

- When reusing the same cookie sheets for several batches of cookies, allow them to cool before placing more dough on them. Dough will soften and begin to spread on a hot sheet.

DECORATING MAGIC

Sometimes all it takes is that special finishing touch to make treats go from drab to dazzling. Here are some simple tips for dressing up your cookies.

Chocolate

Nothing makes a cookie more irresistible than being partially or completely covered in chocolate! Simply dip cookies in melted chocolate (milk, semisweet, white, or some of each), or use a spoon or fork to drizzle it over the cookies. Then place them on waxed paper until the chocolate is set. Or, melt the chocolate in a small, resealable, plastic food storage bag; cut off a very tiny corner of the bag, and squeeze out the chocolate in patterns or designs over the cookies.

Melting Chocolate

Make sure the utensils you use for melting chocolate are completely dry. Moisture, whether from utensils or a drop of water, can make the chocolate become stiff and grainy, or "seize." If this does happen, add ½ teaspoon vegetable shortening (not butter) for each ounce of chocolate, and stir until smooth. Chocolate scorches easily and cannot be used once it is scorched. Follow one of these three methods for successful melting.

Double Boiler: This is the safest method because it prevents scorching. Place the chocolate in the top of a double boiler or in a bowl over hot, not boiling, water; stir until smooth. (Make sure the water remains just below a simmer and is one inch below the top pan.) Make sure no steam or water gets into the chocolate.

Direct Heat: Place the chocolate in a heavy saucepan and melt over very low heat, stirring constantly. Remove the chocolate from the heat as soon as it is melted. Be sure to watch the chocolate carefully, since it is easily scorched with this method.

Microwave Oven: Place 4 to 6 unwrapped 1-ounce squares of chocolate or 1 cup of chocolate chips in a small microwavable bowl. Microwave at HIGH 1 to 1½ minutes. Stir after 1 minute, and then at 30-second intervals after the first minute. Be sure to stir microwaved chocolate, since it retains its original shape even when melted.

Glazes

Plain cookies get a boost of sweetness with a powdered sugar glaze. Use the glaze white, or tint it with food coloring to fit the occasion.

Simply combine 1 cup sifted powdered sugar and 5 teaspoons milk in a small bowl. Add ½ teaspoon vanilla extract or other flavoring, if desired. Stir until smooth and tint with food coloring, if desired. If the glaze is too thin, add additional powdered sugar; if it is too thick, add additional milk, ½ teaspoon at a time.

Nuts & Coconut

Whole, halved, sliced or chopped nuts can add extra flavor and crunch to any type of cookie. Toasted and tinted coconut can add color and flavor to otherwise plain treats.

Toasting Nuts & Coconut

To toast, spread nuts or coconut in a thin layer on an ungreased cookie sheet. Bake in a preheated 325°F oven 7 to 10 minutes or until golden, stirring occasionally to promote even browning and prevent burning. Toasted nuts will darken and become crisper as they cool. Allow nuts and coconut to cool before using.

Tinting Coconut

Tinted coconut is a festive decoration for cookies. To tint coconut, dilute a few drops of liquid food coloring with ½ teaspoon milk or water in a small bowl. Add 1 to 1⅓ cups flaked coconut and toss with a fork until coconut is evenly tinted.

Sugars, Sprinkles & Candies

The possibilities are endless—and easy! Simply sprinkle cookies with coarse sugar, colored sugars or sprinkles before baking. Or, after baking, cookies can be dusted with powdered sugar, or frosted and then topped with colored sugars or sprinkles.

STORING AND FREEZING

- Store soft cookies and crisp cookies separately at room temperature to prevent changes in texture and flavor.
- Keep soft cookies in airtight containers. If they begin to dry out, add a piece of apple or bread to the container to help the cookies retain moisture. Remember to remove the piece of apple or bread after two to three days.
- Store crisp cookies in containers with loose-fitting lids to prevent moisture build-up. If they become soggy, heat undecorated cookies in a 300°F oven for 3 to 5 minutes to restore crispness.
- Store cookies with sticky glazes, fragile decorations and icings in single layers between sheets of waxed paper.
- Bar cookies and brownies can be stored in their baking pans and covered with aluminum foil or plastic wrap when cool.
- As a rule, crisp cookies freeze better than soft, moist cookies. Rich, buttery bar cookies and brownies are an exception to this rule, since they freeze extremely well.
- Freeze baked cookies in airtight containers or freezer bags for up to six months.
- Thaw cookies and brownies unwrapped, at room temperature.
- Meringue-based cookies do *not* freeze well, and chocolate-dipped cookies will discolor if frozen.

THE PERFECT COOKIE PACKAGE

Homemade cookies are a thoughtful gift for any occasion. And simple cookies can be made extraordinary when tucked into unique packages and lavished with decorative accessories.

Baskets & Boxes: These versatile hold-alls are available in a wide variety of materials and sizes. Large, sturdy ones are well-suited for packing entire gift themes.

Gift Bags: These handy totes come in many sizes and colors. Pack individual cookies in smaller bags; pack goodie-filled canisters or tins in larger bags.

Tins: Metal containers with tight-fitting lids are perfect for cookies. They also hold up well when sent through the mail.

Cellophane: Cellophane is an indispensable material for hard-to-wrap gifts such as plates of cookies. Gather the ends and secure them with a multitude of pretty ribbon.

Decorative Papers: Papers come in a variety of colors and finishes, and many can be enhanced with rubber stamps.

Gift Tags: Assorted metal and paper tags come in handy when making personalized notes for your gifts. They also make great labels for storing tips and serving suggestions, or even for the recipe itself.

Raffia: Use raffia as ribbon to tie boxes and tins with rustic bows.

Ribbons, Strings and Satin Cords: Thick, colorful ribbons, metallic strings and thin, shiny cords add a touch of glamour to any kind of wrapping paper.

Rubber Stamps: Stamps with holiday or food themes, when paired with colorful inks, are perfect for decorating plain papers, gift tags and personalized note and recipe cards.

SPECIAL DELIVERY

When you can't be with the ones you love, bake them some cookies! Keep the following tips in mind when shipping those special treats.

- Prepare soft, moist cookies that can handle jostling, rather than crisp cookies that may crumble.
- Brownies and bar cookies are generally sturdy, but it is best not to ship any with moist fillings and frostings.
- Wrap each type of cookie separately to retain flavors and textures.

- Bar cookies should be packed in layers the size of the container, or they can be sent in a covered foil pan, as long as the pan is well-cushioned inside the shipping box.
- Place wrapped cookies as tightly as possible in snug rows inside a sturdy shipping box or container.
- Fill the bottom of the shipping container with an even layer of packing material. Do not use popped popcorn or puffed cereal, as they may attract insects. Place crumpled waxed paper, newspaper or paper toweling in between layers of wrapped cookies. Fill any crevices with packing material, and add a final layer at the top of the box.
- Ship the container to arrive as soon as possible.

Drop by the
COOKIE JAR

Monster Cookies

1¼ cups firmly packed light brown sugar
  1 cup granulated sugar
  ¾ Butter Flavor* CRISCO® Stick or ¾ cup Butter Flavor
     CRISCO® all-vegetable shortening
  3 eggs
1½ cups crunchy peanut butter
  1 tablespoon light corn syrup
  2 teaspoons baking soda
  1 teaspoon pure vanilla extract
4½ cups quick oats, uncooked
  1 cup (6-ounce package) semi-sweet chocolate chips

*Butter Flavor Crisco is artificially flavored.

1. Heat oven to 350°F. Place sheets of foil on countertop for cooling cookies.

2. Combine brown sugar, granulated sugar and ¾ cup shortening in large bowl. Beat at medium speed of electric mixer until well blended. Beat in eggs. Beat in peanut butter, corn syrup, baking soda and vanilla. Stir in oats and chocolate chips with spoon.

3. Fill ice cream scoop that holds ¼ cup with dough (or use ¼-cup measure). Level with knife. (Or form dough into 2-inch balls.) Drop 3 inches apart onto ungreased baking sheet.

4. Bake at 350°F for 11 to 13 minutes or until just beginning to brown. *Do not overbake.* Cool on baking sheet for 2 minutes. Remove cookies to foil to cool completely.

Makes about 2½ dozen cookies

Monster Cookies

Oatmeal Cookies

1 cup all-purpose flour
1 teaspoon baking powder
½ teaspoon baking soda
½ teaspoon salt
¼ cup MOTT'S® Cinnamon Apple
   Sauce
2 tablespoons margarine
½ cup granulated sugar
½ cup firmly packed light brown sugar
1 egg
1 teaspoon vanilla extract
1⅓ cups uncooked rolled oats
½ cup raisins (optional)

1. Preheat oven to 375°F. Spray cookie sheet with nonstick cooking spray.

2. In small bowl, combine flour, baking powder, baking soda and salt.

3. In large bowl, place apple sauce. Cut in margarine with pastry blender or fork until margarine breaks into pea-sized pieces. Add granulated sugar, brown sugar, egg and vanilla; stir until well blended.

4. Add flour mixture to apple sauce mixture; stir until well blended. Fold in oats and raisins, if desired.

5. Drop rounded teaspoonfuls of dough 2 inches apart onto prepared cookie sheet.

6. Bake 10 to 12 minutes or until lightly browned. Cool 5 minutes on cookie sheet. Remove to wire rack; cool completely.

Makes 3 dozen cookies

Gingersnaps

2½ cups all-purpose flour
1½ teaspoons ground ginger
1 teaspoon baking soda
1 teaspoon ground allspice
½ teaspoon salt
1½ cups sugar
2 tablespoons margarine, softened
½ cup MOTT'S® Apple Sauce
¼ cup GRANDMA'S® Molasses

1. Preheat oven to 375°F. Spray cookie sheet with nonstick cooking spray.

2. In medium bowl, sift together flour, ginger, baking soda, allspice and salt.

3. In large bowl, beat sugar and margarine with electric mixer at medium speed until blended. Whisk in apple sauce and molasses.

4. Add flour mixture to apple sauce mixture; stir until well blended.

5. Drop rounded tablespoonfuls of dough 1 inch apart onto prepared cookie sheet. Flatten each slightly with moistened fingertips.

6. Bake 12 to 15 minutes or until firm. Cool completely on wire rack.

Makes 3 dozen cookies

Top to bottom: Oatmeal Cookies and Gingersnaps

Brian's Buffalo Cookies

1 Butter Flavor* CRISCO® Stick or
   1 cup Butter Flavor CRISCO®
   all-vegetable shortening, melted,
   plus additional for greasing
1 cup granulated sugar
1 cup firmly packed brown sugar
2 tablespoons milk
1 teaspoon vanilla
2 eggs
2 cups all-purpose flour
1 teaspoon baking powder
1 teaspoon baking soda
½ teaspoon salt
1 cup rolled oats (quick or
   old-fashioned), uncooked
1 cup corn flakes, crushed to about
   ½ cup
1 cup semi-sweet chocolate chips
½ cup chopped pecans
½ cup flake coconut

Butter Flavor Crisco is artificially flavored.

1. Heat oven to 350°F. Grease baking sheets with shortening. Place sheets of foil on countertop for cooling cookies.

2. Combine 1 cup shortening, granulated sugar, brown sugar, milk and vanilla in large bowl. Beat at low speed of electric mixer until well blended. Add eggs; beat at medium speed until well blended.

3. Combine flour, baking powder, baking soda and salt. Add gradually to shortening mixture at low speed. Stir in oats, corn flakes, chocolate chips, nuts and coconut.

Fill ice cream scoop that holds ¼ cup with dough (or use ¼ cup measuring cup). Level with knife. Drop 3 inches apart onto prepared baking sheets.

4. Bake at 350°F for 13 to 15 minutes or until lightly browned around edges but still slightly soft in center. *Do not overbake.* Cool 3 minutes on baking sheets before removing to foil with wide, thin pancake turner to cool completely.

Makes 2 to 2½ dozen cookies

Peanut Chip Cookies

1½ cups packed dark brown sugar
   1 cup PETER PAN® Crunchy Peanut
     Butter
 ¾ cup butter
 ¾ cup granulated sugar
 ¼ cup water
 1 egg
1¼ teaspoons vanilla extract
  2 cups rolled oats
1½ cups all-purpose flour
1½ teaspoons baking powder
 ¼ teaspoon salt
 1 cup semi-sweet chocolate chips

In large mixer bowl, beat *first* 4 ingredients until creamy and well blended. Beat in water, egg and vanilla. In medium bowl, mix *remaining* ingredients. Stir into peanut butter mixture until well blended. Drop by heaping teaspoonfuls onto greased baking sheets. Bake at 350°F 12 to 15 minutes or until lightly browned around edges. Cool on wire racks and store in an airtight container.

Makes 4 dozen cookies

Brian's Buffalo Cookies

Carrot Oatmeal Cookies

COOKIES
  1 cup firmly packed light brown sugar
  ¾ Butter Flavor* CRISCO® Stick or
     ¾ cup Butter Flavor CRISCO®
     all-vegetable shortening, melted,
     plus additional for greasing
  ½ cup granulated sugar
  ⅓ cup molasses
  1 egg
  1 teaspoon ground cinnamon
  1 cup cooked mashed carrots, cooled
  2 cups all-purpose flour
  2 cups oats (quick or old-fashioned,
     uncooked)
  1 teaspoon baking soda
  ½ cup chopped walnuts
  ½ cup raisins

DRIZZLE (OPTIONAL)
  ¼ to ½ container cream cheese cake
     frosting

*Butter Flavor Crisco is artificially flavored.

1. Heat oven to 350°F. Grease baking sheet with shortening. Place sheets of foil on countertop for cooling cookies.

2. For cookies, combine brown sugar, ¾ cup shortening, granulated sugar, molasses, egg and cinnamon in large bowl. Beat at medium speed of electric mixer until well blended. Beat in carrots.

3. Combine flour, oats and baking soda. Add gradually to creamed mixture at low speed. Beat until well blended. Stir in nuts and raisins with spoon. Drop by tablespoonfuls 2 inches apart onto prepared baking sheet.

4. Bake at 350°F for 11 to 13 minutes or until light brown around edges and center is just set. *Do not overbake.* Cool 2 minutes on baking sheet. Remove cookies to foil to cool completely.

5. For drizzle (if used), place frosting in heavy resealable plastic sandwich bag. Cut tiny tip off corner of bag. Squeeze out to drizzle over cookies.

         Makes about 4 dozen cookies

HELPFUL HINT

When measuring molasses, lightly spray the measuring cup with nonstick cooking spray first. That way all the molasses will go into your dough, instead of clinging to the inside of the cup.

Hawaiian Drops

¾ cup (1½ sticks) butter or margarine, softened
¾ cup granulated sugar
¾ cup firmly packed light brown sugar
2 large eggs
1 teaspoon vanilla extract
2 cups quick-cooking or old-fashioned oats, uncooked
1½ cups all-purpose flour
1 teaspoon baking powder
1 teaspoon baking soda
1¾ cups "M&M's"® Chocolate Mini Baking Bits
1 cup shredded coconut
1 cup coarsely chopped macadamia nuts

Preheat oven to 350°F. Cream butter and sugars until light and fluffy; beat in eggs and vanilla. Combine oats, flour, baking powder and baking soda; blend into creamed mixture. Stir in remaining ingredients. Drop by rounded tablespoonfuls onto greased cookie sheets. Bake 13 to 15 minutes or until edges are golden brown. Cool 1 minute on cookie sheets; cool completely on wire racks. Store in tightly covered container.

Makes about 6 dozen cookies

Hawaiian Drops

Glazed Oatmeal Raisin Coffee Cookies

COOKIES

1¼ Butter Flavor* CRISCO® Stick or
   1¼ cups Butter Flavor CRISCO®
   all-vegetable shortening
¾ cup firmly packed light brown sugar
½ cup granulated sugar
1 egg
¼ cup coffee flavor liqueur
1 teaspoon pure vanilla extract
1¾ cups all-purpose flour
1½ teaspoons ground cinnamon
1¼ teaspoons baking soda
½ teaspoon ground nutmeg
3 cups oats (quick or old-fashioned,
   uncooked)
1½ cups raisins
¾ cup sliced almonds

DRIZZLE

1 cup confectioners' sugar
1 tablespoon coffee flavor liqueur
1 teaspoon cold coffee

Butter Flavor Crisco is artificially flavored.

1. Heat oven to 375°F. Place sheets of foil on countertop for cooling cookies.

2. For cookies, combine 1¼ cups shortening, brown sugar and granulated sugar in large bowl. Beat at medium speed of electric mixer until well blended. Beat in egg, ¼ cup liqueur and vanilla.

3. Combine flour, cinnamon, baking soda and nutmeg. Add gradually to creamed mixture at low speed. Stir in oats, raisins

and nuts. Drop by tablespoonfuls 2 inches apart onto ungreased baking sheet.

4. Bake at 375°F for 9 to 10 minutes. *Do not overbake.* Cool 2 minutes on baking sheet. Remove cookies to foil to cool completely.

5. For drizzle, combine confectioners' sugar, 1 tablespoon liqueur and coffee in medium bowl. Add additional liquid if needed to make thick drizzle. Stir until smooth. Drizzle over cooled cookies.

Makes about 4 dozen cookies

Raisin Spice Drops

¾ cup (1½ sticks) margarine, softened
⅔ cup granulated sugar
⅔ cup firmly packed brown sugar
2 eggs
1 teaspoon vanilla
2½ cups QUAKER® Oats (quick or old
   fashioned, uncooked)
1¼ cups all-purpose flour
1 teaspoon ground cinnamon
½ teaspoon baking soda
½ teaspoon salt (optional)
¼ teaspoon ground nutmeg
⅔ cup raisins
½ cup chopped nuts

Preheat oven to 350°F. In large bowl, beat margarine and sugars until fluffy. Blend in eggs and vanilla. Add remaining ingredients; mix well. Drop dough by teaspoonfuls onto ungreased cookie sheet. Bake 8 to 10 minutes or until light golden brown. Cool on wire rack. Store tightly covered.

Makes about 4½ dozen cookies

Glazed Oatmeal Raisin Coffee Cookies

Oatmeal Coconut Chocolate Chip Cookies

bef icing 2.33
.15
2.18

Made 63

COOKIES

1 Butter Flavor* CRISCO® Stick or
    1 cup Butter Flavor CRISCO®
    all-vegetable shortening plus
    additional for greasing *56*
1 cup granulated sugar *15*
½ cup firmly packed light brown sugar *7*
2 eggs *4*
2 teaspoons pure vanilla extract
2 cups all-purpose flour *18*
1 teaspoon salt
1 teaspoon baking soda
⅔ cup quick oats, uncooked *3*
½ cup flake coconut *12* *tbsp=1.5*
1 cup semi-sweet chocolate chips *32*
147

CHOCOLATE COATING

1 cup semi-sweet chocolate chips *32*
2 teaspoons Butter Flavor CRISCO®
    Stick or 2 teaspoons Butter Flavor *175*
    CRISCO® all-vegetable shortening
+ Set

*Butter Flavor Crisco is artificially flavored.

1. Heat oven to 375°F. Grease baking sheet with shortening. Place sheets of foil on countertop for cooling cookies.

2. For cookies, combine 1 cup shortening, granulated sugar, brown sugar, eggs and vanilla in large bowl. Beat at medium speed of electric mixer until well blended.

3. Combine flour, salt and baking soda. Add gradually to creamed mixture at low speed.

Beat until well blended. Stir in oats, coconut and 1 cup chocolate chips with spoon. Drop by teaspoonfuls 2 inches apart onto prepared baking sheet.

4. Bake at 375°F for 10 to 12 minutes or until light brown. *Do not overbake.* Cool 2 minutes on baking sheet. Remove cookies to foil to cool completely.

5. For chocolate coating, melt 1 cup chocolate chips and 2 teaspoons shortening (see Melting/Drizzling procedure).

6. Spread thin coating of melted chocolate on back of each cookie. Place upside down on waxed paper to allow coating to harden.

Makes about 6 dozen cookies

63 cookies

Melting/Drizzling Procedure: For melting or drizzling, choose one of these easy methods. Start with chips and Butter Flavor* Crisco® all-vegetable shortening (if called for), then: place in small microwave-safe measuring cup or bowl. Microwave at 50% (MEDIUM). Stir after 1 minute. Repeat until smooth. Drizzle from tip of spoon. **OR,** place in heavy resealable plastic sandwich bag. Seal. Microwave at 50% (MEDIUM). Check every minute until melted. Knead bag until smooth. Cut tiny tip off corner of bag. Squeeze out to drizzle. **OR,** place in small saucepan. Melt on range top on very low heat. Stir until smooth. Drizzle from tip of spoon.

Oatmeal Coconut Chocolate Chip Cookies

Prized Peanut Butter Crunch Cookie

1 Butter Flavor* CRISCO® Stick or
   1 cup Butter Flavor CRISCO®
   all-vegetable shortening
2 cups firmly packed brown sugar
1 cup extra crunchy peanut butter
4 egg whites, slightly beaten
1 teaspoon vanilla
2 cups all-purpose flour
1 teaspoon baking soda
½ teaspoon baking powder
2 cups crisp rice cereal
1½ cups chopped peanuts
   1 cup quick oats (not instant or
     old-fashioned)
   1 cup flake coconut

Butter Flavor Crisco is artificially flavored.

1. Heat oven to 350°F. Place sheets of foil on countertop for cooling cookies.

2. Combine 1 cup shortening, sugar and peanut butter in large bowl. Beat at medium speed of electric mixer until blended. Beat in egg whites and vanilla.

3. Combine flour, baking soda and baking powder. Mix into creamed mixture at low speed until just blended. Stir in, one at a time, rice cereal, nuts, oats and coconut with spoon. Drop rounded tablespoonfuls of dough 2 inches apart onto ungreased baking sheet.

4. Bake at 350°F, one baking sheet at a time, for 8 to 10 minutes, or until set. *Do not overbake.* Remove cookies to foil to cool.

Makes about 4 dozen cookies

Sunflower Cookies

1 cup sunflower margarine
1 cup granulated sugar
1 cup packed brown sugar
2 eggs
1 teaspoon vanilla
2 cups all-purpose flour
1 teaspoon baking soda
½ teaspoon baking powder
¼ teaspoon salt
2 cups old-fashioned or quick-cooking
   oatmeal
1 cup flaked coconut
1 cup sunflower seeds (roasted, salted
   or unsalted)

In medium bowl, combine sunflower margarine, granulated sugar and brown sugar; beat until well blended. Add eggs and vanilla. Stir together flour, baking soda, baking powder and salt; add to margarine mixture. Stir in oatmeal, coconut and sunflower seeds. Drop by rounded tablespoons onto *ungreased* baking sheet. Bake at 350°F 8 to 10 minutes or until cookies are golden brown around edges. Remove from baking sheets. Cool.

Makes about 4 dozen cookies

Variation: Substitute chocolate chips or raisins for the coconut.

Favorite recipe from **National Sunflower Association**

Prized Peanut Butter Crunch Cookies

The First Family's Chocolate Chip Oatmeal Cookies

½ cup packed light brown sugar
⅓ cup Dried Plum Purée (recipe follows) or prepared prune butter or 1 jar (2½ ounces) first-stage baby food dried plums
¼ cup granulated sugar
2 tablespoons vegetable shortening
1 egg white
1 teaspoon vanilla
¾ cup all-purpose flour
½ teaspoon salt
½ teaspoon baking soda
1 cup rolled oats
⅔ cup semisweet chocolate chips

Preheat oven to 375°F. Coat baking sheets with vegetable cooking spray. In bowl, beat brown sugar, dried plum purée, granulated sugar, shortening, egg white and vanilla at high speed 1 minute. Mix flour, salt and baking soda; stir into sugar mixture. Stir in rolled oats and chocolate chips. (Batter will be stiff.) Drop tablespoonfuls of dough 2 inches apart onto prepared baking sheets. Bake 10 minutes or until golden brown. Let stand on baking sheets 1 minute; remove to wire racks to cool.

Makes 2 dozen cookies

Dried Plum Purée: Mix 1⅓ cups (8 ounces) pitted dried plums and 6 tablespoons hot water in container of food processor. Pulse on and off until smooth. Store leftovers in covered container in refrigerator for up to 2 months.

Favorite recipe from **California Dried Plum Board**

Butterscotch Walnut Crisps

2 cups (12-ounce package) NESTLÉ® TOLL HOUSE® Butterscotch Flavored Morsels, divided
¾ cup (1½ sticks) butter
¾ cup sugar
1 egg
2 cups quick oats, uncooked
1 cup all-purpose flour
1 teaspoon baking soda
¼ teaspoon salt
1 cup chopped walnuts

PREHEAT oven to 350°F. In medium saucepan, combine 1 cup Nestlé® Toll House® Butterscotch Flavored Morsels and butter. Cook over low heat until morsels melt and mixture is smooth. Remove from heat; cool 5 minutes. Transfer to large mixer bowl. Add sugar and egg; beat until creamy. Gradually add oats, flour, baking soda and salt. Stir in remaining Nestlé® Toll House® Butterscotch Flavored Morsels and walnuts. Drop by slightly rounded measuring tablespoonfuls onto ungreased cookie sheets. Bake 10 to 12 minutes, until edges are golden brown. Cool on wire racks.

Makes about 3½ dozen cookies

Oatmeal Raisin Cookies

¼ cup (4 tablespoons) margarine, softened
3 tablespoons granulated sugar *or* 1¼ teaspoons EQUAL® Measure (5 packets) *or* 2 tablespoons fructose
¼ cup egg substitute *or* 2 egg whites
¾ cup unsweetened applesauce
¼ cup frozen unsweetened apple juice concentrate, thawed
1 teaspoon vanilla
1 cup all-purpose flour
1 teaspoon baking soda
½ teaspoon ground cinnamon
¼ teaspoon salt (optional)
1½ cups QUAKER® Oats (quick or old fashioned, uncooked)
⅓ cup raisins, chopped

Heat oven to 350°F. Lightly spray large cookie sheet with vegetable oil cooking spray. Beat together margarine and sugar until creamy. Beat in egg substitute. Add applesauce, apple juice concentrate and vanilla; beat well. Blend in combined flour, baking soda, cinnamon and salt. Stir in oats and chopped raisins. Drop by rounded teaspoonfuls onto prepared cookie sheet. Bake 15 to 17 minutes or until cookies are firm to the touch and lightly browned. Cool 1 minute on cookie sheet; remove to wire rack. Cool completely. Store in airtight container.   *Makes about 3 dozen cookies*

Fudgy Peanut Butter Jiffy Cookies

2 cups granulated sugar
½ cup evaporated milk
½ cup (1 stick) margarine or butter
¼ cup unsweetened cocoa powder
2½ cups QUAKER® Oats (quick or old fashioned, uncooked)
½ cup peanut butter
½ cup raisins or chopped dates
2 teaspoons vanilla

In large saucepan, combine sugar, milk, margarine and cocoa. Bring to a boil over medium heat, stirring frequently. Continue boiling 3 minutes. Remove from heat. Stir in oats, peanut butter, raisins and vanilla; mix well. Quickly drop by tablespoonfuls onto waxed paper or greased cookie sheet. Let stand until set. Store tightly covered at room temperature.

Makes about 3 dozen cookies

HELPFUL HINT

Before chopping raisins, separate them if they are clumped together, and then put them in the freezer for a few minutes until they are frozen. That way they will be easier to chop.

Double Lemon Delights

2¼ cups all-purpose flour
½ teaspoon baking powder
½ teaspoon salt
1 cup butter, softened
¾ cup granulated sugar
1 egg
2 tablespoons grated lemon peel, divided
1 teaspoon vanilla
  Additional sugar
1 cup powdered sugar
4 to 5 teaspoons lemon juice

1. Preheat oven to 375°F.

2. Combine flour, baking powder and salt in small bowl; set aside. Beat butter and granulated sugar in large bowl of electric mixer on medium speed until light and fluffy. Beat in egg, 1 tablespoon lemon peel and vanilla until well blended. Beat in flour mixture on low speed until blended.

3. Drop dough by level ¼ cupfuls onto ungreased cookie sheets, spacing 3 inches apart. Flatten dough until 3 inches in diameter with bottom of glass that has been dipped in additional sugar.

4. Bake 12 to 14 minutes or until cookies are just set and edges are golden brown. Cool on cookie sheets 2 minutes; transfer to wire racks. Cool completely.

5. Combine powdered sugar, lemon juice and remaining 1 tablespoon lemon peel in small bowl; drizzle mixture over cookies. Let stand until icing is set.
Makes about 1 dozen (4-inch) cookies

Ginger Snap Oats

¾ Butter Flavor* CRISCO® Stick or ¾ cup Butter Flavor CRISCO® all-vegetable shortening plus additional for greasing
1 cup packed brown sugar
½ cup granulated sugar
½ cup molasses
2 teaspoons vinegar
2 eggs
1¼ cups all-purpose flour
1 tablespoon ground ginger
1½ teaspoons baking soda
½ teaspoon ground cinnamon
¼ teaspoon ground cloves
2¾ cups quick oats (not instant or old-fashioned), uncooked
1½ cups raisins

Butter Flavor Crisco is artificially flavored.

1. Heat oven to 350°F. Grease baking sheets with shortening. Place sheets of foil on countertop for cooling cookies.

2. Combine ¾ cup shortening, brown sugar, granulated sugar, molasses, vinegar and eggs in large mixer bowl. Beat until well blended.

3. Combine flour, ginger, baking soda, cinnamon and cloves. Mix into shortening mixture until well blended. Stir in oats and raisins. Drop dough by rounded teaspoonfuls 2 inches apart onto prepared baking sheets.

4. Bake one baking sheet at a time for 11 to 14 minutes. *Do not overbake.* Cool 2 minutes on cookie sheets. Remove cookies to foil to cool. *Makes 5 dozen cookies*

Double Lemon Delights

Peanut Butter Surprise Cookies

24 miniature peanut butter cups
1 can (14 ounces) sweetened
   condensed milk (not evaporated
   milk)
¾ cup creamy peanut butter
¼ Butter Flavor* CRISCO® Stick or
   ¼ cup Butter Flavor CRISCO®
   all-vegetable shortening
1 egg
1 teaspoon pure vanilla extract
2 cups regular all-purpose baking mix

Butter Flavor Crisco is artificially flavored.

1. Remove wrappers from peanut butter cups. Cut candy into quarters.

2. Combine condensed milk, peanut butter, ¼ cup shortening, egg and vanilla in large bowl. Beat at medium speed of electric mixer until smooth. Add baking mix. Beat until well blended. Stir in candy pieces with spoon. Cover. Refrigerate 1 hour.

3. Heat oven to 350°F. Place sheets of foil on countertop for cooling cookies.

4. Drop dough by slightly rounded teaspoonfuls 2 inches apart onto ungreased baking sheet. Shape into balls with spoon.

5. Bake at 350°F for 7 to 9 minutes or until light brown around edges and center is just set. *Do not overbake.* Cool 2 minutes on baking sheet. Remove cookies to foil to cool completely.

Makes about 4 dozen cookies

Corn Flake Macaroons

4 egg whites
¼ teaspoon cream of tartar
1 teaspoon vanilla
1⅓ cups sugar
1 cup chopped pecans
1 cup shredded coconut
3 cups KELLOGG'S® CORN FLAKES®
   cereal

1. Preheat oven to 325°F. In large bowl, beat egg whites until foamy. Stir in cream of tartar and vanilla. Gradually add sugar, beating until stiff and glossy. Stir in pecans, coconut and Kellogg's Corn Flakes® cereal. Drop by rounded measuring tablespoonfuls onto cookie sheets sprayed with vegetable cooking spray.

2. Bake about 15 minutes or until lightly browned. Remove immediately from cookie sheets. Cool on wire racks.

Makes about 3 dozen cookies

Variation: Fold in ½ cup crushed peppermint candy with pecans and coconut.

Peanut Butter Surprise Cookies

Apricot Cream Cheese Drops

COOKIES

½ Butter Flavor* CRISCO® Stick or
½ cup Butter Flavor CRISCO®
all-vegetable shortening
1 package (3 ounces) cream cheese,
softened
1 tablespoon milk
½ cup apricot preserves
¼ cup firmly packed brown sugar
1¼ cups all-purpose flour
1½ teaspoons baking powder
1½ teaspoons cinnamon
¼ teaspoon salt
½ cup coarsely chopped pecans or
flake coconut

FROSTING

1 tablespoon Butter Flavor CRISCO®
Stick or 1 tablespoon Butter
Flavor CRISCO® all-vegetable
shortening
1 cup powdered sugar
¼ cup apricot preserves
Finely chopped pecans or flake
coconut (optional)

*Butter Flavor Crisco is artificially flavored.

1. Heat oven to 350°F. Grease baking sheet with shortening. Place sheets of foil on countertop for cooling cookies.

2. For cookies, combine ½ cup shortening, cream cheese and milk in large bowl. Beat at medium speed of electric mixer until well blended. Beat in ½ cup apricot preserves and brown sugar.

3. Combine flour, baking powder, cinnamon and salt. Mix into creamed mixture at low speed until just blended. Stir in nuts. Drop 2 level measuring tablespoonfuls of dough into a mound 3 inches apart onto ungreased baking sheet. Repeat for each cookie.

4. Bake at 350°F for 14 minutes, or until set. *Do not overbake.* Cool 2 minutes on baking sheet. Remove cookies to foil to cool completely.

5. For frosting, combine 1 tablespoon shortening, powdered sugar and ¼ cup apricot preserves in small bowl. Stir until well blended. Frost cooled cookies. Sprinkle finely chopped nuts over frosting, if desired.

Makes about 1½ dozen cookies

Walnut Meringues

3 egg whites
Pinch of salt
¾ cup sugar
⅓ cup finely chopped walnuts

Preheat oven to 350°F. Line baking sheet with parchment paper. Place egg whites and salt in large bowl. Beat until soft peaks form. Gradually add sugar, beating until stiff peaks form. Gently fold in walnuts. Drop mounds about 1 inch in diameter 1 inch apart onto prepared baking sheet. Bake 20 minutes or until lightly browned and dry to the touch. Let cool completely before removing from baking sheet. Store in airtight container.

Makes 4 dozen cookies

Orange Drop Cookies

COOKIES

   1 package DUNCAN HINES® Golden
      Sugar Cookie Mix
   1 egg
   1 tablespoon orange juice
   ½ teaspoon grated orange peel
   ¾ cup flaked coconut
   ½ cup chopped pecans

GLAZE

   1 cup confectioners' sugar
   2 teaspoons lemon juice
   2 teaspoons orange juice
   1 teaspoon grated orange peel

1. Preheat oven to 375°F.

2. For cookies, combine cookie mix, buttery flavor packet from Mix, egg, 1 tablespoon orange juice and ½ teaspoon orange peel in large bowl. Stir with spoon until well blended. Stir in coconut and pecans. Drop by rounded teaspoonfuls 2 inches apart onto ungreased cookie sheets. Bake at 375°F for 7 to 8 minutes or until set. Cool 1 minute on cookie sheets. Remove to cooling racks. Cool completely.

3. For glaze, combine confectioners' sugar, lemon juice, 2 teaspoons orange juice and 1 teaspoon orange peel in small bowl. Stir until blended. Drizzle over top of cooled cookies. Allow glaze to set before storing between layers of waxed paper in airtight container.   *Makes about 3 dozen cookies*

Orange Drop Cookies

White Chocolate Biggies

1½ cups butter, softened
1 cup granulated sugar
¾ cup packed light brown sugar
2 eggs
2 teaspoons vanilla
2½ cups all-purpose flour
⅔ cup unsweetened cocoa powder
1 teaspoon baking soda
½ teaspoon salt
1 package (10 ounces) large white
    chocolate chips *or* 1 white
    chocolate bar, cut into pieces
¾ cup pecan halves, coarsely chopped
½ cup golden raisins

1. Preheat oven to 350°F. Lightly grease cookie sheets or line with parchment paper.

2. Beat butter, sugars, eggs and vanilla in large bowl until light and fluffy. Combine flour, cocoa, baking soda and salt in medium bowl; blend into butter mixture until smooth. Stir in white chocolate chips, pecans and raisins.

3. Drop dough by ⅓ cupfuls onto prepared cookie sheets, spacing about 4 inches apart. Press each cookie to flatten slightly.

4. Bake 12 to 14 minutes or until firm in center. Cool 5 minutes on cookie sheets; remove to wire racks to cool completely.

Makes about 2 dozen cookies

Irresistible Peanut Butter Cookies

1¼ cups firmly packed light brown
    sugar
¾ cup creamy peanut butter
½ CRISCO® Stick or ½ cup CRISCO®
    all-vegetable shortening
3 tablespoons milk
1 tablespoon vanilla
1 egg
1¾ cups all-purpose flour
¾ teaspoon baking soda
¾ teaspoon salt

1. Heat oven to 375°F. Place sheets of foil on countertop for cooling cookies.

2. Combine brown sugar, peanut butter, ½ cup shortening, milk and vanilla in large bowl. Beat at medium speed of electric mixer until well blended. Add egg. Beat just until blended.

3. Combine flour, baking soda and salt. Add to creamed mixture at low speed. Mix just until blended.

4. Drop by rounded measuring tablespoonfuls of dough 2 inches apart onto ungreased baking sheet. Flatten slightly in crisscross pattern with tines of fork.

5. Bake one baking sheet at a time at 375°F for 7 to 8 minutes, or until set and just beginning to brown. *Do not overbake.* Cool 2 minutes on baking sheet. Remove cookies to foil to cool completely.

Makes about 3 dozen cookies

Top to bottom: White Chocolate Biggies and Peanut Butter Jumbos (page 36)

Orange Pecan Gems

1 package DUNCAN HINES® Moist
    Deluxe Orange Supreme Cake Mix
1 container (8 ounces) vanilla low fat
    yogurt
1 egg
2 tablespoons butter or margarine,
    softened
1 cup finely chopped pecans
1 cup pecan halves

1. Preheat oven to 350°F. Grease cookie
sheets.

2. Combine cake mix, yogurt, egg, butter
and chopped pecans in large bowl. Beat at
low speed with electric mixer until blended.
Drop by rounded teaspoonfuls 2 inches
apart onto prepared cookie sheets. Press
pecan half onto center of each cookie. Bake
at 350°F for 11 to 13 minutes or until
golden brown. Cool 1 minute on cookie
sheets. Remove to cooling racks. Cool
completely. Store in airtight container.

Makes 4½ to 5 dozen cookies

HELPFUL HINT

To keep pecans fresh-tasting, store
them in an airtight container for
up to 3 months in the
refrigerator, or up to
6 months in the freezer.

Hermits

¾ Butter Flavor* CRISCO® Stick or
    ¾ cup Butter Flavor CRISCO®
    all-vegetable shortening
1½ cups firmly packed brown sugar
  2 tablespoons milk
  3 eggs
2½ cups all-purpose flour
  1 teaspoon salt
  1 teaspoon ground cinnamon
  ¾ teaspoon baking soda
  ¼ teaspoon ground nutmeg
  ⅛ teaspoon ground cloves
  1 cup raisins
  ¾ cup chopped walnuts
    Powdered sugar

Butter Flavor Crisco is artificially flavored.

1. Heat oven to 400°F. Place sheets of foil on
countertop for cooling cookies.

2. Combine ¾ cup shortening, brown sugar
and milk in large bowl. Beat at medium
speed of electric mixer until well blended.
Add eggs one at a time. Beat well after each
addition.

3. Combine flour, salt, cinnamon, baking
soda, nutmeg and cloves. Mix into creamed
mixture at low speed just until blended. Stir
in raisins and nuts.

4. Drop level tablespoonfuls of dough
2 inches apart onto ungreased baking sheet.

5. Bake at 400°F for 7 to 8 minutes, or until
set. *Do not overbake.* Remove cookies to foil
to cool completely. Sift powdered sugar over
cooled cookies.

Makes about 5 dozen cookies

Orange Pecan Gems

Powdered Sugar Cookies

1½ cups (3 sticks) I CAN'T BELIEVE
   IT'S NOT BUTTER!® Spread,
   softened
1⅓ cups powdered sugar
 1 teaspoon vanilla extract
3½ cups all-purpose flour
1⅓ cups chopped walnuts
   Additional powdered sugar

Preheat oven to 350°F.

In large bowl, with electric mixer, beat
I Can't Believe It's Not Butter! Spread and
sugar until light and fluffy, about 5 minutes.
Beat in vanilla, then flour, scraping sides
occasionally, until blended. Stir in walnuts.

On *ungreased* baking sheets, drop dough by
heaping teaspoonfuls, 2 inches apart. With
palm of hand or spoon, gently flatten each
cookie.

Bake 10 minutes or until light golden
around edges. On wire rack, let stand
2 minutes; remove from sheets and cool
completely. Sprinkle with additional sugar.

Makes 7 dozen cookies

FUN FOOD FACT

*Powdered sugar is granulated sugar
that has been ground into a fine
powder which is then mixed
with a little cornstarch to
prevent clumping.*

Peanut Butter Jumbos

½ cup butter, softened
 1 cup granulated sugar
 1 cup packed brown sugar
1½ cups peanut butter
 3 eggs
 2 teaspoons baking soda
 1 teaspoon vanilla
4½ cups uncooked old-fashioned oats
 1 cup (6 ounces) semisweet chocolate
   chips
 1 cup candy-coated chocolate pieces

Preheat oven to 350°F. Lightly grease cookie
sheets or line with parchment paper.

Beat butter, sugars, peanut butter and eggs
in large bowl until well blended. Blend in
baking soda, vanilla and oats until well
mixed. Stir in chocolate chips and candy
pieces.

Scoop out about ⅓ cup dough for each
cookie. Place on prepared cookie sheets,
spacing about 4 inches apart. Press each
cookie to flatten slightly. Bake 15 to
20 minutes or until firm in center. Remove
to wire racks to cool.

Makes about 1½ dozen cookies

Peanut Butter Jumbo Sandwiches:
Prepare cookies as directed. Place ⅓ cup
softened chocolate or vanilla ice cream on
cookie bottom. Top with another cookie.
Lightly press sandwich together. Repeat with
remaining cookies. Wrap sandwiches in
plastic wrap; freeze until firm.

Moist Pumpkin Cookies

½ cup butter, softened
1 cup packed brown sugar
½ cup granulated sugar
1½ cups canned pumpkin (not pumpkin pie filling)
1 egg
1 teaspoon vanilla
2¼ cups all-purpose flour
1¼ teaspoons ground cinnamon
1 teaspoon baking powder
½ teaspoon baking soda
½ teaspoon salt
½ teaspoon ground nutmeg
¾ cup raisins
½ cup chopped walnuts
Powdered Sugar Glaze (recipe follows)

Preheat oven to 350°F. Beat butter and sugars in large bowl until creamy. Beat in pumpkin, egg and vanilla until light and fluffy. Mix in flour, cinnamon, baking powder, baking soda, salt and nutmeg until blended. Stir in raisins and walnuts. Drop heaping tablespoonfuls of dough 2 inches apart onto ungreased cookie sheets.

Bake 12 to 15 minutes or until set. Cool 2 minutes on cookie sheets. Remove to wire racks; cool completely. Drizzle Powdered Sugar Glaze onto cookies. Let glaze set.
Makes about 3½ dozen cookies

Powdered Sugar Glaze: Combine 1 cup powdered sugar and 2 tablespoons milk in small bowl until well blended.

Homemade Coconut Macaroons

3 egg whites
¼ teaspoon cream of tartar
⅛ teaspoon salt
¾ cup sugar
2¼ cups shredded coconut, toasted*
1 teaspoon vanilla

To toast coconut, spread evenly on cookie sheet. Toast in preheated 350°F oven 7 minutes. Stir and toast 1 to 2 minutes more or until light golden brown.

Preheat oven to 325°F. Line cookie sheets with parchment paper or foil. Beat egg whites, cream of tartar and salt in large bowl with electric mixer until soft peaks form. Beat in sugar, 1 tablespoon at a time, until egg whites are stiff and shiny. Fold in coconut and vanilla. Drop tablespoonfuls of dough 4 inches apart onto prepared cookie sheets; spread each into 3-inch circles with back of spoon.

Bake 18 to 22 minutes or until light brown. Cool 1 minute on cookie sheets. Remove to wire racks; cool completely. Store in airtight container. *Makes about 2 dozen cookies*

DECORATE IT!

To make macaroons more festive, stir colored sprinkles into the dough just before baking. Or, dip cookies in melted chocolate for a beautiful and delicious presentation.

Soft Molasses Spice Cookies

2¼ cups all-purpose flour
1 teaspoon baking soda
1 teaspoon ground cinnamon
½ teaspoon ground ginger
¼ teaspoon ground nutmeg
⅛ teaspoon salt
⅛ teaspoon ground cloves
½ cup plus 2 tablespoons butter, softened and divided
½ cup packed dark brown sugar
1 egg
½ cup molasses
1¼ teaspoons vanilla, divided
¼ cup plus 2 to 3 tablespoons milk, divided
¾ cup raisins (optional)
2 cups powdered sugar

Preheat oven to 350°F. Grease cookie sheets. Mix flour, baking soda, cinnamon, ginger, nutmeg, salt and cloves in medium bowl.

Beat ½ cup butter in large bowl with electric mixer at medium speed until smooth and creamy. Gradually beat in brown sugar until blended; increase speed to high and beat until light and fluffy. Beat in egg until fluffy. Beat in molasses and 1 teaspoon vanilla until smooth. Beat in flour mixture at low speed alternately with ¼ cup milk until blended. Stir in raisins, if desired.

Drop rounded tablespoonfuls of dough about 1½ inches apart onto prepared cookie sheets. Bake 12 minutes or until set. Let cookies stand on cookie sheets 5 minutes; transfer to wire racks to cool completely.

For icing, melt remaining 2 tablespoons butter in small saucepan over medium-low heat. Remove from heat; add powdered sugar and stir until blended. Add remaining 2 tablespoons milk and ¼ teaspoon vanilla; stir until smooth. If icing is too thick, add milk, 1 teaspoon at a time, until desired consistency.

Spread icing over tops of cookies. Let stand 15 minutes or until icing is set. Store in airtight container.

Makes about 3 dozen cookies

Lemon Cookies

⅔ cup MIRACLE WHIP® Salad Dressing
1 two-layer yellow cake mix
2 eggs
2 teaspoons grated lemon peel
⅔ cup ready-to-spread vanilla frosting
4 teaspoons lemon juice

• Blend salad dressing, cake mix and eggs at low speed with electric mixer until moistened. Add peel. Beat on medium speed 2 minutes. (Dough will be stiff.)

• Drop rounded teaspoonfuls of dough, 2 inches apart, onto greased cookie sheet.

• Bake at 375°F for 9 to 11 minutes or until lightly browned. (Cookies will still appear soft.) Cool 1 minute; remove from cookie sheet. Cool completely on wire rack.

• Stir together frosting and juice until well blended. Spread on cookies.

Makes about 4 dozen cookies

Soft Molasses Spice Cookies

Orange Marmalade Cookies

COOKIES
 2 cups sugar
 ½ cup shortening
 2 eggs
 1 cup sour cream
 ½ cup SMUCKER'S® Sweet Orange
    Marmalade
 4 cups all-purpose flour
 2 teaspoons baking powder
 1 teaspoon baking soda
 ½ teaspoon salt

ICING
 3 cups powdered sugar
 ½ cup butter or margarine
 ¼ cup Smucker's Sweet Orange
    Marmalade
 Orange juice

Combine sugar, shortening and eggs; beat until well mixed. Add sour cream and ½ cup marmalade; mix well. Add remaining cookie ingredients; mix well. Chill dough.

Drop by rounded teaspoonfuls onto greased cookie sheets. Bake at 400°F for 8 to 10 minutes. Cool.

Combine all icing ingredients, adding enough orange juice for desired spreading consistency (none may be needed). Ice cooled cookies.   *Makes 5 dozen cookies*

Luscious Cookie Drops made with Milky Way® Bars

3 MILKY WAY® Bars (2.15 ounces
    each), chopped, divided
 2 tablespoons milk
 ½ cup butter or margarine, softened
 ⅓ cup packed light brown sugar
 1 egg
 ½ teaspoon vanilla extract
1⅔ cups all-purpose flour
 ½ teaspoon baking soda
 ¼ teaspoon salt
 ½ cup chopped walnuts

Preheat oven to 350°F. Stir 1 Milky Way® Bar with milk in small saucepan over low heat until melted and smooth; cool. In large bowl, beat butter and brown sugar until creamy. Beat in egg, vanilla and melted Milky Way® Bar mixture. Combine flour, baking soda and salt in small bowl. Stir into chocolate mixture. Add remaining chopped Milky Way® Bars and nuts; stir gently. Drop dough by rounded teaspoonfuls onto ungreased cookie sheets.

Bake 12 to 15 minutes or until cookies are just firm to the touch. Cool on wire racks.
          Makes about 2 dozen cookies

Prep Time: 20 minutes
Bake Time: 15 minutes

Spicy Ginger Molasses Cookies

2 cups all-purpose flour
1½ teaspoons ground ginger
1 teaspoon baking soda
½ teaspoon ground cloves
¼ teaspoon salt
¾ cup butter, softened
1 cup sugar
¼ cup molasses
1 egg
   Additional sugar
½ cup yogurt-covered raisins

1. Preheat oven to 375°F.

2. Combine flour, ginger, baking soda, cloves and salt in small bowl; set aside.

3. Beat butter and 1 cup sugar in large bowl of electric mixer at medium speed until light and fluffy. Add molasses and egg; beat until well blended. Gradually beat in flour mixture on low speed just until blended.

4. Drop dough by level ¼ cupfuls onto parchment-lined cookie sheets, spacing 3 inches apart. Flatten each ball of dough until 2 inches in diameter with bottom of glass that has been dipped in additional sugar. Press 7 to 8 yogurt-covered raisins into dough of each cookie.

5. Bake 11 to 12 minutes or until cookies are set. Cool cookies 2 minutes on cookie sheets; slide parchment paper and cookies onto countertop. Cool completely.

Makes about 1 dozen (4-inch) cookies

Spicy Ginger Molasses Cookies

Special Chocolate Chip Sandwiches

1 package DUNCAN HINES®
   Chocolate Chip Cookie Mix
1 egg
⅓ cup vegetable oil
3 tablespoons water
10 ounces chocolate-flavored candy
   coating
⅓ cup chopped sliced natural almonds

1. Preheat oven to 375°F.

2. Combine cookie mix, egg, oil and water in large bowl. Stir until thoroughly blended. Drop by rounded teaspoonfuls 2 inches apart onto ungreased baking sheets. Bake at 375°F for 8 to 10 minutes or until light golden brown. Cool 1 minute on baking sheets. Remove to cooling racks. Cool completely.

3. Place chocolate candy coating in small saucepan. Melt on low heat, stirring frequently until smooth.

4. To assemble, spread about ½ teaspoon melted coating on bottom of one cookie; top with second cookie. Press together to make sandwiches. Repeat with remaining cookies. Dip one-third of each sandwich cookie in remaining melted coating and sprinkle with chopped almonds. Place on cooling racks until coating is set. Store between layers of waxed paper in airtight container.

Makes 29 sandwich cookies

Reese's® Cookies

2 cups all-purpose flour
1 teaspoon baking soda
1 cup shortening or ¾ cup (1½ sticks)
   butter or margarine, softened
1 cup granulated sugar
½ cup packed light brown sugar
1 teaspoon vanilla extract
2 eggs
1⅔ cups (10-ounce package) REESE'S®
   Peanut Butter Chips
⅔ cup HERSHEY₅S Semi-Sweet
   Chocolate Chips or Milk
   Chocolate Chips

1. Heat oven to 350°F. Stir together flour and baking soda.

2. Beat shortening, granulated sugar, brown sugar and vanilla in large bowl until creamy. Add eggs; beat well. Gradually add flour mixture, beating well. Stir in chips. Drop by rounded teaspoons onto ungreased cookie sheet.

3. Bake 8 to 10 minutes or until lightly browned. Cool slightly; remove from cookie sheet to wire rack. Cool completely.

Makes about 5 dozen cookies

Special Chocolate Chip Sandwiches

Malted Dream Drops

½ Butter Flavor* CRISCO® Stick or
½ cup Butter Flavor CRISCO®
all-vegetable shortening plus
additional for greasing
1 cup firmly packed brown sugar
1 egg
1 teaspoon vanilla
½ cup evaporated milk
1¼ cups all-purpose flour
1 cup chocolate malted milk granules
1 teaspoon baking powder
¼ teaspoon salt
1 cup semi-sweet chocolate chips
1 cup coarsely chopped walnuts

Butter Flavor Crisco is artificially flavored.

1. Combine ½ cup shortening and sugar in large bowl. Beat at medium speed of electric mixer until well blended. Beat in egg and vanilla. Add milk. Beat until smooth.

2. Combine flour, malted milk granules, baking powder and salt. Mix into creamed mixture at low speed until just blended. Stir in chocolate chips and nuts. Cover and refrigerate at least 1 hour.

3. Heat oven to 350°F. Grease baking sheet with shortening. Place sheets of foil on countertop for cooling cookies.

4. Drop rounded teaspoonfuls of dough 2 inches apart onto prepared sheet. Bake at 350°F 10 to 12 minutes, or until set. *Do not overbake.* Cool 2 minutes on baking sheet. Remove cookies to foil to cool completely.

Makes about 4 dozen cookies

Hershey's Soft & Chewy Cookies

1 cup (2 sticks) butter (no substitutes)
¾ cup packed light brown sugar
½ cup granulated sugar
¼ cup light corn syrup
1 egg
2 teaspoons vanilla extract
2½ cups all-purpose flour
1 teaspoon baking soda
¼ teaspoon salt
1 package (10 or 12 ounces)
HERSHEY₀S Chips or Baking Bits
(any flavor)

1. Heat oven to 350°F.

2. Beat butter, brown sugar and granulated sugar in large bowl until fluffy. Add corn syrup, egg and vanilla; beat well. Stir together flour, baking soda and salt; gradually add to butter mixture, beating until well blended. Stir in chips or bits. Drop by rounded teaspoons onto ungreased cookie sheet.

3. Bake 8 to 10 minutes or until lightly browned and almost set. Cool slightly and remove from cookie sheet to wire rack. Cool completely. Cookies will be softer on the second day.

Makes about 3½ dozen cookies

Chocolate Chocolate Cookies: Decrease flour to 2¼ cups and add ¼ cup HERSHEY₀S Cocoa or HERSHEY₀S Dutch Processed Cocoa.

Malted Dream Drops and Mocha Chips 'n' Bits (page 46)

Chocolate Hazelnut Cookie Drops

1 cup (2 sticks) butter or margarine, softened
1 cup firmly packed light brown sugar
2 large eggs
1¾ cups all-purpose flour
1 package (4-serving size) chocolate-flavor instant pudding mix
½ teaspoon baking soda
1¾ cups "M&M's"® Semi-Sweet Chocolate Mini Baking Bits
1 cup coarsely chopped toasted hazelnuts or filberts*

To toast hazelnuts, spread in single layer on baking sheet. Bake at 350°F for 7 to 10 minutes or until light golden, stirring occasionally. Remove hazelnuts from pan and cool completely before chopping.

Preheat oven to 350°F. In large bowl cream butter and sugar until light and fluffy; beat in eggs. In small bowl combine flour, pudding mix and baking soda; blend into creamed mixture. Stir in "M&M's"® Semi-Sweet Chocolate Mini Baking Bits and nuts. Drop by teaspoonfuls about 2 inches apart onto ungreased cookie sheets. Bake 8 to 10 minutes or until set. *Do not overbake.* Cool completely on wire racks. Store in tightly covered container.

Makes about 5 dozen cookies

Mocha Chips 'n' Bits

1 Butter Flavor* CRISCO® Stick or 1 cup Butter Flavor CRISCO® all-vegetable shortening
¾ cup granulated sugar
½ cup firmly packed brown sugar
2 tablespoons milk
1 tablespoon instant coffee
1 teaspoon vanilla
2 eggs
2⅓ cups all-purpose flour
1½ tablespoons unsweetened cocoa powder
1 teaspoon baking soda
½ teaspoon salt
1 cup coarsely chopped pecans
1 cup milk chocolate big chips
¾ cup raisins
¾ cup flake coconut

Butter Flavor Crisco is artificially flavored.

1. Heat oven to 375°F. Place sheets of foil on countertop for cooling cookies.

2. Combine shortening, granulated sugar, brown sugar, milk, instant coffee and vanilla in bowl. Beat until blended. Beat in eggs.

3. Combine flour, cocoa, baking soda and salt. Mix into creamed mixture until just blended. Stir in nuts, chocolate chips, raisins and coconut. Drop rounded tablespoonfuls 2 inches apart onto ungreased baking sheet.

4. Bake at 375°F for 10 to 12 minutes. *Do not overbake.* Let stand 2 minutes on baking sheet. Remove cookies to foil to cool.

Makes about 3½ dozen cookies

Top to bottom: Polka Dot Macaroons (page 50) and Chocolate Hazelnut Cookie Drops

Island Cookies

1⅔ cups all-purpose flour
¾ teaspoon baking powder
½ teaspoon baking soda
½ teaspoon salt
¾ cup (1½ sticks) butter or margarine, softened
¾ cup packed brown sugar
⅓ cup granulated sugar
1 teaspoon vanilla extract
1 egg
2 cups (11½-ounce package) NESTLÉ® TOLL HOUSE® Milk Chocolate Morsels
1 cup flaked coconut, toasted if desired
¾ cup macadamia nuts or walnuts, chopped

PREHEAT oven to 375°F. Combine flour, baking powder, baking soda and salt in small bowl.

BEAT butter, brown sugar, granulated sugar and vanilla in large mixer bowl until creamy. Beat in egg. Gradually blend in flour mixture. Stir in morsels, coconut and nuts. Drop by slightly rounded tablespoons onto ungreased baking sheets.

BAKE for 8 to 11 minutes or until edges are lightly browned. Let stand for 2 minutes. Remove from cookie sheets; cool on wire racks.   *Makes about 2 dozen cookies*

Honey Chocolate Chippers

1 cup honey
1 cup butter or margarine, softened
1 egg yolk
1 teaspoon vanilla extract
2 cups all-purpose flour
1 cup rolled oats
½ teaspoon baking soda
½ teaspoon salt
1 cup chopped toasted pecans
1 cup (6 ounces) semi-sweet chocolate chips

In medium bowl, beat honey and butter until creamy but not fluffy. Beat in egg yolk and vanilla. In separate bowl, combine flour, rolled oats, baking soda and salt. Stir dry ingredients into wet mixture until thoroughly blended. Mix in pecans and chocolate chips. Chill dough for 30 minutes. Drop dough by rounded tablespoons onto ungreased cookie sheets. Flatten each cookie with a spoon. Bake at 350°F for 15 to 20 minutes, or until tops are dry. Cool on wire racks.   *Makes 2 dozen cookies*

Favorite recipe from **National Honey Board**

FUN FOOD FACT

Honey is one of the only foods that will never go bad, no matter how long you keep it. Be sure to store it in a tightly closed jar in a cool, dry place.

Chocolate Orange Granola Cookies

1 cup all-purpose flour
½ teaspoon baking powder
½ teaspoon allspice
½ teaspoon salt
⅔ cup firmly packed brown sugar
½ cup butter, softened
1 egg
1 teaspoon vanilla extract
½ teaspoon grated orange peel
1¼ cups granola cereal
1 cup (6-ounce package) NESTLÉ®
     TOLL HOUSE® Semi-Sweet
     Chocolate Morsels
½ cup flaked coconut
¼ cup chopped nuts

PREHEAT oven to 350°F. In small bowl, combine flour, baking powder, allspice and salt; set aside. In large bowl, combine brown sugar and butter; beat until creamy. Add egg, vanilla extract and orange peel; beat well. Gradually beat in flour mixture. Stir in granola cereal, morsels, coconut and nuts. Drop by rounded tablespoonfuls onto ungreased cookie sheets. Sprinkle with additional coconut, if desired. Bake at 350°F. for 9 to 11 minutes. Cool completely on wire racks.

Makes 1½ dozen (2-inch) cookies

Almond Double Chip Cookies

¾ cup butter, softened
¾ cup packed light brown sugar
1 egg
½ teaspoon almond extract
1½ cups all-purpose flour
¼ teaspoon baking soda
     Dash salt
1 cup (6 ounces) semisweet chocolate
     chips
1 cup (6 ounces) white chocolate chips
½ cup slivered blanched almonds

Preheat oven to 375°F. Line cookie sheets with parchment paper or leave ungreased.

Beat butter and brown sugar in large bowl with electric mixer until creamy. Beat in egg and almond extract.

Combine flour, baking soda and salt in small bowl; blend into butter mixture. Stir in semisweet and white chocolate chips and almonds. Drop by rounded tablespoonfuls, 3 inches apart, onto prepared cookie sheets. Bake 8 to 10 minutes or until lightly browned. Do not overbake. Cool 2 minutes on cookie sheets; remove to wire racks to cool completely.

Makes about 3 dozen cookies

Caramel Lace Chocolate Chip Cookies

¼ **Butter Flavor* CRISCO® Stick or**
¼ **cup Butter Flavor CRISCO® all-vegetable shortening plus additional for greasing**
½ **cup light corn syrup**
1 **tablespoon brown sugar**
½ **teaspoon vanilla**
1½ **teaspoons grated orange peel (optional)**
½ **cup all-purpose flour**
¼ **teaspoon salt**
⅓ **cup semi-sweet chocolate chips**
⅓ **cup coarsely chopped pecans**

*Butter Flavor Crisco is artificially flavored.

1. Heat oven to 375°F. Grease baking sheets with shortening. Place foil on countertop for cooling cookies.

2. Combine ¼ cup shortening, corn syrup, brown sugar, vanilla and orange peel in large bowl. Beat at medium speed of electric mixer until well blended.

3. Combine flour and salt. Mix into creamed mixture at low speed until blended. Stir in chocolate chips and nuts. Drop teaspoonfuls of dough 4 inches apart onto baking sheets.

4. Bake one baking sheet at a time at 375°F for 5 minutes or until edges are golden brown. (Chips and nuts will remain in center while dough spreads out.) *Do not overbake.* Cool 2 minutes on baking sheets.

Lift each cookie edge with spatula. Grasp cookie edge gently and lightly pinch or flute the edge, bringing it up to chips and nuts in center. Work around each cookie until completely fluted. Remove cookies to foil to cool completely.

Makes about 3 dozen cookies

Polka Dot Macaroons

1 **14-ounce bag (5 cups) shredded coconut**
1 **14-ounce can sweetened condensed milk**
½ **cup all-purpose flour**
1¾ **cups "M&M's"® Chocolate Mini Baking Bits**

Preheat oven to 350°F. Grease cookie sheets; set aside. In large bowl combine coconut, condensed milk and flour until well blended. Stir in "M&M's"® Chocolate Mini Baking Bits. Drop by rounded tablespoonfuls about 2 inches apart onto prepared cookie sheets. Bake 8 to 10 minutes or until edges are golden. Cool completely on wire racks. Store in tightly covered container.

Makes about 5 dozen cookies

Caramel Lace Chocolate Chip Cookies

Chocolate Orange Dreams

COOKIES
 1 Butter Flavor* CRISCO® Stick or
   1 cup Butter Flavor CRISCO®
   all-vegetable shortening plus
   additional for greasing
 1 cup granulated sugar
 1 package (3 ounces) cream cheese,
   softened
 2 eggs
 2 teaspoons grated orange peel
 2 teaspoons strained fresh orange
   juice
 ½ teaspoon salt
 2 cups all-purpose flour
 1 cup (6-ounce package) semi-sweet
   chocolate chips

GLAZE
 ½ cup confectioners' sugar
2½ teaspoons strained fresh orange
   juice
1½ teaspoons orange flavor liqueur

Butter Flavor Crisco is artificially flavored.

1. Heat oven to 350°F. Grease baking sheet with shortening. Place sheets of foil on countertop for cooling cookies.

2. For cookies, combine 1 cup shortening, granulated sugar and cream cheese in large bowl. Beat at medium speed of electric mixer until well blended. Beat in eggs, orange peel, 2 teaspoons orange juice and salt. Add flour gradually at low speed. Mix until well blended. Add chocolate chips.

Drop by rounded teaspoonfuls 2 inches apart onto prepared baking sheet.

3. Bake at 350°F for 8 to 10 minutes or until light brown around edges. *Do not overbake.*

4. For glaze (prepare while cookies are baking), combine confectioners' sugar, 2½ teaspoons orange juice and liqueur. Stir until well blended. Brush on cookies immediately upon removing from oven. Cool 2 minutes on baking sheet. Remove cookies to foil to cool completely.
Makes about 4 dozen cookies

Hershey®s Mint Chocolate Cookies

¾ cup (1½ sticks) butter, softened
 1 cup sugar
 1 egg
 1 teaspoon vanilla extract
1½ cups all-purpose flour
 ½ teaspoon baking soda
 ¼ teaspoon salt
1⅔ cups (10-ounce package)
   HERSHEY®S Mint Chocolate Chips

1. Heat oven to 350°F.

2. Beat butter and sugar in bowl until fluffy. Add egg and vanilla; beat well. Stir together flour, baking soda and salt; gradually blend into butter mixture. Stir in chocolate chips. Drop by rounded teaspoonfuls onto ungreased cookie sheet.

3. Bake 8 to 9 minutes or until browned. Cool slightly; remove to wire rack. Cool completely. *Makes 2½ dozen cookies*

Chocolate Orange Dreams

Marbled Mocha Drops

1 cup (2 sticks) butter or margarine, softened
⅔ cup granulated sugar
⅔ cup firmly packed light brown sugar
1 large egg
2 tablespoons instant coffee granules, dissolved in 1 tablespoon water
1 teaspoon vanilla extract
2¼ cups all-purpose flour
1 teaspoon baking soda
½ teaspoon salt
¾ cup coarsely chopped nuts
¼ cup unsweetened cocoa powder
1¾ cups "M&M's"® Semi-Sweet Chocolate Mini Baking Bits

Preheat oven to 350°F. In large bowl cream butter and sugars until light and fluffy; add egg, dissolved coffee mixture and vanilla. In medium bowl combine flour, baking soda and salt. Blend flour mixture and nuts into creamed mixture. Remove half of the dough to small bowl; set aside. Blend cocoa powder into remaining dough. Stir "M&M's"® Semi-Sweet Chocolate Mini Baking Bits into the two doughs, using half for each. Combine two doughs by folding together just enough to marble, about 4 strokes. Drop by heaping tablespoonfuls about 2 inches apart onto ungreased cookie sheets. Bake 10 to 12 minutes or just until set. Do not overbake. Cool 1 minute on cookie sheets; cool completely on wire racks. Store in tightly covered container.

Makes about 2½ dozen cookies

Triple Chipper Monsters

2½ cups all-purpose flour
1 teaspoon baking soda
¾ teaspoon salt
1 cup butter, softened
1 cup packed light brown sugar
½ cup granulated sugar
2 eggs
2 teaspoons vanilla
2 cups semisweet chocolate chips
½ cup white chocolate chips
½ cup butterscotch or peanut butter chips

1. Preheat oven to 350°F.

2. Combine flour, baking soda and salt in medium bowl; set aside.

3. Beat butter, brown sugar and granulated sugar in large bowl of electric mixer at medium speed until light and fluffy. Beat in eggs and vanilla until blended. Gradually beat in flour mixture on low speed until well blended. Stir in chips.

4. Drop dough by scant ¼ cupfuls onto ungreased cookie sheets, spacing 3 inches apart. Lightly flatten dough with fingertips. Bake 12 to 14 minutes or until edges are set and golden brown. Cool cookies 1 to 2 minutes on cookie sheets; transfer to wire racks. Cool completely.

Makes about 22 (4-inch) cookies

Brown Sugar Granola Cookies

¾ cup (1½ sticks) butter or margarine,
   softened
1 cup firmly packed light brown sugar
1 large egg
1 teaspoon vanilla extract
2 cups all-purpose flour
1 teaspoon baking soda
1¾ cups "M&M's"® Chocolate Mini
   Baking Bits
6 KUDOS® Milk Chocolate Granola
   Bars Fudge, chopped

Preheat oven to 350°F. Lightly grease cookie sheets. In large bowl cream butter and sugar until light and fluffy; beat in egg and vanilla. In medium bowl combine flour and baking soda; blend into creamed mixture. Stir in "M&M's"® Chocolate Mini Baking Bits and chopped KUDOS® Milk Chocolate Granola Bars Fudge. Drop dough by tablespoonfuls onto prepared cookie sheets. Bake 11 to 13 minutes. Cool 2 to 3 minutes on cookie sheets; cool completely on wire racks.

Makes about 3½ dozen cookies

Brown Sugar Granola Cookies

Eggnog Crisps

½ cup (1 stick) butter or margarine,
    softened
1 cup granulated sugar
1 large egg
1½ teaspoons brandy extract
1½ cups cake flour
½ cup ground pecans
½ teaspoon ground nutmeg
1¾ cups "M&M's"® Chocolate Mini
    Baking Bits
36 pecan halves

Preheat oven to 375°F. Cream butter and
sugar until light and fluffy; add egg and
brandy extract. Combine flour, ground
pecans and nutmeg; blend into creamed
mixture. Stir in "M&M's"® Chocolate Mini
Baking Bits. Drop by heaping tablespoonfuls
onto greased cookie sheets; top each with
1 pecan half. Bake 10 to 11 minutes or until
edges turn light golden. Cool 1 minute on
cookie sheets.

Makes about 3 dozen cookies

FUN FOOD FACT

Cake flour is made from low-gluten
soft wheat and is high in starch.
It gives baked goods a more
tender texture than all-
purpose flour.

Pudding Drop Cookies

¾ cup sugar
2 eggs
¼ cup margarine or butter, melted
1 cup all-purpose flour
1 (4-serving size) package ROYAL®
    Instant Butterscotch Pudding &
    Pie Filling*
½ cup PLANTERS® Walnuts, chopped
½ cup semisweet chocolate chips

*1 (4-serving size) package ROYAL® Instant Chocolate
or Vanilla Pudding & Pie Filling may be substituted.*

Preheat oven to 375°F. In medium bowl,
with electric mixer at high speed, beat sugar
and eggs until thick and pale yellow. Beat in
margarine or butter until smooth. Stir in
flour and pudding mix until blended. Stir in
walnuts and chocolate chips. Drop batter by
tablespoonfuls, 2 inches apart, onto greased
and floured cookie sheets. Bake for 10 to
12 minutes or until lightly browned. Cool
slightly on cookie sheets. Remove from
sheets; cool completely on wire racks. Store
in airtight container.

Makes about 2 dozen cookies

**Left to right: Patchwork Cream Cheese
Cookies (page 60) and Eggnog Crisps**

Ship-Shape COOKIES

Dandy Candy Oatmeal Cookies

½ Butter Flavor* CRISCO® Stick or ½ cup Butter Flavor
    CRISCO® all-vegetable shortening plus additional for
    greasing
1 jar (12 ounces) creamy peanut butter
1 cup granulated sugar
1 cup firmly packed brown sugar
3 eggs
¾ teaspoon vanilla
¾ teaspoon maple syrup
2 teaspoons baking soda
4½ cups quick oats, uncooked, divided
1 package (8 ounces) candy-coated chocolate pieces

*Butter Flavor Crisco is artificially flavored.

1. Heat oven to 350°F. Grease baking sheet with shortening. Place sheets of foil on countertop for cooling cookies.

2. Combine peanut butter, granulated sugar, brown sugar and ½ cup shortening in large bowl. Beat until well blended and fluffy. Add eggs, vanilla and maple syrup. Beat at high speed 3 to 4 minutes. Add baking soda and 2¼ cups oats; stir. Stir in candy. Stir in remaining 2¼ cups oats. Shape dough into 1½-inch balls. Flatten slightly. Place 2 inches apart on prepared baking sheet.

3. Bake for 9 to 10 minutes for chewy cookies or 11 to 12 minutes for crispy cookies. Cool 2 minutes. Remove cookies to foil to cool completely. *Makes 3½ dozen cookies*

Dandy Candy Oatmeal Cookies

Low Fat Molasses Jumbles

½ cup Dried Plum Purée (recipe
    follows) or prepared prune butter
½ cup sugar
½ cup molasses
1 egg
2 cups all-purpose flour
2 teaspoons ground cinnamon
1 teaspoon ground ginger
½ teaspoon baking soda
½ teaspoon salt
    Additional sugar

Preheat oven to 350°F. Coat baking sheets
with vegetable cooking spray. In large bowl,
mix dried plum purée, sugar and molasses
until well blended. Add egg; mix well.
Combine remaining ingredients except
sugar; stir into dried plum purée mixture
until blended. Roll heaping tablespoonfuls
of dough in additional sugar. Place on baking
sheets, spacing 2 inches apart. With fork,
flatten dough in crisscross fashion until
½ inch thick. Bake in center of oven about
12 to 13 minutes or until set and bottoms
are lightly browned. Remove from baking
sheets to wire racks to cool completely.

Makes 30 (2½-inch) cookies

Dried Plum Purée: Mix 1⅓ cups (8 ounces)
pitted dried plums and 6 tablespoons hot
water in container of food processor. Pulse
on and off until smooth. Store leftovers in
covered container in refrigerator for up to
2 months.

Favorite recipe from **California Dried Plum Board**

Patchwork Cream Cheese Cookies

½ cup (1 stick) butter or margarine,
    softened
3 ounces cream cheese, softened
½ cup granulated sugar
1 large egg
1 teaspoon grated orange zest
1 teaspoon vanilla extract
2 cups all-purpose flour
½ teaspoon baking soda
1¾ cups "M&M's"® Chocolate Mini
    Baking Bits
    Granulated sugar

Preheat oven to 350°F. Cream butter, cream
cheese and sugar until light and fluffy; add
egg, orange zest and vanilla. Combine flour
and baking soda; blend into creamed
mixture. Stir in "M&M's"® Chocolate Mini
Baking Bits. Shape dough into 1-inch balls;
place about 2 inches apart onto greased
cookie sheets. Gently flatten cookies with
bottom of greased glass dipped in sugar.
Bake 12 to 15 minutes.

Makes about 3 dozen cookies

HELPFUL HINT

*To soften cream cheese in your
microwave, place the unwrapped cream
cheese on a microwavable plate. Heat
at MEDIUM (50% power) 15 to
20 seconds or just until
softened. Let stand about
1 minute before using.*

Low Fat Molasses Jumbles

Chocolate Crackles

⅓ cup CRISCO® Oil*
1½ cups granulated sugar
1½ teaspoons vanilla
1 egg
2 egg whites
1⅔ cups all-purpose flour
½ cup unsweetened cocoa powder
1½ teaspoons baking powder
½ teaspoon salt
½ cup confectioners' sugar

Use your favorite Crisco Oil product.

1. Heat oven to 350°F. Place sheets of foil on countertop for cooling cookies.

2. Combine oil, granulated sugar and vanilla in large bowl. Beat at medium speed of electric mixer until blended. Add egg and egg whites. Beat until well blended. Stir in flour, cocoa, baking powder and salt with spoon.

3. Place confectioners' sugar in shallow dish or large plastic food storage bag.

4. Shape dough into 1-inch balls. Roll or shake in confectioners' sugar until coated. Place about 2 inches apart on ungreased baking sheet.

5. Bake at 350°F for 7 to 8 minutes or until almost no indentation remains when touched lightly. (Do not overbake.) Cool on baking sheet 2 minutes. Remove cookies to foil to cool completely.   *Makes 4 dozen cookies*

Hot 'n' Nutty Cookies

¾ cup unsalted butter, softened
1 cup granulated sugar
1 cup packed brown sugar
2 cups peanut butter, smooth *or* crunchy
½ cup macadamia nuts, chopped (optional)
2 eggs
1 teaspoon vanilla extract
1 teaspoon TABASCO® brand Pepper Sauce
3 cups flour
1 teaspoon salt
1 teaspoon baking soda

Preheat oven to 350°F. Lightly butter and flour cookie sheet.

Cream butter, granulated sugar and brown sugar in large bowl. Stir in peanut butter and macadamia nuts; mix until well blended. Add eggs, vanilla and TABASCO® Sauce. Mix until well combined.

Mix together flour, salt and baking soda in another bowl. Add to nut mixture and stir until blended.

Spoon about 1 heaping tablespoon of batter onto prepared cookie sheet. Coat tines of fork in flour and score each cookie in crisscross pattern. Bake 15 to 17 minutes or until edges begin to turn golden. Set aside to cool on racks.   *Makes 2 dozen cookies*

Peanut Butter Cookies

⅓ cup Dried Plum Purée (recipe
    follows) or prepared prune butter
    or 1 jar (2½ ounces) first-stage
    baby food dried plums
⅓ cup granulated sugar
⅓ cup packed brown sugar
¼ cup creamy peanut butter
¼ cup honey
 2 tablespoons vegetable oil
 1 egg white
 1 teaspoon vanilla
1½ cups all-purpose flour
½ teaspoon salt
½ teaspoon baking soda

Preheat oven to 375°F. Coat baking sheets with vegetable cooking spray. Beat dried plum purée, sugars, peanut butter, honey, oil, egg white and vanilla until blended. Beat flour, salt and baking soda into dried plum purée mixture until blended. With moist hands, shape generous tablespoonfuls of dough into balls. Place 3 inches apart on prepared baking sheets. With fork, flatten dough in crisscross fashion until ½ inch thick. Bake 10 to 11 minutes or until golden brown. Let stand on baking sheets 1 minute; remove to wire racks to cool. ***Makes 24 cookies***

Dried Plum Purée: Mix 1⅓ cups (8 ounces) pitted dried plums and 6 tablespoons hot water in container of food processor. Pulse on and off until smooth. Store leftovers in covered container in refrigerator for up to 2 months.

Favorite recipe from **California Dried Plum Board**

Chocolate Chunk Cookies

 3 eggs
 1 cup vegetable oil
¾ cup packed brown sugar
 1 teaspoon baking powder
 1 teaspoon vanilla
¼ teaspoon baking soda
¼ teaspoon salt
2½ cups all-purpose flour
 1 package (12 ounces) semisweet
    chocolate chunks

Preheat oven to 350°F. Lightly grease cookie sheets or line with parchment paper. Beat eggs in large bowl until foamy. Add oil and brown sugar; beat until light and frothy. Blend in baking powder, vanilla, baking soda and salt. Mix in flour until dough is smooth. Stir in chocolate chunks. Shape dough into walnut-sized balls. Place 2 inches apart on prepared cookie sheets. Bake 10 to 12 minutes or until lightly browned. Remove to wire racks to cool.

Makes about 4½ dozen cookies

FUN FOOD FACT

Store chocolate in a cool, dry place. If chocolate gets too warm, the cocoa butter rises to the surface and causes a grayish white appearance, which is called a bloom. The bloom will not affect the chocolate's taste or baking quality.

Gaiety Pastel Cookies

3½ cups flour
 1 teaspoon CALUMET® Baking Powder
1½ cups (3 sticks) butter or margarine
 1 cup sugar
 1 package (4-serving size) JELL-O®
    Brand Gelatin Dessert, any flavor*
 1 egg
 1 teaspoon vanilla
    Additional JELL-O® Brand Gelatin
    Dessert, any flavor*

For best results, use same flavor.

HEAT oven to 400°F.

MIX flour and baking powder in medium bowl. Beat butter in large bowl with electric mixer to soften. Gradually add sugar and 1 package gelatin, beating until light and fluffy. Beat in egg and vanilla. Gradually add flour mixture, beating well after each addition.

SHAPE dough into 1-inch balls. Place on ungreased cookie sheets. Flatten with bottom of glass. Sprinkle with additional gelatin.

BAKE 10 to 12 minutes or until edges are lightly browned. Remove from cookie sheets. Cool on wire racks. Store in tightly covered container.

Makes about 5 dozen cookies

Preparation Time: 40 minutes
Baking Time: 12 minutes

Peanut Butter Orange Blossoms

½ Butter Flavor* CRISCO® Stick or
    ½ cup Butter Flavor CRISCO®
    all-vegetable shortening
½ cup creamy peanut butter
 2 teaspoons grated orange peel
½ cup granulated sugar
½ cup firmly packed dark brown sugar
 1 egg
 1 cup all-purpose flour
1½ teaspoons baking powder
½ teaspoon salt
¼ teaspoon baking soda

Butter Flavor Crisco is artificially flavored.

1. Heat oven to 350°F. Place sheets of foil on countertop for cooling cookies.

2. Combine ½ cup shortening, peanut butter and orange peel in large bowl. Beat at medium speed of electric mixer until well blended. Add granulated sugar, brown sugar and egg. Beat until well blended.

3. Combine flour, baking powder, salt and baking soda. Add to creamed mixture at low speed. Beat until well blended. Shape level measuring tablespoonfuls into balls. Place 2 inches apart on ungreased baking sheet. Dip fork in flour; flatten dough slightly in crisscross pattern.

4. Bake at 350°F for 9 to 11 minutes or until set. *Do not overbake.* Remove cookies to foil to cool completely.

Makes about 3 dozen cookies

Gaiety Pastel Cookies

Super-Duper Chocolate Pecan Cookies

½ cup butter, softened
⅓ cup peanut butter
⅓ cup granulated sugar
⅓ cup packed light brown sugar
1 egg
1 teaspoon vanilla
1¼ cups all-purpose flour
½ teaspoon baking soda
1 package (12 ounces) semisweet chocolate chunks *or* 4 semisweet chocolate bars (3 ounces each), cut into squares
1 cup pecan halves, cut into pieces

Preheat oven to 350°F. Lightly grease two cookie sheets or line with parchment paper. Beat butter, peanut butter, sugars, egg and vanilla in large bowl until light and fluffy. Blend in combined flour and baking soda. Scoop out ⅓ cupfuls of dough, forming into 12 balls. Place on prepared cookie sheets, spacing about 4 inches apart. Press each cookie to flatten slightly. Press chocolate chunks and pecan pieces into cookies, dividing equally. Bake 15 to 17 minutes or until firm in center. Remove to wire racks to cool. ***Makes 1 dozen cookies***

Brandy Nut Cookies

¾ Butter Flavor* CRISCO® Stick or ¾ cup Butter Flavor CRISCO® all-vegetable shortening
½ cup confectioners' sugar
1 egg yolk
2 tablespoons milk
2 tablespoons brandy (optional)**
½ teaspoon pure vanilla extract
1¾ cups all-purpose flour
¾ cup ground toasted walnuts***
½ teaspoon baking powder
⅛ teaspoon salt
Confectioners' sugar

Butter Flavor Crisco is artificially flavored.

**Use 4 tablespoons milk if omitting brandy.*

***To toast nuts, place in single layer in baking pan. Place in 350°F oven for 7 minutes. Stir several times. Cool before using.*

1. Heat oven to 325°F. Place sheets of foil on countertop for cooling cookies. Combine ¾ cup shortening and ½ cup confectioners' sugar in large bowl. Beat at medium speed of electric mixer until well blended. Beat in egg yolk, milk, brandy (if used) and vanilla.

2. Combine flour, nuts, baking powder and salt. Add gradually to creamed mixture at low speed. Beat until well blended. Shape dough into 1-inch balls. Place 2 inches apart on ungreased baking sheet.

3. Bake at 325°F for 13 to 15 minutes or until light brown. *Do not overbake.* Let stand 2 minutes on baking sheet. Remove cookies to foil to cool; sprinkle with confectioners' sugar. ***Makes about 3½ dozen cookies***

Honey Carrot Cookies

1 cup sugar
½ cup butter, softened
2 eggs
3 tablespoons honey
1 teaspoon vanilla
2¼ cups all-purpose flour
2 teaspoons baking soda
½ teaspoon ground nutmeg
¼ teaspoon salt
½ cup shredded carrot

Preheat oven to 325°F. Combine sugar and butter in large bowl. Beat well. Add eggs, honey and vanilla; beat until well mixed. Combine flour, baking soda, nutmeg and salt in medium bowl. Stir dry ingredients into butter mixture; mix well. Stir in carrot. Using well-floured hands, shape rounded teaspoonfuls of dough into 1-inch balls. Place 2 inches apart on ungreased cookie sheets.

Bake 13 to 18 minutes or until edges are lightly browned. Remove immediately to wire racks to cool.

Makes about 3 dozen cookies

Honey Carrot Cookies

Chewy Choco-Peanut Pudgies

COOKIES

1¼ cups firmly packed light brown
   sugar
¾ cup creamy peanut butter
½ CRISCO® Stick or ½ cup CRISCO®
   all-vegetable shortening
3 tablespoons milk
1 tablespoon vanilla
1 egg
1¾ cups all-purpose flour
¾ teaspoon baking soda
¾ teaspoon salt
1½ cups coarsely chopped unsalted
   peanuts (raw or dry roasted)
½ cup granulated sugar

FROSTING

½ cup semi-sweet chocolate chips
½ teaspoon Butter Flavor* CRISCO®
   Stick or ½ teaspoon Butter Flavor
   CRISCO® all-vegetable shortening
½ teaspoon granulated sugar

Butter Flavor Crisco is artificially flavored.

1. Heat oven to 375°F. Place sheets of foil on countertop for cooling cookies.

2. For cookies, combine brown sugar, peanut butter, ½ cup shortening, milk and vanilla in large bowl. Beat at medium speed of electric mixer until well blended. Add egg. Beat just until blended.

3. Combine flour, baking soda and salt. Add to creamed mixture at low speed. Mix just until blended. Stir in nuts.

4. Form dough into 1¼-inch balls. Roll in ½ cup granulated sugar. Place 2 inches apart onto ungreased baking sheet; flatten dough slightly with fork.

5. Bake one baking sheet at a time at 375°F for 7 to 8 minutes, or until set and just beginning to brown. *Do not overbake.* Cool 2 minutes on baking sheet. Remove cookies to foil to cool completely.

6. For frosting, combine chocolate chips, ½ teaspoon shortening and ½ teaspoon granulated sugar in microwave-safe measuring cup. Microwave at 50% (MEDIUM). Stir after 1 minute. Repeat until smooth (or melt on rangetop in small saucepan on very low heat). Drizzle generously over cooled cookies.

Makes about 3 dozen cookies

HELPFUL HINT

Once the chocolate drizzle is completely set, you can store these cookies in single layers between sheets of waxed paper.

Chewy Choco-Peanut Pudgies

Honey Ginger Snaps

2 cups all-purpose flour
1 tablespoon ground ginger
2 teaspoons baking soda
⅛ teaspoon salt
⅛ teaspoon ground cloves
½ cup shortening
¼ cup butter, softened
1½ cups sugar, divided
¼ cup honey
1 egg
1 teaspoon vanilla

Preheat oven to 350°F. Grease cookie sheets. Combine flour, ginger, baking soda, salt and cloves in medium bowl.

Beat shortening and butter in large bowl with electric mixer at medium speed until smooth. Gradually beat in 1 cup sugar until blended; increase speed to high and beat until light and fluffy. Beat in honey, egg and vanilla until fluffy. Gradually stir in flour mixture until blended.

Shape mixture into 1-inch balls. Place remaining ½ cup sugar in shallow bowl; roll balls in sugar to coat. Place 2 inches apart on prepared cookie sheets.

Bake 10 minutes or until golden brown. Let cookies stand on cookie sheets 5 minutes; transfer to wire racks to cool completely. Store in airtight container up to 1 week.

Makes 3½ dozen cookies

Mocha Mint Crisps

1 cup (2 sticks) butter, softened
1 cup sugar
1 egg
¼ cup light corn syrup
¼ teaspoon peppermint extract
1 teaspoon powdered instant coffee
1 teaspoon hot water
2 cups all-purpose flour
6 tablespoons HERSHEY®S Cocoa
2 teaspoons baking soda
¼ teaspoon salt
   Mocha Mint Sugar (recipe follows)

1. Beat butter and sugar in large bowl until fluffy. Add egg, corn syrup and peppermint extract; beat until blended. Dissolve instant coffee in hot water; stir into butter mixture.

2. Stir together flour, cocoa, baking soda and salt; gradually add to butter mixture, beating until well blended. Cover; refrigerate dough until firm enough to shape into balls.

3. Heat oven to 350°F.

4. Shape dough into 1-inch balls. Roll balls in Mocha Mint Sugar. Place on ungreased cookie sheet, about two inches apart.

5. Bake 8 to 10 minutes or until no imprint remains when touched lightly. Cool slightly; remove from cookie sheet to wire rack. Cool completely. *Makes 4 dozen cookies*

Mocha Mint Sugar: Stir together ¼ cup powdered sugar, 2 tablespoons finely crushed hard peppermint candies (about 6 candies) and 1½ teaspoons powdered instant coffee in small bowl.

Honey Ginger Snaps

Pecan Praline Cookies

¾ Butter Flavor* CRISCO® Stick or
¾ cup Butter Flavor CRISCO®
all-vegetable shortening plus
additional for greasing
1½ cups firmly packed brown sugar
 1 egg
 1 teaspoon vanilla
1½ cups all-purpose flour
 1 cup chopped pecans

Butter Flavor Crisco is artificially flavored.

1. Heat oven to 375°F. Grease baking sheet with shortening. Place sheets of foil on countertop for cooling cookies.

2. Combine ¾ cup shortening and brown sugar in large bowl. Beat at medium speed with electric mixer until creamy. Beat in egg and vanilla. Beat until light and fluffy. Add flour and pecans. Stir until well blended.

3. Shape level measuring tablespoons of dough into balls. Flatten to ⅛-inch thickness. Place 1 inch apart on prepared baking sheet.

4. Bake for 7 to 8 minutes or until edges are golden brown. *Do not overbake.* Cool on baking sheet 2 minutes. Remove cookies to foil to cool completely.

Makes 4 dozen cookies

Mrs. J's Chip Cookies

 4 cups crisp rice cereal
 1 milk chocolate crunch bar
   (5 ounces), broken into squares
 2 cups all-purpose flour
 1 teaspoon baking powder
 1 teaspoon baking soda
 ¼ teaspoon salt
 1 cup butter, softened
 1 cup granulated sugar
 1 cup packed light brown sugar
 2 eggs
 1 teaspoon vanilla
 1 package (12 ounces) semisweet
   chocolate chips
1½ cups chopped walnuts

Preheat oven to 375°F. Line cookie sheets with parchment paper or leave ungreased. Process cereal in blender or food processor until pulverized. Add chocolate bar; continue processing until both chocolate and cereal are completely ground. Add flour, baking powder, baking soda and salt; process until blended. Beat butter and sugars in large bowl until well blended. Add eggs; beat until light. Blend in vanilla. Add flour mixture; blend until smooth. Stir in chocolate chips and walnuts until blended. Shape dough into walnut-sized balls. Place 2 inches apart on cookie sheets. Bake 10 to 12 minutes or until firm in center. *Do not overbake.* Remove to wire racks to cool.

Makes about 8 dozen cookies

Cinnamon Crinkles Cookies

TOPPINGS
 2 tablespoons sugar
 ½ teaspoon ground cinnamon
 2 eggs, separated
 1 teaspoon water

COOKIES
 ¾ cup butter or margarine, softened
 1 teaspoon vanilla extract
 1 package DUNCAN HINES® Moist
  Deluxe French Vanilla Flavor Cake
  Mix
 48 whole almonds or pecans halves for
  garnish (optional)

1. Preheat oven to 375°F.

2. For toppings, combine sugar and cinnamon in small bowl; set aside. Combine egg whites and water in another small bowl; beat lightly with fork. Set aside.

3. For cookies, combine butter, egg yolks and vanilla extract in large bowl. Blend in cake mix gradually. Stir until thoroughly blended. Roll 1 level measuring teaspoon of dough into ball. Dip half the ball into egg white mixture, then into cinnamon-sugar mixture. Place ball sugar-side-up on ungreased baking sheet. Press nut on top. Repeat with remaining dough, placing balls 2 inches apart. Bake at 375°F for 9 to 10 minutes or until puffed and edges are light golden brown. Cool 2 minutes on baking sheets. Remove to cooling racks. Store in airtight container.

Makes 48 cookies

Chocolate Molasses Gems

 ¾ cup butter-flavored solid vegetable
  shortening
 1 cup firmly packed dark brown sugar
 ⅓ cup molasses
  1 large egg
 2½ cups all-purpose flour
  2 teaspoons baking soda
  1 teaspoon ground cinnamon
  1 teaspoon ground ginger
 ¼ teaspoon salt
 ¼ teaspoon ground cloves
 1¾ cups "M&M's"® Chocolate Mini
  Baking Bits
  Granulated sugar

Preheat oven to 350°F. In large bowl cream shortening and brown sugar until light and fluffy; beat in molasses and egg. In medium bowl combine flour, baking soda, cinnamon, ginger, salt and cloves; blend into creamed mixture. Stir in "M&M's"® Chocolate Mini Baking Bits. Shape dough into 1½-inch balls; roll in granulated sugar. Place about 2 inches apart onto ungreased cookie sheets. Bake 8 to 10 minutes or until set. Do not overbake. Cool 1 minute on cookie sheets; cool completely on wire racks. Store in tightly covered container.

Makes about 3 dozen cookies

Whole Grain Chippers

1 cup butter, softened
1 cup packed light brown sugar
⅔ cup granulated sugar
2 eggs
1 teaspoon baking soda
1 teaspoon vanilla
  Pinch salt
2 cups uncooked old-fashioned oats
1 cup all-purpose flour
1 cup whole wheat flour
1 package (12 ounces) semisweet
  chocolate chips
1 cup sunflower seeds

Preheat oven to 375°F. Lightly grease cookie sheets or line with parchment paper.

Beat butter with sugars and eggs in large bowl until light and fluffy. Beat in baking soda, vanilla and salt. Blend in oats and flours to make stiff dough. Stir in chocolate chips. Shape rounded teaspoonfuls of dough into balls; roll in sunflower seeds. Place 2 inches apart on prepared cookie sheets.

Bake 8 to 10 minutes or until firm. Do not overbake. Cool a few minutes on cookie sheets; remove to wire racks to cool.

Makes about 6 dozen cookies

Chocolate Mint Sugar Cookie Drops

2½ cups all-purpose flour
1½ teaspoons baking powder
 ¾ teaspoon salt
 1 cup granulated sugar
 ¾ cup vegetable oil
 1 teaspoon vanilla extract
 2 eggs
1½ cups (10-ounce package) NESTLÉ®
  TOLL HOUSE® Mint Chocolate
  Morsels
  Red and green coarse sugar or
  additional granulated sugar
  (optional)

COMBINE flour, baking powder and salt in small bowl; set aside.

COMBINE 1 cup granulated sugar, oil and vanilla in large bowl. Add eggs, 1 at a time, beating well after each addition. Gradually beat in flour mixture. Stir in morsels. Shape rounded teaspoonfuls of dough into 1-inch balls. Roll in coarse sugar or additional granulated sugar. Place on ungreased baking sheets.

BAKE in preheated 350°F. oven for 7 to 9 minutes or until centers are just set. Let stand 2 minutes; remove to wire racks to cool completely.

Makes about 5½ dozen cookies

Whole Grain Chippers

Oatmeal Snowballs

1 Butter Flavor* CRISCO® Stick or
  1 cup Butter Flavor CRISCO®
  all-vegetable shortening
¾ cup confectioners' sugar
2 tablespoons milk
1½ teaspoons vanilla
1¾ cups all-purpose flour
1 cup uncooked oats
½ cup finely chopped pecans
¼ teaspoon salt
  Additional confectioners' sugar

Butter Flavor Crisco is artificially flavored.

1. Heat oven to 325°F. Place sheets of foil on countertop for cooling cookies.

2. For cookies, combine 1 cup shortening, ¾ cup confectioners' sugar, milk and vanilla in large bowl. Beat at medium speed with electric mixer until well blended and fluffy.

3. Combine flour, oats, pecans and salt. Add gradually to creamed mixture at low speed. Shape rounded teaspoonfuls of dough into balls. Place 2 inches apart on ungreased baking sheet.

4. Bake for 15 to 18 minutes or until set and bottoms are light golden brown. *Do not overbake.* Remove cookies to foil. Cool partially. Roll warm cookies in confectioners' sugar. Cool completely. Reroll in confectioners' sugar. ***Makes 4 dozen cookies***

Chocolate Mint Snow-Top Cookies

1½ cups all-purpose flour
1½ teaspoons baking powder
¼ teaspoon salt
1½ cups (10-ounce package) NESTLÉ®
  TOLL HOUSE® Mint Flavored
  Semi-Sweet Chocolate Morsels,
  divided
6 tablespoons butter, softened
1 cup granulated sugar
1½ teaspoons vanilla extract
2 eggs
⅔ cup confectioners' sugar

COMBINE flour, baking powder and salt in small bowl. In small saucepan over low heat, melt 1 cup morsels. In large bowl, cream butter and granulated sugar. Beat in melted morsels and vanilla; beat in eggs. Gradually beat in flour mixture. Stir in remaining ½ cup morsels. Wrap in plastic wrap; freeze for 30 minutes or until firm.

PREHEAT oven to 350°F. Shape dough into 1-inch balls; roll in confectioners' sugar. Place on ungreased cookie sheets. Bake for 10 to 12 minutes or until sides are set but centers are still slightly soft. Let stand for 2 minutes; cool on wire racks.
Makes about 3 dozen cookies

Note: Nestlé® Toll House® Mint Flavored Semi-Sweet Chocolate Morsels may be melted in microwave on HIGH (100% power) for 1½ minutes, stirring once.

Soft Spicy Molasses Cookies

2 cups all-purpose flour
1 cup sugar
¾ cup butter, softened
⅓ cup light molasses
3 tablespoons milk
1 egg
½ teaspoon baking soda
½ teaspoon ground ginger
½ teaspoon ground cinnamon
½ teaspoon ground cloves
⅛ teaspoon salt
  Sugar for rolling

Combine flour, 1 cup sugar, butter, molasses, milk, egg, baking soda, ginger, cinnamon, cloves and salt in large bowl. Beat at low speed of electric mixer 2 to 3 minutes or until well blended, scraping bowl often. Cover; refrigerate until firm enough to handle, at least 4 hours or overnight.

Preheat oven to 350°F. Shape rounded teaspoonfuls of dough into 1-inch balls. Roll in sugar. Place 2 inches apart on ungreased cookie sheets. Bake 10 to 12 minutes or until slightly firm to the touch. Remove immediately.

Makes about 4 dozen cookies

Soft Spicy Molasses Cookies

Peanut Butter Crunchies

1 cup granulated sugar
1 cup firmly packed light brown sugar
1 cup creamy peanut butter
½ Butter Flavor* CRISCO® Stick or
    ½ cup Butter Flavor CRISCO®
    all-vegetable shortening
2 eggs
1½ cups all-purpose flour
½ teaspoon baking soda
1 cup peanut butter chips
⅔ cup almond brickle chips

Butter Flavor Crisco is artificially flavored.

1. Heat oven to 350°F. Place sheets of foil on countertop for cooling cookies.

2. Combine granulated sugar, brown sugar, peanut butter and ½ cup shortening in large bowl. Beat at medium-high speed of electric mixer until well blended. Beat in eggs.

3. Combine flour and baking soda. Add gradually to creamed mixture at low speed. Stir in peanut butter chips and almond brickle chips with spoon. Shape into 1½-inch balls. Place 2 inches apart on ungreased baking sheet. Dip fork in flour; flatten dough slightly in crisscross pattern.

4. Bake at 350°F for 9 to 11 minutes or until bottoms are light brown and set. *Do not overbake.* Cool 5 minutes on baking sheet. Remove cookies to foil to cool completely.

Makes about 3 dozen cookies

Chocolate Chip Cinnamon Crinkles

½ cup butter, softened
½ cup packed brown sugar
¼ cup plus 2 tablespoons granulated
    sugar, divided
1 egg
1 teaspoon vanilla
1 teaspoon cream of tartar
½ teaspoon baking soda
⅛ teaspoon salt
1⅓ cups all-purpose flour
    1 cup (6 ounces) semisweet chocolate
        chips
    2 teaspoons unsweetened cocoa
    1 teaspoon ground cinnamon

Preheat oven to 400°F. Line cookie sheets with parchment paper or leave ungreased.

Beat butter, brown sugar, ¼ cup granulated sugar, egg and vanilla in large bowl until light and fluffy. Beat in cream of tartar, baking soda and salt. Add flour; mix until dough is blended and stiff. Stir in chocolate chips. Combine remaining 2 tablespoons granulated sugar, cocoa and cinnamon in small bowl. Shape rounded teaspoonfuls of dough into balls about 1¼ inches in diameter. Roll balls in cinnamon mixture until coated on all sides. Place 2 inches apart on cookie sheets.

Bake 8 to 10 minutes or until firm. Do not overbake. Remove to wire racks to cool.

Makes about 3½ dozen cookies

Peanut Butter Crunchies

Canned Peanut Butter Candy Cookies

¾ **cup chunky peanut butter**
½ **cup butter, softened**
1 **cup packed light brown sugar**
½ **teaspoon baking powder**
½ **teaspoon baking soda**
1 **egg**
1½ **teaspoons vanilla**
1¼ **cups all-purpose flour**
2 **cups quartered miniature peanut butter cups**
⅓ **cup milk chocolate chips or chopped milk chocolate bar**

1. Beat peanut butter and butter in large bowl of electric mixer at medium speed until well blended. Beat in brown sugar, baking powder and baking soda until blended. Beat in egg and vanilla until well blended. Beat in flour at low speed just until mixed. Stir in peanut butter cups. Cover and refrigerate 1 hour or until firm.

2. Preheat oven to 375°F. For test cookie, measure inside diameter of container. Form ⅓ cup dough into ¼-inch-thick disc, about 2 inches in diameter less than the diameter of container. (One-third cup dough patted into 4-inch disc yields 5-inch cookie. Measure amount of dough used and diameter of cookie before and after baking. Make adjustments before making remaining cookies.)

3. Place dough on ungreased cookie sheets. Bake 10 minutes or until lightly browned. Remove to wire racks; cool completely.

4. Place chocolate chips in small resealable plastic food storage bag; seal bag. Microwave at MEDIUM (50% power) 1 minute. Turn bag over; microwave at MEDIUM 1 minute or until melted. Knead bag until chocolate is smooth. Cut off very tiny corner of bag; pipe chocolate decoratively onto cookies. Let stand until chocolate is set.

5. Stack cookies between layers of waxed paper in container. Store loosely covered at room temperature up to 1 week.

Makes 9 (5-inch) cookies

Lemon Cookies

1 **package DUNCAN HINES® Lemon Supreme Cake Mix**
2 **eggs**
⅓ **cup vegetable oil**
1 **tablespoon lemon juice**
¾ **cup chopped nuts or flaked coconut Confectioners' sugar**

1. Preheat oven to 375°F. Grease cookie sheets.

2. Combine cake mix, eggs, oil and lemon juice in large bowl. Beat at low speed with electric mixer until well blended. Add nuts. Shape into 1-inch balls. Place on prepared cookie sheets, 1 inch apart.

3. Bake 6 to 7 minutes or until lightly browned. Cool 1 minute on cookie sheets. Remove to cooling racks. Sprinkle with confectioners' sugar.

Makes about 3 dozen cookies

Canned Peanut Butter Candy Cookies

Peanut Butter Chocolate Chip Cookies

¼ cup butter or margarine, softened
¼ cup shortening
½ cup REESE'S® Creamy Peanut Butter
½ cup packed light brown sugar
½ cup granulated sugar
 1 egg
1¼ cups all-purpose flour
¾ teaspoon baking soda
½ teaspoon baking powder
 2 cups (12-ounce package)
    HERSHEY‚S Semi-Sweet Chocolate Chips
    Granulated sugar

1. Heat oven to 375°F.

2. Beat butter, shortening, peanut butter, brown sugar, ½ cup granulated sugar and egg in large bowl until fluffy. Stir together flour, baking soda and baking powder; stir into butter mixture. Stir in chocolate chips (if necessary, work chocolate chips into batter with hands).

3. Shape into 1-inch balls; place on ungreased cookie sheet. With fork dipped in granulated sugar flatten slightly in criss-cross pattern.

4. Bake 9 to 11 minutes or just until set. Cool slightly; remove from cookie sheet to wire rack. Cool completely.

Makes about 3 dozen cookies

Snowball Cookies

1 cup margarine or butter, softened
1 cup sugar
1 teaspoon vanilla extract
2 cups all-purpose flour
1½ cups PLANTERS® Pecans, finely ground
 ¼ teaspoon salt
 ½ cup powdered sugar

1. Beat margarine or butter, sugar and vanilla in large bowl with mixer at medium speed until creamy. Blend in flour, pecans and salt. Refrigerate 1 hour.

2. Shape dough into 1-inch balls. Place on ungreased baking sheets, 2 inches apart. Bake in preheated 350°F oven for 10 to 12 minutes. Remove from sheets; cool on wire racks. Dust with powdered sugar. Store in airtight container.

Makes 6 dozen cookies

Prep Time: 15 minutes
Chill Time: 1 hour
Cook Time: 10 minutes
Total Time: 1 hour and 25 minutes

DECORATE IT!

To dust cookies with powdered sugar, place the powdered sugar in a small strainer and gently shake the strainer over the cooled cookies.

Butterscotch Chewy Cookies

¾ cup (1½ sticks) butter or margarine, softened
1 cup packed light brown sugar
¼ cup light corn syrup
1 egg
1⅔ cups (10-ounce package) HERSHEY®S Butterscotch Chips, divided
2½ cups all-purpose flour
2 teaspoons baking soda
¼ teaspoon salt
1 to 1¼ cups finely ground nuts
Butterscotch Chip Drizzle (recipe follows)

1. Beat butter and brown sugar in large bowl until creamy. Add corn syrup and egg; blend well. Reserve ⅔ cup butterscotch chips for glaze. Microwave remaining 1 cup butterscotch chips in small microwave-safe bowl at HIGH (100%) 1 minute; stir. If necessary, microwave at HIGH an additional 15 seconds at a time, stirring after each heating, just until chips are melted when stirred. Blend into butter mixture.

2. Stir together flour, baking soda and salt; gradually add to butterscotch mixture, blending well. Refrigerate 1 hour or until dough is firm enough to handle.

3. Heat oven to 350°F. Shape dough into 1-inch balls; roll in nuts, lightly pressing nuts into dough. Place on ungreased cookie sheet.

4. Bake 8 to 10 minutes or until golden around edges. Cool several minutes; remove from cookie sheet to wire rack. Cool completely. Prepare Butterscotch Chip Drizzle; drizzle over cookies.

Makes about 5 dozen cookies

Butterscotch Chip Drizzle

⅔ cup HERSHEY®S Butterscotch Chips (reserved from cookies)
1½ teaspoons shortening (do *not* use butter, margarine, spread or oil)

Place reserved butterscotch chips and shortening in small microwave-safe bowl. Microwave at HIGH (100%) 1 minute; stir. If necessary, microwave at HIGH an additional 15 seconds at a time, stirring after each heating, just until chips are melted when stirred.

HELPFUL HINT

To reduce the risk of overprocessing when grinding nuts in a food processor, add a small amount of the flour or sugar from the recipe. If they are overprocessed, nuts will become nut butter.

Peanut Butter Jewels

1 package DUNCAN HINES® Peanut
    Butter Cookie Mix
1 egg
¼ cup vegetable oil
1 tablespoon water
⅓ cup sugar
⅓ cup cocktail peanuts, finely chopped
    Strawberry jam
    Apricot preserves

1. Preheat oven to 375°F.

2. Combine cookie mix, peanut butter flavor
packet from Mix, egg, oil and water in large
bowl. Stir until thoroughly blended. Shape
dough into 48 (1-inch) balls. Roll half the
balls in sugar and half in chopped peanuts.
Place 2 inches apart on ungreased cookie
sheets. Make indentation in center of each
ball with finger or handle end of wooden
spoon. Fill with ¼ teaspoon strawberry jam
or apricot preserves. Bake at 375°F for 8 to
10 minutes or until light golden brown.
Cool 1 minute on cookie sheets. Remove to
wire racks. Cool completely. Store in airtight
containers.   ***Makes 4 dozen cookies***

Tip: For a delicious flavor variation, try
seedless red raspberry or blackberry jam.

Thumbprint Cookies

¾ cup butter or margarine, softened
¾ cup firmly packed brown sugar
1 egg, unbeaten
1 teaspoon vanilla
1½ cups quick-cooking rolled oats
1½ cups all-purpose flour
1 teaspoon baking soda
½ teaspoon salt
    Flaked coconut (about 1½ cups)
1 can SOLO® or 1 jar BAKER®
    Raspberry Filling or any other
    fruit filling

Preheat oven to 350°F.

In large bowl, cream butter, sugar, egg and
vanilla until very light and fluffy. Add oats;
blend well. Combine flour, baking soda and
salt. Add to creamed mixture; mix until well
blended.

Shape dough into 1-inch balls; roll in coconut.
Place 1½ inches apart on ungreased cookie
sheets. Make depression in center of each
ball with thumb; fill with raspberry filling.
Bake 15 minutes or until golden. Cool on
wire racks.   ***Makes 42 to 48 cookies***

Peanut Butter Jewels

Fruited Oat Thumbprints

1½ Butter Flavor* CRISCO® Sticks or
    1½ cups Butter Flavor CRISCO®
    all-vegetable shortening
1 cup firmly packed light brown sugar
1 egg
1 tablespoon pure vanilla extract
2½ cups oats (quick or old-fashioned,
    uncooked)
  2 cups all-purpose flour
  ½ teaspoon salt
1¾ cups finely chopped pecans
  ⅔ cup fruit preserves

Butter Flavor Crisco is artificially flavored.

1. Heat oven to 350°F. Place sheets of foil on countertop for cooling cookies.

2. Combine 1½ cups shortening and brown sugar in large bowl. Beat at medium speed of electric mixer until well blended. Beat in egg and vanilla.

3. Combine oats, flour and salt. Add gradually to creamed mixture at low speed. Beat until well blended. Shape into 1-inch balls. Roll in nuts. Place 2 inches apart on ungreased baking sheet. Press thumb in centers. Fill with preserves.

4. Bake at 350°F for 12 to 15 minutes or until light golden brown. *Do not overbake.* Cool 2 minutes on baking sheet. Remove cookies to foil to cool completely.

        Makes about 4½ dozen cookies

Jam Thumbprint Gems

1½ cups all-purpose flour
  1 teaspoon baking powder
  ½ teaspoon salt
  ½ teaspoon ground cinnamon
  ¼ teaspoon ground cloves
  ¼ cup MOTT'S® Natural Apple Sauce
  2 tablespoons vegetable shortening
  ½ cup plus 1 tablespoon powdered
    sugar, divided
  1 egg
  ½ teaspoon vanilla extract
  ½ cup strawberry or other favorite
    flavor preserves

1. Preheat oven to 400°F. Spray cookie sheet with nonstick cooking spray.

2. In large bowl, combine flour, baking powder, salt and spices.

3. In large bowl, whisk together apple sauce and shortening until shortening breaks into pea-sized pieces. Add ½ cup powdered sugar; stir. Add egg and vanilla; mix well.

4. Add flour mixture to apple sauce mixture; stir until well blended. (Mixture will be stiff.)

5. Using flour-coated hands, roll teaspoonfuls of dough into balls. Place 1 inch apart on prepared cookie sheet. Press thumb gently into center of each ball. Spoon ½ teaspoon preserves into each indentation.

6. Bake 12 to 15 minutes or until lightly browned. Cool completely on wire rack; sprinkle with remaining 1 tablespoon powdered sugar.   ***Makes 2 dozen cookies***

Peanut Butter Thumbprints

1¼ cups firmly packed light brown
    sugar
¾ cup creamy peanut butter
½ **CRISCO® Stick or** ½ **cup CRISCO®**
    all-vegetable shortening
3 tablespoons milk
1 tablespoon vanilla extract
1 egg
1¾ cups all-purpose flour
¾ teaspoon baking soda
¾ teaspoon salt
    Granulated sugar
¼ cup strawberry jam, stirred

1. Heat oven to 375°F. Place sheets of foil on countertop for cooling cookies.

2. Place brown sugar, peanut butter, ½ cup shortening, milk and vanilla in large bowl. Beat at medium speed of electric mixer until well blended. Add egg; beat until blended.

3. Combine flour, baking soda and salt. Add to shortening mixture; beat at low speed just until blended.

4. Shape dough into 1-inch balls. Roll in granulated sugar. Place 2 inches apart on ungreased cookie sheets.

5. Bake one cookie sheet at a time at 375°F for 6 minutes. Press centers of cookies immediately with back of measuring teaspoon. Bake 3 minutes longer or until cookies are set and just beginning to brown. *Do not overbake.* Cool 2 minutes on baking sheet. Spoon jam into center of each cookie. Remove cookies to foil to cool completely.

Makes about 4 dozen cookies

Peanut Butter Thumbprints

Raspberry Pecan Thumbprints

2 cups all-purpose flour
1 cup pecan pieces, finely chopped
and divided
½ teaspoon ground cinnamon
¼ teaspoon ground allspice
⅛ teaspoon salt
1 cup butter, softened
½ cup packed light brown sugar
2 teaspoons vanilla
⅓ cup seedless raspberry jam

Preheat oven to 350°F. Combine flour,
½ cup pecans, cinnamon, allspice and salt in
medium bowl.

Beat butter in large bowl until smooth.
Gradually beat in brown sugar; beat until
light and fluffy. Beat in vanilla until blended.
Beat in flour mixture just until blended.

Form dough into 1-inch balls; flatten
slightly and place on ungreased cookie
sheets. Press down with thumb in center of
each ball to form indentation. Pinch together
any cracks in dough. Fill each indentation
with generous ¼ teaspoon jam. Sprinkle
filled cookies with remaining ½ cup pecans.

Bake 14 minutes or until just set. Let cookies
stand on cookie sheets 5 minutes; transfer
to wire racks to cool completely. Store in
airtight container at room temperature.
Cookies are best the day after baking.

Makes 3 dozen cookies

Peanut Butter and Jelly Thumbprints

1½ cups all-purpose flour
½ cup sugar
½ teaspoon baking soda
¼ teaspoon salt
¾ cup PETER PAN® Creamy Peanut
Butter
¼ cup butter, softened
¼ cup honey
1 tablespoon milk
KNOTT'S BERRY FARM® Grape Jelly
or any favorite flavor

In large bowl, combine flour, sugar, baking
soda and salt. Add peanut butter and butter;
mix until crumbly. Stir in honey and milk.
Shape into 1-inch balls. Place 2 inches apart
on ungreased baking sheets. Press thumb
into center of each ball; place *½ teaspoon*
jelly in each thumbprint. Bake at 375°F for
8 to 10 minutes. Cool on baking sheets
1 minute before removing to wire racks.
Store in airtight container.

Makes 2 dozen cookies

Raspberry Pecan Thumbprints

Double Peanut Butter Supremes

COOKIES

1¼ cups firmly packed light brown
    sugar
¾ cup creamy peanut butter
½ CRISCO® Stick or ½ cup CRISCO®
    all-vegetable shortening
3 tablespoons milk
1 tablespoon vanilla
1 egg
1¾ cups all-purpose flour
¾ teaspoon salt
¾ teaspoon baking soda
    Granulated sugar

FILLING

1 package (8 ounces) cream cheese,
    softened
½ cup creamy peanut butter
⅓ cup granulated sugar
1 egg, slightly beaten
    Dash salt
1 cup semi-sweet miniature chocolate
    chips

1. For cookies, combine brown sugar, ¾ cup peanut butter, ½ cup shortening, milk and vanilla in large bowl. Beat at medium speed of electric mixer until well blended. Add 1 egg. Beat just until blended.

2. Combine flour, salt and baking soda. Add to shortening mixture at low speed. Mix just until blended. Cover and refrigerate 1 hour.

3. Heat oven to 375°F. Place sheets of foil on countertop for cooling cookies.

4. For filling, combine cream cheese, ½ cup peanut butter, granulated sugar, 1 egg and salt. Beat at medium speed of electric mixer until blended. Stir in miniature chips.

5. Form dough into 1-inch balls. Roll in granulated sugar. Place 2 inches apart on ungreased baking sheets. Press thumb gently in center of each cookie. Fill center with rounded teaspoon of filling.

6. Bake one baking sheet at a time at 375°F for 7 to 8 minutes or until set and just beginning to brown. *Do not overbake.* Cool 2 minutes on baking sheets. Remove cookies to foil to cool completely.

Makes about 3 dozen cookies

FUN FOOD FACT

Peanut butter is a blend of ground roasted peanuts, vegetable oil and salt. Some commercial brands also contain sugar or a stabilizer that prevents the oil from separating.

Butter Pecan Crisps

1 cup unsalted butter, softened
¾ cup granulated sugar
¾ cup packed brown sugar
½ teaspoon salt
2 eggs
1 teaspoon vanilla
1½ cups finely ground pecans
2½ cups sifted all-purpose flour
1 teaspoon baking soda
30 pecan halves
4 squares (1 ounce each) semisweet
   chocolate
1 tablespoon shortening

Preheat oven to 375°F. Beat butter, sugars and salt in large bowl until light and fluffy. Add eggs, 1 at a time, beating well after each addition. Beat in vanilla and ground pecans. Combine flour and baking soda in small bowl. Gradually stir flour mixture into butter mixture. Spoon dough into large pastry bag fitted with ⅜-inch round tip; fill bag halfway. Shake down dough to remove air bubbles. Hold bag perpendicular to, and about ½ inch above, parchment paper-lined cookie sheets. Pipe dough into 1¼ inch balls, spacing 3 inches apart. Cut each pecan half lengthwise into 2 slivers. Press 1 sliver in center of each dough ball.

Bake 9 to 12 minutes or until lightly browned. Cool 5 minutes on cookie sheets. Remove to wire racks; cool completely. Melt chocolate and shortening in small heavy saucepan over low heat; stir to blend. Drizzle chocolate mixture over cookies. Let stand until chocolate is set.

Makes about 5 dozen cookies

Gingerbread Teddies

1 cup butter or margarine
⅔ cup JACK FROST® Light Brown
   Sugar, packed
⅓ cup JACK FROST® Granulated Sugar
½ cup molasses
1 egg, beaten
2 teaspoons vanilla
4 cups all-purpose flour
¾ teaspoon baking soda
1½ teaspoons ground cinnamon
1 teaspoon ground ginger
½ teaspoon ground cloves
   Chocolate chips

In saucepan, combine butter, sugars and molasses. Heat and stir over medium heat until butter is melted and sugars are dissolved. Pour into large mixing bowl; cool 10 minutes. Add egg and vanilla; mix well. Stir together flour, baking soda, cinnamon, ginger and cloves. Add to butter mixture; beat until well mixed. Divide dough in half. Wrap in plastic wrap; chill at least 2 hours.

For each bear, shape dough into one 3-inch ball, one 2-inch ball, six ¾-inch balls and five ½-inch balls. On ungreased cookie sheet, flatten 3-inch ball to ½-inch thickness for body. Attach 2-inch ball for head; flatten. Attach ¾-inch balls for arms, legs and ears. Place ½-inch balls at end of arms and legs to make paws. Add last ball to face to make nose. Use chocolate chips for eyes and navel. Melt 1 to 2 tablespoons chocolate chips. Using decorator's tip, pipe on mouth.

Bake in 350°F oven for 10 minutes or until lightly browned. Remove and cool on wire rack.

Makes 4 large cookies

Almond Rice Madeleines

1 cup whole blanched almonds, lightly toasted
¾ cup flaked coconut
1½ cups sugar
3 cups cooked rice, chilled
3 egg whites
Fresh raspberries
Frozen nondairy whipped topping (optional)

Preheat oven to 350°F. Spray madeleine pans* with nonstick cooking spray.

Place almonds in food processor fitted with metal blade; process until finely ground. Add coconut and sugar to processor; process until coconut is finely minced. Add rice; pulse to blend. Add egg whites; pulse to blend. Spoon mixture evenly into prepared madeleine pans, filling to tops.

Bake 25 to 30 minutes or until lightly browned. Cool completely in pans on wire racks. Cover and refrigerate 2 hours or until ready to serve. Run sharp knife around each shell; gently remove from pan. Invert onto serving plates. Serve with raspberries and whipped topping, if desired.

Makes about 3 dozen cookies

Substitute miniature muffin tins for madeleine pans, if desired.

Favorite recipe from **USA Rice Federation**

Chocolate-Dipped Almond Horns

1 can SOLO® Almond Paste
3 egg whites
½ cup sugar
½ teaspoon almond extract
¼ cup plus 2 tablespoons all-purpose flour
½ cup sliced almonds
5 squares (1 ounce each) semisweet chocolate, melted and cooled

Preheat oven to 350°F. Grease 2 cookie sheets; set aside. Break almond paste into small pieces and place in medium bowl or food processor container. Add egg whites, sugar and almond extract. Beat with electric mixer or process until mixture is very smooth. Add flour and beat or process until blended.

Spoon almond mixture into pastry bag fitted with ½-inch (#8) plain tip. Pipe mixture into 5- or 6-inch crescent shapes on prepared cookie sheets, about 1½ inches apart. Sprinkle with sliced almonds.

Bake 13 to 15 minutes or until edges are golden brown. Cool on cookie sheets on wire racks 2 minutes. Remove from cookie sheets and cool completely on wire racks. Dip ends of cookies in melted chocolate and place on aluminum foil. Let stand until chocolate is set.

Makes about 16 cookies

Almond Rice Madeleines

Inside-Out Peanut Butter Cookie Cups

COOKIES
1¼ cups firmly packed light brown
    sugar
¾ cup creamy peanut butter
½ CRISCO® Stick or ½ cup CRISCO®
    all-vegetable shortening plus
    additional for greasing
3 tablespoons milk
1 tablespoon vanilla
1 egg
1¾ cups all-purpose flour
¾ teaspoon baking soda
¾ teaspoon salt

FILLING
1 cup (6 ounces) semi-sweet chocolate
    chips
1 teaspoon Butter Flavor* CRISCO®
    Stick or 1 teaspoon Butter Flavor
    CRISCO® all-vegetable shortening
¼ cup finely chopped peanuts

Butter Flavor Crisco is artificially flavored.

1. For cookies, place brown sugar, peanut butter, ½ cup shortening, milk and vanilla in large bowl. Beat at medium speed of electric mixer until well blended. Add egg; beat just until blended.

2. Combine flour, baking soda and salt. Add to shortening mixture; beat at low speed just until blended. Refrigerate about 1 hour or until firm.

3. Heat oven to 375°F. Grease mini-muffin pans. Place sheets of foil on countertop for cooling cookies.

4. Shape dough into 1-inch balls. Place each ball in prepared mini-muffin cup (1¾ inches in diameter). Press dough onto bottom and sides of cup to within ½ inch of top.

5. Bake at 375°F for 7 to 8 minutes or until cookies are set and just beginning to brown. *Do not overbake.* Cool 10 minutes on cooling racks. Remove cookie cups carefully to foil to cool completely.

6. For filling, place chocolate chips and 1 teaspoon shortening in medium microwave-safe bowl. Microwave at 50% (MEDIUM) for 1 to 2 minutes or until chips are shiny and soft. Stir until smooth. Spoon about ½ teaspoon chocolate mixture into center of each cookie. Sprinkle with chopped peanuts. Cool completely.

Makes about 3½ dozen cookie cups

FUN FOOD FACT

Brown sugar is a mixture of granulated sugar and molasses that adds a rich flavor to baked goods. Dark brown sugar has more molasses in it, and will actually give foods a darker color. Light brown sugar has a milder flavor and lighter color than the dark variety.

Top to bottom: Bananaramas (page 358) and Inside-Out Peanut Butter Cookie Cups

Chocolate Almond Biscotti

2 cups (12-ounce package) NESTLÉ®
TOLL HOUSE® Semi-Sweet
Chocolate Morsels, divided
2 cups all-purpose flour
¼ cup NESTLÉ® TOLL HOUSE® Baking
Cocoa
1½ teaspoons baking powder
¼ teaspoon baking soda
¼ teaspoon salt
½ cup granulated sugar
½ cup packed brown sugar
¼ cup (½ stick) butter or margarine,
softened
½ teaspoon vanilla extract
½ teaspoon almond extract
3 eggs
1 cup slivered almonds, toasted
Chocolate Coating (recipe follows,
optional)

MICROWAVE 1 cup morsels in small, microwave-safe bowl on HIGH (100%) power for 1 minute; stir. Microwave at additional 10- to 20-second intervals, stirring until smooth; cool to room temperature. Combine flour, cocoa, baking powder, baking soda and salt in medium bowl.

BEAT granulated sugar, brown sugar, butter, vanilla and almond extracts until crumbly. Add eggs one at a time, beating well after each addition. Beat in melted chocolate. Gradually beat in flour mixture. Stir in nuts. Chill for 15 minutes or until firm.

SHAPE dough into two (3-inch-wide by 1-inch-high) loaves with floured hands on 1 large or 2 small greased baking sheets.

BAKE in preheated 325°F. oven for 40 to 50 minutes or until firm. Cool on baking sheets for 15 minutes. Cut into ¾-inch-thick slices; turn slices onto their sides. Bake for 10 minutes on each side until dry. Remove to wire racks to cool completely.

Makes about 2½ dozen cookies

Chocolate Coating: MICROWAVE *remaining* 1 cup morsels and 2 tablespoons shortening in medium, microwave-safe bowl on HIGH (100%) power for 1 minute; stir. Microwave at 10- to 20-second intervals, stirring until smooth. Dip biscotti halfway into chocolate coating, pushing mixture up with spatula; shake off excess. Place on waxed paper-lined tray. Chill for 10 minutes or until chocolate is set. Store in airtight containers in cool place or in refrigerator.

HELPFUL HINT

To toast nuts, spread them in a single layer on a baking sheet and toast them in a preheated 350°F oven for 8 to 10 minutes. Watch carefully, and stir them once or twice for even browning.

Linzer Cookies

2½ cups all-purpose flour
½ cup finely ground almonds
1 teaspoon baking powder
1 teaspoon salt
1 cup (2 sticks) I CAN'T BELIEVE IT'S NOT BUTTER!® Spread
1⅓ cups plus ¼ cup granulated sugar
2 eggs
½ teaspoon almond extract
1 jar (12 ounces) raspberry jam
Confectioners' sugar

Preheat oven to 350°F. Grease baking sheets; set aside. In medium bowl, combine flour, almonds, baking powder and salt; set aside.

In bowl, with electric mixer, beat I Can't Believe It's Not Butter! Spread and 1⅓ cups granulated sugar until light and fluffy, about 5 minutes. Beat in eggs and almond extract. Beat in flour mixture just until blended. On prepared sheets, drop dough by rounded tablespoonfuls, 2 inches apart.

In bowl, place remaining ¼ cup granulated sugar. Dip moistened bottom of flat glass in sugar. With glass, flatten one cookie. Repeat with remaining cookies, dipping glass just in sugar before flattening each cookie.

Bake 9 minutes or until lightly golden around edges. On wire rack, cool 2 minutes; remove from sheets and cool completely.

With 1-inch cookie cutter, cut hole in center of ½ of the cookies. Spread jam on bottom side of each remaining whole cookie; top each with cut-out cookie. Sprinkle with confectioners' sugar.

Makes 1½ dozen cookies

Roasted Honey Nut Sandwich Cookies

1½ cups quick oats
½ cup all-purpose flour
½ teaspoon baking powder
½ teaspoon baking soda
⅛ teaspoon salt
½ cup Roasted Honey Nut SKIPPY® Creamy Peanut Butter
½ cup (1 stick) margarine or butter, softened
½ cup granulated sugar
½ cup packed brown sugar
1 egg
½ teaspoon vanilla
Cookie Filling (recipe follows)

1. Preheat oven to 350°F. In bowl, combine oats, flour, baking powder, baking soda and salt. In large bowl, with mixer at medium speed, beat peanut butter, margarine and sugars until blended. Beat in egg and vanilla. Stir in oat mixture until well mixed.

2. Shape dough by heaping teaspoonfuls into balls; place 2 inches apart on ungreased cookie sheets. Flatten to 2-inch rounds.

3. Bake 8 minutes or until golden brown. Cool 3 minutes on cookie sheets. Remove to wire racks; cool completely.

4. Spread bottoms of half the cookies with heaping teaspoonfuls of Cookie Filling; top with remaining cookies.

Makes 2½ dozen sandwich cookies

Cookie Filling: In bowl, stir 1 cup Roasted Honey Nut SKIPPY® Creamy Peanut Butter and ½ cup confectioners' sugar until smooth.

Nutty Sunflower Cookies

1 package (20 ounces) refrigerated
   peanut butter cookie dough
⅓ cup all-purpose flour
½ cup semisweet chocolate chips
½ cup unsalted sunflower seeds
   Yellow and green icing

1. Remove dough from wrapper. Combine dough and flour in large bowl until well blended. Divide dough into 8 equal sections. Preheat oven to 375°F.

2. For each sunflower, divide 1 dough section in half. Roll one half into ball; flatten on ungreased cookie sheet to 2½-inch thickness. Roll other half into 5-inch long rope. Cut 2 inches from rope for stem. Cut remaining 3 inches into 10 equal sections; roll into small balls. Arrange stem and small balls around large ball on cookie sheet as shown in photo. Repeat with remaining dough.

3. Bake 10 to 11 minutes or until lightly browned. Cool 4 minutes on cookie sheets. Remove to wire racks; cool completely.

4. Melt chocolate chips in microwavable bowl at HIGH 1½ minutes or until smooth, stirring after 1 minute. Spread melted chocolate in center of each cookie; sprinkle with sunflower seeds. Decorate petals with yellow icing. Decorate stem with green icing or additional melted chocolate, if desired.

Makes 8 large cookies

Double Almond Butter Cookies

DOUGH
   2 cups butter, softened
2½ cups powdered sugar, divided
   4 cups all-purpose flour
   2 teaspoons vanilla

FILLING
   ⅔ cup BLUE DIAMOND® Blanched
      Almond Paste
   ¼ cup packed light brown sugar
   ½ cup BLUE DIAMOND® Chopped
      Natural Almonds, toasted
   ¼ teaspoon vanilla

For dough, beat butter and 1 cup powdered sugar until smooth. Gradually beat in flour. Beat in 2 teaspoons vanilla. Chill dough ½ hour.

For filling, combine almond paste, brown sugar, almonds and ¼ teaspoon vanilla.

Preheat oven to 350°F. Shape dough around ½ teaspoon filling mixture to form 1-inch balls. Place on ungreased cookie sheets.

Bake 15 minutes. Cool on wire racks. Roll cookies in remaining 1½ cups powdered sugar or sift over cookies.

Makes about 8 dozen cookies

Nutty Sunflower Cookies

Wonderful BAR COOKIES

Lemon-Cranberry Bars

½ cup frozen lemonade concentrate, thawed
½ cup spoonable sugar substitute
¼ cup margarine
 1 egg
1½ cups all-purpose flour
 2 teaspoons grated lemon peel
½ teaspoon baking soda
½ teaspoon salt
½ cup dried cranberries

1. Preheat oven to 375°F. Lightly coat 8-inch square baking pan with nonstick cooking spray; set aside.

2. Combine lemonade concentrate, sugar substitute, margarine and egg in medium bowl; mix well. Add flour, lemon peel, baking soda and salt; stir well. Stir in dried cranberries; spoon into prepared pan.

3. Bake 20 minutes or until light brown. Cool completely in pan on wire rack. Cut into 16 squares.   *Makes 16 bars*

Lemon-Cranberry Bars

Minty Shortbread Squares

1½ cups (3 sticks) butter, softened
1½ cups powdered sugar
　2 teaspoons mint extract, divided
　3 cups all-purpose flour
　½ cup unsweetened cocoa powder
1¾ cups "M&M's"® Chocolate Mini
　　Baking Bits, divided
　1 16-ounce container prepared white
　　frosting
　Several drops green food coloring

Preheat oven to 325°F. Lightly grease 15×10×1-inch baking pan; set aside. In large bowl cream butter and sugar until light and fluffy; add 1 teaspoon mint extract. In medium bowl combine flour and cocoa powder; blend into creamed mixture. Stir in 1 cup "M&M's"® Chocolate Mini Baking Bits. Dough will be stiff. Press dough into prepared baking pan with lightly floured fingers. Bake 16 to 18 minutes. Cool completely. Combine frosting, remaining 1 teaspoon mint extract and green food coloring. Spread frosting over shortbread; sprinkle with remaining ¾ cup "M&M's"® Chocolate Mini Baking Bits. Cut into squares. Store in tightly covered container.

Makes 36 squares

Outlandish Oatmeal Bars

¾ Butter Flavor* CRISCO® Stick or
　¾ cup Butter Flavor CRISCO®
　all-vegetable shortening plus
　additional for greasing
¾ cup firmly packed brown sugar
½ cup granulated sugar
　1 egg
¼ cup apple butter
　2 tablespoons milk
1¼ cups all-purpose flour
½ teaspoon baking soda
½ teaspoon salt
2½ cups quick oats (not instant or
　　old-fashioned)
　1 cup raspberry preserves, stirred
¾ cup white chocolate baking chips

Butter Flavor Crisco is artificially flavored.

1. Heat oven to 350°F. Grease 13×9×2-inch pan with shortening. Combine ¾ cup shortening, sugars, egg, apple butter and milk in large bowl. Beat until well blended.

2. Mix flour, baking soda and salt. Stir into creamed mixture until blended. Stir in oats, 1 cup at a time, until blended.

3. Spread ½ of the dough in bottom of pan. Spread with preserves to ¼ inch of sides. Mix baking chips in remaining dough. Drop by spoonfuls over preserves. Spread evenly.

4. Bake at 350°F for 30 to 35 minutes, or until golden. (Center will be soft.) *Do not overbake.* Run spatula around pan edge to loosen before cooling. Cool in pan on rack. Cut into bars. *Makes 3 dozen bars*

Minty Shortbread Squares

Autumn Apple Bars

CRUST
   Milk
   1 egg yolk (reserve egg white)
   2½ cups all-purpose flour
   1 teaspoon salt
   1 cup butter, softened

FILLING
   1 cup graham cracker crumbs
   8 cups tart cooking apples, peeled,
      cored and sliced to ¼-inch
      thickness (about 8 to 10 medium)
   1 cup plus 2 tablespoons granulated
      sugar, divided
   2½ teaspoons ground cinnamon, divided
   ¼ teaspoon ground nutmeg
   1 egg white
   1 teaspoon ground cinnamon

DRIZZLE
   1 cup powdered sugar
   1 to 2 tablespoons milk
   ½ teaspoon vanilla

1. Preheat oven to 350°F. For crust, add enough milk to egg yolk to measure ⅔ cup; set aside. Combine flour and salt in medium bowl. Cut in butter until crumbly using pastry blender or two knives. With fork, stir in milk mixture until dough forms ball; divide into 2 halves. Roll out ½ to 15×10-inch rectangle on lightly floured surface. Place on bottom of ungreased 15×10×1-inch jelly-roll pan.

2. For filling, sprinkle graham cracker crumbs over top of dough; layer apple slices over crumbs. Combine 1 cup granulated sugar, 1½ teaspoons cinnamon and nutmeg in small bowl; sprinkle over apples.

3. Roll out remaining dough into 15×10½-inch rectangle; place over apples. With fork, beat egg white in small bowl until foamy; brush over top crust. Stir together remaining 2 tablespoons granulated sugar and remaining 1 teaspoon cinnamon in another small bowl; sprinkle over crust. Bake 45 to 60 minutes or until lightly browned.

4. For drizzle, stir together all ingredients in small bowl. Drizzle over top; cut into bars.

Makes about 3 dozen bars

S'More Cookie Bars

¾ **cup (1½ sticks) IMPERIAL® Spread,**
   melted
3 cups graham cracker crumbs
1 package (6 ounces) semi-sweet
   chocolate chips (1 cup)
1 cup butterscotch chips
1 cup mini marshmallows
1 can (14 ounces) sweetened
   condensed milk

Preheat oven to 350°F.

In 13×9-inch baking dish, combine spread with crumbs; press to form even layer. Sprinkle evenly with chocolate chips, then butterscotch chips, then marshmallows. Pour condensed milk evenly over mixture.

Bake 25 minutes or until bubbly. On wire rack, let cool completely. To serve, cut into squares. ***Makes 2 dozen bars***

Autumn Apple Bars

Almond Toffee Triangles

Bar Cookie Crust (page 132)
⅓ cup KARO® Light or Dark Corn
    Syrup
⅓ cup packed brown sugar
 3 tablespoons margarine or butter
¼ cup heavy or whipping cream
1½ cups sliced almonds
 1 teaspoon vanilla

1. Preheat oven to 350°F. Prepare Bar Cookie Crust.

2. Meanwhile, in medium saucepan combine corn syrup, brown sugar, margarine and cream. Bring to a boil over medium heat; remove from heat. Stir in almonds and vanilla. Pour over hot crust; spread evenly.

3. Bake 12 minutes or until set and golden. Cool completely on wire rack. Cut into 2-inch squares; cut diagonally in half for triangles.   ***Makes about 48 triangles***

Prep Time: 30 minutes
Bake Time: 27 minutes, plus cooling

DECORATE IT!

For an easy glaze for bar cookies, sprinkle them with chocolate chips immediately after baking, then cover with foil. After 3 to 4 minutes, remove the foil and spread the melted chips over the bars.

Banana Chocolate Chip Bars

1 cup plus 2 tablespoons all-purpose
    flour
1 cup plus 2 tablespoons rolled oats
¼ cup plus 2 tablespoons chopped
    almonds, toasted
½ teaspoon baking soda
¼ teaspoon salt
¾ cup packed brown sugar
½ cup margarine
 2 small, ripe DOLE® Bananas, peeled
½ cup chocolate chips
½ teaspoon grated orange peel

• Combine flour, oats, almonds, baking soda and salt.

• Beat sugar and margarine until light and fluffy. Add flour mixture and beat until well combined. Press half of mixture in 8-inch square baking pan coated with vegetable spray. Bake in 350°F oven 10 to 12 minutes. Cool.

• Dice bananas (1½ cups). Combine with chocolate chips and orange peel. Spread over cooked crust. Top with remaining flour mixture. Press lightly. Bake 20 to 25 minutes until golden.

• Cut into bars.   ***Makes 12 bars***

Prep Time: 20 minutes
Bake Time: 35 minutes

Cranberry Cheese Bars

2 cups all-purpose flour
1½ cups quick-cooking or old-fashioned oats, uncooked
¾ cup plus 1 tablespoon firmly packed light brown sugar, divided
1 cup (2 sticks) butter, softened
1¾ cups "M&M's"® Chocolate Mini Baking Bits, divided
1 8-ounce package cream cheese
1 14-ounce can sweetened condensed milk
¼ cup lemon juice
1 teaspoon vanilla extract
2 tablespoons cornstarch
1 16-ounce can whole berry cranberry sauce

Preheat oven to 350°F. Grease 13×9×2-inch baking pan; set aside. In large bowl combine flour, oats, ¾ cup sugar and butter; mix until crumbly. Reserve 1½ cups crumb mixture for topping. Stir ½ cup "M&M's"® Chocolate Mini Baking Bits into remaining crumb mixture; press into prepared pan. Bake 15 minutes. Cool completely. In bowl beat cream cheese until light and fluffy; mix in condensed milk, lemon juice and vanilla until smooth. Pour over crust. In small bowl combine remaining 1 tablespoon sugar, cornstarch and cranberry sauce. Spoon over cream cheese mixture. Stir remaining 1¼ cups "M&M's"® Chocolate Mini Baking Bits into reserved crumb mixture. Sprinkle over cranberry mixture. Bake 40 minutes. Let cool; chill before cutting. Store covered in refrigerator. *Makes 32 bars*

Cranberry Cheese Bars

Peanut Butter and Jelly Crispies

½ Butter Flavor* CRISCO® Stick or
  ½ cup Butter Flavor CRISCO®
  all-vegetable shortening plus
  additional for greasing
½ cup crunchy peanut butter
½ cup granulated sugar
½ cup firmly packed light brown sugar
 1 egg
1¼ cups all-purpose flour
½ teaspoon baking powder
½ teaspoon baking soda
¼ teaspoon salt
 2 cups crisp rice cereal
   Honey roasted peanuts, finely
     chopped (optional)
   Jelly, any flavor

Butter Flavor Crisco is artificially flavored.

1. Heat oven to 375°F. Grease 13×9×2-inch pan with shortening. Place cooling rack on countertop for cooling bars.

2. Combine ½ cup shortening, peanut butter, granulated sugar and brown sugar in large bowl. Beat at medium speed of electric mixer until well blended. Beat in egg.

3. Combine flour, baking powder, baking soda and salt. Add gradually to creamed mixture at low speed. Beat until well blended. Add cereal. Mix just until blended. Press into greased pan. Sprinkle with nuts, if desired.

4. Score dough into bars about 2¼×2 inches. Press thumb in center of each. Fill indentation with ¼ to ½ teaspoon jelly.

5. Bake at 375°F for 12 to 15 minutes or until golden brown. *Do not overbake.* Remove pan to cooling rack. Cool 2 to 3 minutes. Cut into bars. Cool completely.

Makes about 2 dozen bars

Layered Chocolate Cheesecake Squares

1 package (9.2 ounces) JELL-O®
  No Bake Chocolate Silk Pie
1 package (11.1 ounces) JELL-O®
  No Bake Real Cheesecake
½ cup (1 stick) butter or margarine,
  melted
1⅔ cups cold milk
1½ cups cold milk

MIX crumbs from both packages and butter thoroughly with fork in medium bowl until crumbs are well moistened. Press firmly onto bottom of foil-lined 13×9-inch pan.

PREPARE Chocolate Silk Pie and Cheesecake fillings, separately, as directed on each package. Spread chocolate filling evenly over crust; top with cheesecake filling.

REFRIGERATE at least 1 hour. Garnish as desired. *Makes 15 servings*

Preparation Time: 20 minutes
Refrigerating Time: 1 hour

Peanut Butter and Jelly Crispies

Gingerbread Apple Bars

1 cup applesauce
½ cup raisins
⅓ cup unsulfured light molasses
1 teaspoon baking soda
2 eggs
¼ cup sugar
¼ cup CRISCO® Oil*
1½ cups all-purpose flour
1 teaspoon ground cinnamon
½ teaspoon ground ginger
¼ teaspoon ground cloves
⅛ teaspoon salt

Use your favorite Crisco Oil product.

1. Heat oven to 350°F. Oil 8-inch square pan lightly.

2. Place applesauce and raisins in small saucepan. Cook and stir on low heat until mixture comes to a boil. Remove from heat. Stir in molasses and baking soda. Cool slightly.

3. Combine eggs and sugar in large bowl. Beat in ¼ cup oil gradually.

4. Combine flour, cinnamon, ginger, cloves and salt in small bowl. Add to egg mixture alternately with applesauce mixture, beginning and ending with flour mixture. Spoon into pan.

5. Bake at 350°F for 30 minutes or until toothpick inserted in center comes out clean. Cool in pan on cooling rack. Cut into bars. Serve warm or at room temperature.

Makes 1 dozen bars

Championship Chocolate Chip Bars

1½ cups all-purpose flour
½ cup packed light brown sugar
½ cup (1 stick) cold butter or margarine
2 cups (12-ounce package) HERSHEY₃S Semi-Sweet Chocolate Chips, divided
1 can (14 ounces) sweetened condensed milk (*not* evaporated milk)
1 egg
1 teaspoon vanilla extract
1 cup chopped nuts

1. Heat oven to 350°F.

2. Stir together flour and brown sugar in medium bowl; with pastry blender, cut in butter until mixture resembles coarse crumbs. Stir in ½ cup chocolate chips; press mixture onto bottom of 13×9×2-inch baking pan. Bake 15 minutes.

3. Meanwhile, in large bowl, combine sweetened condensed milk, egg and vanilla. Stir in remaining 1½ cups chips and nuts. Spread over baked crust. Continue baking 25 minutes or until golden brown. Cool completely in pan on wire rack. Cut into bars.

Makes about 36 bars

Absolutely Wonderful Pecan Bars

1½ cups quick or old-fashioned oats
1½ cups all-purpose flour
  2 cups JACK FROST® Dark Brown
     Sugar, packed, divided
1½ cups butter (we do not recommend
     margarine), divided
1½ cups or 1 (7-ounce) package pecan
     halves
  1 cup JACK FROST® Granulated Sugar
  ⅓ cup heavy cream
  2 teaspoons vanilla

In large bowl, combine oats, flour and 1 cup dark brown sugar. Cut ½ cup butter into mixture until coarse and crumbly. Press into 13×9-inch baking pan. Place pecans evenly over crumb mixture.

In heavy saucepan, combine remaining 1 cup brown sugar, granulated sugar and 1 cup butter. Bring to a rolling boil over medium heat, stirring constantly. Boil 3 minutes; remove from heat. Stir in cream and vanilla until well blended; pour over pecans. Bake in preheated 350°F oven 35 to 40 minutes. Cool in pan; cut into bars.

Makes 48 bars

FUN FOOD FACT

Pecans are native to the United States, and are a member of the hickory family. They are widely grown in Georgia, Oklahoma and Texas.

Chocolate Raspberry Streusel Squares

1½ cups all-purpose flour
1½ cups QUAKER® Oats (quick or old
     fashioned, uncooked)
  ½ cup granulated sugar
  ½ cup firmly packed brown sugar
  1 teaspoon baking powder
  ¼ teaspoon salt (optional)
  1 cup (2 sticks) margarine or butter,
     chilled and cut into pieces
  1 cup raspberry preserves or jam
     (about 10 ounces)
  1 cup (6 ounces) semisweet chocolate
     pieces
  ¼ cup chopped almonds
  ½ cup (3 ounces) semisweet chocolate
     pieces or 1 bar (4 ounces) white
     chocolate, melted* (optional)

*To melt, place chocolate in microwavable bowl. Microwave at HIGH 1 to 2 minutes, stirring every 30 seconds until smooth. Or, place in top part of dry double boiler over hot, not boiling, water; stir until smooth.

Heat oven to 375°F. In bowl, mix flour, oats, sugars, baking powder and salt. Cut in margarine with pastry blender until mixture is crumbly. Reserve 1 cup oat mixture for streusel; set aside. Press remaining oat mixture onto bottom of ungreased 9-inch square baking pan. Bake 10 minutes. Spread preserves over crust; sprinkle with chocolate pieces. Mix reserved oat mixture and almonds; sprinkle over chocolate pieces, patting gently. Bake 30 to 35 minutes or until golden. Cool completely. Drizzle with melted chocolate, if desired. Let chocolate set before cutting.

Makes 36 bars

Cherry Butterscotch Bars

2 cups plus 1 tablespoon all-purpose flour, divided
¾ cup packed brown sugar
¾ cup butter, softened
2 eggs
¼ cup butterscotch chips, melted
1 teaspoon baking powder
1 teaspoon vanilla
¼ teaspoon salt
½ cup chopped drained maraschino cherries
½ cup butterscotch chips
   Maraschino cherries, butterscotch chips and powdered sugar for garnish

1. Preheat oven to 350°F. Grease and flour 13×9-inch baking pan.

2. Combine 2 cups flour, brown sugar, butter, eggs, melted butterscotch chips, baking powder, vanilla and salt in large bowl. Beat at low speed of electric mixer, scraping bowl often, until well mixed, 1 to 2 minutes.

3. Mix chopped cherries and remaining 1 tablespoon flour in small bowl. Stir cherries and ½ cup butterscotch chips into butter mixture. Spread batter in prepared pan.

4. Bake 25 to 35 minutes or until edges are lightly browned. Cool completely. Sprinkle with additional cherries, chips and powdered sugar, if desired. Cut into bars.

Makes about 3 dozen bars

Pecan Pie Bars

Bar Cookie Crust (page 132)
2 eggs
¾ cup KARO® Light or Dark Corn Syrup
¾ cup sugar
2 tablespoons margarine or butter, melted
1 teaspoon vanilla
1¼ cups coarsely chopped pecans

1. Preheat oven to 350°F. Prepare Bar Cookie Crust.

2. Meanwhile, in large bowl beat eggs, corn syrup, sugar, margarine and vanilla until well blended. Stir in pecans. Pour over hot crust; spread evenly.

3. Bake 20 minutes or until filling is firm around edges and slightly firm in center. Cool completely on wire rack. Cut into 2×1½-inch bars. *Makes about 32 bars*

Prep Time: 30 minutes
Bake Time: 35 minutes, plus cooling

Chocolate Pecan Pie Bars: Follow recipe for Pecan Pie Bars. Add ½ cup (3 ounces) semisweet chocolate chips, melted, to egg mixture. Complete as recipe directs.

Cherry Butterscotch Bars

Fruit and Nut Bars

1 cup unsifted all-purpose flour
1 cup quick oats
⅔ cup brown sugar
2 teaspoons baking soda
½ teaspoon salt
½ teaspoon cinnamon
⅔ cup buttermilk
3 tablespoons vegetable oil
2 egg whites, lightly beaten
1 Washington Golden Delicious apple, cored and chopped
½ cup dried cranberries or raisins, chopped
¼ cup chopped nuts
2 tablespoons flaked coconut (optional)

1. Heat oven to 375°F. Lightly grease 9-inch square baking pan. In large mixing bowl, combine flour, oats, brown sugar, baking soda, salt and cinnamon; stir to blend.

2. Add buttermilk, oil and egg whites; beat with electric mixer just until mixed. Stir in apple, dried fruit and nuts; spread evenly in pan and top with coconut, if desired. Bake 20 to 25 minutes or until cake tester inserted in center comes out clean. Cool and cut into 10 bars. ***Makes 10 bars***

Favorite recipe from **Washington Apple Commission**

Chewy Rocky Road Bars

1½ cups finely crushed unsalted pretzels
¾ cup (1½ sticks) butter or margarine, melted
1 can (14 ounces) sweetened condensed milk (not evaporated milk)
2 cups miniature marshmallows
1 cup HERSHEY₃S Butterscotch Chips
1 cup HERSHEY₃S Semi-Sweet Chocolate Chips
1 cup MOUNDS® Sweetened Coconut Flakes
¾ cup chopped nuts

1. Heat oven to 350°F.

2. Combine crushed pretzels and butter in small bowl; lightly press mixture into bottom of 13×9×2-inch baking pan. Pour sweetened condensed milk evenly over crumb mixture. Top with marshmallows, butterscotch chips, chocolate chips, coconut and nuts. Press toppings firmly into sweetened condensed milk.

3. Bake 25 to 30 minutes or until lightly browned. Cool completely in pan on wire rack. Cut into bars.

Makes about 36 bars

Luscious Lemon Bars

CRUST
- ¼ cup CRISCO® Oil*
- ¼ cup granulated sugar
- ¼ teaspoon salt (optional)
- 1 cup all-purpose flour
- 1½ teaspoons skim milk

FILLING
- 1 egg
- 1 egg white
- 1 cup granulated sugar
- 2 teaspoons grated lemon peel
- 3 tablespoons fresh lemon juice
- 2 tablespoons all-purpose flour
- ½ teaspoon baking powder

DRIZZLE
- ¾ cup confectioners' sugar
- 1 tablespoon skim milk
- ½ teaspoon vanilla
- ¼ teaspoon grated lemon peel

Use your favorite Crisco Oil product.

1. Heat oven to 350°F. Oil bottom of 8-inch square pan lightly. Place cooling rack on countertop.

2. *For crust,* combine ¼ cup oil, granulated sugar and salt (if used) in large bowl. Beat at medium speed of electric mixer until well blended. Add flour and milk. Stir with spoon until well mixed and crumbly. Spoon into pan. Press evenly onto bottom.

3. Bake at 350°F for 15 minutes. *Do not overbake.*

4. *For filling,* combine egg, egg white, granulated sugar, lemon peel, lemon juice, flour and baking powder in medium bowl. Beat at high speed 3 minutes. Pour over hot baked crust.

5. Bake at 350°F for 25 minutes or until light golden brown. *Do not overbake.* Remove pan to cooling rack. Loosen from edge while still warm. Cool completely.

6. *For drizzle,* combine confectioners' sugar, milk, vanilla and lemon peel in small bowl. Drizzle over top. Allow to stand before cutting into bars.   *Makes 2 dozen bars*

Nutty Chocolate Chunk Bars

- 3 eggs
- 1 cup JACK FROST® Granulated Sugar
- 1 cup JACK FROST® Brown Sugar, packed
- 1 cup oat bran
- 1 cup crunchy peanut butter
- ¾ cup butter, softened
- 2 teaspoons baking soda
- 2 teaspoons vanilla
- 3½ cups quick-cooking oats
- 1 package (12 ounces) semi-sweet chocolate chunks
- 1 cup Spanish peanuts

In large bowl, beat eggs, granulated sugar and brown sugar. Add oat bran, peanut butter, butter, baking soda and vanilla. Mix well. Stir in oats, chocolate chunks and peanuts. Spread mixture into greased 15×10×2-inch pan. Bake in 350°F oven 20 to 25 minutes.   *Makes 36 bars*

Chocolate Orange Gems

⅔ cup butter-flavored solid vegetable shortening
¾ cup firmly packed light brown sugar
1 large egg
¼ cup orange juice
1 tablespoon grated orange zest
2¼ cups all-purpose flour
½ teaspoon baking powder
½ teaspoon baking soda
½ teaspoon salt
1¾ cups "M&M's"® Chocolate Mini Baking Bits
1 cup coarsely chopped pecans
⅓ cup orange marmalade
Vanilla Glaze (recipe follows)

Preheat oven to 350°F. In large bowl cream shortening and sugar until light and fluffy; beat in egg, orange juice and orange zest. In medium bowl combine flour, baking powder, baking soda and salt; blend into creamed mixture. Stir in "M&M's"® Chocolate Mini Baking Bits and nuts. Reserve 1 cup dough; spread remaining dough into ungreased 13×9×2-inch baking pan. Spread marmalade evenly over top of dough to within ½ inch of edges. Drop reserved dough by teaspoonfuls randomly over marmalade. Bake 25 to 30 minutes or until light golden brown. *Do not overbake.* Cool completely; drizzle with Vanilla Glaze. Cut into bars. Store in tightly covered container. *Makes 24 bars*

Vanilla Glaze: Combine 1 cup powdered sugar and 1 to 1½ tablespoons warm water until desired consistency. Place glaze in resealable plastic sandwich bag; seal bag. Cut a tiny piece off one corner of the bag (not more than ⅛ inch). Drizzle glaze over cookies.

Chocolate Orange Gems

Cocoa Brownie Cookie Bars

 4 egg whites
 ⅓ cup CRISCO® Oil*
 ¼ cup nonfat vanilla yogurt
 1 teaspoon vanilla
1⅓ cups granulated sugar
 ½ cup unsweetened cocoa powder
1¼ cups all-purpose flour
 ¼ teaspoon salt
 1 tablespoon confectioners' sugar

Use your favorite Crisco Oil product.

1. Heat oven to 350°F. Oil bottom of 9-inch square pan lightly. Place cooling rack on top of counter.

2. Place egg whites in large bowl. Beat with spoon until slightly frothy. Add ⅓ cup oil, yogurt and vanilla. Mix well. Add sugar and cocoa. Mix well. Add flour and salt. Mix until blended. Pour into pan.

3. Bake at 350°F for 26 to 28 minutes or until done. *Do not overbake.* Remove to cooling rack to cool completely.

4. Sprinkle with confectioners' sugar. Cut into bars.   ***Makes 2 dozen bars***

Easy Apricot Oatmeal Bars

1½ cups all-purpose flour
 ¾ cup firmly packed brown sugar
 1 teaspoon baking powder
 1 cup cold butter or margarine
1½ cups quick-cooking oats, uncooked
 ½ cup flaked coconut
 ½ cup coarsely chopped walnuts
 1 can SOLO® or 1 jar BAKER® Apricot, Raspberry or Strawberry Filling

Preheat oven to 350°F. Grease 13×9-inch baking pan; set aside.

Combine flour, brown sugar and baking powder in medium bowl. Cut in butter until mixture resembles coarse crumbs. Add oats, coconut and walnuts; mix until crumbly. Press half of mixture into bottom of prepared pan. Spoon apricot filling over crumb mixture. Sprinkle remaining crumb mixture over apricot layer.

Bake 25 to 30 minutes or until lightly browned. (Center may seem soft but will set when cool.) Cool completely in pan on wire rack. Cut into 2×1½-inch bars.

Makes about 3 dozen bars

Clockwise from top left: Cocoa Brownie Cookie Bars, Gingerbread Apple Bars (page 110) and Luscious Lemon Bars (page 116)

Awesome Apricot Oatmeal Bars

⅔ **cup chopped dried apricots**
⅔ **cup water**
½ **cup apricot preserves**
1 **tablespoon granulated sugar**
½ **teaspoon almond extract**
1 **Butter Flavor* CRISCO® Stick or**
  1 cup Butter Flavor CRISCO®
  all-vegetable shortening
1½ **cups firmly packed brown sugar**
1½ **cups all-purpose flour**
1½ **cups quick oats (not instant or**
  old-fashioned)
1 **teaspoon baking powder**
½ **teaspoon salt**

*Butter Flavor Crisco is artificially flavored.

1. Combine apricots and water in small covered saucepan. Cook on medium heat about 10 minutes. Remove lid. Cook until apricots are tender and water has evaporated. Add preserves, granulated sugar and almond extract. Stir until preserves melt. Cool to room temperature.

2. Heat oven to 350°F. Place cooling rack on countertop.

3. Combine 1 cup shortening, brown sugar, flour, oats, baking powder and salt in large bowl. Mix at low speed of electric mixer until well blended and crumbly.

4. Press ½ of the mixture in bottom of ungreased 13×9×2-inch pan. Spread filling evenly over crust. Sprinkle remaining mixture over filling. Press down gently.

5. Bake at 350°F for 30 minutes, or until crust is golden brown. *Do not overbake.* Remove pan to rack. Cool slightly. Run spatula around edge of pan to loosen. Cut into 2×1½-inch bars. Cool in pan on cooling rack.   *Makes 3 dozen bars*

Chocolate Peanutty Crumble Bars

½ **cup butter or margarine**
1 **cup all-purpose flour**
¾ **cup instant oats, uncooked**
⅓ **cup firmly packed brown sugar**
½ **teaspoon baking soda**
½ **teaspoon vanilla extract**
4 **SNICKERS® Bars (2.07 ounces each),**
  cut into 8 slices each

Preheat oven to 350°F. Grease bottom of an 8-inch square pan. Melt butter in large saucepan. Remove from heat and stir in flour, oats, brown sugar, baking soda and vanilla. Blend until crumbly. Press ⅔ of the mixture into prepared pan. Arrange SNICKERS® Bar slices in pan, about ½ inch from the edge of pan. Finely crumble the remaining mixture over the sliced SNICKERS® Bars. Bake for 25 minutes or until edges are golden brown. Cool in pan on cooling rack. Cut into bars or squares to serve.   *Makes 24 bars*

**Top to bottom: Awesome Apricot Oatmeal Bars
and Outlandish Oatmeal Bars (page 102)**

Chocolate Chip Pecan Squares

½ Butter Flavor* CRISCO® Stick or
   ½ cup Butter Flavor CRISCO®
   all-vegetable shortening plus
   additional for greasing
½ cup firmly packed brown sugar
 1 egg
 1 tablespoon milk
 1 teaspoon vanilla
¾ cup all-purpose flour
 2 cups milk chocolate chips**, divided
¾ cup chopped pecans, divided

Butter Flavor Crisco is artificially flavored.

**You may substitute semi-sweet chocolate chips for the milk chocolate chips.*

1. Heat oven to 350°F. Grease 8×8×2-inch pan with shortening. Place cooling rack on countertop.

2. Combine ½ cup shortening, sugar, egg, milk and vanilla in large bowl. Beat at medium speed of electric mixer until well blended.

3. Mix in flour at low speed. Stir in 1 cup chocolate chips and ½ cup nuts. Spread in pan.

4. Bake at 350°F for 25 to 30 minutes, or until lightly browned. Remove from oven. Sprinkle with 1 cup chocolate chips. Wait 5 minutes, or until chips soften. Spread evenly. Sprinkle ¼ cup nuts over top. Cool in pan on cooling rack. Cut into 2×2-inch squares. ***Makes 16 squares***

Banana Split Bars

 2 extra-ripe, medium DOLE® Bananas,
   peeled
 2 cups all-purpose flour
 1 cup granulated sugar
¾ teaspoon baking soda
½ teaspoon salt
½ teaspoon ground cinnamon
 1 can (8 ounces) DOLE® Crushed
   Pineapple, undrained
 2 eggs
½ cup vegetable oil
 1 teaspoon vanilla extract
¼ cup maraschino cherries, drained,
   halved
   Creamy Vanilla Frosting (recipe
   follows)

Preheat oven to 350°F. In food processor or blender container, process bananas until puréed (1 cup). In large bowl, combine flour, granulated sugar, baking soda, salt and cinnamon. Add puréed bananas, pineapple with juice, eggs, oil and vanilla. Mix until well blended. Stir in cherries. Pour into greased and floured 13×9-inch baking pan. Bake 30 to 35 minutes. Cool in pan on wire rack. Spread with Creamy Vanilla Frosting. Cut into bars. ***Makes about 36 bars***

Creamy Vanilla Frosting

¼ cup margarine, melted
 3 to 4 tablespoons milk
 3 cups powdered sugar
 1 teaspoon vanilla extract

In small bowl, combine margarine and milk. Stir in powdered sugar and vanilla. Beat until smooth.

Chewy Hazelnut Bars

1 pound JACK FROST® Dark Brown
    Sugar (2⅓ cups, packed)
¾ cup (1½ sticks) butter
2 eggs
2 teaspoons vanilla
2 cups all-purpose flour
2 teaspoons baking powder
½ teaspoon salt
1 cup chopped hazelnuts*
1 cup semi-sweet chocolate chips

Substitute pecans or walnuts if desired.

In microwave-safe bowl, heat brown sugar and butter on HIGH about 2 minutes or until butter melts. Let cool to room temperature.

In medium bowl, beat brown sugar mixture, eggs and vanilla until well blended. In large bowl, combine flour, baking powder and salt; add to butter mixture. Stir in nuts and chocolate chips. Spread mixture evenly into buttered 11×8-inch baking pan. Bake in preheated 350°F oven 35 to 40 minutes.

Cool completely and cut into 2-inch squares.   ***Makes 20 bars***

HELPFUL HINT

Always use the pan size called for in the recipe. Substituting a different pan will affect the bars' texture. A smaller pan will give the bars a more cakelike texture; a larger pan will produce flatter bars with a drier texture.

Carrot & Spice Bars

1 cup low-fat (1%) milk
¼ cup margarine or butter
1 cup bran flakes cereal
2 eggs
1 jar (2½ ounces) puréed baby food
    carrots
¾ cup grated carrot
⅓ cup golden raisins, coarsely chopped
1 teaspoon grated orange peel
1 teaspoon vanilla
2 cups all-purpose flour
¾ cup sugar
1 teaspoon baking soda
1 teaspoon ground cinnamon
¼ cup orange juice
¼ cup toasted pecans, chopped

1. Preheat oven to 350°F. Lightly coat 13×9-inch baking pan with nonstick cooking spray; set aside.

2. Combine milk and margarine in large microwavable bowl. Microwave at HIGH 1 minute or until margarine is melted; add cereal. Let stand 5 minutes. Add eggs; whisk to blend. Add puréed carrots, grated carrot, raisins, orange peel and vanilla.

3. Combine flour, sugar, baking soda and cinnamon in medium bowl. Add to carrot mixture, stirring until thoroughly blended. Spread into prepared pan.

4. Bake 25 minutes or until toothpick inserted in center comes out clean. Insert tines of fork into cake at 1-inch intervals. Spoon orange juice over cake. Sprinkle with pecans; press into cake.

Makes 40 servings

Wild Rice Applesauce Bars

2 cups well-cooked wild rice, chopped
1 cup buttermilk or sour milk, divided
1 cup unsweetened applesauce
¼ cup vegetable oil
¾ cup shortening
1 cup firmly packed brown sugar
6 egg whites
2 teaspoons vanilla
2½ cups all-purpose flour
1 teaspoon baking soda
1 teaspoon salt
1 teaspoon cinnamon
1 cup chopped nuts
Powdered sugar

Preheat oven to 350°F. Grease bottom of 15×10×1-inch baking pan. In medium bowl, combine wild rice, ½ cup buttermilk, applesauce and oil; set aside. In large bowl, combine shortening, brown sugar, egg whites and vanilla with electric mixer; beat at high speed 5 minutes or until smooth and creamy. Add remaining ½ cup buttermilk; beat at low speed until well blended. Add flour, baking soda, salt and cinnamon; beat at low speed until well blended. Stir in wild rice mixture and nuts. Spread in prepared pan. Bake 20 to 25 minutes or until toothpick inserted in center comes out clean. Sprinkle with powdered sugar. Cool completely.   *Makes 48 bars*

Favorite recipe from **Minnesota Cultivated Wild Rice Council**

Caramel Oatmeal Chewies

1¾ cups quick or old-fashioned oats
1¾ cups all-purpose flour, divided
¾ cup packed brown sugar
½ teaspoon baking soda
¼ teaspoon salt (optional)
¾ cup (1½ sticks) butter or margarine, melted
1 cup chopped nuts
2 cups (12-ounce package) NESTLÉ® TOLL HOUSE® Semi-Sweet Chocolate Morsels
1 cup caramel ice-cream topping

COMBINE oats, 1½ cups flour, brown sugar, baking soda and salt in large bowl; stir to break up brown sugar. Stir in butter, mixing until well blended. Reserve *1 cup* oat mixture; press remaining oat mixture onto bottom of greased 13×9-inch baking pan.

BAKE in preheated 350°F. oven for 10 to 12 minutes or until light brown; cool on wire rack for 10 minutes. Sprinkle with nuts and morsels. Mix caramel topping with remaining ¼ cup flour in small bowl; drizzle over morsels to within ¼ inch of pan edges. Sprinkle with reserved oat mixture.

BAKE at 350°F. for 18 to 22 minutes or until golden brown. Cool in pan on wire rack; chill until firm.

Makes about 2½ dozen bars

Wild Rice Applesauce Bars

Raspberry Vanilla Nut Bars

1⅔ cups (10-ounce package)
    HERSHEY₅S Premier White Chips,
    divided
¾ cup (1½ sticks) butter or margarine
2¼ cups all-purpose flour
¾ cup sugar
3 eggs
¾ teaspoon baking powder
1⅔ cups (10-ounce package)
    HERSHEY₅S Raspberry Chips,
    divided
½ cup chopped pecans
    Double Drizzle (recipe follows)

1. Heat oven to 350°F. Grease 13×9×2-inch baking pan.

2. Reserve 2 tablespoons white chips for drizzle. Mix remaining white chips and butter in microwave-safe bowl. Microwave at HIGH (100%) 1½ minutes; stir. If necessary, microwave an additional 15 seconds at a time, stirring after each heating, just until chips are melted when stirred. In bowl, mix flour, sugar, eggs and baking powder. Add white chip mixture; beat well. Reserve 2 tablespoons raspberry chips for drizzle. Chop remaining raspberry chips in food processor (use pulsing motion); stir into batter with pecans. Spread in prepared pan.

3. Bake 25 minutes or until edges pull away from sides of pan and top surface is golden. Cool completely in pan on wire rack. Prepare Double Drizzle; using one flavor at a time, drizzle over bars. Cut into bars.

Makes about 24 bars

Double Drizzle

2 tablespoons HERSHEY₅S Premier
    White Chips (reserved from bars)
1 teaspoon shortening (do *not* use
    butter, margarine, spread or oil),
    divided
2 tablespoons HERSHEY₅S Raspberry
    Chips (reserved from bars)

Place 2 tablespoons HERSHEY₅S Premier White Chips and ½ teaspoon shortening (do not use butter, margarine, spread or oil) in small microwave-safe bowl. Microwave at HIGH (100%) 30 seconds; stir. If necessary, microwave at HIGH an additional 15 seconds at a time, stirring after each heating, just until chips are melted when stirred. Repeat procedure with raspberry chips and remaining ½ teaspoon shortening.

Peanut Butter and Chocolate Bars: Omit HERSHEY₅S Premier White Chips; replace with 1⅔ cups REESE'S® Peanut Butter Chips. Omit HERSHEY₅S Raspberry Chips; replace with 1⅔ cups HERSHEY₅S Semi-Sweet Chocolate Chips. Omit chopped pecans; replace with chopped peanuts.

Butterscotch and Chocolate Bars: Omit HERSHEY₅S Premier White Chips; replace with 1⅔ cups HERSHEY₅S Butterscotch Chips. Omit HERSHEY₅S Raspberry Chips; replace with 1⅔ cups HERSHEY₅S Semi-Sweet Chocolate Chips. Omit chopped pecans; replace with chopped walnuts.

Coconut Almond Bars

CRUST
1½ cups all-purpose flour
1 cup butter, softened
½ cup sugar
½ cup ground almonds
½ teaspoon almond extract

FILLING
1 cup sugar
1 egg
2 tablespoons all-purpose flour
½ teaspoon baking powder
½ teaspoon salt
2 teaspoons vanilla
1 cup flaked coconut
¾ cup lightly toasted slivered almonds, divided
2 teaspoons milk

CRUST
Preheat oven to 350°F. Combine all crust ingredients in small bowl. Beat at low speed of electric mixer, scraping bowl often, until particles are fine, 2 to 3 minutes. Press on bottom of 13×9-inch baking pan. Bake 15 to 20 minutes or until edges are lightly browned.

FILLING
Combine sugar, egg, flour, baking powder, salt and vanilla in small bowl. Beat at medium speed of electric mixer, scraping bowl often, until well mixed, 1 to 2 minutes. Stir in coconut, ½ cup nuts and milk. Pour over hot crust. Sprinkle top with remaining ¼ cup nuts. Bake an additional 20 to 25 minutes or until lightly browned.

Makes about 36 bars

Coconut Almond Bars

Oasis Date Bars

½ cup (1 stick) butter or margarine, softened
¾ cup firmly packed light brown sugar
2 large eggs
2 teaspoons vanilla extract
1½ cups all-purpose flour
½ cup shredded coconut
1 teaspoon baking powder
1¾ cups "M&M's"® Chocolate Mini Baking Bits, divided
1 cup chopped pitted dates
½ cup chopped almonds
Lemon Glaze (recipe follows)

Preheat oven to 350°F. Lightly grease 13×9×2-inch baking pan; set aside. In large bowl cream butter and sugar until light and fluffy; beat in eggs and vanilla. In separate bowl combine flour, coconut and baking powder; blend into creamed mixture. Stir in 1¼ cups "M&M's"® Chocolate Mini Baking Bits, dates and nuts. Dough will be stiff. Spread into prepared pan; sprinkle with remaining ½ cup "M&M's"® Chocolate Mini Baking Bits. Bake 35 to 40 minutes or until toothpick inserted in center comes out clean. Cool completely; drizzle with Lemon Glaze. Cut into bars. Store in tightly covered container. *Makes 24 bars*

Lemon Glaze: Combine 1 cup powdered sugar, 2 tablespoons lemon juice and 1 tablespoon grated lemon zest until smooth. Place in resealable plastic sandwich bag; seal bag. Cut a tiny piece off one corner of the bag (not more than ⅛ inch). Drizzle glaze over bars.

Chocolate Macadamia Bars

12 squares (1 ounce each) bittersweet chocolate *or* 1 package (12 ounces) semisweet chocolate chips
1 package (8 ounces) cream cheese, softened
⅔ cup whipping cream or undiluted evaporated milk
1 cup chopped macadamia nuts or almonds
1 teaspoon vanilla, divided
1 cup butter, softened
1½ cups sugar
1 egg
3 cups all-purpose flour
1 teaspoon baking powder
¼ teaspoon salt

Preheat oven to 375°F. Lightly grease 13×9-inch baking pan.

Mix chocolate, cream cheese and whipping cream in large heavy saucepan. Stir over low heat until chocolate is melted and mixture is smooth. Remove from heat; stir in nuts and ½ teaspoon vanilla. Set aside.

Beat butter and sugar in large bowl. Beat in egg and remaining ½ teaspoon vanilla. Add flour, baking powder and salt; blend well. Press half of butter mixture on bottom of prepared pan. Spread chocolate mixture evenly over top. Sprinkle remaining butter mixture over chocolate.

Bake 35 to 40 minutes or until golden brown. Cool in pan on wire rack. Cut into 2×1½-inch bars. *Makes 36 bars*

Oasis Date Bars

White Chip Meringue Dessert Bars

CRUST
  2 cups all-purpose flour
  ½ cup powdered sugar
  1 cup (2 sticks) butter or margarine,
    softened

TOPPING
  2 cups (12-ounce package) NESTLÉ®
    TOLL HOUSE® Premier White
    Morsels
1¼ cups coarsely chopped nuts, divided
  3 egg whites
  1 cup packed brown sugar

FOR CRUST
COMBINE flour, powdered sugar and
butter with pastry blender or two knives in
medium bowl until crumbly. Press evenly
onto bottom of ungreased 13×9-inch
baking pan.

BAKE in preheated 375°F. oven for 10 to
12 minutes or until set. Remove from oven.

FOR TOPPING
SPRINKLE morsels and 1 cup nuts over hot
crust.

BEAT egg whites in small mixer bowl until
frothy. Gradually add brown sugar. Beat
until stiff peaks form when beaters are lifted.
Carefully spread meringue over morsels and
nuts. Sprinkle with *remaining* nuts.

BAKE at 375°F. for 15 to 20 minutes or
until golden brown. Serve warm or cool on
wire rack.   *Makes about 2 dozen bars*

Apple Crumb Squares

  2 cups QUAKER® Oats (quick or old
    fashioned, uncooked)
1½ cups all-purpose flour
  1 cup packed brown sugar
  ¾ cup (12 tablespoons) butter or
    margarine, melted
  1 teaspoon ground cinnamon
  ½ teaspoon baking soda
  ½ teaspoon salt (optional)
  ¼ teaspoon ground nutmeg
  1 cup applesauce
  ½ cup chopped nuts

Preheat oven to 350°F. In large bowl,
combine all ingredients except applesauce
and nuts; mix until crumbly. Reserve 1 cup
oats mixture. Press remaining mixture on
bottom of greased 13×9-inch metal baking
pan. Bake 13 to 15 minutes; cool. Spread
applesauce over partially baked crust.
Sprinkle reserved 1 cup oats mixture over
top; sprinkle with nuts. Bake 13 to
15 minutes or until golden brown. Cool in
pan on wire rack; cut into 2-inch squares.

Makes about 2 dozen bars

HELPFUL HINT

*To melt ½ cup (1 stick) of butter in the
microwave, place the butter in a
microwavable dish. Cover lightly
with plastic wrap and heat at
HIGH 1 to 1½ minutes.*

White Chip Meringue Dessert Bars

Chocolate Chip Walnut Bars

Bar Cookie Crust (recipe follows)
2 eggs
½ cup KARO® Light or Dark Corn Syrup
½ cup sugar
2 tablespoons margarine, melted
1 cup (6 ounces) semisweet chocolate chips
¾ cup chopped walnuts

1. Preheat oven to 350°F. Prepare Bar Cookie Crust.

2. Meanwhile, in medium bowl beat eggs, corn syrup, sugar and margarine until well blended. Stir in chocolate chips and walnuts. Pour over hot crust; spread evenly.

3. Bake 15 to 18 minutes or until set. Cool completely on wire rack. Cut into 2×1½-inch bars.   *Makes about 32 bars*

Bar Cookie Crust

MAZOLA NO STICK® Cooking Spray
2 cups flour
½ cup (1 stick) cold margarine, cut into pieces
⅓ cup sugar
¼ teaspoon salt

1. Preheat oven to 350°F. Spray 13×9-inch baking pan with cooking spray.

2. In bowl, beat flour, margarine, sugar and salt until mixture resembles coarse crumbs. Press firmly into bottom and ¼ inch up sides of prepared pan.

3. Bake 15 minutes or until golden brown. Top with filling. Complete as recipe directs.

Strawberry Pecan Jumbles

1¼ cups all-purpose flour
½ cup CREAM OF WHEAT Cereal (1-minute, 2½-minute or 10-minute stovetop cooking)
⅓ cup PLANTERS Pecans, chopped
⅓ cup sugar
½ teaspoon DAVIS Baking Powder
½ cup margarine or butter, melted
1 egg, slightly beaten
1 teaspoon vanilla extract
½ cup strawberry preserves

1. Mix flour, cereal, pecans, sugar and baking powder in large bowl; stir in margarine or butter, egg and vanilla until crumbly. Reserve ½ cup dough.

2. Press remaining dough on bottom of greased 9×9×2-inch baking pan. Spread strawberry preserves evenly over dough; crumble reserved dough over preserves.

3. Bake at 375°F for 18 to 20 minutes or until golden brown. Cool completely in pan on wire rack. Cut into bars to serve.

Makes 18 bars

Clockwise from top left: Pecan Pie Bars (page 112), Almond Toffee Triangles (page 106) and Chocolate Chip Walnut Bars

Oatmeal Chocolate Cherry Bars

½ cup (1 stick) butter or margarine, softened
¼ cup solid vegetable shortening
1 cup firmly packed light brown sugar
1 large egg
1 teaspoon vanilla extract
2½ cups quick-cooking or old-fashioned oats, uncooked
1 cup all-purpose flour
1 teaspoon baking soda
1¾ cups "M&M's"® Chocolate Mini Baking Bits, divided
1 cup dried cherries, plumped*

To plump cherries, pour 1½ cups boiling water over cherries and let stand 10 minutes. Drain well and use as directed.

Preheat oven to 350°F. Lightly grease 13×9×2-inch baking pan; set aside. In large bowl cream butter and shortening until light and fluffy; beat in sugar, egg and vanilla. In medium bowl combine oats, flour and baking soda; blend into creamed mixture. Stir in 1¼ cups "M&M's"® Chocolate Mini Baking Bits and cherries. Spread batter evenly in prepared pan; top with remaining ½ cup "M&M's"® Chocolate Mini Baking Bits. Bake 25 to 30 minutes or until toothpick inserted in center comes out clean. Cool completely. Cut into squares. Store in tightly covered container.

Makes 24 bars

Lemon Bars

CRUST
1 cup all-purpose flour
½ cup powdered sugar
¼ cup MOTT'S® Natural Apple Sauce
2 tablespoons margarine, melted

LEMON FILLING
1 cup granulated sugar
2 egg whites
1 whole egg
⅓ cup MOTT'S® Natural Apple Sauce
1 teaspoon grated lemon peel
¼ cup lemon juice
3 tablespoons all-purpose flour
½ teaspoon baking powder
Additional powdered sugar (optional)

1. Preheat oven to 350°F. Spray 8-inch square pan with nonstick cooking spray.

2. To prepare crust, in small bowl, combine 1 cup flour and powdered sugar. Add ¼ cup apple sauce and margarine. Stir with fork until mixture resembles coarse crumbs. Press evenly into bottom of prepared pan. Bake 10 minutes.

3. To prepare lemon filling, in bowl, beat granulated sugar, egg whites and whole egg until thick and smooth. Add ⅓ cup apple sauce, lemon peel, lemon juice, 3 tablespoons flour and baking powder. Beat until blended. Pour lemon filling over baked crust.

4. Bake 20 to 25 minutes or until lightly browned. Cool completely on wire rack. Sprinkle with powdered sugar, if desired; cut into bars.   *Makes 14 servings*

Oatmeal Chocolate Cherry Bars

Delightful Peanut Butter Marshmallow Cookie Bars

COOKIE BASE
¾ **cup firmly packed light brown sugar**
½ **Butter Flavor* CRISCO® Stick or**
　　½ **cup Butter Flavor CRISCO®**
　　all-vegetable shortening plus
　　additional for greasing
½ **cup crunchy peanut butter**
¼ **cup granulated sugar**
1 **egg**
1¼ **cups all-purpose flour**
1 **teaspoon baking powder**
¼ **teaspoon salt**

TOPPING
½ **cup creamy peanut butter**
4 **cups miniature marshmallows**
½ **cup chocolate flavor syrup**

*Butter Flavor Crisco is artificially flavored.

1. For cookie base, combine brown sugar, ½ cup shortening, crunchy peanut butter, granulated sugar and egg in large bowl. Beat at medium speed of electric mixer until well blended.

2. Combine flour, baking powder and salt. Add gradually to creamed mixture at low speed. Beat until well blended. Cover. Refrigerate 15 minutes.

3. Heat oven to 350°F. Grease 13×9×2-inch glass baking dish with shortening. Place cooling rack on countertop. Press chilled cookie base into prepared dish.

4. Bake at 350°F for 20 minutes or until light brown. *Do not overbake.* Cool 2 to 3 minutes.

5. For topping, place creamy peanut butter in microwave-safe measuring cup. Microwave at HIGH for 1 minute. Pour over baked surface. Spread to cover. Cover with marshmallows. Drizzle chocolate syrup over marshmallows. Return to oven. Bake 5 minutes or until marshmallows are light brown. *Do not overbake.* Loosen from sides of dish with knife. Remove dish to cooling rack. Cool completely. Cut with sharp greased knife into bars about 2×2 inches.

Makes about 2 dozen bars

Oreo® Decadence Bars

1 **(8-ounce) package OREO® Crunchies**
2 **tablespoons margarine or butter, melted**
¾ **cup white chocolate chips**
¾ **cup miniature marshmallows**
¾ **cup PLANTERS® Walnuts, chopped**
1 **(14-ounce) can sweetened condensed milk**

1. Preheat oven to 350°F. Combine Crunchies and margarine or butter in small bowl. Sprinkle 1 cup crumb mixture over bottom of lightly greased 8×8×2-inch baking pan. Sprinkle with white chocolate chips, marshmallows and walnuts; top with remaining crumb mixture. Pour condensed milk evenly over crumbs.

2. Bake at 350°F for 30 minutes. Cool completely in pan. Cut into bars; store in airtight container. *Makes 16 bars*

Fabulous Fruit Bars

1½ **cups all-purpose flour, divided**
1½ **cups sugar, divided**
   ½ **cup MOTT'S® Apple Sauce, divided**
   ½ **teaspoon baking powder**
   2 **tablespoons margarine**
   ½ **cup chopped peeled apple**
   ½ **cup chopped dried apricots**
   ½ **cup chopped cranberries**
   1 **whole egg**
   1 **egg white**
   1 **teaspoon lemon juice**
   ½ **teaspoon vanilla extract**
   1 **teaspoon ground cinnamon**

1. Preheat oven to 350°F. Spray 13×9-inch baking pan with nonstick cooking spray.

2. In medium bowl, combine 1¼ cups flour, ½ cup sugar, ⅓ cup apple sauce and baking powder. Cut in margarine with pastry blender or fork until mixture resembles coarse crumbs.

3. In large bowl, combine apple, apricots, cranberries, remaining apple sauce, whole egg, egg white, lemon juice and vanilla.

4. In small bowl, combine remaining 1 cup sugar, ¼ cup flour and cinnamon. Add to fruit mixture, stirring just until mixed.

5. Press half of crumb mixture evenly into bottom of prepared pan. Top with fruit mixture. Sprinkle with remaining crumb mixture.

6. Bake 40 minutes or until lightly browned. Broil, 4 inches from heat, 1 to 2 minutes or until golden brown. Cool on wire rack 15 minutes; cut into 16 bars.

Makes 16 servings

Fabulous Fruit Bars

Chippy Cheeseys

BASE

1¼ cups firmly packed brown sugar

¾ Butter Flavor* CRISCO® stick or
   ¾ cup Butter Flavor CRISCO®
   all-vegetable shortening plus
   additional for greasing

2 tablespoons milk

1 egg

1 tablespoon vanilla

2 cups all-purpose flour

1 teaspoon salt

¾ teaspoon baking soda

1 cup semi-sweet mini chocolate chips

1 cup finely chopped walnuts

FILLING

2 (8-ounce) packages cream cheese,
   softened

2 eggs

¾ cup granulated sugar

1 teaspoon vanilla

Butter Flavor Crisco is artificially flavored.

1. Heat oven to 375°F. Grease 13×9-inch pan with shortening. Place cooling rack on countertop.

2. For base, combine brown sugar and ¾ cup shortening in large mixer bowl. Beat at medium speed of electric mixer until creamy. Beat in milk, 1 egg and 1 tablespoon vanilla.

3. Combine flour, salt and baking soda. Add gradually to creamed mixture at low speed. Stir in chocolate chips and nuts with spoon. Spread half of dough in prepared pan. Bake 8 minutes. *Do not overbake.*

4. For filling, combine cream cheese, eggs, sugar and vanilla in medium mixer bowl. Beat at medium speed of electric mixer until smooth. Pour over hot crust.

5. Roll remaining half of dough into 13×9-inch rectangle between sheets of waxed paper. Remove top sheet. Flip dough over onto filling. Remove waxed paper.

6. Bake 40 minutes or until top is set and light golden brown. *Do not overbake.* Remove pans to cooling rack to cool to room temperature. Cut into bars about 2×1¾ inches. Refrigerate.

Makes about 30 bars

HELPFUL HINT

Bar cookies look best when they are cut neatly into uniform sizes. Measure the bars with a ruler, and use a knife to score the surface. Then cut the bars along the score lines with a sharp knife.

Chippy Cheeseys

Tropical Coconut Squares

1 cup butter, softened
½ cup granulated sugar
2 egg yolks
¼ teaspoon salt
2¼ cups plus 3 tablespoons all-purpose flour, divided
½ teaspoon baking powder
1½ cups packed light brown sugar
3 eggs
1 teaspoon vanilla
1½ cups macadamia nuts
2 cups flaked coconut

Preheat oven to 350°F. Grease 15×10-inch jelly-roll pan.

Beat butter and granulated sugar in large bowl until light and fluffy. Beat in egg yolks and salt. Gradually add 2¼ cups flour; beat until well blended. Spread dough in prepared pan. Bake 16 to 18 minutes or until golden brown.

Combine remaining 3 tablespoons flour and baking powder in small bowl. Beat brown sugar and whole eggs in large bowl until very thick. Beat in vanilla. Gradually add flour mixture; beat until blended. Stir in nuts.

Spread batter evenly over hot crust; sprinkle with coconut. Return pan to oven; bake 20 to 22 minutes or until top is golden brown and puffed. Remove pan to wire rack to cool completely. Cut into 2-inch squares. Store squares tightly covered at room temperature.

Makes about 40 squares

Orange Chess Bars

CRUST
1 package DUNCAN HINES® Moist Deluxe Orange Supreme Cake Mix
½ cup vegetable oil
⅓ cup chopped pecans

TOPPING
1 pound confectioners' sugar (3½ to 4 cups)
1 (8-ounce) package cream cheese, softened
2 eggs
2 teaspoons grated orange peel

1. Preheat oven to 350°F. Grease 13×9-inch baking pan.

2. For crust, combine cake mix, oil and pecans in large bowl. Stir until blended (mixture will be crumbly). Press in bottom of prepared pan.

3. For topping, combine confectioners' sugar and cream cheese in large bowl. Beat at low speed with electric mixer until blended. Add eggs and orange peel. Beat at low speed until blended. Pour over crust. Bake 30 to 35 minutes or until topping is set. Cool. Refrigerate until ready to serve. Cut into bars. ***Makes about 24 bars***

Tropical Coconut Squares

Scrumptious Minted Brownies

**1 package DUNCAN HINES® Chocolate Lovers Chewy
  Fudge Brownie Mix**
1 egg
⅓ cup water
⅓ cup vegetable oil
48 chocolate créme de menthe candy wafers, divided

1. Preheat oven to 350°F. Grease bottom of 13×9-inch pan.

2. Combine brownie mix, egg, water and oil in large bowl. Stir
with spoon until well blended, about 50 strokes. Spread in
prepared pan. Bake at 350°F for 25 minutes or until set. Place
30 candy wafers evenly over hot brownies. Let stand for 1 minute
to melt. Spread candy wafers to frost brownies. Score frosting into
36 bars by running tip of knife through melted candy. (Do not cut
through brownies.) Cut remaining 18 candy wafers in half
lengthwise; place halves on each scored bar. Cool completely. Cut
into bars. *Makes 36 brownies*

Scrumptious Minted Brownies

Bittersweet Pecan Brownies with Caramel Sauce

BROWNIE
 ¾ **cup all-purpose flour**
 ¼ **teaspoon baking soda**
 4 **squares (1 ounce each) bittersweet or unsweetened chocolate, coarsely chopped**
 ½ **cup (1 stick) plus 2 tablespoons I CAN'T BELIEVE IT'S NOT BUTTER!® Spread**
 ¾ **cup sugar**
 2 **eggs**
 ½ **cup chopped pecans**

CARAMEL SAUCE
 ¾ **cup firmly packed light brown sugar**
 6 **tablespoons I CAN'T BELIEVE IT'S NOT BUTTER!® Spread**
 ⅓ **cup whipping or heavy cream**
 ½ **teaspoon apple cider vinegar or fresh lemon juice**

For brownie, preheat oven to 325°F. Line 8-inch square baking pan with aluminum foil, then grease and flour foil; set aside.

In small bowl, combine flour and baking soda; set aside.

In medium microwave-safe bowl, microwave chocolate and I Can't Believe It's Not Butter! Spread at HIGH (Full Power) 1 minute or until chocolate is melted; stir until smooth. With wooden spoon, beat in sugar, then eggs. Beat in flour mixture. Evenly spread into prepared pan; sprinkle with pecans.

Bake 31 minutes or until toothpick inserted in center comes out clean. On wire rack, cool completely. To remove brownies, lift edges of foil. Cut brownies into 4 squares, then cut each square into 2 triangles.

For caramel sauce, in medium saucepan, bring brown sugar, I Can't Believe It's Not Butter! Spread and cream just to a boil over high heat, stirring frequently. Cook 3 minutes. Stir in vinegar. To serve, pour caramel sauce around brownie and top, if desired, with vanilla or caramel ice cream.

Makes 8 servings

Buffalo Bill Brownies

 1 **(4-serving size) package ROYAL® Chocolate Pudding & Pie Filling**
 2 **cups heavy cream**
 ¼ **cup raspberry preserves**
 1 **prepared brownie mix baked in 9-inch square pan**
 ¼ **cup semisweet chocolate chips**
 1 **tablespoon margarine or butter**

1. Heat pudding, heavy cream and preserves to a boil in small saucepan over medium heat; boil 1 minute. Pour pudding over baked brownie; set aside.

2. Melt chocolate chips and margarine or butter in small saucepan over medium heat. Drizzle over pudding. Refrigerate until firm, about 2 hours. Cut into 3-inch squares.

Makes 9 servings

Bittersweet Pecan Brownies with Caramel Sauce

Brownie Candy Cups

**1 package DUNCAN HINES® Double
    Fudge Brownie Mix**
2 eggs
⅓ cup water
¼ cup vegetable oil
30 miniature peanut butter cup candies

Preheat oven to 350°F. Place 30 (2-inch) foil liners in muffin pans or on cookie sheets.

Combine brownie mix, fudge packet from Mix, eggs, water and oil in large bowl. Stir with spoon until well blended, about 50 strokes. Place 2 level tablespoonfuls batter into each foil liner. Bake 10 minutes. Remove from oven. Push 1 peanut butter cup candy in center of each cupcake until even with surface of cupcake. Bake 5 to 7 minutes or until candy is softened. Remove to cooling racks. Cool completely.

Makes 30 brownie cups

DECORATE IT!

Cookies, brownies and bars make great gifts. Place them in a paper-lined tin or on a decorative plate; cover with plastic wrap and tie with a colorful ribbon. For a special touch, include the recipe.

Marble Brownies

**½ cup plus 2 tablespoons all-purpose
    flour, divided**
½ cup unsweetened cocoa powder
1 teaspoon baking powder
½ teaspoon salt
1¾ cups sugar, divided
2 tablespoons margarine, softened
½ cup MOTT'S® Natural Apple Sauce
3 egg whites, divided
1½ teaspoons vanilla extract, divided
**4 ounces low fat cream cheese
    (Neufchâtel), softened**

1. Preheat oven to 350°F. Spray 8-inch square baking pan with nonstick cooking spray.

2. In small bowl, sift together ½ cup flour, cocoa, baking powder and salt.

3. In large bowl, beat 1½ cups sugar and margarine with electric mixer at medium speed until blended. Whisk in apple sauce, 2 egg whites and 1 teaspoon vanilla.

4. Add flour mixture to apple sauce mixture; stir until well blended. Pour batter into prepared pan.

5. In small bowl, beat cream cheese and remaining ¼ cup sugar with electric mixer at medium speed until blended. Stir in remaining egg white, 2 tablespoons flour and ½ teaspoon vanilla. Pour over brownie batter; run knife through batters to marble.

6. Bake 35 to 40 minutes or until firm. Cool on wire rack 15 minutes; cut into 12 bars.

Makes 12 servings

Brownie Candy Cups

Brownie Candy Cups

1 package DUNCAN HINES® Double Fudge Brownie Mix
2 eggs
⅓ cup water
¼ cup vegetable oil
30 miniature peanut butter cup candies

Preheat oven to 350°F. Place 30 (2-inch) foil liners in muffin pans or on cookie sheets.

Combine brownie mix, fudge packet from Mix, eggs, water and oil in large bowl. Stir with spoon until well blended, about 50 strokes. Place 2 level tablespoonfuls batter into each foil liner. Bake 10 minutes. Remove from oven. Push 1 peanut butter cup candy in center of each cupcake until even with surface of cupcake. Bake 5 to 7 minutes or until candy is softened. Remove to cooling racks. Cool completely.

Makes 30 brownie cups

DECORATE IT!

Cookies, brownies and bars make great gifts. Place them in a paper-lined tin or on a decorative plate; cover with plastic wrap and tie with a colorful ribbon. For a special touch, include the recipe.

Marble Brownies

½ cup plus 2 tablespoons all-purpose flour, divided
½ cup unsweetened cocoa powder
1 teaspoon baking powder
½ teaspoon salt
1¾ cups sugar, divided
2 tablespoons margarine, softened
½ cup MOTT'S® Natural Apple Sauce
3 egg whites, divided
1½ teaspoons vanilla extract, divided
4 ounces low fat cream cheese (Neufchâtel), softened

1. Preheat oven to 350°F. Spray 8-inch square baking pan with nonstick cooking spray.

2. In small bowl, sift together ½ cup flour, cocoa, baking powder and salt.

3. In large bowl, beat 1½ cups sugar and margarine with electric mixer at medium speed until blended. Whisk in apple sauce, 2 egg whites and 1 teaspoon vanilla.

4. Add flour mixture to apple sauce mixture; stir until well blended. Pour batter into prepared pan.

5. In small bowl, beat cream cheese and remaining ¼ cup sugar with electric mixer at medium speed until blended. Stir in remaining egg white, 2 tablespoons flour and ½ teaspoon vanilla. Pour over brownie batter; run knife through batters to marble.

6. Bake 35 to 40 minutes or until firm. Cool on wire rack 15 minutes; cut into 12 bars.

Makes 12 servings

Brownie Candy Cups

Cheesecake Marble Brownies

6 squares (1 ounce each) semisweet
 chocolate
¾ cup (1½ sticks) IMPERIAL® Spread,
 softened, divided
1¾ cups all-purpose flour, divided
1 teaspoon baking powder
½ teaspoon salt
2 cups sugar, divided
4 eggs, divided
1½ teaspoons vanilla extract, divided
1 package (8 ounces) cream cheese,
 softened

Preheat oven to 350°F. Grease 13×9-inch
baking pan; set aside.

In medium saucepan, melt chocolate with
½ cup spread over low heat, stirring
occasionally. Remove from heat and let cool
slightly. In medium bowl, blend 1½ cups
flour, baking powder and salt; set aside.

In bowl, with wire whisk, beat 1¼ cups
sugar, 3 eggs and ½ teaspoon vanilla. Stir
egg mixture, then flour mixture, into cooled
chocolate mixture. Spread in prepared pan.

In medium bowl, with electric mixer, beat
cream cheese, remaining ¾ cup sugar and
¼ cup spread until smooth. Beat in remaining
egg and 1 teaspoon vanilla, then remaining
¼ cup flour. Spoon over chocolate batter
and gently spread in even layer. With knife
tip, gently marble in cream cheese mixture.

Bake 30 minutes or until set. On wire rack,
cool completely. To serve, cut into bars.

Makes 24 brownies

Divine Double Dark Brownies

½ cup KARO® Light or Dark Corn
 Syrup
½ cup (1 stick) margarine or butter
5 squares (1 ounce each) semisweet
 chocolate
¾ cup sugar
3 eggs
1 cup all-purpose flour
1 cup chopped walnuts
1 teaspoon vanilla
 Chocolate Glaze (recipe follows)

1. Preheat oven to 350°F. Grease and flour
one 9-inch round cake pan.

2. In large saucepan over medium heat,
bring corn syrup and margarine to a boil,
stirring occasionally; remove from heat. Stir
in chocolate until melted. Add sugar; stir in
eggs, one at a time, until blended. Add flour,
nuts and vanilla. Pour into prepared pan.

3. Bake 30 minutes or until wooden pick
or cake tester inserted in center comes out
clean. Cool in pan 10 minutes. Remove from
pan; cool completely on wire rack.

4. Prepare Chocolate Glaze; pour over top
and spread on side. Let stand 1 hour.

Makes 8 servings

Chocolate Glaze: In small saucepan over
low heat, melt 3 squares (1 ounce each)
semisweet chocolate and 1 tablespoon
margarine or butter, stirring often. Remove
from heat. Stir in 2 tablespoons KARO®
Light or Dark Corn Syrup and 1 teaspoon
milk until smooth.

Chocolate Caramel Pecan Squares

1 (14-ounce) package caramels, wrappers removed
⅔ cup evaporated milk, divided
1 (18.25-ounce) package German chocolate cake mix (pudding style)
½ cup butter or margarine, melted
1 (6-ounce) package semi-sweet chocolate chips
1 cup chopped pecans, divided

Preheat oven to 350°F. Melt caramels with ⅓ cup evaporated milk in medium saucepan over low heat until smooth, stirring occasionally. Combine cake mix, butter and remaining ⅓ cup evaporated milk. Press half the cake mixture into greased 13×9-inch baking pan. Bake 6 minutes. Remove from oven. Sprinkle top with chocolate chips and ½ cup pecans. Top with caramel mixture, spreading to edges of pan. Spoon remaining cake mixture over top and sprinkle with remaining ½ cup pecans. Bake 20 minutes more. Cut into squares. Serve warm or cool completely. Store in airtight container.

Makes 24 bar cookies

Serving Suggestion: Serve warm with vanilla frozen yogurt.

Favorite recipe from **Bob Evans®**

Chocolate Caramel Pecan Squares

Kickin' Brownies

½ cup hazelnuts
¾ cup butter
2 cups sugar
¾ cup cocoa powder
3 eggs, lightly beaten
2 teaspoons vanilla
1 cup all-purpose flour
1½ cups fresh raspberries
   White Ganache (recipe follows)
   Chocolate Ganache (recipe follows)
3 to 4 tablespoons raspberry jam

1. Preheat oven to 350°F. Spread nuts in single layer on baking sheet. Bake 10 to 12 minutes or until skins begin to flake off; cool slightly. Wrap nuts in towel; rub to remove skins. Cool completely. Place nuts in food processor. Process using on/off pulsing action until finely chopped, but not pasty. Set aside. Grease 2 (8-inch) square pans. Line bottoms with foil; grease foil. Set aside.

2. Melt butter in saucepan over medium heat. Remove from heat. Stir in sugar and cocoa powder until blended. Stir in eggs and vanilla until smooth. Stir in flour until blended. Pour batter into prepared pans. Press raspberries into batter.

3. Bake 15 to 20 minutes or until center is just set. Do not overbake. Cool brownies in pans on wire rack.

4. Run knife around pan edges to loosen brownies. Hold wire rack over top of 1 pan; invert to release brownie. Remove foil; discard. Place plate over brownie; invert.

5. Prepare White Ganache and Chocolate Ganache. Reserve 2 tablespoons White

Ganache; spread remaining over brownie. Spread raspberry jam on top of ganache.

6. Unmold remaining brownie as directed in Step 4. Place flat side down on bottom layer, pressing gently to seal. Spread Chocolate Ganache evenly over top layer. Drizzle reserved 2 tablespoons White Ganache over top. Sprinkle with hazelnuts. Cut into 16 squares.   *Makes 16 brownies*

White Ganache

1 cup (6 ounces) white chocolate chips
   or chopped white chocolate
3 tablespoons whipping cream
½ teaspoon almond extract

Mix ½ cup white chocolate chips and cream in saucepan. Heat and stir over medium heat until chips are half melted. Remove saucepan from heat. Stir in remaining ½ cup white chips and almond extract until mixture is smooth. Keep warm (ganache is semi-firm at room temperature).   *Makes ¾ cup*

Chocolate Ganache

2 tablespoons whipping cream
1 tablespoon butter
½ cup (2 ounces) semisweet chocolate
   chips or chopped chocolate
½ teaspoon vanilla

Mix cream and butter in saucepan. Heat and stir over medium heat until mixture boils. Remove saucepan from heat. Stir in chocolate chips and vanilla until mixture is smooth, returning to heat for 20- to 30-second intervals, as needed to melt chocolate. Keep warm (ganache is semi-firm at room temperature).   *Makes ¾ cup*

Kickin' Brownies

Rich 'n' Creamy Brownie Bars

BROWNIES
1 package DUNCAN HINES®
    Chocolate Lovers Double Fudge
    Brownie Mix
2 eggs
⅓ cup water
¼ cup vegetable oil plus additional for
    greasing
½ cup chopped pecans

TOPPING
1 package (8 ounces) cream cheese,
    softened
2 eggs
1 pound (3½ cups) confectioners'
    sugar
1 teaspoon vanilla extract

1. Preheat oven to 350°F. Grease bottom of
13×9-inch pan.

2. For brownies, combine brownie mix,
fudge packet from Mix, 2 eggs, water and oil
in large bowl. Stir with spoon until well
blended, about 50 strokes. Stir in pecans.
Spread evenly in prepared pan.

3. For topping, beat cream cheese in large
bowl at medium speed with electric mixer
until smooth. Beat in 2 eggs, confectioners'
sugar and vanilla extract until smooth.
Spread evenly over brownie mixture. Bake
at 350°F for 45 to 50 minutes or until edges
and top are golden brown and shiny. Cool
completely in pan. Refrigerate until well
chilled. Cut into bars.

Makes about 48 bars

Oatmeal Brownies

⅔ cup granulated sugar
⅓ cup water
3 tablespoons CRISCO® Oil*
½ teaspoon vanilla
2 egg whites, lightly beaten
½ cup all-purpose flour
⅓ cup quick oats (not instant or old
    fashioned)
¼ cup unsweetened cocoa powder
¾ teaspoon baking powder
⅛ teaspoon salt
1 teaspoon confectioners' sugar

Use your favorite Crisco Oil product.

1. Heat oven to 350°F. Oil 8-inch square pan
lightly. Place cooling rack on countertop.

2. Combine granulated sugar, water, oil and
vanilla in medium bowl. Stir well. Add egg
whites. Stir well.

3. Combine flour, oats, cocoa, baking
powder and salt. Add to sugar mixture,
stirring well. Pour into prepared pan.

4. Bake at 350°F for 23 minutes or until
toothpick inserted in center comes out
clean. *Do not overbake.* Cool. Sprinkle with
confectioners' sugar. Cut into bars.

Makes about 12 brownies

Rich 'n' Creamy Brownie Bars

Cherry White Chip Brownies

½ **cup chopped maraschino cherries, well drained**
⅓ **cup butter or margarine, softened**
¾ **cup sugar**
2 **eggs**
2 **tablespoons light corn syrup**
1 **tablespoon kirsch (cherry brandy)** *or*
    1 **teaspoon vanilla extract and**
    1 **teaspoon almond extract**
⅔ **cup all-purpose flour**
⅓ **cup HERSHEY®S Cocoa or HERSHEY®S Dutch Processed Cocoa**
¼ **teaspoon baking powder**
1 **cup HERSHEY®S Premier White Chips**
⅓ **cup chopped slivered almonds**
    White Chip Drizzle (recipe follows, optional)
    Maraschino cherry halves, well drained (optional)

1. Heat oven to 350°F. Line 9-inch square baking pan with foil, extending foil over edges of pan. Grease and flour foil.

2. Pat chopped cherries dry between layers of paper towels. Beat butter, sugar, eggs, corn syrup and kirsch in small bowl until blended. Stir together flour, cocoa and baking powder; gradually add to butter mixture, beating until blended. Stir in chopped cherries, white chips and almonds. Pour batter into prepared pan.

3. Bake 25 to 30 minutes or until brownies begin to pull away from sides of pan. Cool completely in pan. Cover; refrigerate until firm.

4. Use foil to lift brownies out of pan; peel off foil. Cut brownies into shapes with cookie cutters or cut into squares.

5. Prepare White Chip Drizzle, if desired; garnish brownies with drizzle and cherry halves, if desired. Refrigerate until drizzle is set. Cut into bars. Refrigerate leftover brownies.   ***Makes about 16 brownies***

White Chip Drizzle

⅔ **cup HERSHEY®S Premier White Chips**
1 **teaspoon shortening (do *not* use butter, margarine, spread or oil)**

Place white chips and shortening in small microwave-safe bowl. Microwave at HIGH (100%) 30 seconds; stir. If necessary, microwave at HIGH an additional 15 seconds, stirring after each heating, just until chips are melted when stirred.

FUN FOOD FACT

Maraschino cherries are sweet cherries that have been pitted and soaked in sugar syrup. Then they are flavored and dyed a vivid red or green.

Orange Cappuccino Brownies

¾ cup butter
2 squares (1 ounce each) semisweet
   chocolate, coarsely chopped
2 squares (1 ounce each) unsweetened
   chocolate, coarsely chopped
1¾ cups granulated sugar
1 tablespoon instant espresso powder
   or instant coffee granules
3 eggs
¼ cup orange-flavored liqueur
2 teaspoons grated orange peel
1 cup all-purpose flour
1 package (12 ounces) semisweet
   chocolate chips
2 tablespoons shortening

Preheat oven to 350°F. Grease 13×9-inch baking pan.

Melt butter and chopped chocolates in large heavy saucepan over low heat, stirring constantly. Stir in granulated sugar and espresso powder. Remove from heat. Cool slightly. Beat in eggs, one at a time. Whisk in liqueur and orange peel. Beat flour into chocolate mixture just until blended. Spread batter evenly in prepared pan.

Bake 25 to 30 minutes or until center is just set. Remove pan to wire rack. Meanwhile, melt chocolate chips and shortening in small heavy saucepan over low heat, stirring constantly. Immediately, spread hot chocolate mixture over warm brownies. Let cool completely in pan on wire rack. Cut into 2-inch squares.

Makes about 2 dozen brownies

Marbled Peanut Butter Brownies

½ cup butter, softened
¼ cup peanut butter
1 cup packed light brown sugar
½ cup granulated sugar
3 eggs
1 teaspoon vanilla
2 cups all-purpose flour
2 teaspoons baking powder
⅛ teaspoon salt
1 cup chocolate-flavored syrup
½ cup coarsely chopped salted mixed
   nuts

Preheat oven to 350°F. Lightly grease 13×9-inch pan. Beat butter and peanut butter in large bowl until blended; stir in sugars. Beat in eggs, one at a time, until well blended. Blend in vanilla. Combine flour, baking powder and salt in small bowl. Stir into butter mixture. Spread half of batter evenly in prepared pan. Spread syrup over top. Spoon remaining batter over syrup. Swirl with knife or spatula to create marbled effect. Sprinkle with chopped nuts. Bake 35 to 40 minutes or until lightly browned. Cool in pan on wire rack. Cut into 2-inch squares. *Makes about 2 dozen brownies*

Rocky Road Brownies

1 cup HERSHEY₂S Semi-Sweet
    Chocolate Chips
1¼ cups miniature marshmallows
  1 cup chopped nuts
  ½ cup (1 stick) butter or margarine
  1 cup sugar
  1 teaspoon vanilla extract
  2 eggs
  ½ cup all-purpose flour
  ⅓ cup HERSHEY₂S Cocoa
  ½ teaspoon baking powder
  ½ teaspoon salt

1. Heat oven to 350°F. Grease 9-inch square baking pan.

2. Stir together chocolate chips, marshmallows and nuts; set aside. Place butter in large microwave-safe bowl. Microwave at HIGH (100% power) 1 to 1½ minutes or until melted. Add sugar, vanilla and eggs, beating with spoon until well blended. Add flour, cocoa, baking powder and salt; blend well. Spread batter into prepared pan.

3. Bake 22 minutes. Sprinkle chocolate chip mixture over top. Continue baking 5 minutes or until marshmallows have softened and puffed slightly. Cool completely. With wet knife, cut into squares.

Makes about 20 brownies

Raspberry Fudge Brownies

½ cup (1 stick) butter
  3 squares (1 ounce each) bittersweet
    chocolate*
  1 cup sugar
  2 eggs
  1 teaspoon vanilla
  ¾ cup all-purpose flour
  ¼ teaspoon baking powder
    Dash salt
  ½ cup sliced or slivered almonds
  ½ cup raspberry preserves
  1 cup (6 ounces) milk chocolate chips

Bittersweet chocolate is available in specialty food stores. One square unsweetened chocolate plus two squares semisweet chocolate may be substituted.

Preheat oven to 350°F. Grease and flour 8-inch square baking pan.

Melt butter and bittersweet chocolate in heavy saucepan over low heat. Remove from heat; let cool. Beat sugar, eggs and vanilla in large bowl until light. Beat in chocolate mixture. Stir in flour, baking powder and salt until just blended. Spread ¾ of batter in prepared pan; sprinkle almonds over top.

Bake 10 minutes. Remove from oven; spread preserves over almonds. Spoon remaining batter over preserves, smoothing top. Bake 25 to 30 minutes or just until top feels firm.

Remove from oven; sprinkle chocolate chips over top. Let stand 1 to 2 minutes or until chips melt; spread over brownies. Cool completely in pan on wire rack.

Makes 16 brownies

Rocky Road Brownies

Moist and Minty Brownies

1¼ cups all-purpose flour
½ teaspoon baking soda
¼ teaspoon salt
¾ cup granulated sugar
½ cup (1 stick) butter or margarine
2 tablespoons water
1½ cups (10-ounce package) NESTLÉ®
  TOLL HOUSE® Mint-Chocolate
  Morsels, divided
1 teaspoon vanilla extract
2 eggs

COMBINE flour, baking soda and salt in small bowl; set aside. Combine sugar, butter and water in medium saucepan. Bring *just to a boil* over medium heat, stirring constantly; remove from heat.* Add *1 cup* morsels and vanilla; stir until smooth. Add eggs, one at a time, stirring well after each addition. Stir in flour mixture and *remaining* morsels. Spread into greased 9-inch-square baking pan.

BAKE in preheated 350°F. oven for 20 to 30 minutes or until center is set. Cool in pan on wire rack (center will sink).

Makes about 16 brownies

Or, combine sugar, butter and water in medium microwave-safe bowl. Microwave on HIGH (100% power) for 3 minutes, stirring halfway through cooking time. Stir until smooth. Proceed as above.

German Chocolate Brownies

1½ cups PLANTERS® Pecan Halves, divided
2¼ cups packed brown sugar, divided
4 eggs
¾ cup margarine or butter, melted
4 ounces unsweetened chocolate, melted
2 teaspoons vanilla extract
1 cup all-purpose flour
½ teaspoon salt
1 cup flaked coconut, divided
1 (16-ounce) can prepared vanilla frosting

1. Reserve 24 pecan halves for garnish; coarsely chop remaining pecans.

2. Blend 2 cups brown sugar and eggs; stir in margarine or butter, chocolate and vanilla. Mix in flour and salt until well blended. Stir in ½ cup coconut and ¾ cup chopped pecans.

3. Pour batter into lightly greased 13×9×2-inch baking pan. Bake at 350°F 30 minutes. Cool completely in pan on wire rack.

4. Mix frosting, remaining ¼ cup brown sugar, ½ cup coconut and chopped pecans in small bowl; spread over brownies. Cut into 24 pieces; top each with 1 pecan half. Store in airtight container.

Makes 24 brownies

Moist and Minty Brownies

Double "Topped" Brownies

BROWNIES

   1 package DUNCAN HINES®
      Chocolate Lovers Double Fudge
      Brownie Mix
   2 eggs
   ⅓ cup water
   ¼ cup vegetable oil plus additional for
      greasing
   ½ cup flaked coconut
   ½ cup chopped nuts

FROSTING

   3 cups confectioners' sugar
   ⅓ cup shortening
   1½ teaspoons vanilla extract
   2 to 3 tablespoons milk

TOPPING

   3 squares (3 ounces) unsweetened
      chocolate
   1 tablespoon butter or margarine

1. Preheat oven to 350°F. Grease bottom of 13×9-inch pan.

2. For brownies, combine brownie mix, fudge packet from Mix, eggs, water and oil in large bowl. Stir with spoon until well blended, about 50 strokes. Stir in coconut and nuts. Spread in prepared pan. Bake at 350°F 27 to 30 minutes or until set; cool.

3. For frosting, combine confectioners' sugar, shortening and vanilla extract. Stir in milk, 1 tablespoon at a time, until frosting is of spreading consistency. Spread over cooled brownies. Refrigerate until frosting is firm, about 30 minutes.

4. For topping, melt chocolate and butter in small bowl over hot water; stir until smooth. Drizzle over frosting. Refrigerate until chocolate is firm, about 15 minutes. Cut into bars.   *Makes about 48 brownies*

Rocky Road Squares

   1 package (21.5 ounces) fudge
      brownie mix calling for ½ cup
      water
   Vegetable oil, per package directions
   Egg(s), per package directions
   ½ cup CARNATION® Evaporated Milk
   2 cups miniature marshmallows
   1½ cups coarsely chopped DIAMOND®
      Walnuts
   1 cup (6 ounces) NESTLÉ® TOLL
      HOUSE® Semi-Sweet Chocolate
      Morsels

PREPARE brownie mix according to package directions, using oil and egg(s); substitute evaporated milk for water. Spread into greased 13×9-inch baking pan. Bake according to package directions; do not overbake. Remove from oven. Top with marshmallows, walnuts and morsels.

BAKE for 3 to 5 minutes or just until topping is warm and begins to melt together. Cool for 20 to 30 minutes before cutting into squares.   *Makes 24 brownies*

Double "Topped" Brownies

Sour Cream Brownies

BROWNIES
1 cup water
1 cup butter
3 tablespoons unsweetened cocoa
 powder
2 cups all-purpose flour
2 cups granulated sugar
1 teaspoon baking soda
½ teaspoon salt
1 (8-ounce) container sour cream
2 eggs

FROSTING
4 cups sifted powdered sugar
3 tablespoons unsweetened cocoa
 powder
½ cup butter, softened
6 tablespoons milk
1 cup chopped nuts

For brownies, preheat oven to 350°F. Grease 15×10×1-inch pan; set aside. Mix water, butter and cocoa in saucepan. Cook and stir until mixture comes to a boil. Remove from heat. Mix flour, granulated sugar, baking soda and salt in bowl; set aside. Beat sour cream and eggs. Add hot cocoa mixture; beat well. Beat in flour mixture. Pour into prepared pan. Bake 25 to 30 minutes or until brownie springs back when touched. Cool.

For frosting, mix powdered sugar and cocoa in bowl; set aside. Beat butter in medium bowl until creamy. Add powdered sugar mixture alternately with milk, beating well after each addition. Spread over cooled brownies. Sprinkle nuts over frosting.

Makes about 40 brownies

Favorite recipe from **Wisconsin Milk Marketing Board**

Brownie Fudge

4 squares (1 ounce each) unsweetened
 chocolate
1 cup butter
2 cups sugar
4 eggs
1 cup all-purpose flour
1 cup chopped walnuts
2 teaspoons vanilla
 Fudge Topping (recipe follows)

Preheat oven to 350°F. Grease 13×9-inch baking pan. Melt chocolate and butter in saucepan over low heat, stirring often; cool. Beat sugar and eggs in bowl until fluffy. Blend chocolate mixture into egg mixture. Stir in flour, walnuts and vanilla. Spread in prepared pan. Bake 25 to 35 minutes or just until set. Do not overbake. Meanwhile, prepare Fudge Topping. Remove brownies from oven. Immediately pour topping evenly over hot brownies. Cool in pan on wire rack. Place in freezer until firm. Cut into 1-inch squares.

Makes 9 dozen brownies

Fudge Topping

4½ cups sugar
1 can (12 ounces) evaporated milk
⅓ cup butter
1 jar (7 ounces) marshmallow creme
12 ounces semisweet chocolate chips
12 ounces milk chocolate chips
2 teaspoons vanilla
2 cups walnuts, coarsely chopped

Bring sugar, milk and butter to a boil in saucepan over medium heat; boil 5 minutes, stirring constantly. Remove from heat; add marshmallow creme, chocolate chips and vanilla. Beat until smooth. Stir in walnuts.

Almond Brownies

½ cup (1 stick) butter
2 squares (1 ounce each) unsweetened baking chocolate
2 large eggs
1 cup firmly packed light brown sugar
¼ teaspoon almond extract
½ cup all-purpose flour
1½ cups "M&M's"® Chocolate Mini Baking Bits, divided
½ cup slivered almonds, toasted and divided
Chocolate Glaze (recipe follows)

Preheat oven to 350°F. Grease and flour 8×8×2-inch baking pan; set aside. In small saucepan melt butter and chocolate over low heat; stir to blend. Remove from heat; let cool. In medium bowl beat eggs and brown sugar until well blended; stir in chocolate mixture and almond extract. Add flour. Stir in 1 cup "M&M's"® Chocolate Mini Baking Bits and ¼ cup almonds. Spread batter evenly in prepared pan. Bake 25 to 28 minutes or until firm in center. Cool completely on wire rack. Prepare Chocolate Glaze. Spread over brownies; decorate with remaining ½ cup "M&M's"® Chocolate Mini Baking Bits and remaining ¼ cup almonds. Cut into bars. Store in tightly covered container. *Makes 16 brownies*

Chocolate Glaze: In small saucepan over low heat combine 4 teaspoons water and 1 tablespoon butter until it comes to a boil. Stir in 4 teaspoons unsweetened cocoa powder. Stir in ½ cup powdered sugar until smooth. Remove from heat; stir in ¼ teaspoon vanilla extract. Let cool slightly.

Almond Brownies

Butterscotch Brownies

1 cup butterscotch chips
½ cup packed light brown sugar
¼ cup butter, softened
2 eggs
½ teaspoon vanilla
1 cup all-purpose flour
½ teaspoon baking powder
¼ teaspoon salt
1 cup semisweet chocolate chips

Preheat oven to 350°F. Grease 9-inch square baking pan. Melt butterscotch chips in small saucepan over low heat, stirring constantly; set aside.

Beat brown sugar and butter in large bowl until light and fluffy. Beat in eggs, one at a time, scraping down side of bowl after each addition. Beat in melted butterscotch chips and vanilla. Combine flour, baking powder and salt in small bowl; add to butter mixture. Beat until well blended. Spread batter evenly in prepared pan.

Bake 20 to 25 minutes or until golden brown and center is set. Remove pan from oven and immediately sprinkle with chocolate chips. Let stand about 4 minutes or until chocolate is melted. Spread chocolate evenly over top. Place pan on wire rack; cool completely. Cut into 2¼-inch squares.

Makes about 16 brownies

White Chocolate Brownies

6 tablespoons butter
5 squares (1 ounce each) white chocolate, divided
1 large egg
½ cup granulated sugar
¾ cup all-purpose flour
¾ teaspoon vanilla extract
¼ teaspoon salt
1¼ cups "M&M's"® Semi-Sweet Chocolate Mini Baking Bits, divided
½ cup chopped walnuts

Preheat oven to 325°F. Lightly grease 8×8×2-inch baking pan; set aside. In small saucepan melt butter and 4 squares white chocolate over low heat; stir to blend. Remove from heat; let cool slightly. In medium bowl beat egg and sugar until light; stir in white chocolate mixture, flour, vanilla and salt. Spread batter evenly in prepared pan. Sprinkle with ¾ cup "M&M's"® Semi-Sweet Chocolate Mini Baking Bits and walnuts. Bake 35 to 37 minutes or until firm in center. Cool completely on wire rack. Place remaining 1 square white chocolate in small microwave-safe bowl. Microwave at HIGH 20 seconds; stir. Repeat as necessary until white chocolate is completely melted, stirring at 10-second intervals. Drizzle over brownies and sprinkle with remaining ½ cup "M&M's"® Semi-Sweet Chocolate Mini Baking Bits. Cut into bars. Store in tightly covered container.

Makes 16 brownies

Butterscotch Brownies

Decadent Blonde Brownies

1½ cups all-purpose flour
1 teaspoon baking powder
½ teaspoon salt
¾ cup granulated sugar
¾ cup packed light brown sugar
½ cup butter, softened
2 large eggs
2 teaspoons vanilla
1 package (10 ounces) semisweet chocolate chunks*
1 jar (3½ ounces) macadamia nuts, coarsely chopped, to measure ¾ cup

*If chocolate chunks are not available, cut 1 (10-ounce) thick chocolate candy bar into ½-inch pieces to equal 1½ cups.

Preheat oven to 350°F. Grease 13×9-inch baking pan. Combine flour, baking powder and salt in small bowl; set aside.

Beat granulated sugar, brown sugar and butter in large bowl with electric mixer at medium speed until light and fluffy. Beat in eggs and vanilla. Add flour mixture. Beat at low speed until well blended. Stir in chocolate chunks and macadamia nuts. Spread batter evenly into prepared pan. Bake 25 to 30 minutes or until golden brown. Remove pan to wire rack; cool completely. Cut into 3¼×1½-inch bars.

Makes 2 dozen brownies

Apple Date Nut Blondies

2 medium Granny Smith apples, peeled, cored and finely chopped
2½ cups all-purpose flour, divided
¾ Butter Flavor* CRISCO® Stick or ¾ cup Butter Flavor CRISCO® all-vegetable shortening plus additional for greasing
1 cup firmly packed light brown sugar
2 eggs
2 tablespoons pure vanilla extract
2 teaspoons baking powder
½ teaspoon salt
½ cup finely chopped pecans
½ cup finely chopped dates
Confectioners' sugar

*Butter Flavor Crisco is artificially flavored.

1. Heat oven to 350°F. Grease 15×10×1-inch jelly roll pan with shortening. Place cooling rack on countertop. Toss apples with ¼ cup flour.

2. Beat ¾ cup shortening and brown sugar in bowl at medium speed of electric mixer until well blended. Beat in eggs and vanilla. Mix remaining 2¼ cups flour, baking powder and salt. Add to creamed mixture at low speed. Beat until blended. Fold in apple mixture, nuts and dates. Spread in pan.

3. Bake at 350°F 25 to 30 minutes or until toothpick inserted in center comes out clean. *Do not overbake.* Remove pan to rack. Cool. Cut into 2½×1½-inch bars. Dust with confectioners' sugar just before serving.

Makes about 3 dozen bars

Decadent Blonde Brownies

Blonde Brickle Brownies

1⅓ cups all-purpose flour
½ teaspoon baking powder
¼ teaspoon salt
2 eggs
½ cup granulated sugar
½ cup firmly packed brown sugar
⅓ cup butter or margarine, melted
1 teaspoon vanilla
¼ teaspoon almond extract
1⅓ cups (8-ounce package) HEATH®
   BITS, divided
½ cup chopped pecans (optional)

1. Heat oven to 350°F. Grease 8-inch square baking pan.

2. Mix flour with baking powder and salt; set aside. Beat eggs well in large bowl. Gradually beat in granulated sugar and brown sugar until thick and creamy. Add butter, vanilla and almond extract; mix well. Gently stir in flour mixture until mixed. Fold in ⅔ cup Heath Bits and nuts. Pour into prepared pan.

3. Bake 30 minutes. Remove from oven; immediately sprinkle remaining ⅔ cup bits over top. Cool completely in pan on wire rack. Cut into squares.

Makes about 16 brownies

Pear Blondies

1 cup packed brown sugar
¼ cup butter or margarine, melted
1 egg
½ teaspoon vanilla
¾ cup all-purpose flour
½ teaspoon baking powder
½ teaspoon salt
1 cup chopped firm-ripe fresh
   Northwest Anjou, Bosc, Bartlett,
   Nelis or Seckel pears
⅓ cup semisweet chocolate chips

Preheat oven to 350°F. Grease 8-inch square baking pan. Set aside.

Combine brown sugar, butter, egg and vanilla in medium bowl; blend well. Combine flour, baking powder and salt in small bowl; stir into brown sugar mixture. Stir in pears and chips. Spread in prepared baking pan. Bake 30 to 35 minutes or until golden brown. Cool completely in pan on wire rack. Cut into 2-inch squares.

Makes 16 squares

Favorite recipe from **Pear Bureau Northwest**

HELPFUL HINT

For easy removal of brownies and bar cookies (and no cleanup!), line the baking pan with foil and leave at least 3 inches hanging over each end. Use the foil to lift out the treats; place them on a cutting board and carefully remove the foil. Then simply cut them into pieces.

Fabulous Blonde Brownies

1¾ cups all-purpose flour
1 teaspoon baking powder
¼ teaspoon salt
1 cup (6 ounces) white chocolate chips
1 cup (4 ounces) blanched whole
   almonds, coarsely chopped
1 cup English toffee bits
⅔ cup butter, softened
1½ cups packed light brown sugar
2 eggs
2 teaspoons vanilla

Preheat oven to 350°F. Grease 13×9-inch baking pan.

Combine flour, baking powder and salt in small bowl; mix well. Combine white chocolate chips, almonds and toffee bits in medium bowl; mix well.

Beat butter and brown sugar in large bowl until light and fluffy. Beat in eggs and vanilla. Add flour mixture; beat until well blended. Stir in ¾ cup white chocolate chip mixture. Spread evenly in prepared pan.

Bake 20 minutes. Immediately sprinkle remaining white chocolate chip mixture evenly over brownies. Press lightly. Bake 15 to 20 minutes or until toothpick inserted into center comes out clean. Cool brownies completely in pan on wire rack. Cut into 2×1½-inch bars.

Makes 3 dozen brownies

Fabulous Blonde Brownies

Double-Decker Confetti Brownies

¾ cup (1½ sticks) butter or margarine, softened
1 cup granulated sugar
1 cup firmly packed light brown sugar
3 large eggs
1 teaspoon vanilla extract
2½ cups all-purpose flour, divided
2½ teaspoons baking powder
½ teaspoon salt
⅓ cup unsweetened cocoa powder
1 tablespoon butter or margarine, melted
1 cup "M&M's"® Semi-Sweet Chocolate Mini Baking Bits, divided

Preheat oven to 350°F. Lightly grease 13×9×2-inch baking pan; set aside. In large bowl cream ¾ cup butter and sugars until light and fluffy; beat in eggs and vanilla. In medium bowl combine 2¼ cups flour, baking powder and salt; blend into creamed mixture. Divide batter in half. Blend together cocoa powder and melted butter; stir into one half of the dough. Spread cocoa dough evenly into prepared baking pan. Stir remaining ¼ cup flour and ½ cup "M&M's"® Semi-Sweet Chocolate Mini Baking Bits into remaining dough; spread evenly over cocoa dough in pan. Sprinkle with remaining ½ cup "M&M's"® Semi-Sweet Chocolate Mini Baking Bits. Bake 25 to 30 minutes or until edges start to pull away from sides of pan. Cool completely. Cut into bars. Store in tightly covered container.

Makes 24 brownies

"Blondie" Brownies

½ Butter Flavor* CRISCO® Stick or ½ cup Butter Flavor CRISCO® all-vegetable shortening plus additional for greasing
1 tablespoon milk
1 cup firmly packed brown sugar
1 egg
1 cup all-purpose flour
½ teaspoon baking powder
⅛ teaspoon salt
1 teaspoon vanilla
½ cup chopped walnuts

Butter Flavor Crisco is artificially flavored.

1. Heat oven to 350°F. Grease 8×8×2-inch pan with shortening. Place cooling rack on countertop.

2. Combine ½ cup shortening and milk in large microwave-safe bowl. Microwave at 50% (MEDIUM). Stir after 1 minute. Repeat until melted (or melt on rangetop in large saucepan on low heat). Stir in sugar. Stir in egg quickly. Combine flour, baking powder and salt. Stir into sugar mixture. Stir in vanilla and nuts. Spread in prepared pan.

3. Bake at 350°F for 27 to 30 minutes, or until toothpick inserted in center comes out clean. *Do not overbake.* Cool in pan on cooling rack. Cut into 2×2-inch squares.

Makes 16 squares

Double-Decker Confetti Brownies

White Chocolate & Almond Brownies

12 ounces white chocolate, broken into pieces
1 cup unsalted butter
3 eggs
¾ cup all-purpose flour
1 teaspoon vanilla
½ cup slivered almonds

Preheat oven to 325°F. Grease and flour 9-inch square pan. Melt white chocolate and butter in large saucepan over low heat, stirring constantly. (Do not be concerned if the white chocolate separates.) Remove from heat when chocolate is just melted. With electric mixer, beat in eggs until mixture is smooth. Beat in flour and vanilla. Spread batter evenly in prepared pan. Sprinkle almonds evenly over top. Bake 30 to 35 minutes or just until set in center. Cool completely in pan on wire rack. Cut into 2-inch squares.

Makes about 16 brownies

FUN FOOD FACT

White chocolate is not really chocolate at all because it lacks chocolate liquor (the main component in unsweetened chocolate). White chocolate is cocoa butter with added sugar, milk and flavorings (often vanilla or vanillin). It is more delicate than other chocolates and burns easily.

Butterscotch Brownies

2 eggs
2 cups firmly packed brown sugar
½ Butter Flavor* CRISCO® Stick or
**   ½ cup Butter Flavor CRISCO®**
**   all-vegetable shortening, melted,**
**   plus additional for greasing**
1 teaspoon vanilla
1½ cups all-purpose flour
2 teaspoons baking powder
½ teaspoon salt
1 cup finely chopped walnuts or
**   pecans**

*Butter Flavor Crisco is artificially flavored.

1. Heat oven to 350°F. Grease 13×9×2-inch pan with shortening. Place cooling rack on countertop.

2. Beat eggs in large bowl at medium speed with electric mixer until light and foamy. Add brown sugar, ½ cup shortening and vanilla. Beat until creamy.

3. Combine flour, baking powder and salt. Add gradually to egg mixture at low speed until blended. Mix in walnuts. (Dough will be stiff.) Spread in prepared pan.

4. Bake for 25 to 30 minutes or until top is light brown and toothpick inserted in center comes out clean. Cool 10 to 15 minutes on cooling rack. Cut into bars about 2½×2 inches.   ***Makes 2 dozen bars***

Left to right: Brownie Fudge (page 174) and White Chocolate & Almond Brownies

Chocolate Marbled Blondies

½ cup (1 stick) butter or margarine, softened
½ cup firmly packed light brown sugar
1 large egg
2 teaspoons vanilla extract
1½ cups all-purpose flour
1¼ teaspoons baking soda
1 cup "M&M's"® Chocolate Mini Baking Bits, divided
4 ounces cream cheese, softened
2 tablespoons granulated sugar
1 large egg yolk
¼ cup unsweetened cocoa powder

Preheat oven to 350°F. Lightly grease 9×9×2-inch baking pan; set aside. In large bowl cream butter and brown sugar until light and fluffy; beat in egg and vanilla. In medium bowl combine flour and baking soda; blend into creamed mixture. Stir in ⅔ cup "M&M's"® Chocolate Mini Baking Bits; set aside. Dough will be stiff. In separate bowl beat together cream cheese, granulated sugar and egg yolk until smooth; stir in cocoa powder until well blended. Place chocolate-cheese mixture in six equal portions evenly onto bottom of prepared pan. Place reserved dough around cheese mixture and swirl slightly with tines of fork. Pat down evenly on top. Sprinkle with remaining ⅓ cup "M&M's"® Chocolate Mini Baking Bits. Bake 25 to 30 minutes or until toothpick inserted in center comes out with moist crumbs. Cool completely. Cut into bars. Store in refrigerator in tightly covered container.

Makes 16 bars

Colorful Blondies

1 cup (2 sticks) butter or margarine, softened
1½ cups firmly packed light brown sugar
1 large egg
1 teaspoon vanilla extract
2 cups all-purpose flour
½ teaspoon baking soda
1¾ cups "M&M's"® Semi-Sweet or Milk Chocolate Mini Baking Bits
1 cup chopped walnuts or pecans

Preheat oven to 350°F. Lightly grease 13×9×2-inch baking pan; set aside. In large bowl cream butter and sugar until light and fluffy; beat in egg and vanilla. In medium bowl combine flour and baking soda; add to creamed mixture just until combined. Dough will be stiff. Stir in "M&M's"® Chocolate Mini Baking Bits and nuts. Spread dough into prepared baking pan. Bake 30 to 35 minutes or until toothpick inserted in center comes out with moist crumbs. Do not overbake. Cool completely. Cut into bars. Store in tightly covered container.

Makes 24 bars

Chocolate Marbled Blondies

Slice 'n' Bake BEAUTIES

Pinwheel Cookies

½ cup shortening plus additional for greasing
⅓ cup plus 1 tablespoon butter, softened and divided
2 egg yolks
½ teaspoon vanilla
1 package DUNCAN HINES® Moist Deluxe Fudge Marble
   Cake Mix

1. Combine ½ cup shortening, ⅓ cup butter, egg yolks and vanilla in large bowl. Mix at low speed of electric mixer until blended. Set aside cocoa packet from cake mix. Gradually add cake mix. Blend well.

2. Divide dough in half. Add cocoa packet and remaining 1 tablespoon butter to one half of dough. Knead until well blended and chocolate colored.

3. Roll out yellow dough between two pieces of waxed paper into 18×12×⅛-inch rectangle. Repeat for chocolate dough. Remove top pieces of waxed paper from chocolate and yellow doughs. Place yellow dough directly on top of chocolate dough. Remove remaining layers of waxed paper. Roll up jelly-roll fashion, beginning at wide side. Refrigerate 2 hours.

4. Preheat oven to 350°F. Grease cookie sheets.

5. Cut dough into ⅛-inch slices. Place sliced dough 1 inch apart on prepared cookie sheets. Bake 9 to 11 minutes or until lightly browned. Cool 5 minutes on cookie sheets. Remove to cooling racks. *Makes about 3½ dozen cookies*

Pinwheel Cookies

Lip-Smacking Lemon Cookies

½ cup butter, softened
1 cup sugar
1 egg
2 tablespoons lemon juice
2 teaspoons grated lemon peel
2 cups all-purpose flour
1 teaspoon baking powder
⅛ teaspoon salt
   Dash ground nutmeg

Beat butter in large bowl with electric mixer at medium speed until smooth. Add sugar; beat until well blended. Add egg, lemon juice and peel; beat until well blended.

Combine flour, baking powder, salt and nutmeg in large bowl. Gradually add flour mixture to butter mixture at low speed, blending well after each addition.

Shape dough into 2 logs, each about 1½ inches in diameter and 6½ inches long. Wrap each log in plastic wrap. Refrigerate 2 to 3 hours or up to 3 days.

Preheat oven to 350°F. Grease cookie sheets. Cut logs into ¼-inch-thick slices; place 1 inch apart on cookie sheets.

Bake about 15 minutes or until edges are light brown. Transfer to wire rack to cool. Store in airtight container.

Makes 4 dozen cookies

Mini Chip Slice and Bake Cookies

⅓ cup butter or margarine, softened
¾ cup granulated sugar
½ cup packed light brown sugar
1 egg
1 teaspoon vanilla extract
2½ cups all-purpose flour
1 teaspoon baking soda
½ teaspoon baking powder
½ teaspoon salt
2 to 3 tablespoons milk
1 cup HERSHEY®S MINI CHIPS™ Semi-Sweet Chocolate

1. Beat butter, granulated sugar and brown sugar in large bowl on medium speed of mixer until creamy. Add egg and vanilla; beat well. Stir together flour, baking soda, baking powder and salt; gradually add to butter mixture, beating until well blended. Add milk, 1 tablespoon at a time, until dough holds together. Stir in small chocolate chips.

2. Divide dough in half. Shape each half into 1½-inch-thick roll. Wrap tightly in wax paper; refrigerate 5 to 24 hours.

3. Heat oven to 350°F. Lightly grease cookie sheet.

4. Using a sharp knife and a sawing motion, cut rolls into ¼-inch slices. Place on prepared cookie sheet.

5. Bake 8 to 10 minutes or until set. Remove from cookie sheet to wire rack. Cool completely.

Makes about 6 dozen cookies

Lip-Smacking Lemon Cookies

Party Peanut Butter Cookies

1½ cups all-purpose flour
½ cup sugar
½ teaspoon baking soda
¾ cup creamy peanut butter, divided
½ Butter Flavor* CRISCO® Stick or
**   ½ cup Butter Flavor CRISCO®**
**   all-vegetable shortening**
¼ cup light corn syrup
1 teaspoon vanilla extract

*Butter Flavor Crisco is artificially flavored.

1. Combine flour, sugar and baking soda in medium bowl. Cut in ½ cup peanut butter and ½ cup shortening until mixture resembles coarse meal. Stir in syrup and vanilla until blended.

2. Form dough into 2-inch roll. Wrap in waxed paper. Refrigerate 1 hour.

3. Heat oven to 350°F. Place sheets of foil on countertop for cooling cookies.

4. Cut dough into ¼-inch slices. Place ½ of the slices 2 inches apart on ungreased baking sheet. Spread ½ teaspoon peanut butter on each slice. Top with remaining slices. Seal edges with fork.

5. Bake at 350°F for 10 minutes, or until lightly browned. *Do not overbake.* Cool 2 minutes on baking sheet. Remove to foil to cool completely.

Makes about 2 dozen cookies

Peppersass Cookies

2¼ cups flour
½ teaspoon baking soda
½ teaspoon salt
1½ cups sugar, divided
⅔ cup butter *or* margarine, at room
**   temperature**
1 egg
2 teaspoons TABASCO® brand Pepper
**   Sauce**
1 teaspoon vanilla extract

Combine flour, baking soda and salt in small bowl. Beat 1 cup sugar and butter in large bowl with electric mixer at low speed until well blended. Add egg, TABASCO® Sauce, vanilla and flour mixture; beat until smooth.

Divide dough in half; place halves on plastic wrap. Shape each half into log about 1½ inches in diameter. Cover and refrigerate until firm, 2 to 3 hours or overnight.

Preheat oven to 350°F. Place remaining ½ cup sugar in shallow dish. Cut dough logs into ¼-inch-thick slices; dip each slice in sugar. Place slices 1 inch apart on ungreased cookie sheets. Bake 10 to 12 minutes or until cookies are golden around edges. Cool on wire racks.

Makes about 5 dozen cookies

Refrigerator Cookies

½ cup sugar
¼ cup light corn syrup
¼ cup margarine, softened
¼ cup cholesterol-free egg substitute
1 teaspoon vanilla
1¾ cups all-purpose flour
¼ teaspoon baking soda
¼ teaspoon salt
   Cookie decorations (optional)

1. Beat sugar, corn syrup and margarine in large bowl. Add egg substitute and vanilla; mix well. Set aside.

2. Combine flour, baking soda and salt in medium bowl. Add to sugar mixture; mix well. Form dough into 2 (1½-inch-wide) rolls. Wrap in plastic wrap. Freeze 1 hour.

3. Preheat oven to 350°F. Line baking sheets with parchment paper. Cut dough into ¼-inch-thick slices; place 1 inch apart on prepared cookie sheets. Sprinkle with cookie decorations, if desired.

4. Bake 8 to 10 minutes or until edges begin to turn golden brown. Cool on wire racks.

Makes about 4 dozen cookies

Variation: Add 2 tablespoons unsweetened cocoa powder to dough for chocolate cookies.

Refrigerator Cookies

Ice Cream Cookies

2 squares (1 ounce each) unsweetened
  chocolate
1 cup butter, softened
1 cup powdered sugar
4 egg yolks
1 teaspoon vanilla
3 cups all-purpose flour
  Powdered sugar

Melt chocolate in top of double boiler over
hot, not boiling, water. Remove from heat;
cool. Cream butter and 1 cup sugar in large
bowl until blended. Add egg yolks, vanilla
and melted chocolate; beat until light. Blend
in flour to make stiff dough. Divide dough
into 4 parts. Shape each part into a roll
about 1½ inches in diameter. Wrap in
plastic wrap; refrigerate until firm, at least
30 minutes or up to 2 weeks. (For longer
storage, freeze up to 6 weeks.)

Preheat oven to 350°F. Line cookie sheets
with parchment paper or leave ungreased.
Cut rolls into ⅛-inch-thick slices; place
2 inches apart on ungreased cookie sheets.
Bake 8 to 10 minutes or just until set, but
not browned. Remove to wire racks to cool.
Dust with powdered sugar.

Makes about 8 dozen cookies

Ice Cream Cookie Sandwiches: Prepare
and bake cookies as directed; cool
completely. Spread desired amount of
softened ice cream on bottoms of half the
cookies. Top with remaining cookies,
bottom sides down, forming sandwiches.
Dust tops with powdered sugar; serve
immediately. Makes about 4 dozen sandwich
cookies.

Mocha Pecan Pinwheels

½ cup (1 stick) butter, softened
¾ cup packed brown sugar
1 egg
1 teaspoon vanilla
¼ teaspoon baking soda
1¾ cups all-purpose flour
½ cup chopped pecans
1 teaspoon instant espresso coffee
  powder
1 square (1 ounce) unsweetened
  chocolate, melted

Beat butter, brown sugar, egg, vanilla and
baking soda in large bowl, blending well.
Stir in flour to make stiff dough. Remove
half of dough. Blend pecans and coffee
powder into half of dough. Stir melted
chocolate into remaining half of dough.
Cover doughs; refrigerate 30 minutes.

Roll out coffee dough into 15×8-inch
rectangle between 2 sheets of plastic wrap.
Roll chocolate dough out to same dimensions
between 2 more sheets of plastic wrap.
Remove top sheets of plastic wrap. Place
coffee dough on top of chocolate dough.
Remove remaining sheets of plastic wrap.
Roll up firmly, jelly-roll fashion, starting
with long side. Wrap in plastic wrap; freeze
until firm enough to handle.

Preheat oven to 350°F. Cut frozen dough
into ¼-inch slices; place 2 inches apart on
ungreased cookie sheets. Bake 9 to
12 minutes or until set. Remove to wire
racks to cool.

Makes about 5 dozen cookies

Ice Cream Cookie Sandwiches

Slice 'n' Bake Ginger Wafers

½ cup butter, softened
1 cup packed brown sugar
¼ cup light molasses
1 egg
2 teaspoons ground ginger
1 teaspoon grated orange peel
¼ teaspoon salt
¼ teaspoon ground cinnamon
¼ teaspoon ground cloves
2 cups all-purpose flour

1. Beat butter, sugar and molasses in large bowl until light and fluffy. Add egg, ginger, orange peel, salt, cinnamon and cloves; beat until well blended. Stir in flour until well blended. (Dough will be very stiff.)

2. Divide dough in half. Roll each half into 8×1½-inch log. Wrap logs in waxed paper or plastic wrap; refrigerate at least 5 hours or up to 3 days.

3. Preheat oven to 350°F. Cut dough into ¼-inch-thick slices. Place about 2 inches apart on ungreased baking sheets. Bake 12 to 14 minutes or until set. Remove from baking sheets to wire racks to cool.

Makes about 4½ dozen cookies

Serving Suggestion: Dip half of each cookie in melted white chocolate, or drizzle cookies with a glaze of 1¼ cups powdered sugar and 2 tablespoons orange juice. Or, cut cookie dough into ⅛-inch-thick slices and bake. Sandwich melted caramel candy or peanut butter between cooled cookies.

Shapers

2 packages (20 ounces each) refrigerated sugar cookie dough
Red, yellow, green and blue paste food colors
1 container (16 ounces) vanilla frosting

1. Remove dough from wrapper. Cut each roll of dough in half.

2. Beat ¼ of dough and red food color in medium bowl until well blended. Shape red dough into 5-inch log on sheet of waxed paper; set aside.

3. Repeat with remaining dough and food colors. Cover; refrigerate tinted logs 1 hour or until firm.

4. Roll or shape each log on smooth surface to create circular, triangular, square and oval-shaped logs. Use ruler to keep triangle and square sides flat. Cover; refrigerate dough 1 hour or until firm.

5. Preheat oven to 350°F. Cut shaped dough into ¼-inch slices. Place 2 inches apart on ungreased baking sheets. Bake 9 to 12 minutes. Remove to wire racks; cool completely.

6. Spoon frosting into resealable plastic food storage bag; seal. Cut tiny tip from corner of bag. Pipe frosting around each cookie to define shape.

Makes about 6½ dozen cookies

Slice 'n' Bake Ginger Wafers

Rainbows

Christmas Ornament Cookie Dough (page 553)
Red, green, yellow and blue paste food coloring
White frosting and edible gold glitter dust

1. Prepare Christmas Ornament Cookie Dough. Divide dough into 10 equal sections. Combine 4 sections dough and red food coloring in large bowl; blend until smooth.

2. Combine 3 sections dough and green food coloring in medium bowl; blend until smooth.

3. Combine 2 sections dough and yellow food coloring in another medium bowl; blend until smooth.

4. Combine remaining dough and blue food coloring in small bowl; blend until smooth. Wrap each section of dough in plastic wrap. Refrigerate 30 minutes.

5. Shape blue dough into 8-inch log. Shape yellow dough into 8×3-inch rectangle; place on waxed paper. Place blue log in center of yellow rectangle. Fold yellow edges up and around blue log, pinching to seal. Roll to form smooth log.

6. Roll green dough into 8×5-inch rectangle on waxed paper. Place yellow log in center of green rectangle. Fold green edges up and around yellow log. Pinch to seal. Roll gently to form smooth log.

7. Roll red dough into 8×7-inch rectangle. Place green log in center of red rectangle. Fold red edges up and around green log.

Pinch to seal. Roll gently to form smooth log. Wrap in plastic wrap. Refrigerate 1 hour.

8. Preheat oven to 350°F. Grease cookie sheets. Cut log in half lengthwise. Cut each half into ¼-inch-thick slices. Place slices 1 inch apart on prepared cookie sheets. Bake 8 to 12 minutes. (Do not brown.) Cool on cookie sheets 1 minute. Remove to wire racks; cool completely.

9. Pipe small amount of frosting on bottom corner of 1 side of each cookie and sprinkle with glitter dust. Let stand 1 hour or until frosting sets.

Makes about 5 dozen cookies

DECORATE IT!

If you don't have a pastry bag to pipe the frosting onto these cookies, use a plastic food storage bag instead. Place the frosting in the bag; cut off a tiny corner of the bag, and then squeeze the frosting out onto the cookies.

Kaleidoscope Cookies

1 package (20 ounces) refrigerated
    sugar cookie dough
All-purpose flour (optional)
Blue and red liquid food colors
2 tablespoons sprinkles, multi-colored
    coarse sugar or rock sugar,
    divided

1. Remove dough from wrapper. Cut dough into 5 equal sections. Cover and refrigerate 1 section. Sprinkle remaining 4 sections with flour to minimize sticking, if necessary.

2. Add blue food coloring to 1 section in medium bowl; mix until well blended. Repeat with another section of dough and red food coloring. Shape each section into 7½-inch log. Cover and refrigerate.

3. Add 1 tablespoon sprinkles to third section in medium bowl; mix until well blended. Repeat with fourth section of dough and remaining 1 tablespoon sprinkles. Shape each section into 7½-inch log. Cover and refrigerate.

4. Roll out reserved section of plain dough on sheet of waxed paper to 7½×8½-inch rectangle. Place blue dough log and 1 sprinkled dough log in middle of rectangle. Place remaining sprinkled dough log on top of blue dough log and pink dough log on top of first sprinkled dough log.

5. Bring waxed paper and closest edge of plain dough up and over tops of logs. Press together gently. Repeat with opposite side, overlapping plain dough edges. Press together gently. Wrap waxed paper around dough and twist ends to secure.

6. Freeze 20 minutes. Preheat oven to 350°F. Grease cookie sheets.

7. Remove waxed paper. Cut log with sharp knife into ½-inch slices. Place 2 inches apart on prepared cookie sheets.

8. Bake 15 to 17 minutes or until edges are lightly browned. Remove to wire racks; cool completely. ***Makes about 15 cookies***

Domino® Sugar Cookies

1 cup DOMINO® Granulated Sugar
1 cup (2 sticks) butter or margarine,
    softened
1 egg
1 tablespoon vanilla
2¼ cups all-purpose flour
1 teaspoon baking soda
    Additional DOMINO® Granulated
    Sugar

In large bowl, blend sugar and butter. Beat in egg and vanilla until light and fluffy. Mix in flour and baking soda. Divide dough in half. Shape each half into roll about 1½ inches in diameter. Wrap and refrigerate for 1 hour until chilled.* Cut rolls into ¼-inch slices. Place on ungreased baking sheet and sprinkle generously with additional sugar. Bake in 375°F oven for 10 to 12 minutes or until lightly browned around edges. Cool on wire rack. ***Makes about 3 dozen cookies***

Tip: To chill dough quickly, place in freezer for 30 minutes.

Choco-Coco Pecan Crisps

½ cup butter, softened
1 cup packed light brown sugar
1 egg
1 teaspoon vanilla
1½ cups all-purpose flour
1 cup chopped pecans
⅓ cup unsweetened cocoa
½ teaspoon baking soda
1 cup flaked coconut

Cream butter and brown sugar in large bowl until light and fluffy. Beat in egg and vanilla. Combine flour, pecans, cocoa and baking soda in small bowl until well blended. Add to creamed mixture, blending until stiff dough is formed. Sprinkle coconut on work surface. Divide dough into 4 parts. Shape each part into a roll about 1½ inches in diameter; roll in coconut until thickly coated. Wrap in plastic wrap; refrigerate until firm, at least 1 hour or up to 2 weeks. (For longer storage, freeze up to 6 weeks.)

Preheat oven to 350°F. Cut rolls into ⅛-inch-thick slices. Place 2 inches apart on ungreased cookie sheets. Bake 10 to 13 minutes or until firm, but not overly browned. Remove to wire racks to cool.

Makes about 6 dozen cookies

Almond Cream Cheese Cookies

1 (3-ounce) package cream cheese, softened
1 cup butter, softened
1 cup sugar
1 egg yolk
1 tablespoon milk
⅛ teaspoon almond extract
2½ cups sifted cake flour
1 cup BLUE DIAMOND® Sliced Natural Almonds, toasted

Beat cream cheese with butter and sugar until fluffy. Blend in egg yolk, milk and almond extract. Gradually mix in flour. Gently stir in almonds. (Dough will be sticky.) Divide dough in half; place each half on large sheet of waxed paper. Working through waxed paper, shape each half into 12×1½-inch roll. Chill until very firm.

Preheat oven to 325°F. Cut rolls into ¼-inch slices. Bake on ungreased cookie sheets 10 to 15 minutes or until edges are golden. (Cookies will not brown.) Cool on wire racks. *Makes about 4 dozen cookies*

Choco-Coco Pecan Crisps

Peanut Butter and Jelly Sandwich Cookies

**1 package (18 ounces) refrigerated
    sugar cookie dough
1 tablespoon unsweetened cocoa
    powder
    All-purpose flour (optional)
¾ cup creamy peanut butter
½ cup grape jam or jelly**

1. Remove dough from wrapper. Reserve ¼ section of dough; cover and refrigerate remaining ¾ section of dough. Combine reserved dough and cocoa in small bowl; cover and refrigerate.

2. Shape remaining ¾ section dough into 5½-inch log. Sprinkle with flour to minimize sticking, if necessary. Remove chocolate dough from refrigerator; roll on sheet of waxed paper to 9½×6½-inch rectangle. Place dough log in center of rectangle.

3. Bring waxed paper edges and chocolate dough up and together over log. Press gently on top and sides of dough so entire log is wrapped in chocolate dough. Flatten log slightly to form square. Wrap in waxed paper. Freeze 10 minutes.

4. Preheat oven to 350°F. Remove waxed paper. Cut dough into ¼-inch slices. Place slices 2 inches apart on ungreased cookie sheets. Reshape dough edges into square, if necessary. Press dough slightly to form indentation so dough resembles slice of bread.

5. Bake 8 to 11 minutes or until lightly browned. Remove from oven and straighten cookie edges with spatula. Cool 2 minutes on cookie sheets. Remove to wire racks; cool completely.

6. To make sandwich, spread about 1 tablespoon peanut butter on bottom of 1 cookie. Spread about ½ tablespoon jam over peanut butter; top with second cookie, pressing gently. Repeat with remaining cookies. *Makes 11 sandwich cookies*

HELPFUL HINT

Make up your own favorite flavor combinations for these tasty sandwiches. Instead of the grape jam, use another flavor of jam. Or try honey, marshmallow creme or chocolate frosting.

Peanut Butter and Jelly Sandwich Cookies

Tic-Tac-Toe Cookies

¾ **cup (1½ sticks) butter, softened**
¾ **cup granulated sugar**
1 **large egg**
1 **teaspoon vanilla extract**
2¼ **cups all-purpose flour**
½ **teaspoon baking powder**
¼ **teaspoon salt**
4 **squares (1 ounce each) semi-sweet chocolate, melted**
¼ **cup powdered sugar**
1 **teaspoon water**
½ **cup "M&M's"® Chocolate Mini Baking Bits**

In large bowl cream butter and granulated sugar until light and fluffy; beat in egg and vanilla. In small bowl combine flour, baking powder and salt; blend into creamed mixture. Reserve half of dough. Stir chocolate into remaining dough. Wrap and refrigerate doughs 30 minutes. Working with one dough at a time on lightly floured surface, roll or pat into 7×4½-inch rectangle. Cut dough into 9 (7×½-inch) strips. Repeat with remaining dough. Place one strip chocolate dough on sheet of plastic wrap. Place one strip vanilla dough next to chocolate dough. Place second strip of chocolate dough next to vanilla dough to make bottom layer. Prepare second row by stacking strips on first row, alternating vanilla dough over chocolate and chocolate dough over vanilla. Repeat with third row to complete 1 bar. Repeat entire process with remaining dough strips, starting with vanilla dough, to complete second bar. Wrap both bars and refrigerate 1 hour. Preheat oven to 350°F. Lightly grease cookie sheets. Cut bars crosswise into ¼-inch slices. Place 2 inches apart on prepared cookie sheets. Bake 10 to 12 minutes. Cool on cookie sheets 2 minutes; cool completely on wire racks. In small bowl combine powdered sugar and water until smooth. Using icing to attach, decorate cookies with "M&M's"® Chocolate Mini Baking Bits to look like Tic-Tac-Toe games. Store in tightly covered container.

Makes 4 dozen cookies

DECORATE IT!

Decorating these delicious bars is a great rainy-day activity, so keep some of this dough prepared in bars for fun at a moment's notice. Tightly wrapped bars of dough can be stored in the refrigerator for up to one week or frozen for up to six weeks.

Tic-Tac-Toe Cookies

Cinnamon Nut Chocolate Spirals

1½ cups all-purpose flour
¼ teaspoon salt
⅓ cup butter, softened
¾ cup sugar, divided
1 egg
1 cup mini semisweet chocolate chips
1 cup very finely chopped walnuts
2 teaspoons ground cinnamon
3 tablespoons butter

Mix flour and salt in bowl; set aside. Beat ⅓ cup butter and ½ cup sugar in large bowl until light and fluffy. Beat in egg. Add flour mixture. Dough will be stiff. (If necessary, knead dough by hand until it forms ball.)

Roll out dough between 2 sheets of waxed paper into 12×10-inch rectangle. Remove waxed paper from top of rectangle.

Mix chips, walnuts, remaining ¼ cup sugar and cinnamon in bowl. Melt 3 tablespoons butter; pour hot butter over chocolate chip mixture; mix well. (Chips will partially melt.) Spoon mixture over dough. Spread evenly, leaving ½-inch border on long edges.

Using bottom sheet of waxed paper and starting at long side, roll up dough jelly-roll style, removing waxed paper as you roll. Wrap in plastic wrap; chill 30 to 60 minutes.

Preheat oven to 350°F. Grease cookie sheets. Unwrap dough. Cut dough into ½-inch slices. Place slices 2 inches apart on prepared cookie sheets. Bake 14 minutes or until edges are golden. Cool completely on wire racks.

Makes 2 dozen cookies

Orange Pecan Refrigerator Cookies

2⅓ cups all-purpose flour
½ teaspoon baking soda
¼ teaspoon salt
½ cup butter or margarine, softened
½ cup packed brown sugar
½ cup granulated sugar
1 egg, lightly beaten
Grated peel of 1 SUNKIST® Orange
3 tablespoons fresh squeezed orange juice
¾ cup pecan pieces

In bowl, stir together flour, baking soda and salt. In large bowl, blend together butter, brown sugar and granulated sugar. Add egg, orange peel and juice; beat well. Stir in pecans. Gradually beat in flour mixture. (Dough will be stiff.) Divide mixture in half and shape each half (on long piece of waxed paper) into roll about 1¼ inches in diameter and 12 inches long. Roll up tightly in waxed paper. Chill several hours or overnight.

Cut into ¼-inch slices and arrange on lightly greased cookie sheets. Bake at 350°F for 10 to 12 minutes or until lightly browned. Cool on wire racks.

Makes about 6 dozen cookies

Chocolate Filled Sandwich Cookies: Cut each roll into ⅛-inch slices and bake as above. When cool, to make each sandwich cookie, spread about 1 teaspoon canned chocolate fudge frosting on bottom side of 1 cookie; cover with second cookie of same shape. Makes 4 dozen sandwich cookies.

Cappuccino Cookies

1 cup butter, softened
2 cups packed brown sugar
2 tablespoons milk
2 tablespoons instant coffee granules
2 eggs
1 teaspoon rum extract
½ teaspoon vanilla
4 cups all-purpose flour
1 teaspoon baking powder
½ teaspoon ground nutmeg
¼ teaspoon salt
   Chocolate sprinkles or melted
     semisweet and/or white chocolate
     chips (optional)

Beat butter in large bowl with electric mixer at medium speed until smooth. Add brown sugar; beat until well blended.

Heat milk in small saucepan over low heat; add coffee granules, stirring to dissolve. Add milk mixture, eggs, rum extract and vanilla to butter mixture. Beat at medium speed until well blended.

Combine flour, baking powder, nutmeg and salt in large bowl. Gradually add flour mixture to butter mixture, beating at low speed after each addition until blended.

Shape dough into 2 logs, about 2 inches in diameter and 8 inches long. (Dough will be soft; sprinkle lightly with flour if too sticky to handle.)

Roll logs in chocolate sprinkles, if desired, coating evenly (⅓ cup sprinkles per roll). Or, leave rolls plain and dip cookies in melted chocolate after baking. Wrap each log in plastic wrap; refrigerate overnight.

Preheat oven to 350°F. Grease cookie sheets. Cut rolls into ¼-inch-thick slices; place 1 inch apart on cookie sheets. (Keep unbaked rolls and sliced cookies chilled until ready to bake.)

Bake 10 to 12 minutes or until edges are browned. Transfer to wire racks to cool. Dip plain cookies in melted semisweet or white chocolate, if desired. Store in airtight container. ***Makes about 5 dozen cookies***

HELPFUL HINT

Always shape the refrigerator dough into rolls before chilling. Shaping is easier if you first place the dough on a piece of waxed paper or plastic wrap. If desired, you can gently press chopped nuts, flaked coconut, colored sugar or sprinkles into the roll. Before chilling, wrap the rolls securely in plastic wrap to keep air from penetrating the dough, causing it to dry out.

Chocolate-Dipped Cinnamon Thins

1¼ cups all-purpose flour
1½ teaspoons ground cinnamon
¼ teaspoon salt
1 cup unsalted butter, softened
1 cup powdered sugar
1 egg
1 teaspoon vanilla
4 ounces broken bittersweet chocolate candy bar, melted

1. Combine flour, cinnamon and salt in bowl; set aside. Beat butter in bowl until light and fluffy. Add powdered sugar, egg and vanilla; beat well. Add flour mixture. Beat until blended.

2. Place dough on sheet of waxed paper. Using waxed paper to hold dough, roll it back and forth to form a log, about 12 inches long and 2½ inches wide. Wrap in plastic wrap. Refrigerate 2 hours or until firm.

3. Preheat oven to 350°F. Cut dough into ¼-inch-thick slices. Place 2 inches apart on ungreased cookie sheets. Bake 10 minutes or until set. Let cookies stand on cookie sheets 2 minutes. Remove cookies with spatula to wire racks; cool completely.

4. Dip each cookie into chocolate, coating 1 inch up sides. Transfer to wire racks or waxed paper; stand at cool room temperature about 40 minutes or until chocolate is set.

5. Store cookies between sheets of waxed paper at cool room temperature or in refrigerator. These cookies do not freeze well. ***Makes about 2 dozen cookies***

Chocolate & Peanut Butter Tweed Cookies

1 cup butter, softened
½ cup packed light brown sugar
¼ cup granulated sugar
1 egg
¼ teaspoon baking soda
2½ cups all-purpose flour
½ cup peanut butter chips, chopped*
½ cup semisweet chocolate chips, chopped*

*Chips can be chopped in a food processor.

Beat butter and sugars in large bowl with electric mixer at medium speed until smooth. Add egg and baking soda; beat until light and fluffy. Stir in flour until dough is smooth. Blend in chopped chips. Divide dough into 4 parts. Shape each part into roll, about 1½ inches in diameter. Wrap in plastic wrap; refrigerate until firm, at least 1 hour or up to 2 weeks. (For longer storage, freeze up to 6 weeks.)

Preheat oven to 375°F. Lightly grease cookie sheets or line with parchment paper. Cut rolls into ⅛-inch-thick slices; place 2 inches apart on prepared cookie sheets. Bake 10 to 12 minutes or until lightly browned. Remove to wire racks to cool.

Makes about 6 dozen cookies

Chocolate-Dipped Cinnamon Thins

Mint Chocolate Pinwheels

1¼ cups all-purpose flour
  1 teaspoon baking powder
 ½ teaspoon salt
 ⅔ cup butter, softened
  1 cup sugar
  1 egg
  1 teaspoon vanilla
  1 cup uncooked quick oats
  1 cup mint chocolate chips

1. Stir together flour, baking powder and salt in small bowl.

2. Beat butter and sugar in large bowl with electric mixer at medium speed until light and fluffy. Add egg and vanilla; beat well. Gradually add flour mixture. Beat at low speed. Stir in oats.

3. Place chocolate chips in 1-cup glass measure. Microwave at HIGH about 2 minutes or until melted, stirring after 1½ minutes. Divide cookie dough in half. Add melted chocolate to one half; mix well.

4. Roll out each half of dough between 2 sheets of waxed paper into 15×10-inch rectangles. Remove waxed paper from top of each rectangle.

5. Place chocolate dough over plain dough; remove bottom sheet of waxed paper from bottom of chocolate dough. Starting at long side, tightly roll up dough jelly-roll fashion, removing waxed paper as you roll. Wrap dough in plastic wrap; refrigerate at least 2 hours, or up to 24 hours.

6. Preheat oven to 350°F. Lightly grease cookie sheets; set aside.

7. Unwrap log. Cut dough into ¼-inch slices. Place 3 inches apart on prepared cookie sheets.

8. Bake 10 to 12 minutes or until set. Remove cookies with spatula to wire racks; cool completely. Store tightly covered at room temperature or freeze up to 3 months.

Makes about 3 dozen cookies

HELPFUL HINT

Use gentle pressure and a back-and-forth sawing motion when slicing rolls of refrigerator dough, so the cookies will keep their nice round shape. Rotating the roll while slicing also prevents one side from flattening.

Spiced Wafers

½ cup butter, softened
1 cup sugar
1 egg
2 tablespoons milk
1 teaspoon vanilla
1¾ cups all-purpose flour
2 teaspoons baking powder
1 teaspoon ground cinnamon
½ teaspoon ground nutmeg
¼ teaspoon ground cloves
    Red hot candies or red colored sugar for garnish (optional)

Beat butter in large bowl with electric mixer at medium speed until smooth. Add sugar; beat until well blended. Add egg, milk and vanilla; beat until well blended.

Combine flour, baking powder, cinnamon, nutmeg and cloves in large bowl. Gradually add flour mixture to butter mixture at low speed, blending well after each addition.

Shape dough into 2 logs, each about 2 inches in diameter and 6 inches long. Wrap each log in plastic wrap. Refrigerate 2 to 3 hours or overnight.

Preheat oven to 350°F. Grease cookie sheets. Cut logs into ¼-inch-thick slices; decorate with candies or colored sugar, if desired. (Or leave plain and decorate with icing later.) Place at least 2 inches apart on cookie sheets.

Bake 11 to 13 minutes or until edges are light brown. Transfer to wire racks to cool. Store in airtight container.

Makes 4 dozen cookies

Spiced Wafers

Fruitcake Slices

1 cup butter, softened
1 cup powdered sugar
1 egg
1 teaspoon vanilla
1½ cups coarsely chopped candied fruit
    (fruitcake mix)
½ cup coarsely chopped walnuts
2½ cups all-purpose unsifted flour,
    divided
¾ to 1 cup flaked coconut
    Maraschino cherry halves (optional)

Beat butter in large bowl with electric mixer at medium speed until smooth. Add powdered sugar; beat until well blended. Add egg and vanilla; beat until well blended.

Combine candied fruit and walnuts in medium bowl. Stir ¼ cup flour into fruit mixture. Add remaining 2¼ cups flour to butter mixture; beat at low speed until blended. Stir in fruit mixture with spoon.

Shape dough into 2 logs, each about 2 inches in diameter and 5½ inches long. Spread coconut evenly on sheet of waxed paper. Roll logs in coconut, coating evenly. Wrap each log in plastic wrap. Refrigerate 2 to 3 hours or overnight.

Preheat oven to 350°F. Grease cookie sheets. Cut logs into ¼-inch-thick slices; place 1 inch apart on cookie sheets.

Bake 13 to 15 minutes or until edges are golden brown. Transfer to wire racks to cool. Decorate with cherry halves, if desired. Store in airtight container.

Makes about 4 dozen cookies

Peanut Butter and Chocolate Spirals

1 package (20 ounces) refrigerated
    sugar cookie dough
1 package (20 ounces) refrigerated
    peanut butter cookie dough
¼ cup unsweetened cocoa powder
⅓ cup peanut butter-flavored chips,
    chopped
¼ cup all-purpose flour
⅓ cup miniature chocolate chips

1. Remove each dough from wrapper. Place sugar cookie dough and cocoa in large bowl; mix with fork to blend. Stir in peanut butter chips.

2. Place peanut butter cookie dough and flour in another large bowl; mix with fork to blend. Stir in chocolate chips. Divide each dough in half; cover and refrigerate 1 hour.

3. Roll each dough on floured surface to 12×6-inch rectangle. Layer each half of peanut butter dough onto each half of chocolate dough. Roll up doughs, starting at long end to form 2 (12-inch) rolls. Wrap in plastic wrap; refrigerate 1 hour.

4. Preheat oven to 375°F. Cut dough into ½-inch-thick slices. Place cookies 2 inches apart on ungreased cookie sheets.

5. Bake 10 to 12 minutes or until lightly browned. Remove to wire racks; cool completely. *Makes 4 dozen cookies*

Fruitcake Slices

Checkerboard Bars

½ cup hazelnuts (2½ ounces)
4 ounces bittersweet or semisweet
    chocolate candy bar, broken into
    pieces
2¼ cups all-purpose flour
½ teaspoon baking powder
¼ teaspoon salt
¾ cup butter, softened
¾ cup sugar
2 eggs, divided
1 teaspoon vanilla

Preheat oven to 350°F. To remove skins from hazelnuts, spread in single layer on baking sheet. Bake 10 to 12 minutes or until toasted and skins begin to flake off; let cool slightly. Wrap hazelnuts in heavy kitchen towel; rub against towel to remove as much of skins as possible.

Place hazelnuts in food processor; process until finely chopped, but not pasty. Melt chocolate in small bowl over very hot water, stirring until smooth.

Combine flour, baking powder and salt in medium bowl. Beat butter and sugar in large bowl with electric mixer at medium speed until light and fluffy. Beat in 1 egg and vanilla. Gradually add flour mixture; beat well.

Reserve 1¼ cups dough. Stir chocolate and nuts into remaining dough. Wrap both doughs in plastic wrap and refrigerate 20 minutes.

Unwrap and roll out chocolate dough on lightly floured surface to ⅓-inch thickness with floured rolling pin. Cut dough into twelve 4×¾-inch strips. Reroll scraps as necessary, until all dough has been cut into strips. Repeat process with vanilla dough.

To assemble, beat remaining egg in small dish. Place one strip of chocolate dough on sheet of plastic wrap. Brush edge with egg. Place one strip of vanilla dough next to chocolate dough. Brush edge with egg. Repeat with one more chocolate strip and one more vanilla strip to make bottom layer. Brush top with egg.

Prepare second row by stacking strips on first row, alternating vanilla dough over chocolate, and chocolate dough over vanilla. Brush edge of each strip and top layer with egg. Repeat with third row to complete 1 checkerboard bar. Repeat entire process with remaining dough strips to complete second checkerboard bar. Cover with plastic wrap; refrigerate 1 hour or until firm enough to slice.

Preheat oven to 350°F. Grease cookie sheets. Cut checkerboard bar crosswise with long, sharp knife into ¼-inch slices. Place 2 inches apart on prepared cookie sheets.

Bake 10 to 12 minutes or until set. Cool cookies on cookie sheets 2 minutes. Remove cookies to wire racks; cool completely. Store tightly covered at room temperature, or freeze up to 3 months.

Makes 2 dozen bars

Checkerboard Bars

Chocolate-Cherry Slice 'n' Bake Cookies

¾ cup (1½ sticks) butter, softened
1 cup sugar
1 egg
1½ teaspoons vanilla extract
2¼ cups all-purpose flour
2 teaspoons baking powder
½ teaspoon salt
¼ cup finely chopped maraschino
   cherries
½ teaspoon almond extract
   Red food color
⅓ cup HERSHEY'S Cocoa
¼ teaspoon baking soda
4 teaspoons water
   Cocoa Almond Glaze (recipe
   follows)

1. Beat butter, sugar, egg and vanilla in large bowl until fluffy. Stir together flour, baking powder and salt; gradually add to butter mixture, beating until mixture forms a smooth dough. Remove 1¼ cups dough to medium bowl; blend in cherries, almond extract and about 6 drops food color.

2. Stir together cocoa and baking soda. Add with water to remaining dough; blend until smooth. Divide chocolate dough in half; roll each half between two sheets of wax paper, forming 12×4½-inch rectangle. Remove top sheet of wax paper. Divide cherry mixture in half; with floured hands, shape each half into 12-inch roll. Place one roll in center of each rectangle; wrap chocolate dough around roll, forming one large roll. Wrap in plastic wrap. Refrigerate about 6 hours or until firm.

3. Heat oven to 350°F.

4. Cut rolls into ¼-inch-thick slices; place on ungreased cookie sheet. Bake 7 minutes or until set. Cool 1 minute; remove from cookie sheet to wire rack. Cool completely. Prepare Cocoa Almond Glaze; decorate cookies.   *Makes about 7½ dozen cookies*

Cocoa Almond Glaze

2 tablespoons butter or margarine
2 tablespoons HERSHEY'S Cocoa
2 tablespoons water
1 cup powdered sugar
⅛ teaspoon almond extract

Melt butter in small saucepan over low heat. Add cocoa and water; stir constantly until mixture thickens. *Do not boil.* Remove from heat. Add sugar and almond extract, beating until smooth and of desired consistency.

Chocolate Mint Sandwiches

2 squares (1 ounce each) unsweetened
   chocolate
½ cup butter, softened
1 cup packed light brown sugar
1 egg
1 teaspoon vanilla
⅛ teaspoon baking soda
2 cups all-purpose flour
   Creamy Mint Filling (recipe follows)

Melt chocolate in top of double boiler over
hot, not boiling, water. Remove from heat;
cool. Cream butter and brown sugar in large
bowl. Beat in egg, vanilla, melted chocolate
and baking soda until light and fluffy. Stir in
flour to make stiff dough. Divide dough into
four parts. Shape each part into roll about
1½ inches in diameter. Wrap in plastic wrap;
refrigerate at least 1 hour or up to 2 weeks.
(For longer storage, freeze up to 6 weeks.)

Preheat oven to 375°F. Cut rolls into ⅛-inch
slices; place 2 inches apart on ungreased
cookie sheets. Bake 6 to 7 minutes or until
firm. Remove to wire racks to cool. Prepare
Creamy Mint Filling. Spread filling on
bottoms of half the cookies. Top with
remaining cookies, bottom sides down.

Makes about 3 dozen sandwich cookies

Creamy Mint Filling

2 tablespoons butter or margarine,
   softened
1½ cups powdered sugar
3 to 4 tablespoons light cream or
   half-and-half
¼ teaspoon peppermint extract
   Few drops green food coloring

Cream butter, powdered sugar and cream in
small bowl until smooth. Stir in peppermint
extract and food coloring; blend well.

FUN FOOD FACT

*Also called coffee cream, light cream
contains about 20 percent fat, although
the fat content can go as high as
30 percent. Even though it will not
whip, light cream can replace whipping
cream in many recipes, such as sauces,
ice creams, soups and puddings. Light
cream is not always available.
If it is not available in your
area, substitute half-and-
half for it.*

Classic Refrigerator Sugar Cookies

1 cup butter, softened
1 cup sugar
1 egg
1 teaspoon vanilla
2 cups all-purpose flour
2 teaspoons baking powder
  Dash nutmeg
¼ cup milk
  Colored sprinkles or melted
    semisweet chocolate chips*
    (optional)

*To dip 24 cookies, melt 1 cup chocolate chips in small saucepan over very low heat until smooth.

Beat butter in large bowl with electric mixer at medium speed until smooth. Add sugar; beat until well blended. Add egg and vanilla; beat until well blended.

Combine flour, baking powder and nutmeg in medium bowl. Add flour mixture and milk alternately to butter mixture, beating at low speed after each addition until well blended.

Shape dough into 2 logs, each about 2 inches in diameter and 6 inches long. Roll logs in colored sprinkles, if desired, coating evenly (about ¼ cup sprinkles per roll). Or, leave logs plain and decorate cookies with melted chocolate after baking. Wrap each log in plastic wrap. Refrigerate 2 to 3 hours or overnight.

Preheat oven to 350°F. Grease cookie sheets. Cut logs into ¼-inch-thick slices; place 1 inch apart on prepared cookie sheets.

(Keep unbaked logs and sliced cookies chilled until ready to bake.)

Bake 8 to 10 minutes or until edges are golden brown. Transfer to wire racks to cool.

Dip plain cookies in melted chocolate, or drizzle chocolate over cookies with fork or spoon, if desired. Set cookies on wire racks until chocolate is set. Store in airtight container. ***Makes about 4 dozen cookies***

HELPFUL HINT

When reusing the same cookie sheets for several batches of cookies, cool the cookie sheets completely before placing more dough on them. Dough will soften and begin to spread on a hot sheet.

Classic Refrigerator Sugar Cookies

Basic Icebox Cookie Dough

1 cup butter or margarine, softened
1 cup sugar
1 egg
1 teaspoon vanilla
2½ cups flour
1 teaspoon baking powder
½ teaspoon salt

Cream butter and sugar; beat in egg and vanilla. Combine flour, baking powder and salt. Gradually add to creamed mixture and mix well.   ***Makes 4½ cups dough***

Maraschino Cherry Cookies: Add ½ cup chopped well-drained maraschino cherries to basic dough; divide dough in half. Form dough into 2 logs, 1½ inches in diameter. Wrap in waxed paper and refrigerate at least 6 hours. Cut into ¼-inch slices. Place on *ungreased* baking sheets. Bake at 375°F 8 to 10 minutes. Remove to cooling rack. Repeat with remaining dough. Makes 6 to 7 dozen cookies.

Maraschino Date Pinwheels: Combine 8 ounces cut-up pitted dates and ¼ cup water in small saucepan; bring to a boil. Reduce heat; simmer until thickened. Add ¾ cup chopped drained maraschino cherries; mix well and cool. Divide dough in half. Roll out each half to 12×10-inch rectangle on lightly floured surface. Spread half of cooled filling on each rectangle. Roll up beginning at long ends. Pinch ends of rolls to seal. Wrap in waxed paper and refrigerate at least 6 hours. Cut rolls into ¼-inch slices. Place 1 to 1½ inches apart on *ungreased* baking sheet. Bake at 375°F about 10 to 14 minutes or until lightly browned. Remove to cooling rack. Makes 6 to 7 dozen cookies.

Maraschino Thumbprint Cookies: Shape dough into balls, using 2 teaspoons dough for each cookie. Press thumb in center of each ball. Place whole well-drained maraschino cherry in center of each depression. Brush with beaten egg white. If desired, roll each ball in beaten egg white, then in finely chopped pecans before pressing with thumb and filling with cherry. Bake at 375°F 12 to 15 minutes. Remove to cooling rack. Makes 5 dozen cookies.

Favorite recipe from **Cherry Marketing Institute**

HELPFUL HINT

Make sure ingredients such as fruit and nuts are finely chopped before adding them to the dough. This will make slicing the chilled dough much easier.

Cardamom-Chocolate Sandwiches

1½ cups all-purpose flour
1 teaspoon ground cardamom
½ teaspoon baking soda
½ teaspoon salt
¾ cup plus 2 tablespoons butter,
    softened and divided
¾ cup packed light brown sugar
¼ cup half-and-half
½ cup milk chocolate chips
2 tablespoons milk
1 cup sifted powdered sugar

Combine flour, cardamom, baking soda and salt in small bowl. Beat ¾ cup butter and brown sugar until light and fluffy. Beat in half-and-half. Add flour mixture; blend well.

Spoon dough down center of sheet of waxed paper. Using waxed paper, shape and roll dough into smooth 10-inch round log. If dough is too soft, refrigerate 1 hour and reroll log until smooth. Wrap securely. Refrigerate about 4 hours or until firm.

Preheat oven to 375°F. Cut dough into ¼-inch slices. Place 2 inches apart on ungreased cookie sheets. Bake 10 to 12 minutes or until edges are golden brown and cookies are set. Cool on cookie sheets 2 minutes. Cool completely on wire racks.

Microwave chocolate chips and remaining 2 tablespoons butter in microwavable bowl at HIGH 1½ minutes or until melted; stir after 1 minute. Beat in milk and powdered sugar. Spread over bottoms of half the cookies; top with remaining cookies.

Makes 1 dozen sandwich cookies

Cardamom-Chocolate Sandwiches

Date Pinwheel Cookies

1¼ cups dates, pitted and finely chopped
¾ cup orange juice
½ cup granulated sugar
1 tablespoon butter
3 cups plus 1 tablespoon all-purpose flour, divided
2 teaspoons vanilla, divided
4 ounces cream cheese
¼ cup shortening
1 cup packed brown sugar
2 eggs
1 teaspoon baking soda
½ teaspoon salt

1. Heat dates, orange juice, granulated sugar, butter and 1 tablespoon flour in saucepan over medium heat. Cook and stir 10 minutes or until thick; remove from heat. Stir in 1 teaspoon vanilla; set aside to cool.

2. Beat cream cheese, shortening and brown sugar about 3 minutes in large bowl until light and fluffy. Add eggs and remaining 1 teaspoon vanilla; beat 2 minutes longer.

3. Combine remaining 3 cups flour, baking soda and salt in medium bowl. Add to shortening mixture; stir just until blended. Divide dough in half. Roll one half of dough on lightly floured surface into 12×9-inch rectangle. Spread half of date mixture over dough. Spread evenly, leaving ¼-inch border at top short edge. Starting at short side, tightly roll up dough jelly-roll style. Wrap in plastic wrap; freeze for at least 1 hour. Repeat with remaining dough.

4. Preheat oven to 350°F. Grease cookie sheets. Unwrap dough. Using heavy thread or dental floss, cut dough into ¼-inch slices. Place slices 1 inch apart on prepared cookie sheets.

5. Bake 12 minutes or until lightly browned. Let cookies stand on cookie sheets 2 minutes. Remove cookies to wire racks; cool completely.   *Makes 6 dozen cookies*

P.B. Swirls

½ cup shortening
1 cup sugar
½ cup crunchy peanut butter
1 egg
2 teaspoons milk
1¼ cups sifted flour
½ teaspoon salt
½ teaspoon baking soda
1 (6-ounce) package chocolate chips

Preheat oven to 375°F. Cream shortening and sugar. Beat in peanut butter, egg and milk. In separate bowl, mix flour, salt and baking soda. Mix dry ingredients into peanut butter mixture. Place dough on lightly greased waxed paper. Using your hands, shape dough into a rectangle. Melt chocolate chips and spread over dough. Starting at long edge, roll up dough like a jelly roll. Chill ½ hour. Slice into ¼-inch slices. Place on ungreased cookie sheet. Bake at 375°F for 8 to 10 minutes.

Makes 2 dozen cookies

Favorite recipe from **Peanut Advisory Board**

Date Pinwheel Cookies

Charming Cookie
CUTOUTS

Black & White Hearts

¾ **cup sugar**
1 **cup butter, softened**
1 **package (3 ounces) cream cheese, softened**
1 **egg**
1½ **teaspoons vanilla**
3 **cups all-purpose flour**
1 **cup semisweet chocolate chips**
2 **tablespoons shortening**

1. Combine sugar, butter, cream cheese, egg and vanilla in large bowl. Beat at medium speed of electric mixer, scraping bowl often, until light and fluffy. Add flour; beat until well mixed. Divide dough in half; wrap each half in waxed paper. Refrigerate 2 hours or until firm.

2. Preheat oven to 375°F. Roll out dough to 1¼-inch thickness on lightly floured surface. Cut out with lightly floured heart-shaped cookie cutters. Place 1 inch apart on ungreased cookie sheets. Bake 7 to 10 minutes or until edges are very lightly browned. Remove immediately to wire racks to cool completely.

3. Melt chocolate chips and shortening in small saucepan over low heat 4 to 6 minutes or until melted. Dip half of each heart into melted chocolate. Refrigerate on cookie sheets or trays lined with waxed paper until chocolate is firm. Store, covered, in refrigerator.

Makes about 3½ dozen cookies

Black & White Hearts

Lemony Butter Cookies

½ cup butter, softened
½ cup sugar
1 egg
1½ cups all-purpose flour
2 tablespoons fresh lemon juice
1 teaspoon grated lemon peel
½ teaspoon baking powder
⅛ teaspoon salt
   Additional sugar

Beat butter and sugar in large bowl with electric mixer at medium speed until creamy. Beat in egg until light and fluffy. Mix in flour, lemon juice and peel, baking powder and salt. Cover; refrigerate about 2 hours or until firm.

Preheat oven to 350°F. Roll out dough, small portion at a time, on well-floured surface to ¼-inch thickness. (Keep remaining dough in refrigerator.) Cut with 3-inch round cookie cutter. Transfer to ungreased cookie sheets. Sprinkle with sugar.

Bake 8 to 10 minutes or until edges are lightly browned. Cool 1 minute on cookie sheets. Remove to wire racks; cool completely. Store in airtight container.

Makes about 2½ dozen cookies

Berry Treasures

2½ cups all-purpose flour
½ cup sugar
⅔ cup butter
1 egg
½ teaspoon salt
¼ teaspoon baking soda
2 tablespoons milk
1½ teaspoons vanilla
¾ cup mixed berry preserves
   Additional sugar

1. Preheat oven to 350°F. Combine flour, sugar, butter, egg, salt, baking soda, milk and vanilla in large bowl. Beat 3 to 4 minutes, scraping bowl often, until well mixed.

2. Roll out dough, ½ at a time, to ⅛-inch thickness on well-floured surface. Cut out cookies with 2½-inch round cookie cutter. Place ½ of cookies 2 inches apart on ungreased cookie sheets; place level teaspoonful preserves in center of each cookie.

3. Make small "X" or cutout with very small cookie cutter in top of each remaining cutout. Place over preserves; press edges together with fork. Sprinkle with sugar.

4. Bake 11 to 13 minutes or until edges are very lightly browned. Remove cookies immediately to wire racks to cool completely.

Makes about 2 dozen sandwich cookies

Lemony Butter Cookies

Cookie Bowl and Cookie Fruit

1 cup butter, softened
1½ cups sugar
2 whole eggs
2 teaspoons grated orange peel
2 teaspoons vanilla
5 cups all-purpose flour
1 teaspoon baking powder
½ teaspoon salt
1 cup sour cream
4 egg yolks, divided
4 teaspoons water, divided
Red, yellow, blue and green liquid food colors

1. Beat butter and sugar in large bowl at high speed of electric mixer until light and fluffy. Add whole eggs, orange peel and vanilla; mix until well blended.

2. Combine flour, baking powder and salt in another large bowl. Add half of flour mixture to butter mixture; mix at low speed until well blended. Add sour cream; mix well. Add remaining flour mixture; mix well.

3. Divide dough into 4 equal sections. Cover; refrigerate several hours or overnight.

4. Place 1 egg yolk in each of 4 separate bowls. Add 1 teaspoon water and food color to each; beat lightly. Set aside.

5. Preheat oven to 375°F. Roll 1 section of dough on well-floured surface to 12-inch circle. Carefully transfer dough to inverted 1½-quart ovenproof bowl. Press overlapping portions of dough together; trim edges. Paint sides of bowl as desired, using small, clean craft paintbrushes and egg yolk paint.

6. Place bowl on wire rack and then on cookie sheet. Bake 20 to 25 minutes or until lightly browned. Cool completely on bowl.

7. Roll remaining dough on well-floured surface to ⅛-inch thickness. Cut with fruit-shaped cookie cutters. Place 2 inches apart on ungreased cookie sheets. Paint as desired with egg yolk paint.

8. Bake 10 to 12 minutes or until edges are lightly browned. Remove to wire racks; cool completely.

Makes 1 bowl and 4 dozen cookies

HELPFUL HINT

When making cutout cookies, dip the cookie cutters in flour before each use. That way the cookie dough will not stick to the cookie cutters.

Cookie Bowl and Cookie Fruit

Almond Hearts

**1 package DUNCAN HINES® Golden
  Sugar Cookie Mix**
¾ cup ground almonds
2 egg yolks
⅓ cup vegetable oil
1½ tablespoons water
**14 ounces (6 cubes) vanilla flavored
  candy coating**
Pink candy coating, for garnish

1. Preheat oven to 375°F.

2. Combine cookie mix, ground almonds, egg yolks, oil and water in large bowl. Stir until thoroughly blended.

3. Divide dough in half. Roll half the dough between 2 sheets of waxed paper into 11-inch circle. Slide onto flat surface. Refrigerate about 15 minutes. Repeat with remaining dough. Loosen top sheet of waxed paper from dough. Turn over and remove second sheet of waxed paper. Cut dough with 2½-inch heart cookie cutter. Place cut-outs 2 inches apart on ungreased cookie sheets. (Roll leftover cookie dough to ⅛-inch thickness between sheets of waxed paper. Chill before cutting.) Repeat with remaining dough circle. Bake at 375°F for 6 to 8 minutes or until light golden brown. Cool 1 minute on cookie sheets. Remove to cooling racks. Cool completely.

4. Place vanilla candy coating in 1-quart saucepan on low heat; stir until melted and smooth. Dip half of one heart cookie into candy coating. Allow excess to drip back into pan. Place cookie on waxed paper. Repeat with remaining cookies. Place pink candy coating in small saucepan on low heat. Stir until melted and smooth. Pour into pastry bag fitted with small writing tip. Decorate tops of cookies as desired. Allow candy coating to set before storing between layers of waxed paper in airtight container.

Makes about 5 dozen cookies

Moons and Stars

1 cup butter, softened
1 cup sugar
1 egg
2 teaspoons lemon peel
½ teaspoon almond extract
3 cups all-purpose flour
½ cup ground almonds
**Assorted colored icings, hard
  candies and colored sprinkles**

1. Preheat oven to 350°F. Grease cookie sheets.

2. Beat butter, sugar, egg, lemon peel and almond extract in large bowl at medium speed of electric mixer until light and fluffy.

3. Combine flour and almonds in medium bowl. Add flour mixture to butter mixture; stir just until combined.

4. Roll dough on lightly floured surface to ⅛- to ¼-inch thickness. Cut out cookies using moon and star cookie cutters. Place cookies 2 inches apart on prepared cookie sheets.

5. Bake 7 to 9 minutes or until set but not browned. Cool on cookie sheets 2 minutes. Remove to wire racks; cool completely.

6. Decorate cookies with icings, candies and sprinkles as desired.

Makes about 4 dozen cookies

Frosted Sugar Cookies

10 tablespoons margarine, softened
 1 cup sugar
 2 egg whites
 1 teaspoon vanilla
 2 cups all-purpose flour
 1 teaspoon baking powder
 ½ teaspoon salt
   Vanilla Frosting (recipe follows)
   Ground nutmeg or cinnamon

1. Preheat oven to 375°F. Spray cookie sheets with nonstick cooking spray.

2. Beat margarine and sugar in large bowl with electric mixer until fluffy. Beat in egg whites and vanilla.

3. Combine flour, baking powder and salt in medium bowl. Add flour mixture to margarine mixture; mix well. Refrigerate 3 to 4 hours.

4. Roll out dough on generously floured surface to ¼-inch thickness (dough will be soft). Cut decorative shapes out of dough with 2-inch cutters and place on prepared cookie sheets.

5. Bake 8 to 10 minutes or until cookies turn golden brown. Remove from cookie sheets to wire racks; cool completely. Meanwhile, prepare Vanilla Frosting.

6. Frost cookies; sprinkle with nutmeg or cinnamon.   *Makes 7 dozen cookies*

Vanilla Frosting

2 cups powdered sugar
2 to 3 tablespoons fat-free (skim)
   milk, divided
1 teaspoon vanilla

Mix powdered sugar, 2 tablespoons milk and vanilla in medium bowl with fork. Add additional 1 tablespoon milk until desired spreading consistency is reached.
        Makes about ½ cup frosting

HELPFUL HINT

To get the most cookies out of rolled dough, cut cookies as close together as possible. Place the cutouts on the cookie sheets and press the remaining dough scraps together, being careful not to overhandle them. Re-roll this leftover dough, and continue to cut more cookies.

Linzer Sandwich Cookies

1⅓ cups all-purpose flour
¼ teaspoon baking powder
¼ teaspoon salt
¾ cup granulated sugar
½ cup butter, softened
1 large egg
1 teaspoon vanilla
Powdered sugar (optional)
Seedless raspberry jam

Place flour, baking powder and salt in small bowl; stir to combine. Beat granulated sugar and butter in medium bowl with electric mixer at medium speed until light and fluffy. Beat in egg and vanilla. Gradually add flour mixture. Beat at low speed until dough forms. Divide dough in half; cover and refrigerate 2 hours or until firm.

Preheat oven to 375°F. Working with 1 portion at a time, roll out dough on lightly floured surface to ³/₁₆-inch thickness. Cut dough into desired shapes with floured cookie cutters. Cut out equal numbers of each shape. (If dough becomes too soft, refrigerate several minutes before continuing.) Cut 1-inch centers out of half the cookies of each shape. Reroll trimmings and cut out more cookies. Place cookies 1½ to 2 inches apart on ungreased cookie sheets. Bake 7 to 9 minutes or until edges are lightly brown. Let cookies stand on cookie sheets 1 to 2 minutes. Remove cookies to wire racks; cool completely.

Sprinkle cookies with holes with powdered sugar, if desired. Spread 1 teaspoon jam on flat side of whole cookies, spreading almost to edges. Place cookies with holes, flat side down, over jam. Store tightly covered at room temperature or freeze up to 3 months.

Makes about 2 dozen sandwich cookies

Butter Cookies

¾ cup butter, softened
¼ cup granulated sugar
¼ cup packed light brown sugar
1 egg yolk
1¾ cups all-purpose flour
¾ teaspoon baking powder
⅛ teaspoon salt

1. Combine butter, sugars and egg yolk in medium bowl. Add flour, baking powder and salt; mix well. Cover; refrigerate until firm, about 4 hours or overnight.

2. Preheat oven to 350°F.

3. Roll dough on lightly floured surface to ¼-inch thickness; cut into desired shapes with cookie cutters. Place on ungreased cookie sheets.

4. Bake 8 to 10 minutes or until edges begin to brown. Remove to wire racks; cool completely.

Makes about 2 dozen cookies

Linzer Sandwich Cookies

Colorful Sugar Cutouts

½ cup (1 stick) butter or margarine
¼ cup solid vegetable shortening
1 cup granulated sugar
2 large eggs
½ teaspoon vanilla extract
2¾ cups all-purpose flour
½ teaspoon baking powder
¼ teaspoon baking soda
¼ teaspoon salt
   Vanilla Icing (recipe follows)
   "M&M's"® Chocolate Mini Baking
   Bits for decoration

In bowl cream butter, shortening and sugar until fluffy; beat in eggs and vanilla. In medium bowl mix flour, baking powder, baking soda and salt; blend into creamed mixture. Wrap and refrigerate dough 2 to 3 hours. Preheat oven to 350°F. Working with half the dough at a time on floured surface, roll to ⅛-inch thickness. Cut into shapes using 3-inch cookie cutters. Carefully transfer to ungreased cookie sheets. Bake 8 to 10 minutes. Cool completely on wire racks. Frost with Vanilla Icing and decorate with "M&M's"® Chocolate Mini Baking Bits.

Makes about 4 dozen cookies

Vanilla Icing: Beat 6 tablespoons butter and 4 cups powdered sugar until well blended; add ½ teaspoon vanilla extract. Blend in 3 to 4 tablespoons milk, one tablespoon at a time, until of spreading consistency. Divide icing among 3 bowls. Add red food coloring to one and green to another until of desired color. Leave third portion white.

Pecan Toffee Filled Ravioli Cookies

1 cup packed brown sugar
¼ cup butter, melted
½ cup chopped pecans
2 tablespoons all-purpose flour
   Butter Cookie Dough (page 552)

1. For filling, stir brown sugar into melted butter in large bowl until well blended. Add pecans and flour; mix well. Transfer filling to waxed paper; shape into 7½-inch square. Cut into 36 (1¼-inch) pieces. Refrigerate 1 hour or overnight.

2. Prepare 2 recipes Butter Cookie Dough. Cover; refrigerate about 4 hours or until firm. Roll half of dough on well-floured sheet of waxed paper to 12-inch square. Repeat with second half of dough. If dough becomes soft, refrigerate 1 hour.

3. Preheat oven to 350°F. Lightly score 1 layer of dough at 2-inch intervals to form 36 squares. Place 1 square of filling in center of each square. Carefully place second layer of dough over filling squares. Press down gently between rows. Cut with knife, ravioli wheel or pastry cutter. Transfer filled ravioli to ungreased cookie sheets.

4. Bake 14 to 16 minutes or until lightly browned. Cool on cookie sheets 5 minutes. Remove to wire racks; cool completely.

Makes 3 dozen cookies

Sandwich Cookies

1 package (20 ounces) refrigerated cookie dough, any flavor
All-purpose flour (optional)
Any combination of colored frostings, peanut butter or assorted ice creams for filling
Colored sprinkles, chocolate-covered raisins, miniature candy-coated chocolate pieces and other assorted small candies for decoration

1. Preheat oven to 350°F. Grease cookie sheets.

2. Remove dough from wrapper. Cut dough into 4 equal sections. Reserve 1 section; refrigerate remaining 3 sections.

3. Roll reserved dough to ¼-inch thickness. Sprinkle with flour to minimize sticking, if necessary.

4. Cut out cookies using ¾-inch round or fluted cookie cutter. Transfer cookies to prepared cookie sheets, placing about 2 inches apart. Repeat steps with remaining dough.

5. Bake 8 to 11 minutes or until edges are lightly browned. Remove to wire racks; cool completely.

6. To make sandwich, spread about 1 tablespoon desired filling on flat side of 1 cookie to within ¼ inch of edge. Top with second cookie, pressing gently. Roll side of sandwich in desired decorations. Repeat with remaining cookies.

Makes 20 to 24 sandwich cookies

Sandwich Cookies

Butterfly Cookies

2¼ cups all-purpose flour
¼ teaspoon salt
1 cup sugar
¾ cup (1½ sticks) butter, softened
1 egg
1 teaspoon vanilla
1 teaspoon almond extract
White frosting, assorted food colorings, colored sugars, assorted small decors, gummy fruit and hard candies for decoration

1. Combine flour and salt in medium bowl; set aside.

2. Beat sugar and butter in large bowl at medium speed of electric mixer until fluffy. Beat in egg, vanilla and almond extract. Gradually add flour mixture. Beat at low speed until well blended. Divide dough in half. Cover; refrigerate 30 minutes or until firm.

3. Preheat oven to 350°F. Grease cookie sheets. Roll half of dough on lightly floured surface to ¼-inch thickness. Cut out cookies using butterfly cookie cutters. Repeat with remaining dough.

4. Bake 12 to 15 minutes or until edges are lightly browned. Remove to wire racks; cool completely.

5. Tint portions of white frosting with assorted food colorings. Spread desired colors of frosting over cookies. Decorate as desired.   ***Makes 20 to 22 cookies***

Cream Cheese Cutout Cookies

1 cup butter, softened
1 (8-ounce) package cream cheese, softened
1½ cups sugar
1 egg
1 teaspoon vanilla
½ teaspoon almond extract
3½ cups all-purpose flour
1 teaspoon baking powder
Almond Frosting (recipe follows)

In large bowl beat butter and cream cheese until well combined. Add sugar; beat until fluffy. Add egg, vanilla and almond extract; beat well. In medium bowl mix flour and baking powder. Add flour mixture to cream cheese mixture; beat until well combined. Divide dough in half. Cover and chill 1½ hours or until dough is easy to handle. On floured surface roll dough to ⅛-inch thickness. Cut with cookie cutters. Place on ungreased cookie sheets. Bake in 375°F oven 8 to 10 minutes or until done. Remove to wire racks; cool. Decorate with Almond Frosting.   ***Makes about 90 cookies***

Almond Frosting: In bowl beat 2 cups sifted powdered sugar, 2 tablespoons softened butter and ¼ teaspoon almond extract until smooth. Beat in enough milk (4 to 5 teaspoons) until frosting is of piping consistency. For spreadable frosting, add a little more milk. Stir in a few drops of food coloring, if desired.

Favorite recipe from **Wisconsin Milk Marketing Board**

Butterfly Cookies

Festive Rugelach

1½ cups (3 sticks) butter or margarine, softened
12 ounces cream cheese, softened
3½ cups all-purpose flour, divided
½ cup powdered sugar
¾ cup granulated sugar
1½ teaspoons ground cinnamon
1¾ cups "M&M's"® Chocolate Mini Baking Bits, divided
Powdered sugar

Preheat oven to 350°F. Lightly grease cookie sheets; set aside. In large bowl cream butter and cream cheese. Slowly work in 3 cups flour. Divide dough into 6 equal pieces and shape into squares. Lightly flour dough, wrap in waxed paper and refrigerate at least 1 hour. Combine remaining ½ cup flour and ½ cup powdered sugar. Remove one piece of dough at a time from refrigerator; roll out on surface dusted with flour-sugar mixture to 18×5×⅛-inch-thick strip. Combine granulated sugar and cinnamon. Sprinkle dough strip with 2 tablespoons cinnamon-sugar mixture. Sprinkle about ¼ cup "M&M's"® Chocolate Mini Baking Bits on wide end of each strip. Roll dough starting at wide end to completely enclose baking bits. Cut strip into 1½-inch lengths; place seam-side down about 2 inches apart on prepared cookie sheets. Repeat with remaining ingredients. Bake 16 to 18 minutes or until golden. Cool completely on wire racks. Sprinkle with powdered sugar. Store in tightly covered container.

Makes about 6 dozen cookies

Variation: For crescent shapes, roll each piece of dough into 12-inch circle. Sprinkle with cinnamon-sugar mixture. Cut into 12 wedges. Place about ½ teaspoon "M&M's"® Chocolate Mini Baking Bits at wide end of each wedge and roll up to enclose baking bits. Place seam-side down on prepared cookie sheets and proceed as directed.

FUN FOOD FACT

Rugelach refers to small, crescent-shaped eastern European pastries or cookies. They are usually made with a cream cheese dough that is cut into triangles and shaped around a filling of raisins (or other dried fruit) and nuts, jam, chocolate, or sweetened ground poppy seed paste. Rugelach are often part of the Jewish celebration of Hanukkah.

Festive Rugelach

Cut-Out Sugar Cookies

1¼ cups granulated sugar
  1 Butter Flavor* CRISCO® Stick or
    1 cup Butter Flavor CRISCO®
    all-vegetable shortening
  2 eggs
¼ cup light corn syrup or regular
    pancake syrup
  1 tablespoon vanilla extract
  3 cups all-purpose flour plus
    4 tablespoons, divided
¾ teaspoon baking powder
½ teaspoon baking soda
½ teaspoon salt
    Granulated sugar or colored sugar
    crystals

*Butter Flavor Crisco is artificially flavored.

1. Combine sugar and 1 cup shortening in large bowl. Beat at medium speed of electric mixer until well blended. Add eggs, syrup and vanilla. Beat until well blended and fluffy.

2. Combine 3 cups flour, baking powder, baking soda and salt. Add gradually to shortening mixture at low speed. Mix until well blended.

3. Divide dough into 4 quarters. Wrap each quarter of dough with plastic wrap. Chill at least 1 hour. Keep refrigerated until ready to use.

4. Heat oven to 375°F. Place sheets of foil on countertop for cooling cookies.

5. Spread 1 tablespoon flour on large sheet of waxed paper. Place one quarter of dough on floured paper. Flatten slightly with hands. Turn dough over and cover with another large sheet of waxed paper. Roll dough to ¼-inch thickness. Remove top sheet of waxed paper. Cut out with floured cutters. Place 2 inches apart on ungreased baking sheets. Repeat with remaining dough.

6. Sprinkle with granulated sugar or colored sugar crystals, or leave plain to frost or decorate when cooled.

7. Bake one baking sheet at a time at 375°F for 5 to 9 minutes, depending on size of cookies (bake smaller, thinner cookies closer to 5 minutes; larger cookies closer to 9 minutes). *Do not overbake.* Cool 2 minutes on baking sheets. Remove cookies to foil to cool completely, then frost and decorate, if desired.   ***Makes 3 to 4 dozen cookies***

FUN FOOD FACT

Granulated sugar, made from highly refined cane or beet sugar, is the most common form of sugar for table use and cooking purposes. Crystallized or pearl sugar is a coarse granulation that is usually used for decorating purposes.

Peanut Butter Cut-Out Cookies

½ cup butter or margarine
1 cup REESE'S® Peanut Butter Chips
⅔ cup packed light brown sugar
1 egg
¾ teaspoon vanilla extract
1⅓ cups all-purpose flour
¾ teaspoon baking soda
½ cup finely chopped pecans
    Chocolate Chip Glaze (recipe follows)

1. Place butter and peanut butter chips in medium saucepan; cook over low heat, stirring constantly, until melted. Pour into large bowl; add brown sugar, egg and vanilla, beating until well blended. Stir in flour, baking soda and pecans, blending well. Refrigerate 15 to 20 minutes or until firm enough to roll.

2. Heat oven to 350°F.

3. Roll a small portion of dough at a time on lightly floured board, or between 2 pieces of wax paper to ¼-inch thickness. (Keep remaining dough in refrigerator.) With cookie cutters, cut dough into desired shapes; place on ungreased cookie sheets.

4. Bake 7 to 8 minutes or until almost set (do not overbake). Cool 1 minute; remove from cookie sheets to wire racks. Cool completely. Drizzle Chocolate Chip Glaze onto each cookie; allow to set.

Makes about 3 dozen cookies

Chocolate Chip Glaze: Place 1 cup HERSHEY₂S Semi-Sweet Chocolate Chips and 1 tablespoon shortening (do not use butter, margarine spread or oil) in small microwave-safe bowl. Microwave at HIGH (100%) 1 minute; stir. If necessary, microwave at HIGH an additional 15 seconds at a time, stirring after each heating, just until chips are melted and mixture is smooth.

HELPFUL HINT

To roll out cookie dough, place the dough (which should be in the shape of a disc) on a floured surface, such as a counter, pastry cloth or a large cutting board. Lightly flour your hands and the rolling pin. Place the rolling pin across the center of the dough. With several light strokes, roll the rolling pin away from you toward the edge of the dough. Turn the dough a quarter turn and roll again from the center to the edge. Repeat this process until the dough is the desired thickness. If the dough becomes sticky, dust it and the rolling pin with flour. If the dough sticks to the floured surface, gently fold back the edge of the dough and dust the surface underneath the dough with more flour.

Peanut Butter and Jelly Sandwich Surprises

COOKIES
1½ cups all-purpose flour
  ½ cup plus 1 tablespoon sugar
  ½ teaspoon baking soda
  ¼ teaspoon salt
  ½ cup creamy peanut butter
  ⅓ Butter Flavor* CRISCO® Stick or
    ⅓ cup Butter Flavor CRISCO®
    all-vegetable shortening
  3 tablespoons milk
  1 egg yolk
  1 teaspoon pure vanilla extract
  Grape jelly

TOPPING
  Sugar

*Butter Flavor Crisco is artificially flavored.

1. For cookies, combine flour, ½ cup plus 1 tablespoon sugar, baking soda and salt in large bowl. Cut in peanut butter and ⅓ cup shortening using pastry blender (or 2 knives) until mixture resembles coarse meal.

2. Combine milk, egg yolk and vanilla in small bowl. Beat with fork until blended. Add to flour mixture. Beat at low speed of electric mixer until well blended. Divide dough in half. Wrap with plastic wrap. Refrigerate at least 1 hour.

3. Heat oven to 350°F. Place sheets of foil on countertop for cooling cookies.

4. Roll each half of dough between sheets of plastic wrap to ⅛-inch thickness. Cut with 2½-inch heart-shaped cookie cutter. Place half the cut-outs 1 inch apart on ungreased baking sheets. Place about ½ measuring teaspoon jelly in center of each. Top with remaining cut-outs. Press edges with fork. Prick top several times with toothpick.

5. For topping, sprinkle lightly with sugar.

6. Bake at 350°F for 10 to 11 minutes or until golden brown. *Do not overbake.* Sprinkle again with sugar. Cool on baking sheet 5 minutes. Remove cookies to foil to cool completely.

Makes about 2 dozen cookies

Peanut Butter and Jelly Sandwich Surprises

Gingerbread Cookies

¾ cup light or dark molasses
¾ cup margarine or butter
¾ cup packed light brown sugar
4½ cups all-purpose flour
1 tablespoon ground ginger
2 teaspoons ground cinnamon
1 teaspoon DAVIS® Baking Powder
½ teaspoon baking soda
½ teaspoon ground nutmeg
¼ cup egg substitute
   Decorator icing, raisins and assorted candies, optional

1. Heat molasses, margarine or butter, and brown sugar in saucepan over medium heat to a boil, stirring occasionally. Remove from heat; cool.

2. Mix flour, ginger, cinnamon, baking powder, baking soda and nutmeg in large bowl. Blend egg substitute into molasses mixture. Stir molasses mixture into flour mixture until smooth. Wrap dough; refrigerate 1 hour.

3. Divide dough in half. Roll each half of dough to ¼-inch thickness on floured surface. Cut with floured 5×3-inch gingerbread people cutters. Place on lightly greased baking sheets.

4. Bake in preheated 350°F oven for 10 to 12 minutes or until lightly browned. Remove from sheets; cool on wire racks. Decorate as desired with icing, raisins and candies.

Makes 2 dozen cookies

Prep Time: 30 minutes
Chill Time: 1 hour
Bake Time: 10 minutes

Nutty Spice Cookies

½ cup light molasses
⅓ cup sugar
¼ cup egg substitute
¼ cup water
2 tablespoons canola or vegetable oil
2¼ cups all-purpose flour
1 teaspoon baking soda
1 teaspoon ground ginger
½ teaspoon ground nutmeg
½ teaspoon ground cinnamon
¼ teaspoon ground cloves
⅓ cup chopped walnuts

Spray cookie sheets lightly with nonstick cooking spray; set aside. Stir molasses, sugar, egg substitute, water and oil in medium bowl until sugar is dissolved. Sift flour, baking soda, ginger, nutmeg, cinnamon and cloves into large bowl; stir to combine. Add molasses mixture; stir with wooden spoon until smooth. (Dough will be stiff.) Refrigerate, covered, at least 2 hours or up to 2 days.

Preheat oven to 375°F. Roll out dough into 12-inch square on floured surface. If dough cracks, press together. Sprinkle walnuts evenly over dough, pressing nuts into dough with fingers. Cut square into 8 lengthwise strips, and then 8 crosswise strips to form 64 squares.

Place cookies 1 inch apart on prepared cookie sheets. Bake, 1 sheet at a time, 8 minutes or until edges begin to brown. Remove cookies to wire racks; cool completely. Store in airtight container.

Makes about 5½ dozen cookies

Gingerbread Cookies

Spicy Rum Corn Crisps

1 cup (2 sticks) butter or margarine, softened
¾ cup firmly packed light brown sugar
1 teaspoon vanilla extract
½ teaspoon rum extract
1½ cups all-purpose flour
¾ cup yellow cornmeal
1 teaspoon ground ginger
1 teaspoon ground nutmeg
¼ teaspoon ground allspice
¼ teaspoon ground black pepper
1¾ cups "M&M's"® Chocolate Mini Baking Bits, divided

Preheat oven to 350°F. In large bowl cream butter and sugar until light and fluffy. Blend in vanilla and rum extracts. In medium bowl combine flour, cornmeal, ginger, nutmeg, allspice and pepper; stir into creamed mixture just until blended. Stir in 1 cup "M&M's"® Chocolate Mini Baking Bits. On lightly floured surface, carefully roll dough into 12×8-inch rectangle. Press remaining ¾ cup "M&M's"® Chocolate Mini Baking Bits into top before cutting into 48 pieces. Transfer to ungreased cookie sheets. Bake 12 to 14 minutes or until lightly browned. Cool completely on wire racks. Store in tightly covered container.

Makes about 4 dozen cookies

Gingerbread Cookies

½ cup shortening
⅓ cup packed light brown sugar
¼ cup dark molasses
1 egg white
½ teaspoon vanilla
1½ cups all-purpose flour
½ teaspoon baking soda
¼ teaspoon baking powder
½ teaspoon salt
1 teaspoon ground cinnamon
½ teaspoon ground ginger

1. Beat shortening, brown sugar, molasses, egg white and vanilla in large bowl at high speed of electric mixer until smooth. Combine flour, baking soda, baking powder, salt and spices in small bowl. Add to shortening mixture; mix well. Cover; refrigerate until firm, about 8 hours or overnight.

2. Preheat oven to 350°F. Grease cookie sheets.

3. Roll dough on lightly floured surface to ⅛-inch thickness. Cut into desired shapes with cookie cutters. Place on prepared cookie sheets.

4. Bake 6 to 8 minutes or until edges begin to brown. Remove to wire racks; cool completely.

Makes about 2½ dozen cookies

Spicy Rum Corn Crisps

Chocolate Gingerbread Boys and Girls

2 cups (12-ounce package) NESTLÉ® TOLL HOUSE® Semi-Sweet Chocolate Morsels, divided
2¾ cups GOLD MEDAL® All-Purpose Flour
1 teaspoon baking soda
½ teaspoon salt
½ teaspoon ground ginger
½ teaspoon ground cinnamon
3 tablespoons butter or margarine, softened
3 tablespoons granulated sugar
½ cup molasses
¼ cup water
1 container (16 ounces) prepared vanilla frosting, colored as desired or colored icing in tubes

MICROWAVE 1½ cups morsels in medium microwave-safe bowl on HIGH (100% power) 1 minute; stir. Microwave for 10- to 20-second intervals, stirring until smooth; cool to room temperature. Combine flour, baking soda, salt, ginger and cinnamon in medium bowl.

BEAT butter and sugar in small mixer bowl until creamy; beat in molasses and melted chocolate. Gradually add flour mixture alternately with water, beating until smooth. Cover and chill 1 hour or until firm.

ROLL ½ of dough to ¼-inch thickness on floured surface with floured rolling pin. Cut into gingerbread boy and girl shapes; place on ungreased baking sheets. Repeat with remaining dough.

BAKE in preheated 350°F. oven 5 to 6 minutes or until edges are set but centers are slightly soft. Let stand 2 minutes. Remove to wire racks to cool completely.

DECORATE with colored frosting and melted chocolate.

Makes about 2½ dozen cookies

To Pipe Chocolate: PLACE remaining ½ cup morsels in heavy-duty plastic bag. Microwave on HIGH 45 seconds; knead. Microwave 10 seconds; knead until smooth. Cut tiny corner from bag; squeeze to pipe.

DECORATE IT!

To make cutout cookies into holiday ornaments, gently press a plastic drinking straw into the top of each cookie immediately after removing the baked cookies from the oven. Once all the cookies have a hole pressed into them, remove the cookies from the cookie sheets to cool completely on wire racks. Frost and decorate the cookies as desired, and let the frosting set. Then, tie pretty ribbons through the holes, and hang the ornaments.

Festive Lebkuchen

3 tablespoons butter
1 cup packed brown sugar
¼ cup honey
1 egg
 Grated peel and juice of 1 lemon
3 cups all-purpose flour
2 teaspoons ground allspice
½ teaspoon baking soda
½ teaspoon salt
 Powdered Sugar Icing (page 556)

Melt butter with brown sugar and honey in medium saucepan over low heat, stirring constantly. Pour into large bowl. Cool 30 minutes. Add egg, lemon peel and juice; beat 2 minutes with electric mixer at high speed. Stir in flour, allspice, baking soda and salt until well blended. Cover; refrigerate overnight or up to 3 days.

Preheat oven to 350°F. Grease cookie sheets. Roll out dough to ½-inch thickness on lightly floured surface with lightly floured rolling pin. Cut out with 3-inch cookie cutters. Transfer to prepared cookie sheets. Bake 15 to 18 minutes until edges are light brown. Cool 1 minute. Remove to wire racks; cool completely. Prepare Powdered Sugar Icing; decorate cookies as desired. Store in airtight container.

Makes 1 dozen cookies

Cocoa Gingerbread Cookies

¼ cup butter, softened
2 tablespoons shortening
⅓ cup packed brown sugar
¼ cup dark molasses
1 egg
1½ cups all-purpose flour
¼ cup unsweetened cocoa powder
½ teaspoon baking soda
½ teaspoon ground ginger
½ teaspoon ground cinnamon
¼ teaspoon salt
¼ teaspoon ground nutmeg
⅛ teaspoon ground cloves
 Royal Icing (page 556)

Preheat oven to 400°F. Lightly grease cookie sheets or line with parchment paper. Cream butter, shortening, brown sugar and molasses in large bowl. Add egg; beat until light. Combine flour, cocoa, baking soda, ginger, cinnamon, salt, nutmeg and cloves in small bowl. Blend into creamed mixture until smooth. (If dough is too soft to handle, cover and refrigerate until firm.) Roll out dough ¼ inch thick on lightly floured surface. Cut out with cookie cutters. Place 2 inches apart on prepared cookie sheets. Bake 8 to 10 minutes or until firm. Remove to wire racks to cool. Prepare Royal Icing. Spoon into pastry bag fitted with small tip. Decorate cookies with icing.

Makes about 6 dozen cookies

Gingerbread Bears

3½ cups all-purpose flour
  2 teaspoons ground cinnamon
1½ teaspoons ground ginger
  1 teaspoon salt
  1 teaspoon baking soda
  1 teaspoon ground allspice
  1 cup butter, softened
  1 cup packed brown sugar
  1 teaspoon vanilla
  ⅓ cup molasses
  2 eggs
    Assorted cookie nonpareils
      (optional)
    Ornamental Frosting (page 554) or
      prepared creamy or gel-type
      frostings in tubes (optional)
    Colored sugar and assorted candies
      (optional)

Place flour, cinnamon, ginger, salt, baking soda and allspice in medium bowl; stir to combine. Set aside. Beat butter, brown sugar and vanilla in large bowl with electric mixer at medium speed about 5 minutes or until light and fluffy. Beat in molasses and eggs until well blended. Beat in flour mixture at low speed until well blended. Divide dough into 3 equal portions; cover and refrigerate at least 2 hours or up to 24 hours.

Preheat oven to 350°F. Grease large cookie sheets; set aside. Working with 1 portion at a time, roll out dough on lightly floured surface to ⅛-inch thickness. Cut out dough with 3-inch bear-shaped cookie cutter. Place cookies 1 inch apart on prepared cookie sheets. Roll dough scraps into small balls and ropes to make eyes and noses and to decorate bears. Decorate bears with nonpareils, if desired. Bake 10 minutes or until bottoms of cookies are golden brown. Let stand on cookie sheets 1 minute. Remove cookies to wire racks; cool completely.

Prepare Ornamental Frosting, if desired. Pipe or spread frosting on cooled cookies to decorate. Decorate with assorted nonpareils, colored sugar and assorted candies as desired. Store tightly covered at room temperature.

Makes about 3½ dozen cookies

FUN FOOD FACT

Nonpareils are the tiny, colored, sugar balls used for decorating baked goods and candies. "Nonpareil" can also refer to a candy made up of a flat chocolate circle which is covered with these tiny sugar balls.

Gingerbread Bears

No-Bake SENSATIONS

S'More Snack Treats

44 HONEY MAID® Honey Graham squares (2 sleeves)
3 tablespoons margarine or butter
1 (10-ounce) package marshmallows
¾ cup miniature semisweet chocolate chips

1. Break grahams into bite-size pieces; set aside.

2. Heat margarine or butter in large saucepan over medium heat until melted. Add marshmallows, stirring constantly until melted.

3. Stir broken crackers into marshmallow mixture to coat evenly. Spread mixture into lightly greased 13×9×2-inch pan; sprinkle with chocolate chips, pressing lightly with greased hands.

4. Refrigerate at least 20 minutes before cutting into squares.

Makes 12 treats

Preparation Time: 15 minutes
Cook Time: 20 minutes
Chill Time: 20 minutes
Total Time: 55 minutes

S'more Snack Treats

No-Bake Gingersnap Balls

20 gingersnap cookies (about 5 ounces)
3 tablespoons dark corn syrup
2 tablespoons creamy peanut butter
⅓ cup powdered sugar

1. Place cookies in large resealable plastic food storage bag; crush finely with rolling pin or meat mallet.

2. Combine corn syrup and peanut butter in medium bowl. Add crushed gingersnaps; mix well. (Mixture should hold together without being sticky. If mixture is too dry, stir in additional 1 tablespoon corn syrup.)

3. Shape mixture into 24 (1-inch) balls; roll in powdered sugar.   *Makes 8 servings*

Cool Cookie-wiches

1 tub (8 ounces) COOL WHIP®
     Whipped Topping, thawed
24 cookies
     Multi-colored sprinkles
     Finely crushed chocolate cookies

SPREAD whipped topping about ¾ inch thick on 1 cookie. Place another cookie lightly on top. Roll or lightly press edges in sprinkles or crushed cookies. Repeat with remaining ingredients.

FREEZE 4 hours or until firm. Wrap individually and store in freezer for up to 2 weeks.   *Makes 12 servings*

Cocoa Fruit Balls

2½ cups (about 12 ounces) mixed dried fruits, such as apples, apricots, pears and prunes
1¼ cups (8 ounces) dried Mission figs
1 cup MOUNDS® Sweetened Coconut Flakes
½ cup HERSHEY®S Cocoa
2 tablespoons orange juice
2 tablespoons honey
¼ cup powdered sugar

1. Remove pits from prunes and stems from figs, if necessary. Process dried fruits, figs and coconut using metal blade of food processor until ground and almost paste-like (or put through fine blade of food grinder).

2. Combine cocoa, orange juice and honey with fruit mixture in large bowl; mix well. Cover; refrigerate until chilled.

3. Shape mixture into 1¼-inch balls. Store in airtight container at room temperature for 3 to 4 days. Store in airtight container in refrigerator or freezer for longer storage.

4. Roll in powdered sugar just before serving.   *Makes 3 dozen balls*

No-Bake Gingersnap Balls

No-Bake Pineapple Marmalade Squares

1 cup graham cracker crumbs
½ cup plus 2 tablespoons sugar, divided
¼ cup light margarine, melted
1 cup fat free or light sour cream
4 ounces light cream cheese, softened
¼ cup orange marmalade or apricot fruit spread, divided
1 can (20 ounces) DOLE® Crushed Pineapple
1 envelope unflavored gelatin

• Mix graham cracker crumbs, 2 tablespoons sugar and margarine in 8-inch square glass baking dish; pat mixture firmly and evenly onto bottom of dish. Freeze 10 minutes.

• Beat sour cream, cream cheese, remaining ½ cup sugar and 1 tablespoon marmalade in medium bowl until smooth and blended; set aside.

• Drain pineapple; reserve ¼ cup juice.

• Sprinkle gelatin over reserved juice in small saucepan; let stand 1 minute. Cook and stir over low heat until gelatin dissolves.

• Beat gelatin mixture into sour cream mixture until well blended. Spoon mixture evenly over crust.

• Stir together pineapple and remaining 3 tablespoons marmalade in small bowl until blended. Evenly spoon over sour cream filling. Cover and refrigerate 2 hours or until firm.

Makes 16 servings

S'Mores on a Stick

1 (14-ounce) can EAGLE® BRAND Sweetened Condensed Milk (NOT evaporated milk)
1½ cups milk chocolate mini chips, divided
1 cup miniature marshmallows
11 whole graham crackers, halved crosswise
Toppings: chopped peanuts, mini candy-coated chocolate pieces, sprinkles

1. Microwave half of Eagle Brand in microwave-safe bowl at HIGH 1½ minutes. Stir in 1 cup chocolate chips until smooth; stir in marshmallows.

2. Spread evenly by heaping tablespoonfuls onto 11 graham cracker halves. Top with remaining graham cracker halves; place on waxed paper.

3. Microwave remaining Eagle Brand at HIGH 1½ minutes; stir in remaining ½ cup chocolate chips, stirring until smooth. Drizzle mixture over cookies and sprinkle with desired toppings.

4. Let stand for 2 hours; insert a wooden craft stick into center of each cookie.

Makes 11 servings

Prep Time: 10 minutes
Cook Time: 3 minutes

No-Bake Pineapple Marmalade Squares

Peanut Butter Chocolate No-Bake Bars

BARS
- 1 cup peanut butter
- ½ cup light corn syrup
- ½ cup powdered sugar
- 2 tablespoons margarine or butter
- 2 cups QUAKER® Oats (quick or old fashioned, uncooked)

TOPPING
- 1 cup (6 ounces) semisweet chocolate pieces
- 2 tablespoons peanut butter
- ¼ cup chopped peanuts (optional)

1. For bars, in medium saucepan, heat 1 cup peanut butter, corn syrup, powdered sugar and margarine over medium-low heat until margarine is melted, stirring frequently. Remove from heat. Stir in oats; mix well.

2. Spread onto bottom of *ungreased* 8- or 9-inch square pan; set aside.

3. For topping, place chocolate pieces in medium-size microwavable bowl. Microwave on HIGH 1 to 2 minutes, stirring every 30 seconds until smooth.

4. Stir in 2 tablespoons peanut butter until well blended. Spread evenly over oats layer. Sprinkle with chopped nuts, if desired. Chill 30 minutes or until chocolate is set.

5. Cut into bars with sharp knife. If bars are difficult to cut, let stand about 10 minutes. Store tightly covered at room temperature.

Makes 24 bars

Oat & Dried Fruit Balls

- 3 cups uncooked old-fashioned oats
- 1 cup flaked coconut
- 1 cup chopped dried mixed fruit
- ¼ cup sunflower seeds or chopped walnuts
- 1 cup sugar
- ½ cup milk
- ½ cup butter or margarine
- 6 tablespoons unsweetened cocoa powder
- ¼ teaspoon salt
- 1 teaspoon vanilla

Combine oats, coconut, dried fruit and sunflower seeds in large bowl; set aside. Combine sugar, milk, butter, cocoa and salt in 2-quart saucepan until blended. Heat to boiling. Boil 3 minutes, stirring constantly; remove from heat. Stir in vanilla. Pour hot sugar syrup into oat mixture; stir until well blended. When cool enough to handle, shape rounded tablespoonfuls into balls; place on waxed paper until completely cooled and firm.

Makes about 5 dozen balls

Fudgey Cocoa No-Bake Treats

2 cups sugar
½ cup (1 stick) butter or margarine
½ cup milk
⅓ cup HERSHEY'S Cocoa
⅔ cup REESE'S® Crunchy Peanut Butter
3 cups quick-cooking rolled oats
½ cup chopped peanuts (optional)
2 teaspoons vanilla extract

1. Place piece of wax paper or foil on tray or cookie sheet. Combine sugar, butter, milk and cocoa in medium saucepan.

2. Cook over medium heat, stirring constantly, until mixture comes to a rolling boil.

3. Remove from heat; cool 1 minute.

4. Add peanut butter, oats, peanuts, if desired, and vanilla; stir to mix well. Quickly drop mixture by heaping teaspoons onto wax paper or foil. Cool completely. Store in cool, dry place.

Makes about 4 dozen cookies

Prep Time: 20 minutes
Cook Time: 5 minutes
Cool Time: 30 minutes

Chocolate Cereal Bars

6 cups crisp rice cereal
1 cup (6 ounces) semisweet chocolate chips
1 jar (7 ounces) marshmallow creme
2 tablespoons butter or margarine
1 teaspoon vanilla

1. Butter 13×9-inch baking pan; set aside. Place cereal in large heat-proof bowl; set aside.

2. Melt chocolate chips with marshmallow creme and butter in small heavy saucepan over medium heat, stirring occasionally. Remove from heat.

3. Stir in vanilla. Pour chocolate mixture over cereal. Stir until blended. Press into prepared pan; cool.

4. Cut into squares.   *Makes 24 squares*

DECORATE IT!

Sprinkles are a fun and easy way to dress up these crispy bars. Immediately after pressing the cereal mixture into the pan, top with assorted colored sprinkles.

No-Bake Chocolate & Peanut Butter Cookies

1½ cups semi-sweet chocolate chips, divided

2 tablespoons Butter Flavor* CRISCO® Stick or 2 tablespoons Butter Flavor CRISCO® all-vegetable shortening, divided

2½ cups (5-ounce can) chow mein noodles, coarsely broken and divided

½ cup quick oats, uncooked, divided

1⅔ cups (10-ounce package) peanut butter chips, divided

Dried apricots, cut into small pieces (optional)

Butter Flavor Crisco is artificially flavored.

1. Cover tray with waxed paper.

2. Melt 1 cup semi-sweet chocolate chips and 1 tablespoon shortening (see Melting/Drizzling Procedure). Stir in 1¼ cups chow mein noodles and ¼ cup oats. Drop by heaping teaspoonfuls 2 inches apart onto prepared tray. Flatten slightly. Press ⅔ cup peanut butter chips into cookies. Allow to stand until firm.

3. Melt remaining 1 cup peanut butter chips and remaining 1 tablespoon shortening (see Melting/Drizzling Procedure). Stir in remaining 1¼ cups chow mein noodles and remaining ¼ cup oats. Drop and flatten as directed. Press remaining ½ cup chocolate chips into cookies. Garnish with apricots (if used). Allow to stand until firm.

Makes 2 dozen cookies

Melting/Drizzling Procedure: For melting or drizzling, choose one of these easy methods. Start with chips and Butter Flavor* Crisco® all-vegetable shortening (if called for), then: place in small microwave-safe measuring cup or bowl. Microwave at 50% (MEDIUM). Stir after 1 minute. Repeat until smooth. Drizzle from tip of spoon. **OR**, place in heavy resealable plastic sandwich bag. Seal. Microwave at 50% (MEDIUM). Check every minute until melted. Knead bag until smooth. Cut tiny tip off corner of bag. Squeeze out to drizzle. **OR**, place in small saucepan. Melt on range top on very low heat. Stir until smooth. Drizzle from tip of spoon.

No-Bake Chocolate & Peanut Butter Cookies

Special Treat No-Bake Squares

½ cup plus 1 teaspoon butter, divided
¼ cup granulated sugar
¼ cup unsweetened cocoa powder
 1 egg
¼ teaspoon salt
1½ cups graham cracker crumbs
 ¾ cup flaked coconut
 ½ cup chopped pecans
 ⅓ cup butter, softened
 1 package (3 ounces) cream cheese, softened
 1 teaspoon vanilla
 1 cup powdered sugar
 1 (2-ounce) dark sweet or bittersweet candy bar, broken into ½-inch pieces

Line 9-inch square baking pan with foil, shiny side up, allowing 2-inch overhang on sides. Set aside.

For crust, combine ½ cup butter, granulated sugar, cocoa, egg and salt in medium saucepan. Cook over medium heat, stirring constantly, until mixture thickens, about 2 minutes. Remove from heat; stir in graham cracker crumbs, coconut and pecans. Press evenly into prepared pan.

For filling, beat ⅓ cup softened butter, cream cheese and vanilla in small bowl until smooth. Gradually beat in powdered sugar. Spread over crust; refrigerate 30 minutes.

For glaze, place candy bar pieces and remaining 1 teaspoon butter in small resealable plastic food storage bag; seal. Microwave at HIGH 50 seconds. Turn bag over; heat at HIGH 40 to 50 seconds or until melted. Knead bag until candy bar is smooth. Cut tiny corner off bag; drizzle chocolate over filling. Refrigerate until firm, about 20 minutes. Remove foil from pan. Cut into 1½-inch squares.

Makes about 3 dozen squares

Quick No-Bake Brownies

1 cup finely chopped nuts, divided
2 (1-ounce) squares unsweetened chocolate
1 (14-ounce) can EAGLE® BRAND Sweetened Condensed Milk (NOT evaporated milk)
2 to 2½ cups vanilla wafer crumbs (about 48 to 60 wafers)

1. Grease 9-inch square pan with butter. Sprinkle ¼ cup nuts evenly in bottom of pan. In heavy saucepan over low heat, melt chocolate with Eagle® Brand. Cook and stir until mixture thickens, about 10 minutes.

2. Remove from heat; stir in crumbs and ½ cup nuts. Spread evenly in prepared pan.

3. Top with remaining ¼ cup nuts. Chill 4 hours or until firm. Cut into squares. Store loosely covered at room temperature.

Makes 24 brownies

Prep Time: 15 minutes
Chill Time: 4 hours

Special Treat No-Bake Squares

No-Bake Fudgy Brownies

1 (14-ounce) can EAGLE® BRAND Sweetened Condensed Milk (NOT evaporated milk)
2 (1-ounce) squares unsweetened chocolate, cut up
1 teaspoon vanilla extract
2 cups plus 2 tablespoons packaged chocolate cookie crumbs
¼ cup miniature candy-coated milk chocolate candies or chopped nuts

1. Grease 8-inch square baking pan or line with foil; set aside.

2. In medium-sized heavy saucepan, combine Eagle Brand and chocolate; cook and stir over low heat just until boiling. Reduce heat; cook and stir for 2 to 3 minutes more or until mixture thickens. Remove from heat. Stir in vanilla.

3. Stir in 2 cups cookie crumbs. Spread evenly into prepared pan. Sprinkle with remaining cookie crumbs and candies or nuts; press down gently with back of spoon.

4. Cover and chill for 4 hours or until firm. Cut into squares. Store leftovers covered in refrigerator.   *Makes 24 to 36 bars*

Prep Time: 10 minutes
Chill Time: 4 hours

Chocolate Fruit Crispies

6 cups crisp rice cereal
½ cup raisins
½ cup finely chopped dried apricots
1 bag (10 ounces) large marshmallows (about 40)
½ cup (3 ounces) semisweet chocolate morsels
2 tablespoons milk
Vegetable cooking spray

Combine cereal, raisins, and apricots in large bowl; set aside. Combine marshmallows, chocolate, and milk in 2-quart saucepan. Place over low heat and cook, stirring, about 10 minutes or until melted and smooth. Pour over cereal mixture; mix well. Coat 12×8×2-inch baking pan with cooking spray; spread mixture evenly into pan. Press down firmly using fingers coated with cooking spray. Cover and chill until firm. Cut into 1-inch squares.

Makes 8 dozen crispies

Microwave Directions: Combine cereal, raisins, and apricots in large bowl; set aside. Combine marshmallows, chocolate, and milk in 1½-quart microproof dish. Cook, uncovered, on HIGH 1 minute; stir until smooth. Continue as directed above.

Favorite recipe from **USA Rice Federation**

Peanut Butter Crispy Treats

4 cups toasted rice cereal
1¾ cups "M&M's"® Milk Chocolate Mini Baking Bits
4 cups mini marshmallows
½ cup creamy peanut butter
¼ cup butter or margarine
⅛ teaspoon salt

Combine cereal and "M&M's"® Milk Chocolate Mini Baking Bits in lightly greased baking pan; set aside. Melt marshmallows, peanut butter, butter and salt in heavy saucepan over low heat, stirring occasionally until mixture is smooth. Pour melted mixture over cereal mixture, tossing lightly until thoroughly coated. Gently shape into 1½-inch balls with buttered fingers. Place on waxed paper; cool at room temperature until set. Store in tightly covered container.

Makes about 3 dozen treats

Variation: After cereal mixture is thoroughly coated, press into greased 13×9×2-inch pan. Cool completely; cut into bars. Makes 24 bars.

Peanut Butter Crispy Treats

Toffee Creme Sandwich Cookies

1 jar (7 ounces) marshmallow creme
¼ cup toffee baking chips
48 (2-inch) sugar or fudge-striped shortbread cookies
Red and green sprinkles

1. Combine marshmallow creme and toffee chips in medium bowl until well blended. (Mixture will be stiff.)

2. Spread 1 teaspoon marshmallow mixture on bottom of 1 cookie; top with another cookie. Roll side of sandwich cookie in sprinkles. Repeat with remaining marshmallow creme mixture, cookies and sprinkles. *Makes 2 dozen cookies*

Prep Time: 20 minutes

HELPFUL HINT

A metal spatula is a tool with a narrow, thin metal blade attached to a plastic or wooden handle. It is ideal for spreading. Some metal spatulas are rigid, whereas others are more flexible. A flat spatula forms a straight line from handle to blade. An offset spatula is angled near the handle, causing the handle to be raised slightly.

No-Bake Butterscotch Haystacks

1 cup HERSHEY®S Butterscotch Chips
½ cup REESE'S® Peanut Butter Chips
1 tablespoon shortening (do not use butter, margarine, spread or oil)
1½ cups (3-ounce can) chow mein noodles, coarsely broken

1. Line cookie sheet with wax paper. Place butterscotch chips, peanut butter chips and shortening in medium microwave-safe bowl.

2. Microwave at HIGH (100%) 1 minute; stir. If necessary, microwave at HIGH an additional 15 seconds at a time, stirring after each heating, just until chips are melted and mixture is smooth when stirred.

3. Immediately add chow mein noodles; stir to coat. Drop mixture by heaping teaspoons onto prepared cookie sheet or into paper candy cups; let stand until firm. If necessary, cover and refrigerate until firm. Store in refrigerator in tightly covered container. *Makes about 2 dozen cookies*

Chocolate Haystacks: Substitute 1 cup HERSHEY®S Semi-Sweet Chocolate Chips or HERSHEY®S Milk Chocolate Chips for butterscotch chips. Proceed as directed above with peanut butter chips, shortening and chow mein noodles.

Prep Time: 15 minutes
Cook Time: 1 minute
Cool Time: 30 minutes

Toffee Creme Sandwich Cookies

Double Peanut Squares

25 NILLA® Wafers, finely crushed
  (about 1 cup)
½ cup PLANTERS® Dry Roasted
  Peanuts, finely chopped
⅓ cup margarine or butter, melted
2 tablespoons sugar
1 (8-ounce) package regular or light
  cream cheese, softened
¾ cup powdered sugar
½ cup creamy or chunky peanut butter
2 cups prepared whipped topping
  Additional prepared whipped
  topping, for garnish

1. Combine crumbs, peanuts, margarine or butter, and sugar. Reserve 2 tablespoons crumb mixture. Press remaining crumb mixture onto bottom of 8- or 9-inch square baking pan; set aside.

2. Beat cream cheese and powdered sugar in large bowl with electric mixer at medium speed until light and fluffy. Beat in peanut butter until smooth. Fold in whipped topping.

3. Spread evenly over prepared crust. Refrigerate 4 hours or until firm. Garnish with additional whipped topping and reserved crumb mixture.

Makes 9 servings

Monkey Bars

3 cups miniature marshmallows
½ cup honey
⅓ cup butter
¼ cup peanut butter
2 teaspoons vanilla
¼ teaspoon salt
4 cups crispy rice cereal
2 cups rolled oats, uncooked
½ cup flaked coconut
¼ cup peanuts

Combine marshmallows, honey, butter, peanut butter, vanilla and salt in medium saucepan. Melt mixture over low heat, stirring constantly. Combine rice cereal, oats, coconut and peanuts in 13×9×2-inch baking pan. Pour marshmallow mixture over dry ingredients. Mix until thoroughly coated. Press mixture firmly into pan. Cool completely before cutting.

Makes 2 dozen bars

Microwave Directions: Microwave marshmallows, honey, butter, peanut butter, vanilla and salt in 2-quart microwave-safe bowl on HIGH 2½ to 3 minutes. Continue as above.

Favorite recipe from **National Honey Board**

P. B. Graham Snackers

½ Butter Flavor* CRISCO® Stick or
    ½ cup Butter Flavor CRISCO®
    all-vegetable shortening
2 cups powdered sugar
¾ cup creamy peanut butter
1 cup graham cracker crumbs
½ cup semi-sweet chocolate chips
½ cup graham cracker crumbs or
    crushed peanuts or chocolate
    sprinkles (optional)

Butter Flavor Crisco is artificially flavored.

1. Combine ½ cup shortening, powdered sugar and peanut butter in large bowl. Beat at low speed of electric mixer until well blended. Stir in 1 cup crumbs and chocolate chips. Cover and refrigerate 1 hour.

2. Form dough into 1-inch balls. Roll in ½ cup crumbs. Cover and refrigerate until ready to serve.

Makes about 3 dozen cookies

FUN FOOD FACT

Peanuts are grown throughout the southern part of the United States, and have a soft, thin, netted, tan-colored shell. The nuts have a reddish-brown papery skin, an ivory-colored flesh and a buttery flavor that is intensified by roasting. They are used for snacking, baking and for making peanut butter.

Chewy Chocolate No-Bakes

1 cup (6 ounces) semisweet chocolate
    pieces
16 large marshmallows
⅓ cup (5 tablespoons plus 1 teaspoon)
    margarine or butter
2 cups QUAKER® Oats (quick or old
    fashioned, uncooked)
1 cup (any combination of) raisins,
    diced dried mixed fruit, flaked
    coconut, miniature marshmallows
    or chopped nuts
1 teaspoon vanilla

In large saucepan over low heat, melt chocolate pieces, marshmallows and margarine, stirring until smooth. Remove from heat; cool slightly. Stir in remaining ingredients. Drop by rounded teaspoonfuls onto waxed paper. Chill 2 to 3 hours. Let stand at room temperature about 15 minutes before serving. Store in tightly covered container in refrigerator.

Makes 3 dozen cookies

Microwave Directions: Place chocolate pieces, margarine and marshmallows in large microwavable bowl. Microwave on HIGH 1 to 2 minutes or until mixture is melted and smooth, stirring every 30 seconds. Proceed as recipe directs.

Peanut Butter Bars

COOKIES

1⅔ cups peanut butter chips or
    butterscotch chips
1 cup creamy peanut butter
⅓ cup milk
¼ Butter Flavor* CRISCO® Stick or
    ½ cup Butter Flavor CRISCO®
    all-vegetable shortening
2 cups graham cracker crumbs
1 cup chopped salted peanuts

COATING

1 cup semi-sweet chocolate chips
3 tablespoons Butter Flavor CRISCO®
    Stick or 3 tablespoons Butter
    Flavor CRISCO® all-vegetable
    shortening
Finely chopped salted peanuts

Butter Flavor Crisco is artificially flavored.

1. For cookies, combine peanut butter chips, peanut butter, milk and ¼ cup shortening in medium saucepan. Stir on low heat until mixture is melted and smooth.

2. Combine graham cracker crumbs and 1 cup chopped nuts in large bowl. Pour peanut butter mixture over crumbs. Stir until combined.

3. Spread mixture in ungreased 9×9×2-inch pan. Refrigerate until firm. Cut into bars about 1¾×¾ inches.

4. For coating, melt chocolate chips and 3 tablespoons shortening (see Melting/Drizzling Procedure).

5. Place 1 bar at a time in chocolate. Turn with fork. Lift from chocolate with fork.

Allow excess to drip off. Place on waxed paper-lined baking sheet. Sprinkle top with finely chopped nuts. Return to refrigerator to set chocolate.

Makes about 5 dozen bars

Melting/Drizzling Procedure: For melting or drizzling, choose one of these easy methods. Start with chips and Butter Flavor* Crisco® all-vegetable shortening (if called for), then: place in small microwave-safe measuring cup or bowl. Microwave at 50% (MEDIUM). Stir after 1 minute. Repeat until smooth. Drizzle from tip of spoon. **OR,** place in heavy resealable plastic sandwich bag. Seal. Microwave at 50% (MEDIUM). Check every minute until melted. Knead bag until smooth. Cut tiny tip off corner of bag. Squeeze out to drizzle. **OR,** place in small saucepan. Melt on range top on very low heat. Stir until smooth. Drizzle from tip of spoon.

Peanut Butter Bars

Citrus Cream Bars

1¼ cups finely crushed chocolate
    sandwich cookies
⅔ cup butter, softened, divided
1½ cups powdered sugar
  1 tablespoon milk
1½ teaspoons grated orange peel
  ½ teaspoon lemon peel
  ½ teaspoon vanilla
  ¼ cup semisweet chocolate chips,
    melted

1. Combine cookie crumbs and ⅓ cup butter in medium bowl. Press onto bottom of ungreased 9-inch square baking pan. Refrigerate until firm.

2. Combine powdered sugar, remaining ⅓ cup butter, milk, orange peel, lemon peel and vanilla in small bowl. Beat at medium speed, scraping bowl often, until light and fluffy. Spread over crust.

3. Drizzle melted chocolate over filling. Refrigerate until firm, about 2 hours. Cut into bars. Store leftovers in refrigerator.

Makes about 2 dozen bars

No-Bake Peanutty Chocolate Drops

½ cup (1 stick) butter or margarine
⅓ cup unsweetened cocoa
  1 (14-ounce) can EAGLE® BRAND
    Sweetened Condensed Milk (NOT
    evaporated milk)
2½ cups quick-cooking oats
  1 cup chopped peanuts
  ½ cup peanut butter

1. Line baking sheets with waxed paper. In medium saucepan over medium heat, melt butter; stir in cocoa. Bring mixture to a boil.

2. Remove from heat; stir in remaining ingredients.

3. Drop by teaspoonfuls onto prepared baking sheets; chill 2 hours or until set. Store loosely covered in refrigerator.

Makes about 5 dozen drops

Prep Time: 10 minutes
Chill Time: 2 hours

HELPFUL HINT

If you don't have a food processor, crush cookies quickly and easily in a resealable plastic food storage bag. Place the cookies in the bag and seal. Then press a rolling pin over the bag several times to grind them.

Citrus Cream Bars

No-Bake Cherry Crisps

¼ cup butter, softened
1 cup powdered sugar
1 cup peanut butter
1⅓ cups crisp rice cereal
½ cup maraschino cherries, drained, dried and chopped
¼ cup plus 2 tablespoons mini semisweet chocolate chips
¼ cup chopped pecans
1 to 2 cups flaked coconut (for rolling)

Beat butter, powdered sugar and peanut butter in large bowl. Stir in cereal, cherries, chocolate chips and pecans. Mix well. Shape teaspoonfuls of dough into 1-inch balls. Roll in coconut. Place on cookie sheets and chill in refrigerator 1 hour. Store in refrigerator.

Makes about 3 dozen cookies

Crispy Chocolate Logs

1 cup (6 ounces) semisweet chocolate chips
½ cup butter or margarine
1 package (10 ounces) marshmallows
6 cups crisp rice cereal

Lightly grease 13×9-inch baking pan. Melt chocolate chips and butter in large bowl over hot water, stirring constantly. Add marshmallows; stir until melted. Add cereal; stir until evenly coated with chocolate mixture. Press into prepared pan; cool until mixture is firm. Cut into 2×1½-inch logs.

Makes 36 logs

Chocolate Scotcheroos

1 cup light corn syrup
1 cup sugar
1 cup peanut butter
6 cups KELLOGG'S® RICE KRISPIES® cereal
1 package (6 ounces, 1 cup) semi-sweet chocolate morsels
1 package (6 ounces, 1 cup) butterscotch morsels

1. Place corn syrup and sugar in large saucepan. Cook over medium heat, stirring frequently, until sugar dissolves and mixture begins to boil. Remove from heat. Stir in peanut butter; mix well. Add Kellogg's Rice Krispies® cereal. Stir until well coated. Press mixture into 13×9×2-inch pan coated with cooking spray. Set aside.

2. Melt chocolate and butterscotch morsels together in small saucepan over low heat, stirring constantly. Spread evenly over cereal mixture. Let stand until firm. Cut into bars when cool. *Makes about 48 bars*

No-Bake Cherry Crisps

Nathaniel's Jumble

1 cup creamy peanut butter
6 tablespoons margarine or butter, melted
2¼ cups sifted confectioners' sugar
4 cups popped NEWMAN'S OWN® Natural Flavor Microwave Popcorn
½ cup regular candy-coated chocolate pieces
4 ounce semisweet chocolate, melted
⅓ cup caramel ice cream syrup

LAYER 1

Combine peanut butter and margarine in large mixing bowl. With mixer at low speed, beat in confectioners' sugar, about ½ cup at a time, mixing well. After mixing, knead by hand. Spread into foil-lined 8-inch square pan.

LAYER 2

Place popcorn and candy-coated chocolate pieces in medium bowl. Pour melted chocolate over popcorn mixture; gently mix with spoon until all popcorn is covered with chocolate. Spread popcorn mixture evenly over Layer 1; press slightly to adhere to bottom layer. Drizzle caramel over popcorn mixture.

Refrigerate or freeze until set.

Makes 24 bars

The Original Rice Krispies Treats® Recipe

3 tablespoons margarine
1 package (10 ounces, about 40) regular marshmallows *or* 4 cups miniature marshmallows
6 cups KELLOGG'S® RICE KRISPIES® cereal
Vegetable cooking spray

1. Melt margarine in large saucepan over low heat. Add marshmallows and stir until completely melted. Remove from heat.

2. Add Kellogg's Rice Krispies® cereal. Stir until well coated.

3. Using buttered spatula or waxed paper, press mixture evenly into 13×9×2-inch pan coated with cooking spray. Cut into 2×2-inch squares when cool.

Makes 24 (2-inch-square) treats

Note: Use fresh marshmallows for best results.

Microwave Directions: Microwave margarine and marshmallows at HIGH 2 minutes in microwave-safe mixing bowl. Stir to combine. Microwave at HIGH 1 minute longer. Stir until smooth. Add cereal. Stir until well coated. Press into pan as directed in Step 3.

Funny Face Cookies

4 large cookies (about 4 inches in diameter)
½ cup thawed COOL WHIP® Whipped Topping
Assorted candies and sprinkles
BAKER'S® Semi-Sweet Real Chocolate Chips
Toasted BAKER'S ANGEL FLAKE® Coconut

SPREAD each cookie with about 2 tablespoons of the whipped topping.

DECORATE with candies, sprinkles, chips and coconut to resemble faces. Serve immediately. *Makes 4 servings*

Chipwiches

24 CHIPS AHOY!® Chocolate Chip Cookies
3 cups any flavor ice cream, sherbet, frozen yogurt or whipped topping
Sprinkles, chocolate chips, chopped nuts, toasted or tinted coconut, or other assorted small candies

1. Spread ¼ cup ice cream on flat side of each of 12 cookies. Place remaining cookies on top. Roll or lightly press edges in sprinkles.

2. Freeze until firm, about 4 hours.
Makes 12 servings

Peanut Butter Chipwiches: Spread about 1 tablespoon peanut butter on flat side of each of 12 cookies; top with a banana slice. Place remaining cookies on top. Roll or lightly press edges in sprinkles.

Funny Face Cookies

No-Bake Chocolate Oat Bars

1 cup butter
½ cup packed brown sugar
1 teaspoon vanilla
3 cups uncooked quick oats
1 cup semisweet chocolate chips
½ cup crunchy or creamy peanut butter

Grease 9-inch square baking pan. Melt butter in large saucepan over medium heat. Add brown sugar and vanilla; mix well.

Stir in oats. Cook over low heat 2 to 3 minutes or until ingredients are well blended. Press half of mixture into prepared pan. Use back of large spoon to spread mixture evenly.

Meanwhile, melt chocolate chips in small heavy saucepan over low heat, stirring occasionally. Stir in peanut butter. Pour chocolate mixture over oat mixture in pan; spread evenly with knife or back of spoon. Crumble remaining oat mixture over chocolate layer, pressing down gently. Cover and refrigerate 2 to 3 hours or overnight.

Bring to room temperature before cutting into bars. (Bars can be frozen; let thaw about 10 minutes or more before serving.)

Makes 32 bars

Peanut Butter-Hop-Scotch Treats

4 cups corn flakes
1½ cups "M&M's"® Chocolate Mini Baking Bits, divided
¾ cup butterscotch chips
½ cup creamy peanut butter
¼ cup light corn syrup
4 tablespoons butter, divided
6 squares (1 ounce each) semi-sweet chocolate

Lightly grease 13×9-inch baking pan; set aside. In large bowl combine cereal and 1 cup "M&M's"® Chocolate Mini Baking Bits; set aside. In heavy saucepan melt butterscotch chips, peanut butter, corn syrup and 2 tablespoons butter over low heat, stirring often until mixture is smooth. Pour melted mixture over cereal mixture, tossing lightly until thoroughly coated. Gently press into prepared pan with buttered fingers. In small saucepan melt remaining 2 tablespoons butter and chocolate over low heat. Spread chocolate mixture over cereal mixture; decorate with remaining ½ cup "M&M's"® Chocolate Mini Baking Bits. Store in tightly covered container. *Makes 3 dozen bars*

No-Bake Chocolate Oat Bars

Cheery Chocolate Animal Cookies

1⅔ cups (10-ounce package) REESE'S®
   Peanut Butter Chips
1 cup HERSHEY®S Semi-Sweet
   Chocolate Chips
2 tablespoons shortening (do not use
   butter, margarine, spread or oil)
1 package (20 ounces) chocolate
   sandwich cookies
1 package (11 ounces) animal crackers

1. Line trays or cookie sheets with wax paper.

2. Combine peanut butter chips, chocolate chips and shortening in 2-quart glass measuring cup with handle. Microwave on HIGH (100% power) 1½ to 2 minutes or until chips are melted and mixture is smooth when stirred. Using fork, dip each cookie into melted chip mixture; gently tap fork on side of cup to remove excess chocolate.

3. Place coated cookies on prepared trays; top each cookie with an animal cracker. Chill until chocolate is set, about 30 minutes. Store in airtight container in a cool, dry place.   ***Makes about 4 dozen cookies***

No-Bake Banana Peanut Butter Fudge Bars

1 ripe, large DOLE® Banana
⅔ cup butter or margarine
2 teaspoons vanilla extract
2½ cups rolled oats
½ cup packed brown sugar
1 cup semisweet chocolate chips
½ cup peanut butter

• Finely chop banana (1¼ cups). Melt butter in large skillet over medium heat; stir in vanilla. Add oats and brown sugar. Heat and stir 5 minutes. Set aside ¾ cup oat mixture. Press remaining oat mixture into greased 9-inch square baking pan. Sprinkle banana over crust.

• Melt chocolate chips and peanut butter together over low heat. Pour and spread over banana. Sprinkle with reserved oat mixture; press down lightly. Chill 2 hours before cutting. Store in refrigerator.

Makes 24 bars

FUN FOOD FACT

Bananas are high in fiber and great flavor, but low in calories. Naturally sweet bananas are a good source of vitamin B6, and also contain a wide assortment of other nutrients, including vitamin C and potassium.

Cheery Chocolate Animal Cookies

Toffee Chunk Brownie Cookies

1 cup butter
4 ounces unsweetened chocolate, coarsely chopped
1½ cups sugar
2 eggs
1 tablespoon vanilla
3 cups all-purpose flour
⅛ teaspoon salt
1½ cups coarsely chopped chocolate-covered toffee bars

Preheat oven to 350°F. Melt butter and chocolate in large saucepan over low heat, stirring until smooth. Remove from heat; cool slightly.

Stir sugar into chocolate mixture until smooth. Stir in eggs until well blended. Stir in vanilla until smooth. Stir in flour and salt just until mixed. Fold in chopped toffee bars.

Drop heaping tablespoonfuls of dough 1½ inches apart onto ungreased cookie sheets.

Bake 12 minutes or until just set. Let cookies stand on cookie sheets 5 minutes; transfer to wire racks to cool completely. Store in airtight container.   *Makes 3 dozen cookies*

Toffee Chunk Brownie Cookies

Chocolate-Coconut-Toffee Delights

½ cup all-purpose flour
¼ teaspoon baking powder
¼ teaspoon salt
1 package (12 ounces) semisweet
     chocolate chips, divided
¼ cup butter, cut into small pieces
¾ cup packed light brown sugar
2 eggs, beaten
1 teaspoon vanilla
1½ cups flaked coconut
1 cup English toffee baking bits

1. Preheat oven to 350°F. Line cookie sheets with parchment paper.

2. Combine flour, baking powder and salt in small bowl; set aside. Place 1 cup chocolate chips in large microwavable bowl. Microwave at HIGH 1 minute; stir. Microwave 30 to 60 seconds more or until chips are melted. Stir well.

3. Add butter to bowl; stir until melted. Beat in brown sugar, eggs and vanilla until well blended. Beat in flour mixture until blended. Stir in coconut, toffee bits and remaining 1 cup chocolate chips.

4. Drop dough by heaping ⅓ cupfuls onto prepared cookie sheets, spacing 3 inches apart. Flatten into 3½-inch circles. Bake 15 to 17 minutes or until edges are just firm to the touch. Cool cookies on cookie sheets 2 minutes; slide parchment paper and cookies onto countertop. Cool completely.

Makes 1 dozen (5-inch) cookies

German Chocolate Oatmeal Cookies

¾ Butter Flavor* CRISCO® Stick or
     ¾ cup Butter Flavor CRISCO®
     all-vegetable shortening plus
     additional for greasing
1 cup firmly packed dark brown sugar
½ cup granulated sugar
2 eggs
2 packages (4 ounces each) German
     chocolate, melted and cooled
1 tablespoon water
1¼ cups all-purpose flour
½ teaspoon baking soda
½ teaspoon salt
3 cups quick oats (not instant or
     old-fashioned)
1 cup coarsely chopped pecans
1 cup flake coconut

*Butter Flavor Crisco is artificially flavored.

1. Heat oven to 375°F. Grease baking sheet with shortening. Place sheets of foil on countertop for cooling cookies.

2. Beat ¾ cup shortening, sugars, eggs, chocolate and water in large bowl until well blended. Mix flour, baking soda and salt. Beat into creamed mixture until blended. Stir in oats, nuts and coconut.

3. Drop rounded tablespoonfuls of dough 2 inches apart onto prepared baking sheet.

4. Bake at 375°F for 10 minutes, or until bottoms are browned, but tops are slightly soft. Cool 2 minutes on baking sheet. Remove cookies to foil to cool completely.

Makes about 4 dozen cookies

Chocolate-Coconut-Toffee Delights

Peanut Butter Cocoa Cookies

1 Butter Flavor* CRISCO® Stick or
   1 cup Butter Flavor CRISCO®
   all-vegetable shortening
1 cup extra crunchy peanut butter
1 cup firmly packed brown sugar
1 cup granulated sugar
2 eggs
1 teaspoon vanilla extract
2 cups all-purpose flour
½ cup unsweetened cocoa powder
1 teaspoon baking powder
1 teaspoon baking soda
1 cup milk chocolate chips

Butter Flavor Crisco is artificially flavored.

1. Heat oven to 350°F. Place sheets of foil on countertop for cooling cookies.

2. Combine 1 cup shortening, peanut butter, brown sugar and granulated sugar in large bowl. Beat at medium speed of electric mixer until well blended. Beat in eggs and vanilla. Beat until blended.

3. Combine flour, cocoa, baking powder and baking soda. Mix into creamed mixture at low speed until just blended. Stir in milk chocolate chips.

4. Drop rounded tablespoonfuls of dough 2 inches apart onto ungreased baking sheet.

5. Bake at 350°F for 10 to 12 minutes, or until edges are lightly browned. *Do not overbake.* Cool 2 minutes on baking sheet. Remove cookies to foil to cool completely.

Makes about 6 dozen cookies

Ultimate Chippers

2½ cups all-purpose flour
   1 teaspoon baking soda
  ½ teaspoon salt
   1 cup butter, softened
   1 cup packed light brown sugar
  ½ cup granulated sugar
   2 eggs
   1 tablespoon vanilla
   1 cup semisweet chocolate chips
   1 cup milk chocolate chips
   1 cup white chocolate chips
  ½ cup coarsely chopped pecans
   (optional)

Preheat oven to 375°F. Combine flour, baking soda and salt in medium bowl.

Beat butter, brown sugar and granulated sugar in large bowl until light and fluffy. Beat in eggs and vanilla. Add flour mixture to butter mixture; beat until well blended. Stir in chips and pecans, if desired.

Drop by heaping teaspoonfuls 2 inches apart onto ungreased cookie sheets. Bake 10 to 12 minutes or until edges are golden brown. Let cookies stand on cookie sheets 2 minutes. Remove cookies to wire racks; cool completely.

Makes about 6 dozen cookies

Butter Toffee Chocolate Chip Crunch

1 cup firmly packed light brown sugar
¾ Butter Flavor* CRISCO® Stick or
    ¾ cup Butter Flavor CRISCO®
    all-vegetable shortening plus
    additional for greasing
1 egg
2 tablespoons sweetened condensed
    milk (not evaporated milk)
1 teaspoon salt
¾ teaspoon baking soda
1 teaspoon pure vanilla extract
1¾ cups all-purpose flour
¾ cup coarsely chopped pecans
½ cup milk chocolate chips
½ cup semi-sweet chocolate chips
2 to 4 bars (1.4 ounces each) toffee
    bars, finely crushed

*Butter Flavor Crisco is artificially flavored.

1. Heat oven to 350°F. Grease baking sheet with shortening. Place sheets of foil on countertop for cooling cookies.

2. Beat brown sugar, 1 cup shortening, egg, sweetened condensed milk, salt, baking soda and vanilla in large bowl until well blended. Add flour gradually. Beat until well blended. Stir in nuts, chocolate chips and crushed toffee bars. Drop by level tablespoonfuls 2 inches apart onto prepared baking sheet.

3. Bake at 350°F for 10 to 12 minutes or until light golden brown. *Do not overbake.* Cool cookies 2 minutes on baking sheet. Remove to foil to cool completely.

Makes 4 dozen cookies

Butter Toffee Chocolate Chip Crunch

Dark Chocolate Dreams

16 ounces bittersweet chocolate candy bars or bittersweet chocolate chips
¼ cup butter
½ cup all-purpose flour
¾ teaspoon ground cinnamon
½ teaspoon baking powder
¼ teaspoon salt
1½ cups sugar
3 eggs
1 teaspoon vanilla
1 package (12 ounces) white chocolate chips
1 cup chopped pecans, lightly toasted

1. Preheat oven to 350°F. Grease cookie sheets.

2. Coarsely chop chocolate bars; place in microwavable bowl. Add butter. Microwave at HIGH 2 minutes; stir. Microwave 1 to 2 minutes, stirring after 1 minute, or until chocolate is melted. Cool to lukewarm.

3. Combine flour, cinnamon, baking powder and salt in small bowl; set aside.

4. Combine sugar, eggs and vanilla in large bowl of electric mixer. Beat at medium-high speed until very thick and mixture turns a pale color, about 6 minutes.

5. Reduce speed to low; beat in chocolate mixture until well blended. Gradually beat in flour mixture until blended. Fold in white chocolate chips and pecans.

6. Drop batter by level ⅓ cupfuls onto prepared cookie sheets, spacing 3 inches apart. Place piece of plastic wrap over dough; flatten dough with fingertips to form 4-inch circles. Remove plastic wrap.

7. Bake 12 minutes or until just firm to the touch and surface begins to crack. *Do not overbake.* Cool cookies 2 minutes on cookie sheets; transfer to wire racks. Cool completely.

Makes 10 to 12 (5-inch) cookies

Note: Cookies may be baked on ungreased cookie sheets lined with parchment paper. Cool cookies 2 minutes on cookie sheets; slide parchment paper and cookies onto countertop. Cool completely.

Chocolate Candy Cookies

⅔ cup MIRACLE WHIP® Salad Dressing
1 two-layer devil's food cake mix
2 eggs
1 (8-ounce) package candy-coated chocolate candies

• Blend salad dressing, cake mix and eggs at low speed with electric mixer until moistened. Beat at medium speed 2 minutes. Stir in chocolate candies. (Dough will be stiff.)

• Drop by rounded teaspoonfuls, 2 inches apart, onto greased cookie sheets.

• Bake at 375°F for 9 to 11 minutes or until almost set. (Cookies will still appear soft.) Cool 1 minute; remove from cookie sheets.

Makes about 4½ dozen cookies

Dark Chocolate Dreams

Chocolate Pistachio Cookies

2 cups shelled pistachio or macadamia nuts, finely chopped, divided
1¾ cups all-purpose flour
¼ cup unsweetened cocoa powder
¾ teaspoon baking soda
½ teaspoon salt
¾ cup plus 1 tablespoon I CAN'T BELIEVE IT'S NOT BUTTER!® Spread, divided
1 cup granulated sugar
¾ cup firmly packed brown sugar
2 eggs
3 squares (1 ounce each) unsweetened chocolate, melted
½ teaspoon vanilla extract
⅛ teaspoon almond extract
1½ squares (1 ounce each) unsweetened chocolate
2 tablespoons confectioners' sugar

Preheat oven to 375°F. Lightly spray baking sheets with I Can't Believe It's Not Butter! Spray; set aside. Reserve 3 tablespoons pistachios for garnish.

In medium bowl, combine flour, cocoa powder, baking soda and salt; set aside.

In large bowl, with electric mixer, beat ¾ cup I Can't Believe It's Not Butter! Spread, granulated sugar and brown sugar until light and fluffy, about 5 minutes. Beat in eggs, one at a time, beating 30 seconds after each addition. Beat in melted chocolate and extracts. Beat in flour mixture just until blended. Stir in pistachios.

On prepared baking sheets, drop dough by rounded tablespoonfuls, 1 inch apart. Bake one sheet at a time 8 minutes or until tops are puffed and dry but still soft when touched. *Do not overbake.* On wire rack, cool 5 minutes; remove from sheets and cool completely.

For icing, in microwave-safe bowl, melt 1½ squares chocolate with remaining 1 tablespoon I Can't Believe It's Not Butter! Spread at HIGH (Full Power) 1 minute or until chocolate is melted; stir until smooth. Stir in confectioners' sugar. Lightly spread ¼ teaspoon icing on each cookie, then sprinkle with reserved pistachios. Let stand 20 minutes before serving.

Makes about 3½ dozen cookies

FUN FOOD FACT

Pistachio nuts have a hard, tan shell which is sometimes dyed pink or blanched white. They are grown in California, Iran, Italy and Turkey. The inside meat has a pale green color and a delicate, subtly-sweet flavor.

Nutty Clusters

2 squares (1 ounce each) unsweetened chocolate
½ cup butter, softened
1 cup granulated sugar
1 egg
⅓ cup buttermilk
1 teaspoon vanilla
1¾ cups all-purpose flour
½ teaspoon baking soda
1 cup mixed salted nuts, chopped
Easy Chocolate Icing (recipe follows)

Preheat oven to 400°F. Melt chocolate in top of double boiler over hot, not boiling, water. Remove from heat; cool. Beat butter and granulated sugar in large bowl until smooth. Beat in egg, melted chocolate, buttermilk and vanilla until light. Stir in flour, baking soda and nuts. Drop dough by teaspoonfuls 2 inches apart onto ungreased cookie sheets. Bake 8 to 10 minutes or until almost no imprint remains when touched. Immediately remove cookies from cookie sheets to wire racks. While cookies bake, prepare Easy Chocolate Icing. Frost cookies while still warm. ***Makes about 4 dozen cookies***

Easy Chocolate Icing

2 squares (1 ounce each) unsweetened chocolate
2 tablespoons butter or margarine
2 cups powdered sugar
2 to 3 tablespoons water

Melt chocolate and butter in small heavy saucepan over low heat, stirring until completely melted. Add powdered sugar and water, mixing until smooth.

Double Chocolate Mint Chip Cookies

1½ cups (10-ounce package) NESTLÉ® TOLL HOUSE® Mint Chocolate Morsels, divided
1¼ cups all-purpose flour
¾ teaspoon baking soda
½ teaspoon salt
½ cup butter, softened
½ cup firmly packed brown sugar
¼ cup granulated sugar
½ teaspoon vanilla extract
1 egg
½ cup chopped nuts

PREHEAT oven to 375°F. Melt over hot (not boiling) water, ¾ cup morsels; stir until smooth. Remove from heat; cool to room temperature.

COMBINE flour, baking soda and salt in small bowl; set aside. In large bowl, combine butter, brown sugar, granulated sugar and vanilla extract; beat until creamy. Add melted morsels and egg; beat well. Gradually add flour mixture to butter mixture. Stir in remaining ¾ cup morsels and nuts. Drop by rounded tablespoonfuls onto ungreased cookie sheets. Bake at 375°F. for 8 to 9 minutes. Allow to stand 2 to 3 minutes; remove from cookie sheets. Cool completely on wire racks.

Makes about 1½ dozen 2-inch cookies

Super Chocolate Cookies

2 cups all-purpose flour
⅓ cup unsweetened cocoa powder
1 teaspoon baking soda
½ teaspoon salt
½ cup butter, softened
½ cup shortening
1⅓ cups packed brown sugar
2 eggs
2 teaspoons vanilla
1 cup candy-coated chocolate pieces
1 cup raisins
¾ cup salted peanuts, coarsely chopped

1. Preheat oven to 350°F. Combine flour, cocoa, baking soda and salt in medium bowl; set aside.

2. Beat butter, shortening and brown sugar in large bowl of electric mixer at medium speed until light and fluffy. Beat in eggs and vanilla until well blended. Gradually add flour mixture, beating at low speed until blended. Stir in candy pieces, raisins and peanuts.

3. Drop dough by ¼ cupfuls onto ungreased cookie sheets, spacing 3 inches apart. Flatten slightly. Bake cookies 13 to 15 minutes or until almost set. Cool 2 minutes on cookie sheets. Transfer to wire racks. Let cool completely.

Makes 18 to 20 (4-inch) cookies

Chocolate-Orange Chip Cookies

1¼ cups packed brown sugar
½ Butter Flavor* CRISCO® STICK or
    ½ cup Butter Flavor CRISCO®
    all-vegetable shortening
2 squares (1 ounce each) unsweetened chocolate, melted and cooled
1 egg
2 tablespoons orange juice concentrate
1 teaspoon grated orange peel
1 teaspoon vanilla extract
1½ cups all-purpose flour
¾ teaspoon baking soda
¼ teaspoon salt
1 cup semi-sweet chocolate chips
½ cup blanched slivered almonds

Butter Flavor Crisco is artificially flavored.

1. Heat oven to 375°F. Place sheets of foil on countertop for cooling cookies.

2. Combine brown sugar, ½ cup shortening and melted chocolate in large bowl. Beat until well blended. Beat in egg, orange juice concentrate, orange peel and vanilla.

3. Combine flour, baking soda and salt. Mix into shortening mixture until well blended. Stir in chocolate chips and nuts.

4. Drop tablespoonfuls of dough 2 inches apart onto ungreased baking sheets.

5. Bake one baking sheet at a time at 375°F for 7 to 9 minutes or until set. *Do not overbake.* Cool 2 minutes on baking sheets. Remove cookies to foil to cool completely.

Makes about 3½ dozen cookies

Super Chocolate Cookies

Dreamy Chocolate Chip Cookies

1¼ cups firmly packed brown sugar
¾ Butter Flavor* CRISCO® Stick or
    ¾ cup Butter Flavor CRISCO®
    all-vegetable shortening
3 eggs, lightly beaten
2 teaspoons vanilla extract
1 (4-ounce) package German sweet
    chocolate, melted, cooled
3 cups all-purpose flour
1 teaspoon baking soda
½ teaspoon salt
1 (11½-ounce) package milk chocolate
    chips
1 (10-ounce) package premium
    semi-sweet chocolate pieces
1 cup chopped macadamia nuts

Butter Flavor Crisco is artificially flavored.

1. Heat oven to 375°F. Place sheets of foil on countertop for cooling cookies.

2. Combine brown sugar, ¾ cup shortening, eggs and vanilla in large bowl. Beat at low speed of electric mixer until blended. Increase speed to high. Beat 2 minutes. Add melted chocolate. Mix until well blended.

3. Combine flour, baking soda and salt. Add to shortening mixture at low speed.

4. Stir in chocolate chips, chocolate pieces and nuts. Drop by rounded tablespoonfuls 3 inches apart onto ungreased baking sheets.

5. Bake at 375°F for 9 to 11 minutes or until set. *Do not overbake.* Cool 2 minutes on baking sheet. Remove cookies to foil to cool completely. ***Makes 3 dozen cookies***

Choco-Cherry Cookies Supreme

⅔ cup all-purpose flour
½ cup unsweetened cocoa powder
1½ teaspoons baking powder
½ teaspoon salt
⅓ cup butter, softened
½ cup granulated sugar
½ cup packed light brown sugar
⅓ cup milk
1 egg
1 teaspoon vanilla
2 cups uncooked quick or
    old-fashioned oats
3 ounces white baking bar or white
    chocolate candy bar, cut into
    ¼-inch pieces
½ cup candied cherries, cut into halves

1. Preheat oven to 375°F. Lightly grease cookie sheets; set aside.

2. Combine flour, cocoa, baking powder and salt in small bowl. Beat butter, granulated sugar and brown sugar in large bowl until light and fluffy, scraping down side of bowl once. Beat in milk, egg and vanilla, scraping down side of bowl once. Beat in flour mixture, scraping down side of bowl occasionally. Stir in oats until well blended. Stir in baking bar pieces and cherries.

3. Drop heaping teaspoonfuls of dough 2 inches apart onto prepared cookie sheets.

4. Bake 10 minutes or until set. Let cookies stand on cookie sheets 1 minute. Remove cookies to wire racks; cool completely. ***Makes about 3 dozen cookies***

Dreamy Chocolate Chip Cookies

Chocolate Walnut Pie Bars

CRUST
1½ cups all-purpose flour
½ cup (1 stick) butter or margarine, softened
¼ cup packed brown sugar

FILLING
3 eggs
¾ cup light corn syrup
¾ cup granulated sugar
2 tablespoons butter or margarine, melted
1 teaspoon vanilla extract
2 cups (12-ounce package) NESTLÉ® TOLL HOUSE® Semi-Sweet Chocolate Morsels
1½ cups coarsely chopped walnuts

FOR CRUST
BEAT flour, butter and brown sugar in small mixer bowl until crumbly. Press into bottom of greased 13×9-inch baking pan.

BAKE in preheated 350°F. oven for 12 to 15 minutes or until lightly browned.

FOR FILLING
BEAT eggs, corn syrup, granulated sugar, butter and vanilla in large mixer bowl. Stir in morsels and nuts; pour over hot crust.

BAKE at 350°F. for 25 to 30 minutes or until set. Cool completely in pan on wire rack. *Makes about 3 dozen bars*

Fudgy Cookie Squares

COOKIE CRUST
1 package DUNCAN HINES® Chocolate Chip Cookie Mix
⅓ cup vegetable oil
1 egg
3 tablespoons water

TOPPING
1 (14-ounce) can sweetened condensed milk
1 (12-ounce) package semisweet chocolate chips
2 tablespoons butter or margarine
1 cup chopped walnuts
1 tablespoon vanilla extract
Walnut halves for garnish

Preheat oven to 350°F.

Combine cookie mix, oil, egg and water in large bowl. Stir until thoroughly blended. Spread into *ungreased* 13×9-inch pan. Bake 15 to 20 minutes or until light golden brown. Cool completely in pan.

Combine milk, chips and butter in medium saucepan. Cook on low heat, stirring constantly, until chips are melted. Remove from heat. Add chopped walnuts and vanilla extract; stir until blended. Spread over cookie crust. Score into squares with tip of knife. Place walnut half on top of each square, if desired. Refrigerate until firm. Cut into squares. Refrigerate until ready to serve.
Makes 24 to 48 squares

Chocolate Walnut Pie Bars

Tri-Layer Chocolate Oatmeal Bars

CRUST

1 cup uncooked rolled oats
½ cup all-purpose flour
½ cup firmly packed light brown sugar
¼ cup MOTT'S® Natural Apple Sauce
1 tablespoon margarine, melted
¼ teaspoon baking soda

FILLING

⅔ cup all-purpose flour
½ teaspoon baking powder
¼ teaspoon salt
¾ cup granulated sugar
¼ cup MOTT'S® Natural Apple Sauce
1 whole egg
1 egg white
2 tablespoons unsweetened cocoa
   powder
1 tablespoon margarine, melted
½ teaspoon vanilla extract
¼ cup low fat buttermilk

ICING

1 cup powdered sugar
1 tablespoon unsweetened cocoa
   powder
1 tablespoon skim milk
1 teaspoon instant coffee powder

1. Preheat oven to 350°F. Spray 8-inch square baking pan with nonstick cooking spray.

2. To prepare crust, in medium bowl, combine oats, ½ cup flour, brown sugar, ¼ cup apple sauce, 1 tablespoon margarine and baking soda. Stir with fork until mixture resembles coarse crumbs. Press evenly into bottom of prepared pan. Bake 10 minutes.

3. To prepare filling, in small bowl, combine ⅔ cup flour, baking powder and salt.

4. In large bowl, combine granulated sugar, ¼ cup apple sauce, whole egg, egg white, 2 tablespoons cocoa, 1 tablespoon margarine and vanilla.

5. Add flour mixture to apple sauce mixture alternately with buttermilk; stir until well blended. Spread filling over baked crust.

6. Bake 25 minutes or until toothpick inserted in center comes out clean. Cool completely on wire rack.

7. To prepare icing, in small bowl, combine powdered sugar, 1 tablespoon cocoa, milk and coffee powder until smooth. Spread evenly over bars. Let stand until set. Run tip of knife through icing to score. Cut into 14 bars.   *Makes 14 servings*

HELPFUL HINT

Fresh milk can be soured and used as a substitute for buttermilk. If a recipe calls for ¼ cup buttermilk, place ¾ teaspoon lemon juice or distilled white vinegar in a measuring cup and add enough milk to measure ¼ cup. Stir and then let the mixture stand at room temperature 5 minutes.

Tri-Layer Chocolate Oatmeal Bars

Sachertorte Squares

1 cup (2 sticks) butter or margarine
1⅔ cups sugar
⅔ cup HERSHEY'S Cocoa
3 eggs
1½ teaspoons vanilla extract
1¼ cups all-purpose flour
¼ teaspoon baking powder
¼ teaspoon salt
½ cup apricot or seedless black
    raspberry preserves
    Satiny Chocolate Glaze (recipe
    follows)
    Sliced almonds

1. Heat oven to 325°F. Line 15½×10½×1-inch jelly-roll pan with wax paper or foil.

2. Melt butter in saucepan. Add sugar and cocoa; stir until well blended. Remove from heat. Add eggs, one at a time, beating well after each addition. Stir in vanilla. Stir together flour, baking powder and salt; gradually add to chocolate mixture, beating until well blended. Spread batter in prepared pan.

3. Bake 16 to 20 minutes or until top springs back when touched lightly in center. Cool 10 minutes; remove from pan to wire rack. Carefully remove wax paper. Cool.

4. Cut in half lengthwise, then crosswise, forming 4 rectangles. Spread preserves over two rectangles. Top with remaining two rectangles. Cut into 1½-inch squares; place on wire rack with wax paper beneath to catch drips while glazing. Prepare Satiny Chocolate Glaze. Spoon glaze over squares, allowing glaze to run down sides. Garnish with almonds.   ***Makes 2½ dozen squares***

Satiny Chocolate Glaze

2 tablespoons butter or margarine
3 tablespoons HERSHEY'S Cocoa
2 tablespoons water
1 cup powdered sugar
½ teaspoon vanilla extract

Melt butter in small saucepan over low heat. Add cocoa and water; stir constantly until mixture thickens. *Do not boil.* Remove from heat; gradually add powdered sugar and vanilla, beating with whisk until smooth and of desired consistency. Add additional water, ½ teaspoon at a time, if needed.

FUN FOOD FACT

"Torte," the German word for cake, refers to a rich, single- or multi-layered, cakelike dessert. Tortes made of multiple layers are usually filled with jam or whipped cream. One of the most well-known tortes is the classic Sacher torte, a rich dessert of chocolate cake layers spread with apricot jam and topped with a chocolate glaze. It was created in Vienna by Franz Sacher in the 1830's.

Double Chocolate Raspberry Bars

BARS
1¾ cups all-purpose flour
1 cup granulated sugar
¼ cup unsweetened cocoa
1 cup cold butter or margarine
1 egg, lightly beaten
1 teaspoon vanilla
1 can SOLO® or 1 jar BAKER®
    Raspberry Filling
1 cup chopped almonds or pecans
6 squares (1 ounce each) semi-sweet
    chocolate, finely chopped, or
    1 package (6 ounces) semi-sweet
    chocolate morsels

GLAZE
1 cup powdered sugar
1 to 2 tablespoons milk

Preheat oven to 350°F. Grease 13×9-inch baking pan; set aside.

For bars, mix flour, granulated sugar and cocoa in medium bowl. Cut in butter until mixture resembles coarse crumbs. Add egg and vanilla; stir well. Set aside 1 cup cocoa mixture. Press remaining mixture into bottom of prepared pan. Top with raspberry filling. Combine reserved cocoa mixture, almonds and chocolate. Sprinkle over filling. Bake 40 minutes. Cool in pan on wire rack.

For glaze, mix powdered sugar and milk in bowl; stir until smooth. Drizzle in zigzag pattern over cooled bars. Let stand until glaze is set. Cut into 2×1½-inch bars.

Makes about 3 dozen bars

Fudgy Chip Bars

50 OREO® Chocolate Sandwich
    Cookies, coarsely crushed
1 cup flaked coconut
1 cup semisweet chocolate chips
¼ cup margarine or butter, melted
1 (14-ounce) can sweetened condensed
    milk
1 teaspoon vanilla extract

1. Combine cookie crumbs, coconut and chocolate chips in bowl. Stir in margarine or butter, condensed milk and vanilla extract. Spread into greased 9×9×2-inch baking pan.

2. Bake at 375°F for 30 minutes or until done. Cool and cut into bars.

Makes 2 dozen bars

Rocky Road Bars

2 cups (12-ounce package) NESTLÉ®
   TOLL HOUSE® Semi-Sweet
   Chocolate Morsels, divided
1½ cups all-purpose flour
1½ teaspoons baking powder
  1 cup granulated sugar
  6 tablespoons (¾ stick) butter or
    margarine, softened
1½ teaspoons vanilla extract
  2 eggs
  2 cups (4 ounces) miniature
    marshmallows
1½ cups coarsely chopped walnuts

MICROWAVE 1 cup morsels in medium, microwave-safe bowl on HIGH (100%) power for 1 minute; stir. Microwave at additional 10- to 20-second intervals; stir until smooth. Cool to room temperature. Combine flour and baking powder in small bowl.

BEAT sugar, butter and vanilla in large mixer bowl until crumbly. Beat in eggs. Add melted chocolate; beat until smooth. Gradually beat in flour mixture. Spread batter into greased 13×9-inch baking pan.

BAKE in preheated 375°F. oven for 16 to 20 minutes or until wooden pick inserted in center comes out still slightly sticky.

REMOVE from oven; sprinkle immediately with marshmallows, nuts and remaining morsels. Return to oven for 2 minutes. Remove from oven; cool in pan on wire rack.   *Makes 2½ dozen bars*

Fudgy Chocolate Mint Oatmeal Squares

1¼ cups all-purpose flour
 ½ teaspoon baking soda
  1 cup packed brown sugar
 ½ cup (1 stick) butter or margarine,
    softened
  1 egg
1½ cups oats
  1 cup chopped nuts
1½ cups (10-ounce package) NESTLÉ®
   TOLL HOUSE® Mint Chocolate
   Morsels
1¼ cups (14-ounce can) CARNATION®
   Sweetened Condensed Milk
  2 tablespoons butter or margarine

COMBINE flour and baking soda in small bowl. Beat sugar and ½ cup butter in large mixer bowl until creamy. Beat in egg. Gradually beat in flour mixture. Stir in oats and nuts. Press 2 cups oat mixture onto bottom of greased 13×9-inch baking pan with dampened fingers.

MELT morsels, sweetened condensed milk and 2 tablespoons butter in heavy saucepan over low heat, stirring constantly until smooth; pour over crust. Crumble remaining oat mixture over filling.

BAKE in preheated 350°F. oven for 25 to 30 minutes or until filling is set and topping begins to brown. Cool in pan on wire rack.
   Makes about 2½ dozen squares

Rocky Road Bars

Spiced Chocolate Pecan Squares

COOKIE BASE
  1 cup all-purpose flour
  ½ cup packed light brown sugar
  ½ teaspoon baking soda
  ¼ cup (½ stick) butter or margarine, softened

TOPPING
  1 package (8 ounces) semi-sweet chocolate baking squares
  2 large eggs
  ¼ cup packed light brown sugar
  ¼ cup light corn syrup
  2 tablespoons *French's®* Worcestershire Sauce
  1 tablespoon vanilla extract
  1½ cups chopped pecans or walnuts, divided

Preheat oven to 375°F. To prepare cookie base, place flour, ½ cup sugar and baking soda in food processor or bowl of electric mixer. Process or mix 10 seconds. Add butter. Process or beat 30 seconds or until mixture resembles fine crumbs. Press evenly into bottom of greased 9-inch baking pan. Bake 15 minutes.

Meanwhile, to prepare topping, place chocolate in microwave-safe bowl. Microwave, uncovered, on HIGH 2 minutes or until chocolate is melted, stirring until chocolate is smooth; set aside.

Place eggs, ¼ cup sugar, corn syrup, Worcestershire and vanilla in food processor or bowl of electric mixer. Process or beat until well blended. Add melted chocolate. Process or beat until smooth. Stir in 1 cup nuts. Pour chocolate mixture over cookie base. Sprinkle with remaining ½ cup nuts. Bake 40 minutes or until toothpick inserted into center comes out with slightly fudgy crumbs. (Cookie will be slightly puffed along edges.) Cool completely on wire rack. To serve, cut into squares.

Makes 16 servings

Double Chocolate Fantasy Bars

  2 cups chocolate cookie crumbs
  ⅓ cup (5⅓ tablespoons) butter or margarine, melted
  1 (14-ounce) can sweetened condensed milk
  1¾ cups "M&M's"® Semi-Sweet Chocolate Mini Baking Bits
  1 cup shredded coconut
  1 cup chopped walnuts or pecans

Preheat oven to 350°F. In large bowl combine cookie crumbs and butter; press mixture onto bottom of 13×9×2-inch baking pan. Pour condensed milk evenly over crumbs. Combine "M&M's"® Semi-Sweet Chocolate Mini Baking Bits, coconut and nuts. Sprinkle mixture evenly over condensed milk; press down lightly. Bake 25 to 30 minutes or until set. Cool completely. Cut into bars. Store in tightly covered container. *Makes 32 bars*

Spiced Chocolate Pecan Squares

Chocolate Chip Peanut Butter Swirl Cookies

COOKIES

½ Butter Flavor* CRISCO® Stick or
    ½ cup Butter Flavor CRISCO®
    all-vegetable shortening
½ cup creamy peanut butter
½ cup firmly packed light brown sugar
⅓ cup granulated sugar
1 egg
1 teaspoon pure vanilla extract
1 cup plus 1 tablespoon all-purpose
    flour
¾ teaspoon baking soda
½ teaspoon salt
1 cup semi-sweet chocolate chips,
    divided

DRIZZLE

⅓ cup semi-sweet chocolate mini chips
1 teaspoon Butter Flavor CRISCO®
    Stick or 1 teaspoon Butter Flavor
    CRISCO® all-vegetable shortening

Butter Flavor Crisco is artificially flavored.

1. Heat oven to 350°F. Place sheets of foil on countertop for cooling cookies.

2. For cookies, combine ½ cup shortening and peanut butter in large bowl. Beat at medium speed of electric mixer until blended. Add brown sugar and granulated sugar. Beat until well blended. Beat in egg and vanilla.

3. Combine flour, baking soda and salt. Add gradually to creamed mixture at low speed. Beat until blended. Divide dough in half.

4. Melt ⅓ cup chocolate chips (see Melting/Drizzling Procedure). Stir into half of dough with spoon. Stir in ⅓ cup chocolate chips.

5. Stir remaining ⅓ cup chocolate chips into plain peanut butter dough.

6. Measure 1 teaspoon of each dough. Press together. Shape into 1-inch ball. Place 2 inches apart on ungreased baking sheet.

7. Bake at 350°F for about 10 minutes or until light brown and almost set. *Do not overbake.* Cool 2 minutes on baking sheet. Remove cookies to foil to cool completely.

8. For drizzle, melt ⅓ cup chocolate chips and 1 teaspoon shortening (see Melting/Drizzling Procedure). Drizzle over cooled cookies.

Makes about 3 dozen cookies

Melting/Drizzling Procedure: For melting or drizzling, choose one of these easy methods. Start with chips and Butter Flavor* Crisco® all-vegetable shortening (if called for), then: place in small microwave-safe measuring cup or bowl. Microwave at 50% (MEDIUM). Stir after 1 minute. Repeat until smooth. Drizzle from tip of spoon. **OR,** place in heavy resealable plastic sandwich bag. Seal. Microwave at 50% (MEDIUM). Check every minute until melted. Knead bag until smooth. Cut tiny tip off corner of bag. Squeeze out to drizzle. **OR,** place in small saucepan. Melt on range top on very low heat. Stir until smooth. Drizzle from tip of spoon.

Chocolate Chip Peanut Butter Swirl Cookies

Choco-Scutterbotch

⅔ Butter Flavor* CRISCO® Stick or
  ⅔ cup Butter Flavor CRISCO®
  all-vegetable shortening
½ cup firmly packed brown sugar
2 eggs
1 package (18¼ ounces) deluxe yellow
  cake mix
1 cup toasted rice cereal
½ cup butterscotch chips
½ cup milk chocolate chunks
½ cup semi-sweet chocolate chips
½ cup coarsely chopped walnuts or
  pecans

Butter Flavor Crisco is artificially flavored.

1. Heat oven to 375°F. Place sheets of foil on countertop for cooling cookies.

2. Combine ⅔ cup shortening and brown sugar in large bowl. Beat at medium speed with electric mixer until well blended. Beat in eggs.

3. Add cake mix gradually at low speed. Mix until well blended. Stir in cereal, butterscotch chips, chocolate chunks, chocolate chips and nuts. Stir until well blended.

4. Shape dough into 1¼-inch balls. Place 2 inches apart on ungreased baking sheet. Flatten slightly. Shape sides to form circle, if necessary.

5. Bake for 7 to 9 minutes or until lightly browned around edges. *Do not overbake.* Cool 2 minutes on baking sheet. Remove cookies to foil to cool completely.

Makes 3 dozen cookies

Marshmallow Sandwich Cookies

⅔ cup butter
1¼ cups sugar
¼ cup light corn syrup
1 egg
1 teaspoon vanilla
2 cups all-purpose flour
½ cup unsweetened cocoa powder
2 teaspoons baking soda
¼ teaspoon salt
  Sugar for rolling
24 large marshmallows

Preheat oven to 350°F. Beat butter and 1¼ cups sugar in large bowl until light and fluffy. Beat in corn syrup, egg and vanilla. Combine flour, cocoa, baking soda and salt in medium bowl; add to butter mixture. Beat until well blended. Cover and refrigerate dough 15 minutes or until firm enough to roll into balls.

Place sugar in shallow dish. Roll tablespoonfuls of dough into 1-inch balls; roll in sugar to coat. Place cookies 3 inches apart on ungreased cookie sheets. Bake 10 to 11 minutes or until set. Remove cookies to wire racks; cool completely.

To assemble sandwiches, place one marshmallow on flat side of one cookie on paper plate. Microwave at HIGH about 12 seconds or until marshmallow is softened. Immediately place another cookie, flat side down, on top of hot marshmallow; press together slightly. Repeat with remaining cookies and marshmallows.

Makes about 2 dozen sandwich cookies

Choco-Scutterbotch

Double Chocolate Cherry Cookies

COOKIES
1½ cups firmly packed light brown
    sugar
⅔ CRISCO® Stick or ⅔ cup CRISCO®
    all-vegetable shortening
1 tablespoon water
1 teaspoon vanilla extract
2 eggs
1½ cups all-purpose flour
⅓ cup unsweetened cocoa powder
½ teaspoon salt
¼ teaspoon baking soda
30 to 40 maraschino cherries

ICING
½ cup semi-sweet chocolate chips or
    white chocolate chips
½ teaspoon CRISCO® Stick or
    CRISCO® all-vegetable shortening

1. Heat oven to 375°F. Place sheets of foil on countertop for cooling cookies.

2. For cookies, place brown sugar, ⅔ cup shortening, water and vanilla in large bowl. Beat at medium speed of electric mixer until well blended. Add eggs; beat well.

3. Combine flour, cocoa, salt and baking soda. Add to shortening mixture; beat at low speed just until blended.

4. Shape rounded measuring tablespoonfuls of dough around each maraschino cherry, covering cherry completely. Place cookies 2 inches apart on ungreased baking sheet.

5. Bake one baking sheet at a time at 375°F for 7 to 9 minutes or until cookies are set.

Do not overbake. Cool 2 minutes on baking sheet. Remove cookies to foil to cool completely.

6. For icing, place chocolate chips and ½ teaspoon shortening in heavy resealable sandwich bag; seal bag. Microwave at 50% power (MEDIUM) for 1 minute. Knead bag. If necessary, microwave at 50% power another 30 seconds at a time until mixture is smooth when bag is kneaded. Cut small tip off corner of bag; drizzle chocolate over cookies.   ***Makes about 3 dozen cookies***

Chocolate Spritz

2 squares (1 ounce each) unsweetened
    chocolate
1 cup butter, softened
½ cup granulated sugar
1 egg
1 teaspoon vanilla
¼ teaspoon salt
2¼ cups all-purpose flour
    Powdered sugar

Preheat oven to 400°F. Line cookie sheets with parchment paper or leave ungreased. Melt chocolate in top of double boiler over hot, not boiling, water. Remove from heat; cool. Beat butter, granulated sugar, egg, vanilla and salt in bowl until light. Blend in melted chocolate and flour until stiff. Fit cookie press with your choice of plate. Load press with dough; press cookies out onto cookie sheets, spacing 2 inches apart.

Bake 5 to 7 minutes or just until very slightly browned around edges. Remove to wire racks to cool. Sprinkle with powdered sugar.   ***Makes about 5 dozen cookies***

Cocoa Crinkle Sandwiches

1¾ cups all-purpose flour
½ cup unsweetened cocoa powder
1 teaspoon baking soda
¼ teaspoon salt
½ cup butter
1¾ cups sugar, divided
2 eggs
2 teaspoons vanilla
1 can (16 ounces) chocolate or favorite
  flavor frosting
½ cup crushed candy canes (optional)

Combine flour, cocoa, baking soda and salt in medium bowl.

Melt butter in large saucepan over medium heat; cool slightly. Add 1¼ cups sugar; whisk until smooth. Whisk in eggs, 1 at a time, until blended. Stir in vanilla until smooth. Stir in flour mixture just until combined. Wrap dough in plastic wrap; refrigerate 2 hours.

Preheat oven to 350°F. Grease cookie sheets. Shape dough into 1-inch balls. Place remaining ½ cup sugar in shallow bowl; roll balls in sugar. Place 1½ inches apart on prepared cookie sheets.

Bake 12 minutes or until cookies are set. Let cookies stand on cookie sheets 5 minutes; transfer to wire racks to cool completely.

Stir frosting until soft and smooth. Place crushed candy canes on piece of waxed paper. Spread about 2 teaspoons frosting over flat side of one cookie. Place second cookie, flat side down, over frosting, pressing down to allow frosting to squeeze out slightly between cookies. Press exposed frosting into crushed candy canes. Repeat with remaining cookies.

Makes about 20 sandwich cookies

Cocoa Crinkle Sandwiches

Chocolate-Raspberry Kolacky

2 squares (1 ounce each) semisweet chocolate, coarsely chopped
1½ cups all-purpose flour
¼ teaspoon baking soda
¼ teaspoon salt
½ cup butter, softened
3 ounces cream cheese or light cream cheese, softened
⅓ cup granulated sugar
1 teaspoon vanilla
Seedless raspberry jam
Powdered sugar

Place chocolate in 1-cup microwavable glass measure. Microwave at HIGH 1 to 1½ minutes or until chocolate is melted, stirring after 1 minute.

Combine flour, baking soda and salt in small bowl; stir well. Beat butter and cream cheese in large bowl with electric mixer at medium speed until well blended. Beat in granulated sugar until light and fluffy. Beat in vanilla and melted chocolate. Gradually add flour mixture. Beat at low speed just until blended. Divide dough in half; flatten each half into disc. Wrap discs separately in plastic wrap. Refrigerate 1 to 2 hours or until firm.

Preheat oven to 375°F. Lightly grease cookie sheets. Roll out each dough disc on well-floured surface to ¼- to ⅛-inch thickness. Cut out with 3-inch round cookie cutter. Place 2 inches apart on prepared cookie sheets. Place rounded ½ teaspoon jam in center of each circle. Bring three edges of dough circles up over jam; pinch edges together to seal, leaving center of triangle slightly open.

Bake 10 minutes or until set. Let cookies stand on cookie sheets 2 minutes. Remove cookies to wire racks; cool completely. Just before serving, sprinkle with powdered sugar. Store tightly covered in refrigerator; let stand 30 minutes at room temperature before serving.

Makes about 1½ dozen cookies

Note: These cookies do not freeze well.

DECORATE IT!

Another way to dress up these cookies is to drizzle them with melted white chocolate. Place 1 or 2 squares of white chocolate in a resealable plastic food storage bag; seal the bag. Microwave at HIGH about 30 seconds; knead chocolate until it is melted. Repeat if necessary, microwaving chocolate for 15- to 20-second intervals. Cut a tiny piece (about ⅛ inch) off one corner of the bag; drizzle white chocolate over cookies.

Chocolate-Raspberry Kolacky

Double Chocolate Chunk Cookies

2 squares (1 ounce each) unsweetened
    chocolate
3 eggs
1 cup vegetable oil
¾ cup packed brown sugar
1 teaspoon baking powder
1 teaspoon vanilla
¼ teaspoon baking soda
¼ teaspoon salt
2⅓ cups all-purpose flour
1 package (12 ounces) semisweet
    chocolate chunks
Melted milk chocolate (optional)

Preheat oven to 350°F. Lightly grease cookie
sheets. Melt unsweetened chocolate in top of
double boiler over hot, not boiling, water.
Remove from heat; cool. Beat eggs in large
bowl until foamy. Add oil and sugar; beat
until light and frothy. Blend in baking
powder, vanilla, baking soda, salt and melted
unsweetened chocolate. Mix in flour until
smooth. Stir in chocolate chunks. Shape
dough into walnut-sized balls. Place
2 inches apart on prepared cookie sheets.
Bake 10 to 12 minutes or until firm in
center. Do not overbake. Remove to wire
racks to cool. Dip cookies halfway in melted
chocolate, if desired; let set.

Makes about 4½ dozen cookies

White Chocolate Chunk Cookies:

Substitute one package (12 ounces) white
chocolate chunks or two white chocolate
candy bars (5 to 6 ounces each), cut into
chunks, for semisweet chocolate chunks.

Fudgy Raisin Pixies

½ cup butter, softened
2 cups granulated sugar
4 eggs
2 cups all-purpose flour, divided
¾ cup unsweetened cocoa powder
2 teaspoons baking powder
½ teaspoon salt
½ cup chocolate-covered raisins
    Powdered sugar

Beat butter and granulated sugar in large
bowl until light and fluffy. Add eggs; mix
until well blended. Combine 1 cup flour,
cocoa, baking powder and salt in small
bowl; add to butter mixture. Mix until well
blended. Stir in remaining 1 cup flour and
chocolate-covered raisins. Cover; refrigerate
until firm, 2 hours or overnight.

Preheat oven to 350°F. Grease cookie sheets.
Coat hands with powdered sugar. Shape
rounded teaspoonfuls of dough into 1-inch
balls; roll in powdered sugar. Place 2 inches
apart on prepared cookie sheets. Bake 14 to
17 minutes or until firm to the touch.
Immediately remove cookies to wire racks;
cool completely.

Makes about 4 dozen cookies

Double Chocolate Chunk Cookies

Swiss Mocha Treats

**2 ounces imported Swiss bittersweet
chocolate candy bar, broken**
**½ cup plus 2 tablespoons butter,
softened and divided**
1 tablespoon instant espresso powder
1 teaspoon vanilla
1¾ cups all-purpose flour
½ teaspoon baking soda
½ teaspoon salt
¾ cup sugar
1 egg
**3 ounces imported Swiss white
chocolate candy bar, broken**

Melt bittersweet chocolate and 2 tablespoons butter in small heavy saucepan over low heat, stirring often. Add espresso powder; stir until dissolved. Remove mixture from heat; stir in vanilla. Let cool to room temperature.

Place flour, baking soda and salt in medium bowl; stir to combine. Beat remaining ½ cup butter and sugar in large bowl with electric mixer at medium speed until light and fluffy. Beat in bittersweet chocolate mixture and egg. Gradually add flour mixture. Beat at low speed until well blended. Cover; refrigerate 30 minutes or until firm.

Preheat oven to 375°F. Roll tablespoonfuls of dough into 1-inch balls. Place balls 3 inches apart on ungreased cookie sheets. Flatten each ball into ½-inch-thick round with fork dipped in sugar. Bake 9 to 10 minutes or until set (do not overbake or cookies will become dry). Immediately remove cookies to wire racks; cool completely.

Place white chocolate in small resealable plastic food storage bag; seal bag. Microwave at MEDIUM (50% power) 1 minute. Turn bag over; microwave at MEDIUM 1 minute or until melted. Knead bag until chocolate is smooth. Cut off very tiny corner of bag; pipe or drizzle white chocolate decoratively onto cooled cookies. Let stand at room temperature 30 minutes or until set. Store tightly covered at room temperature.

Makes about 4 dozen cookies

FUN FOOD FACT

The word "chocolate" originated from the Aztec word, "xocolatl," meaning "bitter water," an unexpected translation, since today chocolate is loved for its sweetness. The Aztec word, however, described an ancient drink made from unsweetened cocoa beans and spices, which was probably rather bitter.

Chocolate Thumbprints

COOKIES
- ½ Butter Flavor* CRISCO® Stick or ½ cup Butter Flavor CRISCO® all-vegetable shortening plus additional for greasing
- ½ cup granulated sugar
- 1 tablespoon milk
- ½ teaspoon vanilla
- 1 egg yolk
- 1 square (1 ounce) unsweetened baking chocolate, melted and cooled
- 1 cup all-purpose flour
- ¼ teaspoon salt
- ⅓ cup semi-sweet chocolate chips

PEANUT BUTTER CREAM FILLING
- 2 tablespoons Butter Flavor CRISCO® Stick or 2 tablespoons Butter Flavor CRISCO® all-vegetable shortening
- ⅓ cup creamy peanut butter
- 1 cup confectioners' sugar
- 2 tablespoons milk
- ½ teaspoon vanilla

Butter Flavor Crisco is artificially flavored.

1. Heat oven to 350°F. Grease baking sheet with shortening. Place sheets of foil on countertop for cooling cookies.

2. For cookies, combine ½ cup shortening, granulated sugar, 1 tablespoon milk, vanilla and egg yolk in large bowl. Beat at medium speed of electric mixer until well blended. Add melted chocolate. Mix well.

3. Combine flour and salt. Add gradually to chocolate mixture at low speed. Mix until blended. Add chocolate chips. Shape dough into 1-inch balls. Place 2 inches apart on prepared baking sheet. Press thumb gently in center of each cookie.

4. Bake at 350°F for 8 minutes. *Do not overbake.* Press centers again with small measuring spoon. Remove cookies to foil to cool completely.

5. For peanut butter cream filling, combine 2 tablespoons shortening and peanut butter in medium bowl. Stir with spoon until blended. Add confectioners' sugar. Stir well. Add 2 tablespoons milk and vanilla. Stir until smooth. Fill centers of cookies.

Makes 2½ dozen cookies

Old-Fashioned Ice Cream Sandwiches

2 squares (1 ounce each) semisweet baking chocolate, coarsely chopped
½ cup butter, softened
½ cup sugar
1 egg
1 teaspoon vanilla
1½ cups all-purpose flour
¼ teaspoon baking soda
¼ teaspoon salt
Softened vanilla or mint chocolate chip ice cream*

One quart of ice cream can be softened in the microwave at HIGH about 20 seconds.

Place chocolate in 1-cup glass measuring cup. Microwave, uncovered, at HIGH 1 to 1½ minutes or until chocolate is melted, stirring after 1 minute; set aside.

Beat butter and sugar in large bowl until light and fluffy. Beat in egg and vanilla. Gradually beat in chocolate. Combine flour, baking soda and salt in small bowl; add to butter mixture. Form dough into two discs; wrap in plastic wrap and refrigerate until firm, at least 2 hours. (Dough may be refrigerated up to 3 days before baking.)

Preheat oven to 350°F. Grease cookie sheets. Roll one dough disc between two sheets of waxed paper to ¼- to ⅛-inch thickness. Remove top sheet of waxed paper; invert dough onto prepared cookie sheet. Score dough into 3×2-inch rectangles. *Do not cut completely through dough.* Cut excess scraps of dough from edges; add to second disc of

dough and repeat rolling and scoring until all of dough is scored. Pierce each rectangle with fork.

Bake 10 minutes or until set. Let cookies stand on cookie sheets 1 minute. Cut through score marks while cookies are still warm. Remove cookies to wire racks; cool completely. Spread half of cookies with softened ice cream; top with remaining cookies. Wrap in plastic wrap and freeze 1 hour or up to 2 days.

Makes about 8 ice cream sandwiches

DECORATE IT!

It's easy to add some color to these delicious sandwiches. Just before baking, brush half the dough rectangles with beaten egg white, and then decorate with colored sprinkles.

Old-Fashioned Ice Cream Sandwiches

Chocolate Macaroons

1 can (8 ounces) almond paste
½ cup powdered sugar
2 egg whites
12 ounces semisweet baking chocolate
    or chips, melted
2 tablespoons all-purpose flour
    Powdered sugar (optional)

Preheat oven to 300°F. Line cookie sheets with parchment paper; set aside.

Beat almond paste, ½ cup powdered sugar and egg whites in large bowl with electric mixer at medium speed for 1 minute, scraping down side of bowl once. Beat in chocolate until well combined. Beat in flour at low speed, scraping down side of bowl once.

Spoon dough into pastry bag fitted with rosette tip. Pipe 1½-inch spirals 1 inch apart on prepared cookie sheets. Pipe all cookies at once; dough will get stiff upon standing.

Bake 20 minutes or until set. Carefully transfer parchment paper with cookies to countertop. Let cookies cool completely.

Peel cookies off parchment paper. Sprinkle powdered sugar over cookies, if desired.

Makes about 3 dozen cookies

Chewy Fingers

¾ Butter Flavor* CRISCO® Stick or
    ¾ cup Butter Flavor CRISCO®
    all-vegetable shortening plus
    additional for greasing
1¼ cups firmly packed light brown
    sugar
1 egg
⅓ cup milk
1½ teaspoons vanilla
3 cups quick oats, uncooked
1 cup all-purpose flour
½ teaspoon baking soda
½ teaspoon salt
¾ cup semi-sweet chocolate chips
4 peanut butter candy bars
    (2.1 ounces each), cut into ¼-inch
    pieces

Butter Flavor Crisco is artificially flavored.

1. Heat oven to 375°F. Grease baking sheets with shortening. Place sheets of foil on countertop for cooling cookies.

2. Beat ¾ cup shortening, brown sugar, egg, milk and vanilla in large bowl at medium speed of electric mixer until well blended.

3. Combine oats, flour, baking soda and salt. Mix into creamed mixture at low speed until blended. Stir in chips and candy pieces.

4. Form dough into 1-inch balls. Place 2 inches apart on prepared baking sheets.

5. Bake one baking sheet at a time at 375°F 10 to 12 minutes, or until lightly browned. *Do not overbake.* Cool 2 minutes on baking sheets. Remove cookies to foil to cool completely. *Makes 2½ dozen cookies*

Chocolate Macaroons

Peach Oatmeal Cookies

¾ cup granulated sugar
¾ cup packed brown sugar
⅔ cup margarine
2 eggs
1½ teaspoons vanilla
1½ cups whole wheat flour
2 teaspoons baking powder
1 teaspoon salt
2½ cups rolled oats
1½ cups diced peeled fresh California
　　peaches
1 cup raisins

1. Preheat oven to 350°F.

2. Beat sugars, margarine, eggs and vanilla in large mixing bowl with electric mixer at medium speed.

3. Combine flour, baking powder and salt in separate bowl. Add to egg mixture and beat at low speed 2 to 3 minutes or until smooth.

4. Stir in oats, peaches and raisins. Drop by tablespoonfuls onto nonstick baking sheet.

5. Bake 10 to 15 minutes or until golden.
Makes 3 dozen cookies

Favorite recipe from **California Tree Fruit Agreement**

Breakfast Cookies

1 Butter Flavor* CRISCO® Stick or
　1 cup Butter Flavor CRISCO®
　all-vegetable shortening
1 cup crunchy peanut butter
¾ cup granulated sugar
¾ cup firmly packed brown sugar
2 eggs, beaten
1½ cups all-purpose flour
1 teaspoon baking powder
1 teaspoon baking soda
1 teaspoon ground cinnamon
1¾ cups quick oats, uncooked
1¼ cups raisins
1 medium Granny Smith apple, finely
　grated, including juice
⅓ cup finely grated carrot
¼ cup flake coconut (optional)

*Butter Flavor Crisco is artificially flavored.

1. Heat oven to 350°F. Place sheets of foil on countertop for cooling cookies.

2. Combine 1 cup shortening, peanut butter and sugars in large bowl. Beat at medium speed with electric mixer until blended. Beat in eggs.

3. Combine flour, baking powder, baking soda and cinnamon. Add gradually to creamed mixture at low speed. Beat until blended. Stir in oats, raisins, apple, carrot and coconut. Drop by measuring tablespoonfuls onto ungreased baking sheet.

4. Bake for 9 to 11 minutes or until just brown around edges. *Do not overbake.* Cool 2 minutes on baking sheet. Remove cookies to foil to cool completely.
Makes 5 to 6 dozen cookies

Fruity Crunchy Sunflower Cookies

½ cup raisins, coarsely chopped
⅓ cup chopped dried apricots
3 tablespoons rum or apple juice
½ cup sunflower margarine or butter
    (1 stick)
¾ cup packed brown sugar
½ cup granulated sugar
1 egg
    Salt
1½ cups all-purpose flour
1½ cups rolled oats
½ teaspoon baking powder
⅓ cup sunflower kernels (raw or
    roasted)

Soak raisins and apricots in rum or apple juice. Cream margarine with electric mixer. Add sugars, egg and pinch of salt. Cream until fluffy. Add flour, oats and baking powder; mix until blended. Mix in sunflower kernels and apricot mixture (do not drain). Spray baking sheet lightly with nonstick spray, if desired. Place rounded teaspoons cookie dough onto baking sheet, leaving space between each cookie. Sprinkle tops of cookies with additional sunflower kernels, if desired. Bake at 375° F for about 10 minutes or until cookies are light brown in color.

Makes 50 cookies

Favorite recipe from **National Sunflower Association**

Double Chocolate Banana Cookies

3 to 4 extra-ripe medium DOLE®
    Bananas
2 cups rolled oats
2 cups sugar
1¾ cups all-purpose flour
½ cup unsweetened cocoa powder
1 teaspoon baking soda
½ teaspoon salt
1¼ cups margarine, melted
2 eggs, slightly beaten
2 cups semisweet chocolate chips
1 cup chopped natural almonds,
    toasted

• Purée bananas in blender; measure 2 cups for recipe.

• Combine oats, sugar, flour, cocoa, baking soda and salt until well mixed. Stir in bananas, margarine and eggs until blended. Stir in chocolate chips and almonds.

• Refrigerate batter 1 hour or until mixture becomes partially firm (batter runs during baking if too soft).

• Preheat oven to 350°F. Measure ¼ cup batter for each cookie; drop onto greased cookie sheet. Flatten slightly with spatula.

• Bake 15 to 17 minutes until cookies are golden brown. Remove to wire rack to cool.

Makes 2½ dozen (3-inch) cookies

Prep Time: 15 minutes
Chill Time: 1 hour
Bake Time: 17 minutes per batch

Rum Fruitcake Cookies

1 cup sugar
¾ cup shortening
3 eggs
⅓ cup orange juice
1 tablespoon rum extract
3 cups all-purpose flour
2 teaspoons baking powder
1 teaspoon baking soda
1 teaspoon salt
2 cups (8 ounces) chopped candied
   mixed fruit
1 cup raisins
1 cup nuts, coarsely chopped

1. Preheat oven to 375°F. Lightly grease cookie sheets; set aside. Beat sugar and shortening in large bowl until fluffy. Add eggs, orange juice and rum extract; beat 2 minutes.

2. Combine flour, baking powder, baking soda and salt in small bowl. Add candied fruit, raisins and nuts. Stir into creamed mixture. Drop dough by rounded teaspoonfuls 2 inches apart onto prepared cookie sheets. Bake 10 to 12 minutes or until golden. Let cookies stand on cookie sheets 2 minutes. Remove to wire racks; cool completely.

Makes about 6 dozen cookies

Pineapple Coconut Snowballs

1 cup sugar
½ Butter Flavor* CRISCO® Stick or
   ½ cup Butter Flavor CRISCO®
   all-vegetable shortening plus
   additional for greasing
1 egg
½ cup well-drained crushed
   pineapple**
2 cups all-purpose flour
¼ teaspoon salt
¼ teaspoon baking soda
1 can (3½ ounces) flake coconut
½ cup coarsely chopped pecans

Butter Flavor Crisco is artificially flavored.

**Place drained pineapple on paper towels.*

1. Heat oven to 375°F. Grease baking sheet with shortening. Place sheets of foil on countertop for cooling cookies.

2. Combine sugar and ½ cup shortening in large bowl. Beat at medium speed with electric mixer until well blended. Beat in egg. Mix in pineapple.

3. Combine flour, salt and baking soda. Add gradually to creamed mixture at low speed. Mix until well blended. Stir in coconut and nuts. Drop by teaspoonfuls 2 inches apart onto prepared baking sheet.

4. Bake at 375°F for 10 to 11 minutes. *Do not overbake.* Cool 2 minutes on baking sheet. Remove cookies to foil to cool completely. *Makes 4 dozen cookies*

Rum Fruitcake Cookies

Double Chocolate Cranberry Chunkies

1¾ cups all-purpose flour
⅓ cup unsweetened cocoa
½ teaspoon baking powder
½ teaspoon salt
1 cup butter, softened
1 cup granulated sugar
½ cup packed brown sugar
1 egg
1 teaspoon vanilla
2 cups semisweet chocolate chunks or
    large chocolate chips
¾ cup dried cranberries or dried tart
    cherries
    Additional granulated sugar

1. Preheat oven to 350°F.

2. Combine flour, cocoa, baking powder and salt in small bowl; set aside. Beat butter, 1 cup granulated sugar and brown sugar in large bowl of electric mixer at medium speed until light and fluffy. Beat in egg and vanilla until well blended. Gradually beat in flour mixture on low speed until blended. Stir in chocolate chunks and cranberries.

3. Drop dough by level ¼ cupfuls onto ungreased cookie sheets, spacing 3 inches apart. Flatten dough until 2 inches in diameter with bottom of glass that has been dipped in additional granulated sugar.

4. Bake 11 to 12 minutes or until cookies are set. Cool cookies 2 minutes on cookie sheets; transfer to wire racks. Cool completely.

Makes about 1 dozen (4-inch) cookies

Apple-Cranberry Crescent Cookies

1¼ cups chopped apples
½ cup dried cranberries
½ cup reduced-fat sour cream
¼ cup cholesterol-free egg substitute
¼ cup margarine or butter, melted
3 tablespoons sugar, divided
1 package quick-rise yeast
1 teaspoon vanilla
2 cups all-purpose flour
1 teaspoon ground cinnamon
1 tablespoon reduced-fat (2%) milk

1. Preheat oven to 350°F. Lightly coat cookie sheet with nonstick cooking spray. Place apples and cranberries in food processor or blender; pulse to finely chop. Set aside.

2. Mix sour cream, egg substitute, margarine and 2 tablespoons sugar in bowl. Add yeast and vanilla. Add flour; stir to form ball. Knead dough 1 minute on floured surface. Cover with plastic wrap; stand 10 minutes.

3. Divide dough into thirds. Roll one portion into 12-inch circle. Spread with ⅓ apple mixture (about ¼ cup). Cut dough to make 8 wedges. Roll up each wedge, beginning at outside edge. Place on prepared cookie sheet; turn ends of cookies to form crescents. Repeat with remaining dough and apple mixture.

4. Combine remaining 1 tablespoon sugar and cinnamon in small bowl. Brush cookies with milk; sprinkle with sugar-cinnamon mixture. Bake 18 to 20 minutes or until lightly browned.   *Makes 2 dozen cookies*

Double Chocolate Cranberry Chunkies

Bananaramas

1¼ cups firmly packed light brown
    sugar
¾ cup creamy peanut butter
½ CRISCO® Stick or ½ cup CRISCO®
    all-vegetable shortening
1 cup mashed banana
3 tablespoons milk
1½ teaspoons vanilla
½ teaspoon almond extract
1 egg
2 cups all-purpose flour
¾ teaspoon baking soda
¾ teaspoon salt
1½ cups milk chocolate chunks or
    semi-sweet chocolate chunks*
1 cup peanuts or coarsely chopped
    pecans (optional)

A combination of milk chocolate and semi-sweet chocolate chunks can be used.

1. Heat oven to 350°F. Place sheets of foil on countertop for cooling cookies.

2. Place brown sugar, peanut butter, ½ cup shortening, banana, milk, vanilla and almond extract in large bowl. Beat at medium speed of electric mixer until well blended. Add egg; beat just until blended.

3. Combine flour, baking soda and salt. Add to shortening mixture; beat at low speed just until blended. Stir in chocolate chunks and nuts, if desired.

4. Drop dough by rounded measuring tablespoonfuls 2 inches apart onto ungreased baking sheets.

5. Bake one baking sheet at a time at 350°F for 11 to 13 minutes or until cookies are light brown around edges. *Do not overbake.* Cool 2 minutes on baking sheets. Remove cookies to foil to cool completely.

Makes about 4 dozen cookies

Pumpkin & Chocolate Chip Cookies

2 cups all-purpose flour
1 teaspoon baking soda
1 teaspoon ground cinnamon
½ teaspoon salt
¼ teaspoon ground nutmeg
¼ teaspoon ground cloves
½ cup solid-pack pumpkin
½ cup granulated sugar
½ cup packed brown sugar
¼ cup caramel-flavored low-fat yogurt
1 egg
½ cup mini semisweet chocolate chips

1. Preheat oven to 350°F. Coat cookie sheets with nonstick cooking spray; set aside.

2. Mix flour, baking soda, cinnamon, salt, nutmeg and cloves in bowl; set aside.

3. Combine pumpkin, sugars, yogurt and egg in large bowl. Blend in flour mixture. Add chocolate chips.

4. Drop dough by teaspoonfuls onto prepared cookie sheets. Bake 10 minutes or until firm to touch. Remove to wire racks and cool completely. *Makes 3 dozen cookies*

Peanut Butter Chip Pineapple Drops

¼ cup (½ stick) butter or margarine, softened
¼ cup shortening
1 cup packed light brown sugar
1 egg
1 teaspoon vanilla extract
2 cups all-purpose flour
1 teaspoon baking powder
½ teaspoon baking soda
½ teaspoon salt
1 can (8 ounces) crushed pineapple, drained
1 cup REESE'S® Peanut Butter Chips
½ cup chopped nuts (optional)
    Red candied cherries, halved

1. Heat oven to 375°F.

2. Beat butter and shortening in large bowl until blended. Add sugar, egg and vanilla; beat until fluffy. Stir together flour, baking powder, baking soda and salt; add to butter mixture, beating until well blended. Stir in pineapple, peanut butter chips and nuts, if desired. Drop by teaspoons onto ungreased cookie sheet. Lightly press cherry half in center of each cookie.

3. Bake 10 to 12 minutes or until lightly browned. Remove from cookie sheet to wire rack. Cool completely.

Makes about 3½ dozen cookies

Peanut Butter Chip Pineapple Drops

Mincemeat Pastries

3½ cups all-purpose flour
¾ cup granulated sugar
½ teaspoon salt
½ cup (1 stick) butter, chilled
8 tablespoons vegetable shortening
1 cup buttermilk
1 cup mincemeat
¼ cup powdered sugar (optional)

1. Mix flour, granulated sugar and salt in large bowl; set aside. Cut butter into 1-inch chunks. Cut butter and shortening into flour mixture with pastry blender until mixture resembles coarse crumbs. Drizzle buttermilk over top; toss until mixture forms a ball.

2. Turn out dough onto floured surface; fold in half and flatten to about ½ inch thick. Knead about eight times. Divide dough in half; press each half into ½-inch-thick disc. Wrap in plastic wrap and chill 30 minutes.

3. Preheat oven to 350°F. Grease cookie sheets; set aside. Let dough rest at room temperature 10 minutes. Roll 1 dough disc into 18×12-inch rectangle on lightly floured work surface. Cut into 24 (3-inch) squares. Place heaping ½ teaspoon mincemeat in center of each square. Fold opposite corners each about ⅔ of the way over filling, overlapping dough corners.

4. Place 2 inches apart on prepared cookie sheets. Repeat with remaining dough.

5. Bake 20 minutes or until lightly browned. Remove cookies to wire racks; cool completely. Sprinkle pastries with powdered sugar, if desired. ***Makes 4 dozen cookies***

Chewy Cherry Chocolate Chip Cookies

½ Butter Flavor* CRISCO® Stick or
    ½ cup Butter Flavor CRISCO®
    all-vegetable shortening
½ cup granulated sugar
½ cup firmly packed brown sugar
½ cup dairy sour cream
1 egg
1 tablespoon maraschino cherry juice
¾ teaspoon vanilla extract
1¼ cups all-purpose flour
½ teaspoon baking soda
¼ teaspoon salt
1 cup semi-sweet chocolate chips
½ cup chopped pecans
¼ cup well-drained chopped
    maraschino cherries

Butter Flavor Crisco is artificially flavored.

1. Heat oven to 375°F. Place sheets of foil on countertop for cooling cookies.

2. Beat ½ cup shortening and sugars in large bowl until well blended. Beat in sour cream, egg, cherry juice and vanilla.

3. Combine flour, baking soda and salt. Mix into creamed mixture until well blended. Stir in chocolate chips, nuts and cherries.

4. Drop rounded tablespoonfuls of dough 2 inches apart onto ungreased baking sheet.

5. Bake at 375°F for 10 to 12 minutes, or until set. *Do not overbake.* Cool 2 minutes on baking sheet. Remove cookies to foil to cool completely. ***Makes 3 dozen cookies***

Mincemeat Pastries

Harvest Pumpkin Cookies

2 cups all-purpose flour
1 teaspoon baking powder
1 teaspoon ground cinnamon
½ teaspoon baking soda
½ teaspoon salt
½ teaspoon ground allspice
1 cup butter, softened
1 cup sugar
1 cup canned pumpkin
1 egg
1 teaspoon vanilla
1 cup chopped pecans
1 cup dried cranberries (optional)
   Pecan halves (about 36)

Preheat oven to 375°F. Combine flour, baking powder, cinnamon, baking soda, salt and allspice in medium bowl.

Beat butter and sugar in large bowl with electric mixer at medium speed until light and fluffy. Beat in pumpkin, egg and vanilla. Gradually add flour mixture. Beat at low speed until well blended. Stir in chopped pecans and cranberries, if desired.

Drop heaping tablespoonfuls of dough 2 inches apart onto ungreased cookie sheets. Flatten slightly with back of spoon. Press one pecan half into center of each cookie.

Bake 10 to 12 minutes or until golden brown. Let cookies stand on cookie sheets 1 minute; transfer to wire racks to cool completely. Store tightly covered at room temperature or freeze up to 3 months.

Makes about 3 dozen cookies

Fruit & Nut Biscotti Toasts

2 cups all-purpose flour
¾ cup sugar
½ cup cornmeal
½ cup finely chopped toasted walnuts
1½ teaspoons baking powder
½ teaspoon baking soda
¾ cup I CAN'T BELIEVE IT'S NOT BUTTER!® Spread, melted and cooled
3 eggs
1½ teaspoons vanilla extract
½ cup finely chopped citron (optional)
¼ cup dried cranberries or raisins

Preheat oven to 325°F. In large bowl, mix flour, sugar, cornmeal, walnuts, baking powder and baking soda; set aside.

In small bowl, with wire whisk, beat I Can't Believe It's Not Butter! Spread, eggs and vanilla. Add to flour mixture, stirring until mixture forms a dough. Stir in citron and cranberries. Chill 1 hour.

On lightly floured surface, knead dough. Divide in half. On greased baking sheet, with floured hands, shape dough into two flat logs, about 14×1½-inches each. Bake 30 minutes or until firm. On wire rack, cool 10 minutes.

On cutting board, cut logs into ½-inch-thick diagonal slices. On baking sheet, arrange cookies cut side down. Bake an additional 20 minutes, turning over once. On wire rack, cool completely. Store in airtight container.

Makes about 2½ dozen toasts

Harvest Pumpkin Cookies

Pumpkin White Chocolate Drops

2 cups butter, softened
2 cups granulated sugar
1 can (16 ounces) solid pack pumpkin
2 eggs
4 cups all-purpose flour
2 teaspoons pumpkin pie spice
1 teaspoon baking powder
½ teaspoon baking soda
1 bag (12 ounces) white chocolate chips
1 container (16 ounces) cream cheese frosting
¼ cup packed brown sugar

1. Preheat oven to 375°F. Grease cookie sheets.

2. Beat butter and granulated sugar in large bowl until light and fluffy. Add pumpkin and eggs; beat until smooth. Add flour, pumpkin pie spice, baking powder and baking soda; beat just until well blended. Stir in white chocolate chips.

3. Drop dough by teaspoonfuls about 2 inches apart onto prepared cookie sheets. Bake about 16 minutes or until set and bottoms are brown. Cool 1 minute on cookie sheets. Remove to wire racks to cool.

4. Combine frosting and brown sugar in small bowl. Spread on warm cookies.

Makes about 6 dozen cookies

Bran Fruit and Nut Cookies

½ cup firmly packed brown sugar
¼ cup oil
2 tablespoons water
2 egg whites, slightly beaten
1 teaspoon ground cinnamon
½ teaspoon baking soda
⅛ teaspoon salt
1 cup flour
1½ cups POST® Raisin Bran Cereal
¼ cup chopped walnuts
¼ cup chopped dried apricots (optional)

MIX sugar, oil, water, egg whites, cinnamon, baking soda and salt in large bowl. Stir in flour and cereal. Mix in walnuts and apricots.

DROP by rounded teaspoons onto lightly greased cookie sheets.

BAKE at 350°F for 10 minutes or until browned. Remove and cool on wire racks. Store in tightly covered container.

Makes 4 dozen cookies

> ## HELPFUL HINT
>
> *When making drop cookies, unless the recipe directs otherwise, space the mounds of dough about 2 inches apart on the cookie sheets to allow for spreading.*

Pumpkin White Chocolate Drops

Chocolate-Coconut Cookies

2 squares (1 ounce each) unsweetened chocolate
½ cup butter, softened
1 cup packed light brown sugar
1 egg
1¼ cups all-purpose flour
¼ teaspoon baking powder
⅛ teaspoon baking soda
  Dash salt
2 cups chopped pecans or walnuts
½ cup flaked coconut
  Pecan halves or red candied cherry halves

Preheat oven to 350°F. Lightly grease cookie sheets or line with parchment paper.

Melt chocolate in top of double boiler over hot, not boiling, water. Remove from heat; cool. Beat butter and brown sugar in large bowl until blended. Add egg and melted chocolate; beat until light. Combine flour, baking powder, baking soda and salt in small bowl. Stir into butter mixture until blended. Mix in chopped pecans and coconut. Drop dough by teaspoonfuls 2 inches apart onto prepared cookie sheets. Press pecan or cherry half into center of each cookie.

Bake 10 to 12 minutes or until firm. Remove to wire racks to cool.

Makes about 4 dozen cookies

Fruitcake Cookies

½ cup butter, softened
¾ cup sugar
½ cup milk
1 egg
2 tablespoons orange juice
1 tablespoon vinegar
2 cups all-purpose flour
1 teaspoon baking powder
½ teaspoon baking soda
¼ teaspoon salt
½ cup chopped walnuts
½ cup chopped candied mixed fruit
½ cup raisins
¼ cup chopped dried pineapple
  Powdered sugar

Preheat oven to 350°F. Grease cookie sheets. Beat butter and sugar in large bowl until creamy. Beat in milk, egg, orange juice and vinegar until blended. Mix in flour, baking powder, baking soda and salt. Stir in walnuts, mixed fruit, raisins and pineapple. Drop rounded tablespoonfuls of dough 2 inches apart onto prepared cookie sheets.

Bake 12 to 14 minutes or until lightly browned around edges. Cool 2 minutes on cookie sheets. Remove to wire racks; cool completely. Dust with powdered sugar. Store in airtight container.

Makes about 2½ dozen cookies

Apricot-Filled Pastries

   Apricot Filling (recipe follows)
2¼ cups flour
   ⅔ cup sugar
   1 cup (2 sticks) cold margarine or
      butter
   2 egg yolks, lightly beaten
   ½ cup sour cream
      Confectioners' sugar

1. Prepare Apricot Filling; set aside.

2. In large bowl combine flour and sugar. With pastry blender or 2 knives, cut in margarine until mixture resembles coarse crumbs. Stir in egg yolks and sour cream until mixed.

3. Turn out dough onto floured surface; knead just until smooth. Divide dough into quarters. Cover; refrigerate 20 minutes.

4. Preheat oven to 375°F. On floured pastry cloth with stockinette-covered rolling pin, roll one piece of dough at a time into 10-inch square. (Keep remaining dough refrigerated.)

5. Cut dough into 2-inch squares. Place ½ teaspoon Apricot Filling diagonally across each square. Moisten 2 opposite corners with water; fold over filling, overlapping slightly. Place on ungreased cookie sheets.

6. Bake 10 to 12 minutes or until edges are lightly browned. Cool on wire racks.

7. Just before serving, sprinkle with confectioners' sugar. Store in tightly covered container up to 3 weeks.

Makes about 8 dozen pastries

Apricot Filling: In 1-quart saucepan bring 1 cup dried apricots and 1 cup water to boil over medium-high heat. Reduce heat; cover and simmer 5 minutes. Drain. Place apricots and ½ cup KARO® Light Corn Syrup in blender container or food processor. Cover and blend on high speed 2 minutes or until smooth. Cool completely.

Prep Time: 90 minutes, plus chilling
Bake Time: 10 minutes, plus cooling

Banana Chocolate Chip Cookies

2 extra-ripe, medium DOLE® Bananas,
   peeled
1 package (17.5 ounces) chocolate
   chip cookie mix
½ teaspoon ground cinnamon
1 egg, lightly beaten
1 teaspoon vanilla extract
1 cup toasted wheat germ

• Mash bananas with fork. Measure 1 cup.

• Combine cookie mix and cinnamon. Stir in contents of enclosed flavoring packet, mashed bananas, egg and vanilla until well blended. Stir in wheat germ.

• Drop batter by heaping tablespoonfuls 2 inches apart onto cookie sheets coated with cooking spray. Shape cookies with back of spoon. Bake in 375°F oven 10 to 12 minutes until lightly browned. Cool on wire racks.

Makes 18 cookies

Apricot Biscotti

3 cups all-purpose flour
1½ teaspoons baking soda
½ teaspoon salt
⅔ cup sugar
3 eggs
1 teaspoon vanilla
½ cup chopped dried apricots*
⅓ cup sliced almonds, chopped
1 tablespoon reduced-fat (2%) milk

*Other chopped dried fruits, such as dried cherries, cranberries or blueberries, may be substituted.

1. Preheat oven to 350°F. Lightly coat cookie sheet with nonstick cooking spray; set aside.

2. Combine flour, baking soda and salt in medium bowl; set aside.

3. Beat sugar, eggs and vanilla in large bowl with electric mixer at medium speed until combined. Add flour mixture; beat well.

4. Stir in apricots and almonds. Turn dough out onto lightly floured work surface. Knead 4 to 6 times. Shape dough into 20-inch log; place on prepared cookie sheet. Brush dough with milk.

5. Bake 30 minutes or until firm. Remove from oven; cool 10 minutes. Diagonally slice into 30 biscotti. Place slices on cookie sheet. Bake 10 minutes; turn and bake additional 10 minutes. Cool on wire racks. Store in airtight container.

Makes 2½ dozen cookies

Cherry Cashew Cookies

1 cup butter or margarine, softened
¾ cup granulated sugar
¾ cup packed brown sugar
2 eggs
1 teaspoon vanilla extract
2¼ cups all-purpose flour
1 teaspoon baking soda
1 package (10 ounces) vanilla milk chips (about 1⅔ cups)
1½ cups dried tart cherries
1 cup broken salted cashews

Preheat oven to 375°F.

In large mixer bowl, combine butter, granulated sugar, brown sugar, eggs and vanilla. Mix with electric mixer on medium speed until thoroughly combined. Combine flour and baking soda; gradually add flour mixture to butter mixture. Stir in vanilla milk chips, dried cherries and cashews. Drop by rounded tablespoonfuls onto ungreased baking sheets.

Bake 12 to 15 minutes or until light golden brown. Cool on wire racks and store in airtight container.

Makes 4½ dozen cookies

Favorite recipe from **Cherry Marketing Institute**

Apricot Biscotti

Date Fudge Cookies

1 cup (6 ounces) semisweet chocolate
    chips
½ cup butter, softened
1 cup granulated sugar
2 eggs
1½ cups all-purpose flour
    Dash salt
1 package (8 ounces) chopped pitted
    dates
½ cup coarsely chopped pecans or
    walnuts
Brown Sugar Icing (recipe follows)

Preheat oven to 375°F. Lightly grease cookie sheets or line with parchment paper. Melt chocolate chips in top of double boiler over hot, not boiling, water. Remove from heat; cool. Cream butter, granulated sugar and eggs in large bowl until smooth. Beat in melted chocolate. Gradually add flour and salt, mixing until smooth. Stir in dates and pecans. Drop dough by rounded teaspoonfuls 2 inches apart onto prepared cookie sheets. Bake 10 to 12 minutes or until slightly firm. Cool 5 minutes on cookie sheets, then remove to wire racks. While cookies bake, prepare Brown Sugar Icing. Spread over cookies while still warm. Cool until icing is set.   ***Makes about 5 dozen cookies***

Brown Sugar Icing

½ cup packed dark brown sugar
¼ cup water
2 squares (1 ounce each) unsweetened
    chocolate
2 cups powdered sugar
¼ cup butter or margarine
1 teaspoon vanilla

Combine brown sugar, water and chocolate in small heavy saucepan. Stir over medium heat until chocolate is melted and mixture boils. Boil 1 minute. Remove from heat; beat in powdered sugar, butter and vanilla. Continue beating until mixture has cooled slightly and thickened. Spread over cookies while icing is still warm.

DECORATE IT!

These cookies make delicious sandwich cookies, too. Spread the bottoms of half the cookies with the icing, and then top with the remaining cookies. Press the cookies together slightly until some of the icing comes out. Then roll the sandwich edges in chopped nuts.

Banana Chocolate Chip Softies

1¼ cups all-purpose flour
  1 teaspoon baking powder
½ teaspoon salt
⅓ cup butter, softened
⅓ cup granulated sugar
⅓ cup firmly packed light brown sugar
  1 ripe medium banana, mashed
  1 egg
  1 teaspoon vanilla
  1 cup milk chocolate chips
½ cup coarsely chopped walnuts
    (optional)

Preheat oven to 375°F. Lightly grease cookie sheets.

Place flour, baking powder and salt in small bowl; stir to combine.

Beat butter and sugars in large bowl with electric mixer at medium speed until light and fluffy. Beat in banana, egg and vanilla. Add flour mixture. Beat at low speed until well blended. Stir in chocolate chips and walnuts, if desired. (Dough will be soft.)

Drop rounded teaspoonfuls of dough 2 inches apart onto prepared cookie sheets.

Bake 9 to 11 minutes or until edges are golden brown. Let cookies stand on cookie sheets 2 minutes. Remove cookies to wire racks; cool completely. Store tightly covered at room temperature.

Makes about 3 dozen cookies

Note: These cookies do not freeze well.

Banana Chocolate Chip Softies

Date-Nut Cookies

1 cup chopped dates
½ cup water
1¾ cups all-purpose flour
½ teaspoon baking powder
⅛ teaspoon salt
½ cup butter, softened
½ cup packed dark brown sugar
1 egg
2 teaspoons rum extract
½ cup walnut pieces, chopped

Soak dates in water in small bowl at least 30 minutes or up to 2 hours.

Preheat oven to 350°F. Grease cookie sheets. Combine flour, baking powder and salt in medium bowl.

Beat butter in large bowl at medium speed until smooth. Gradually beat in brown sugar; increase speed to high and beat until light and fluffy. Beat in egg and rum extract until fluffy. Gradually stir in flour mixture alternately with date mixture, mixing just until combined after each addition. Stir in walnuts until blended.

Drop level tablespoonfuls of dough about 1½ inches apart onto prepared cookie sheets. Bake 14 minutes or until just set. Transfer to wire racks to cool completely. Store in airtight container.

Makes 2 dozen cookies

Butterscotch Fruit Drops

2 cups all-purpose flour
1 teaspoon baking soda
½ teaspoon salt
½ cup (1 stick) butter or margarine, softened
¾ cup firmly packed brown sugar
1 egg
2 tablespoons milk
1 teaspoon grated lemon rind, optional
2 cups (12-ounce package) NESTLÉ® TOLL HOUSE® Butterscotch Flavored Morsels
1 cup diced mixed dried fruit bits or raisins

PREHEAT oven to 350°F. In small bowl, combine flour, baking soda and salt; set aside.

BEAT butter and brown sugar in large mixer bowl until creamy . Blend in egg, milk and lemon rind. Gradually beat in flour mixture. Stir in Nestlé® Toll House® Butterscotch Flavored Morsels and fruit bits. Drop by rounded measuring teaspoonfuls onto ungreased cookie sheets.

BAKE 9 to 11 minutes until golden brown. Let stand 2 minutes. Remove from cookie sheets; cool on wire racks.

Makes about 6 dozen cookies

Date-Nut Cookies

Chocolate Biscotti Nuggets

¾ **cup old-fashioned or quick oats**
2¼ **cups all-purpose flour**
1½ **teaspoons baking powder**
½ **teaspoon salt**
¾ **cup chopped dates**
½ **cup coarsely chopped toasted pecans**
½ **cup honey**
2 **eggs**
1 **teaspoon vanilla**
½ **cup (1 stick) butter, melted**
Grated peel of 2 oranges

CHOCOLATE COATING
1¾ **cups semisweet chocolate chips or white chocolate chips**
4 **teaspoons shortening**

1. Grease baking sheet; set aside. Preheat oven to 350°F.

2. Place oats in food processor; process until oats resemble coarse flour. Combine oats, flour, baking powder and salt in large bowl. Stir in dates and pecans.

3. Whisk together honey, eggs and vanilla in medium bowl. Add melted butter and orange peel. Stir egg mixture into oat mixture just until blended. Turn out dough onto lightly floured surface; flatten slightly. Knead until dough holds together, adding flour if necessary to prevent sticking. Divide dough into 3 equal pieces; shape each piece into 9×½-inch log. Carefully transfer logs to prepared baking sheet, spacing about 2 inches apart. If dough cracks, pat back into shape.

4. Bake logs 25 to 30 minutes or until lightly golden but still soft. Remove from oven. *Reduce oven temperature to 275°F.* Let logs cool on baking sheet 10 minutes. Trim ends using serrated knife. Slice logs on slight diagonal, about ¾ inch thick. Arrange biscotti on their sides on baking sheet. Return to oven and bake 15 to 20 minutes or until lightly golden. Turn biscotti over and bake 10 to 15 minutes longer. Remove biscotti to wire rack to cool completely.

5. Brush individual biscotti with dry pastry brush to remove any loose crumbs. Heat chocolate chips and shortening in small heavy saucepan over very low heat until melted and smooth. Dip half of each biscotti slice into melted chocolate, letting any excess run off. Place on waxed paper. Let stand until set. Store in waxed paper-lined container at room temperature.

Makes about 3 dozen cookies

FUN FOOD FACT

A traditional Italian cookie, biscotti (plural of biscotto) is baked twice. The dough is first formed into a log and baked. The log is then cut into slices, and the slices are baked. This produces the characteristic crunchy texture that is ideal for dipping in coffee or dessert wine.

Chocolate Biscotti Nuggets

Fruit and Cookie Pizza

1 package (18 ounces) refrigerated chocolate chip cookie dough
1 can (20 ounces) DOLE® Pineapple Slices
1 package (8 ounces) light cream cheese
⅓ cup sugar
1 teaspoon vanilla extract
1 DOLE® Banana, peeled, sliced
½ cup DOLE® Mandarin Oranges, drained
½ cup sliced DOLE® Strawberries or Raspberries
2 to 4 tablespoons bottled chocolate sauce

• Press small pieces of cookie dough onto greased 12-inch pizza pan. Bake at 350°F, 10 to 12 minutes or until browned and puffed. Cool completely in pan on wire rack.

• Drain pineapple; reserve 2 tablespoons juice.

• Beat cream cheese, sugar, reserved juice and vanilla in bowl until smooth. Spread over cooled cookie.

• Arrange pineapple slices over cream cheese. Arrange banana slices, oranges and strawberries in pattern over pineapple. Drizzle chocolate sauce over fruit.

Makes 10 servings

Prep Time: 15 minutes
Bake Time: 12 minutes

Peanut Butter & Banana Cookies

¼ cup butter
½ cup mashed ripe banana
½ cup no-sugar-added natural peanut butter
¼ cup thawed frozen unsweetened apple juice concentrate
1 egg
1 teaspoon vanilla
1 cup all-purpose flour
½ teaspoon baking soda
¼ teaspoon salt
½ cup chopped salted peanuts
Whole peanuts (optional)

Preheat oven to 375°F. Beat butter in large bowl until creamy. Add banana and peanut butter; beat until smooth. Blend in apple juice concentrate, egg and vanilla. Beat in flour, baking soda and salt. Stir in chopped peanuts. Drop rounded tablespoonfuls of dough 2 inches apart onto lightly greased cookie sheets; top each with one peanut, if desired. Bake 8 minutes or until set. Cool completely on wire racks. Store in tightly covered container.

Makes 2 dozen cookies

Chocolate Orange Macadamia Cookies

1 Butter Flavor* CRISCO® Stick or
   1 cup Butter Flavor CRISCO®
   all-vegetable shortening
1 cup firmly packed light brown sugar
½ cup granulated sugar
1 egg
2 teaspoons orange extract
2 cups all-purpose flour
1 teaspoon baking soda
1 teaspoon salt
1 bar (7 ounces) dark chocolate, cut
   into ¼-inch pieces
1 cup milk chocolate chips
½ cup flake coconut
⅓ cup chopped macadamia nuts
¼ cup grated orange peel (about
   2 small oranges) spooned lightly
   into cup

Butter Flavor Crisco is artificially flavored.

1. Heat oven to 350°F. Place sheets of foil on countertop for cooling cookies.

2. Combine 1 cup shortening, brown sugar and granulated sugar in large bowl. Beat at medium speed of electric mixer until well blended. Beat in egg and orange extract.

3. Combine flour, baking soda and salt. Add gradually to creamed mixture at low speed. Beat until well blended.

4. Stir in dark chocolate pieces, chocolate chips, coconut, nuts and orange peel with spoon. Shape dough into 1½-inch balls. Place 2 inches apart on ungreased baking sheet.

5. Bake at 350°F for 14 to 16 minutes or until golden brown and just set. *Do not overbake.* Cool on baking sheet 2 minutes. Remove cookies to foil to cool completely.

Makes about 2 dozen cookies

Banana Sandies

2⅓ cups all-purpose flour
  1 cup butter, softened
  ¾ cup granulated sugar
  ¼ cup brown sugar
  ½ cup ¼-inch slices banana (about
    1 medium)
  1 teaspoon vanilla
  ¼ teaspoon salt
  ⅔ cup chopped pecans
    Prepared cream cheese frosting
    Yellow food coloring (optional)

1. Preheat oven to 350°F. Combine flour, butter, sugars, banana slices, vanilla and salt in large bowl. Beat 2 to 3 minutes, scraping bowl often, until well blended. Stir in pecans. Shape rounded teaspoonfuls of dough into 1-inch balls. Place 2 inches apart on greased cookie sheets. Flatten cookies to ¼-inch thickness with bottom of glass dipped in sugar. Bake 12 to 15 minutes or until edges are lightly browned. Remove immediately to wire racks; cool completely.

2. Tint frosting with food coloring, if desired. Spread 1 tablespoon frosting over bottoms of ½ the cookies. Top with remaining cookies.

Makes 2 dozen sandwich cookies

Date-Nut Macaroons

1 (8-ounce) package pitted dates, chopped
1½ cups flaked coconut
1 cup PLANTERS® Pecan Halves, chopped
¾ cup sweetened condensed milk (not evaporated milk)
½ teaspoon vanilla extract

Preheat oven to 350°F.

In medium bowl, combine dates, coconut and nuts; blend in sweetened condensed milk and vanilla. Drop by rounded tablespoonfuls onto greased and floured cookie sheets. Bake 10 to 12 minutes or until light golden brown. Carefully remove from cookie sheets; cool completely on wire racks. Store in airtight container.

Makes about 2 dozen cookies

HELPFUL HINT

Unopened cans of sweetened condensed milk can be stored at room temperature for up to 6 months. Reduced-fat versions are now available and may be substituted for regular sweetened condensed milk in most recipes. Do not substitute evaporated milk, which is not sweet, for condensed milk.

Grape-Filled Cookies

2 cups coarsely chopped California seedless grapes
¼ cup packed brown sugar
½ teaspoon ground cinnamon
1 teaspoon lemon juice
Sugar Cookie Dough (recipe follows)

Combine grapes, sugar and cinnamon in saucepan. Bring to a boil; cook and stir over medium heat 35 minutes or until thickened. Stir in lemon juice; cool. Roll Sugar Cookie Dough to ⅛-inch thickness. Cut into 24 (2½-inch) circles. Place 12 circles on greased cookie sheet. Place heaping teaspoonful of grape mixture on each circle, leaving ⅛-inch border around edges. Place remaining circles on filling; press together with fork. Cut 3 to 5 slits through top circles of dough. Bake at 400°F 6 to 8 minutes or until lightly browned. Cool on wire rack.

Makes about 1 dozen cookies

Sugar Cookie Dough: Beat ⅓ cup butter or margarine and 2 tablespoons sugar until smooth. Beat in 1 egg and ½ teaspoon vanilla. Combine 1 cup all-purpose flour, ¾ teaspoon baking powder and dash salt; stir into butter mixture. Wrap and refrigerate at least 1 hour.

Favorite recipe from **California Table Grape Commission**

Date-Nut Macaroons

Cherry Thumbprint Cookies

¾ cup sugar
½ cup HELLMANN'S® or BEST FOODS® Mayonnaise
½ cup (1 stick) margarine
2 eggs, separated
1 teaspoon vanilla
2 cups all-purpose flour
¼ teaspoon ground nutmeg
1½ cups finely chopped walnuts or almonds
Red and green candied cherries

1. In large bowl, beat sugar, mayonnaise, margarine, egg yolks and vanilla. Beat in flour and nutmeg until well blended. Cover; refrigerate until firm, at least 3 hours.

2. Preheat oven to 350°F. Shape dough into ¾-inch balls.

3. In small bowl, beat egg whites with fork until foamy. Dip each ball into egg whites; roll in nuts. Place 1½ inches apart on greased cookie sheets. Press thumb into centers of balls. Place 1 whole cherry in each center.

4. Bake 15 to 17 minutes or until bottoms are browned. Let cookies cool slightly before removing from cookie sheets to wire racks.

Makes about 5 dozen cookies

Fig Bars

DOUGH
½ cup dried figs
6 tablespoons hot water
1 tablespoon granulated sugar
⅔ cup all-purpose flour
½ cup uncooked quick oats
¾ teaspoon baking powder
¼ teaspoon salt
2 tablespoons oil
3 tablespoons fat-free (skim) milk

ICING
1 ounce reduced-fat cream cheese
⅓ cup powdered sugar
½ teaspoon vanilla

1. Preheat oven to 400°F. Lightly coat cookie sheet with nonstick cooking spray; set aside.

2. Combine figs, water and granulated sugar in food processor or blender; process until figs are finely chopped. Set aside. Combine flour, oats, baking powder and salt in medium bowl. Add oil and just enough milk, 1 tablespoon at a time, until mixture forms a ball.

3. On lightly floured surface, roll dough into 12×9-inch rectangle. Place dough on prepared cookie sheet. Spread fig mixture in 2½-inch-wide strip lengthwise down center of rectangle. Make cuts almost to filling at ½-inch intervals on both 12-inch sides. Fold strips over filling, overlapping and crossing in center. Bake 15 to 18 minutes or until lightly browned.

4. Combine cream cheese, powdered sugar and vanilla in small bowl; mix well. Drizzle over braid. Cut into 12 pieces.

Makes 12 servings

Marvelous Macaroons

1 can (8 ounces) DOLE® Crushed
    Pineapple
1 can (14 ounces) sweetened
    condensed milk
1 package (7 ounces) flaked coconut
½ cup margarine, melted
½ cup chopped almonds, toasted
1 teaspoon grated lemon peel
¼ teaspoon almond extract
1 cup all-purpose flour
1 teaspoon baking powder

• Preheat oven to 350°F. Drain pineapple well, pressing out excess juice with back of spoon. In large bowl, combine drained pineapple, milk, coconut, margarine, almonds, lemon peel and almond extract.

• In small bowl, combine flour and baking powder. Beat into pineapple mixture until blended. Drop heaping tablespoonfuls of dough 1 inch apart onto greased cookie sheets.

• Bake 13 to 15 minutes or until lightly browned. Garnish with whole almonds, if desired. Cool on wire racks. Store in covered container in refrigerator.

Makes about 3½ dozen cookies

Marvelous Macaroons

Elvis Would Have Loved These Peanut Butter Cookies

COOKIES
1¼ cups firmly packed light brown
    sugar
¾ cup creamy peanut butter
½ CRISCO® Stick or ½ cup CRISCO®
    all-vegetable shortening
1 cup mashed banana
3 tablespoons milk
1½ teaspoons vanilla extract
1 egg
2 cups all-purpose flour
¾ teaspoon baking soda
¾ teaspoon salt
1½ cups milk chocolate chunks or
    semi-sweet chocolate chips
1 cup coarsely chopped pecans

FROSTING
2 tablespoons Butter Flavor* CRISCO®
    Stick or 2 tablespoons Butter
    Flavor CRISCO® all-vegetable
    shortening
1½ cups miniature marshmallows
¼ cup creamy peanut butter
½ teaspoon vanilla extract
1¼ cups confectioners' sugar
    Hot water
1 cup peanut butter chips

Butter Flavor Crisco is artificially flavored.

1. Heat oven to 350°F. Place sheets of foil on countertop for cooling cookies.

2. For cookies, place brown sugar, peanut butter, ½ cup shortening, banana, milk and vanilla in large bowl. Beat at medium speed of electric mixer until well blended. Add egg. Beat just until blended.

3. Combine flour, baking soda and salt. Add to shortening mixture. Beat at low speed just until blended. Stir in chocolate chunks and nuts.

4. Drop dough by rounded measuring tablespoonfuls 2 inches apart onto ungreased baking sheets.

5. Bake one baking sheet at a time at 350°F for 11 to 13 minutes or until cookies are light brown around edges. *Do not overbake.* Cool 2 minutes on baking sheet. Remove cookies to foil to cool completely.

6. For frosting, melt 2 tablespoons shortening in medium saucepan on low heat. Add marshmallows and peanut butter. Heat until melted, stirring constantly until well blended. Remove from heat. Stir in vanilla.

7. Place confectioners' sugar in medium bowl. Add marshmallow mixture and 1 tablespoon of hot water at a time, beating until desired consistency. Frost cookies. Sprinkle with peanut butter chips.

Makes about 4 dozen cookies

**Elvis Would Have Loved These
Peanut Butter Cookies**

Around the WORLD

Mexican Chocolate Macaroons

1 package (8 ounces) semisweet baking chocolate, divided
1¾ cups plus ⅓ cup whole almonds, divided
¾ cup sugar
1 teaspoon ground cinnamon
1 teaspoon vanilla
2 egg whites

1. Preheat oven to 400°F. Grease baking sheets; set aside.

2. Place 5 squares chocolate in food processor; process until coarsely chopped. Add 1¾ cups almonds and sugar; process using on/off pulsing action until mixture is finely ground. Add cinnamon, vanilla and egg whites; process just until mixture forms moist dough.

3. Form dough into 1-inch balls (dough will be sticky). Place about 2 inches apart on prepared baking sheets. Press 1 almond on top of each cookie.

4. Bake 8 to 10 minutes or just until set. Cool 2 minutes on baking sheets. Remove cookies from baking sheets to wire racks; cool completely.

5. Heat remaining 3 squares chocolate in small saucepan over very low heat until melted. Spoon chocolate into small resealable plastic food storage bag. Cut small corner off bottom of bag with scissors. Drizzle chocolate over cookies.   ***Makes 3 dozen cookies***

Mexican Chocolate Macaroons

Spanish Churros

1 cup water
¼ cup butter
6 tablespoons sugar, divided
¼ teaspoon salt
1 cup all-purpose flour
2 eggs
    Vegetable oil for frying
1 teaspoon ground cinnamon

Place water, butter, 2 tablespoons sugar and salt in medium saucepan; bring to a boil over high heat. Remove from heat; add flour. Beat with spoon until dough forms ball and releases from side of pan. Vigorously beat in eggs, 1 at a time, until mixture is smooth. Spoon dough into pastry bag fitted with large star tip. Pipe 3×1-inch strips onto waxed-paper-lined baking sheet. Place baking sheet in freezer; freeze 20 minutes.

Pour vegetable oil into 10-inch skillet to ¾-inch depth. Heat oil to 375°F. Transfer frozen dough to hot oil with large spatula. Fry 4 or 5 cookies at a time until deep golden brown, 3 to 4 minutes, turning once. Remove cookies with spatula to paper towels; drain.

Combine remaining 4 tablespoons sugar with cinnamon. Place in paper bag. Add warm cookies, 1 at a time; close bag and shake until cookie is coated with sugar mixture. Remove cookie to wire rack. Repeat with remaining sugar mixture and cookies; cool completely. Store tightly covered at room temperature or freeze up to 3 months.

Makes about 3 dozen cookies

Biscochitos

3 cups all-purpose flour
2 teaspoons aniseed
1½ teaspoons baking powder
½ teaspoon salt
1 cup butter
¾ cup sugar, divided
1 egg
¼ cup orange juice
2 teaspoons ground cinnamon

Preheat oven to 350°F. Combine flour, aniseed, baking powder and salt in medium bowl; set aside. Beat butter in large bowl with electric mixer at medium speed until creamy. Add ½ cup sugar; beat until fluffy. Blend in egg. Gradually add flour mixture alternately with orange juice, mixing well after each addition.

Divide dough in half. Roll out one portion at a time on lightly floured surface to ¼-inch thickness; cover remaining dough to prevent drying. Cut out cookies with fancy cookie cutters 2 to 2½ inches in diameter, adding scraps to remaining dough. If dough becomes too soft to handle, refrigerate briefly. Place cookies 1 inch apart on ungreased baking sheets.

Combine remaining ¼ cup sugar and cinnamon in small bowl; lightly sprinkle over cookies. Bake 8 to 10 minutes or until edges are lightly browned. Let cool on wire racks; store in airtight container.

Makes 4 to 5 dozen cookies

Spanish Churros

Lebkuchen Jewels

¾ cup packed brown sugar
1 egg
1 cup honey
1 tablespoon grated lemon peel
1 teaspoon lemon juice
2¾ cups all-purpose flour
1 teaspoon ground nutmeg
1 teaspoon ground cinnamon
1 teaspoon ground cloves
½ teaspoon baking soda
½ teaspoon salt
1 cup SUN•MAID® Golden Raisins
½ cup each mixed candied fruits and
  citron
1 cup chopped walnuts
  Lemon Glaze (recipe follows)
  Candied cherries and citron, for
  garnish

Preheat oven to 375°F. In large bowl, beat
brown sugar and egg until smooth and fluffy.
Add honey, lemon peel and juice; beat well.
In medium bowl, sift flour with nutmeg,
cinnamon, cloves, baking soda and salt;
gradually mix into egg-sugar mixture on low
speed of electric mixer. Stir in raisins, fruits,
citron and nuts. Spread batter into greased
15×10-inch jelly-roll pan.

Bake 20 minutes or until lightly browned.
Cool slightly in pan; brush with Lemon
Glaze. Cool; cut into diamonds. Decorate
with candied cherries and slivers of citron,
if desired. Store in covered container up to
1 month.   *Makes about 4 dozen cookies*

Lemon Glaze: In bowl, mix 1 cup sifted
powdered sugar with enough lemon juice
(1½ to 2 tablespoons) to make thin glaze.

Old World Pfeffernüsse Cookies

½ cup butter, softened
¾ cup packed brown sugar
½ cup molasses
1 egg
1 tablespoon licorice-flavored liqueur
  (optional)
3¼ cups all-purpose flour
1 teaspoon baking soda
1 teaspoon ground cinnamon
½ teaspoon ground cloves
¼ teaspoon ground nutmeg
  Dash black pepper
  Powdered sugar

Preheat oven to 350°F. Grease cookie sheets.
Beat butter and brown sugar in large bowl
until creamy. Beat in molasses, egg and
liqueur, if desired, until light and fluffy. Mix
in flour, baking soda, cinnamon, cloves,
nutmeg and pepper. Shape level
tablespoonfuls of dough into balls. Place
2 inches apart on prepared cookie sheets.

Bake 12 to 14 minutes or until set. Cool
2 minutes on cookie sheets. Remove to wire
racks; sprinkle with powdered sugar. Cool
completely. Store in airtight containers.
     Makes about 4 dozen cookies

English Thumbprint Cookies

1 cup pecan pieces
1¼ cups all-purpose flour
¼ teaspoon salt
½ cup butter, softened
½ cup firmly packed light brown sugar
1 teaspoon vanilla
1 egg, separated
2 to 3 tablespoons seedless raspberry jam

1. Preheat oven to 350°F. Spread pecans on ungreased baking sheet. Bake 8 to 10 minutes or until golden brown, stirring frequently. Remove pecans from baking sheet and cool. Process cooled pecans in food processor until finely chopped; place in shallow bowl.

2. Place flour and salt in medium bowl; stir to combine. Beat butter and brown sugar in large bowl with electric mixer at medium speed until light and fluffy. Beat in vanilla and egg yolk. Gradually beat in flour mixture. Beat egg white with fork until frothy.

3. Shape dough into 1-inch balls. Roll balls in egg white; roll in nuts to coat. Place balls on ungreased cookie sheets. Press deep indentation in center of each ball with thumb.

4. Bake 8 minutes or until set. Remove cookies from oven; fill each indentation with about ¼ teaspoon jam. Return filled cookies to oven; continue to bake 8 to 10 minutes or until lightly brown. Immediately remove cookies to wire racks; cool completely.

Makes 2½ dozen cookies

Welsh Tea Cakes

¾ cup chopped dried mixed fruit
2 tablespoons brandy or cognac
2¼ cups all-purpose flour
2½ teaspoons ground cinnamon, divided
1 teaspoon baking powder
½ teaspoon baking soda
¼ teaspoon salt
¼ teaspoon ground cloves
1 cup butter, softened
1¼ cups sugar, divided
1 egg
⅓ cup sliced almonds (optional)

1. Preheat oven to 375°F. Combine dried fruit and brandy in medium bowl; let sit at least 10 minutes to plump.

2. Combine flour, 1½ teaspoons cinnamon, baking powder, baking soda, salt and cloves in medium bowl. Beat butter and 1 cup sugar in large bowl until light and fluffy. Beat in egg. Add flour mixture. Beat until well blended. Stir in fruit and brandy mixture.

3. Combine remaining ¼ cup sugar and 1 teaspoon cinnamon in small bowl. Shape heaping teaspoonfuls of dough into 1-inch balls; roll balls in cinnamon-sugar to coat. Place balls 2 inches apart on ungreased cookie sheets.

4. Press balls to ¼-inch thickness, using bottom of glass dipped in granulated sugar. Press 3 almond slices horizontally into center of each cookie, if desired.

5. Bake 10 to 12 minutes or until browned. Remove tea cakes to wire racks; cool completely. Store tightly covered at room temperature.   *Makes 3½ dozen cookies*

English Thumbprint Cookies

Classic Anise Biscotti

4 ounces whole blanched almonds (about ¾ cup)
2¼ cups all-purpose flour
1 teaspoon baking powder
¾ teaspoon salt
¾ cup sugar
½ cup unsalted butter, softened
3 eggs
2 tablespoons brandy
2 teaspoons grated lemon peel
1 tablespoon aniseed

1. Preheat oven to 375°F. Spread almonds on baking sheet. Bake 6 to 8 minutes or until toasted and light brown; turn off oven. Remove almonds from baking sheet; cool. Coarsely chop almonds.

2. Combine flour, baking powder and salt in small bowl. Beat sugar and butter in medium bowl with electric mixer at medium speed until light and fluffy. Add eggs, 1 at a time, beating well after each addition and scraping side of bowl often. Stir in brandy and lemon peel. Add flour mixture; stir until smooth. Stir in chopped almonds and aniseed. Cover and refrigerate dough 1 hour or until firm.

3. Preheat oven to 375°F. Grease large baking sheet. Divide dough in half. Shape ½ of dough into 12×2-inch log on lightly floured surface. (Dough will be fairly soft.) Pat smooth with lightly floured fingertips. Transfer to prepared baking sheet. Repeat with remaining ½ of dough to form second log. Bake 20 to 25 minutes or until logs are light golden brown. Remove baking sheet from oven to wire rack; turn off oven. Cool logs completely.

4. Preheat oven to 350°F. Cut logs diagonally with serrated knife into ½-inch-thick slices. Place slices flat in single layer on 2 ungreased baking sheets.

5. Bake 8 minutes. Turn slices over; bake 10 to 12 minutes or until cut surfaces are light brown and cookies are dry. Remove cookies to wire racks; cool completely. Store cookies in airtight container up to 2 weeks.

Makes about 4 dozen cookies

FUN FOOD FACT

Aniseed is a spice which comes from the anise plant, a relative of parsley. Both the seeds and the leaves of the anise plant have a licorice-like flavor.

Classic Anise Biscotti

Florentine Cookies

¼ **cup unsalted butter**
¼ **cup sugar**
  1 **tablespoon heavy or whipping cream**
¼ **cup sliced blanched almonds, finely**
    chopped
¼ **cup walnuts, finely chopped**
  5 **red candied cherries, finely chopped**
  1 **tablespoon golden or dark raisins,**
    finely chopped
  1 **tablespoon crystallized ginger, finely**
    chopped
  1 **tablespoon diced candied lemon**
    peel, finely chopped
  3 **tablespoons all-purpose flour**
  4 **ounces semisweet chocolate,**
    chopped

1. Preheat oven to 350°F. Grease 2 large baking sheets.

2. Combine butter, sugar and cream in small heavy saucepan. Cook and stir over medium heat until sugar dissolves and mixture boils. Cook and stir 1 minute more; remove from heat. Stir in nuts, fruit, ginger and lemon peel. Add flour; mix well.

3. Spoon heaping teaspoonfuls batter onto prepared baking sheets. Repeat, placing 4 cookies on each baking sheet to allow room for spreading.

4. Bake cookies, 1 baking sheet at a time, 8 to 10 minutes or until deep brown. Remove baking sheet from oven to wire rack. (If cookies have spread unevenly, push in edges with metal spatula to round out shape.) Cool cookies 1 minute or until firm enough to remove from sheet; then quickly and carefully remove cookies to wire racks. Cool.

5. Repeat with remaining batter. (To prevent cookies from spreading too quickly, allow baking sheets to cool before greasing and spooning batter onto sheets.)

6. Bring water in bottom of double boiler just to a boil; remove from heat. Place chocolate in top of double boiler and place over water. Stir chocolate until melted; immediately remove top of double boiler from water. Let chocolate cool slightly.

7. Line large baking sheets with waxed paper. Turn cookies over; spread chocolate on bottoms. Place cookies, chocolate side up, on prepared baking sheets; let stand until chocolate is almost set. Score chocolate in zig-zag pattern with tines of fork. Let stand until completely set, or refrigerate until firm. Serve or store in airtight container in refrigerator.

Makes about 2 dozen cookies

Florentine Cookies

Hazelnut Biscotti

6 raw hazelnuts
2 tablespoons margarine
¼ cup sugar
2 egg whites, lightly beaten
1½ teaspoons vanilla
1½ cups all-purpose flour
½ teaspoon baking powder
½ teaspoon grated orange peel
⅛ teaspoon salt

1. Preheat oven to 375°F. Place hazelnuts in shallow baking pan; toast 7 to 8 minutes or until rich golden brown. Set aside. *Reduce oven temperature to 325°F.* Spray cookie sheets with nonstick cooking spray. Set aside.

2. Combine margarine and sugar in medium bowl; mix well. Add egg whites and vanilla; mix well. Combine flour, baking powder, orange peel and salt in large bowl; mix well. Finely chop toasted hazelnuts; stir into flour mixture. Add egg white mixture to flour mixture; blend well.

3. Divide dough in half. Shape half of dough into log on lightly floured surface. (Dough will be fairly soft.) Transfer to prepared cookie sheet. Repeat with remaining half of dough to form second log. Bake both logs 25 minutes or until wooden pick inserted in center of logs comes out clean. Cool on wire racks. *Reduce oven temperature to 300°F.*

4. When cool enough to handle, cut each log into 8 (½-inch) slices. Place cut sides down on cookie sheets. Bake slices 12 minutes. Turn slices over; bake additional 12 minutes or until golden brown on both sides.

Makes 16 servings

Danish Lemon-Filled Spice Cookies

2¼ cups all-purpose flour
1 teaspoon ground cinnamon
½ teaspoon ground allspice
½ teaspoon ground ginger
½ teaspoon ground nutmeg
¼ teaspoon salt
¾ cup butter, softened
¾ cup sugar plus additional
¼ cup milk
1 egg yolk
1 teaspoon vanilla
Lemon Filling (recipe follows)

Mix flour, spices and salt in medium bowl. Beat butter, sugar, milk, egg yolk and vanilla in large bowl until light and fluffy. Gradually add flour mixture. Beat until dough forms. Cover dough and chill 30 minutes or until firm.

Preheat oven to 350°F. Grease cookie sheets. Shape dough into ½-inch balls; place 2 inches apart on prepared cookie sheets. Flatten balls to ¼-inch thickness with bottom of glass dipped in sugar. Pierce cookies with fork. Bake 10 to 13 minutes or until golden brown. Remove to wire racks; cool.

Prepare Lemon Filling. Spread filling on flat side of half of cookies. Top with remaining cookies, pressing flat sides together. Stand at room temperature until set.

Makes 3 dozen sandwich cookies

Lemon Filling: Beat 2¼ cups powdered sugar, 3 tablespoons lemon juice, 1½ tablespoons softened butter and ½ teaspoon lemon extract until smooth.

Danish Orange Cookies

½ **cup butter, softened**
¼ **cup sugar**
1 **egg**
½ **teaspoon orange extract**
2 **tablespoons grated orange peel**
1½ **cups all-purpose flour**
4 **squares (1 ounce each) semisweet chocolate**

1. Beat butter and sugar in large bowl until light and fluffy. Beat in egg, orange extract and grated peel until well blended. Gradually add flour; beat until well blended. Stir in additional flour, if necessary, to form soft dough. Form dough into disc; wrap in plastic wrap and refrigerate until firm, at least 1 hour or overnight.

2. Preheat oven to 400°F. Grease cookie sheets; set aside.

3. Unwrap dough and place on lightly floured surface. Roll dough to ¼-inch thickness; cut into 2×1-inch bars. Place bars 2 inches apart on prepared cookie sheets. Gently press dough trimmings together; reroll and cut out more cookies. (Rerolled dough will produce slightly tougher cookies than first rolling.)

4. Bake 10 minutes or until lightly browned. Remove cookies to wire racks; cool completely.

5. Melt chocolate in 1-cup glass measure in microwave at MEDIUM (50% power) 1½ to 2 minutes, stirring occasionally. Dip one end of each cookie into chocolate, coating ½ way up side. Scrape excess chocolate on bottom of cookie back into cup. Transfer cookies to waxed paper; let stand at room temperature 1 hour or until set.

6. Store tightly covered between sheets of waxed paper at room temperature.

Makes about 2½ dozen bars

Danish Orange Cookies

Danish Cookie Rings

½ cup blanched almonds
2 cups all-purpose flour
¾ cup sugar
¼ teaspoon baking powder
1 cup butter, cut into small pieces
1 egg
1 tablespoon milk
1 tablespoon vanilla
15 candied red cherries
15 candied green cherries

Grease cookie sheets; set aside. Process almonds in food processor until ground, but not pasty. Place almonds, flour, sugar and baking powder in large bowl. Cut butter into flour mixture with pastry blender or 2 knives until mixture is crumbly.

Beat egg, milk and vanilla in small bowl with fork until well blended. Add egg mixture to flour mixture; stir until soft dough forms.

Spoon dough into pastry bag fitted with medium star tip. Pipe 3-inch rings, 2 inches apart, onto prepared cookie sheets. Refrigerate rings 15 minutes or until firm.

Preheat oven to 375°F. Cut red cherries into quarters. Cut green cherries into halves; cut each half into 4 slivers. Press red cherry quarter onto each ring where ends meet. Arrange 2 green cherry slivers on either side of red cherry to form leaves. Bake 8 to 10 minutes or until golden. Remove cookies to wire racks; cool completely. Store tightly covered at room temperature.

Makes about 5 dozen cookies

Almond Chinese Chews

1 cup granulated sugar
3 eggs
1 can SOLO® or 1 jar BAKER® Almond Filling
¾ cup all-purpose flour
1 teaspoon baking powder
¼ teaspoon salt
Powdered sugar

Preheat oven to 300°F. Grease 13×9-inch baking pan; set aside.

Beat granulated sugar and eggs in medium bowl with electric mixer until thoroughly blended. Add almond filling; beat until blended. Stir flour, baking powder and salt until mixed; fold into almond mixture. Spread batter evenly in prepared pan.

Bake 40 to 45 minutes or until wooden toothpick inserted in center comes out clean. Cool completely in pan on wire rack. Cut into 2×1½-inch bars; dust with powdered sugar.

Makes about 3 dozen bars

Danish Cookie Rings

Norwegian Pepper Cookies

4 to 4½ cups all-purpose flour, divided
1 teaspoon baking soda
1 teaspoon ground cardamom
1 teaspoon ground cinnamon
1 teaspoon ground cloves
½ teaspoon black pepper
½ teaspoon salt
½ cup butter, softened
2½ cups powdered sugar
4 eggs
3 tablespoons lemon juice
1 tablespoon grated lemon peel
½ teaspoon almond extract
½ cup diced candied citron, finely chopped
Lemon Glaze (recipe follows)

1. Combine 4 cups flour, baking soda, cardamom, cinnamon, cloves, pepper and salt in medium bowl. Beat butter and half of powdered sugar in large bowl with electric mixer at medium speed until light and fluffy, scraping down side of bowl once. Beat in eggs and remaining powdered sugar, scraping down side of bowl once.

2. Gradually add flour mixture. Beat at low speed until well blended, scraping down side of bowl once. Beat in lemon juice, lemon peel and almond extract. Stir in citron and enough remaining flour until stiff dough forms.

3. Shape tablespoonfuls of dough into 1-inch balls. Place balls on large baking sheets or tray; cover with plastic wrap and refrigerate until firm, 2 hours or overnight.

4. Preheat oven to 350°F. Grease cookie sheets. Place balls 1 inch apart on prepared cookie sheets. Bake 13 to 15 minutes or until firm and light golden brown. Remove cookies to wire racks.

5. Meanwhile, prepare Lemon Glaze. While still warm, brush cookies with Lemon Glaze. Let stand at room temperature 1 hour or until set.

6. Store tightly covered at room temperature or freeze up to 3 months.

Makes about 7 dozen cookies

Lemon Glaze

2 cups sifted powdered sugar
3 to 4 tablespoons lemon juice

Place powdered sugar and lemon juice in large bowl. Stir until smooth and spreadable. If mixture is too stiff, add more lemon juice.

Makes about ½ cup glaze

FUN FOOD FACT

Citron is a citrus fruit (or the peel of the fruit) which resembles a large lemon. Citron is grown for its thick peel, since the pulp of the fruit is too sour for eating. It is most often available candied.

Norwegian Almond Squares

1¾ cups all-purpose flour
1 cup sugar
¼ cup ground almonds
1 cup butter, softened
1 egg
1 teaspoon ground cinnamon
½ teaspoon salt
1 egg white
¾ cup sliced almonds

Preheat oven to 350°F. Combine flour, sugar, ground almonds, butter, egg, cinnamon and salt in medium bowl. Beat at low speed of electric mixer, scraping bowl often, until well mixed, 2 to 3 minutes. Press dough onto ungreased cookie sheet to ¹⁄₁₆-inch thickness.

Beat egg white with fork in small bowl until foamy. Brush over dough; sprinkle with sliced almonds. Bake 12 to 15 minutes or until very lightly browned. Immediately cut into 2-inch squares and remove from pan. Cool; store in tightly covered container.

Makes about 3½ dozen squares

Norwegian Wreaths

1 hard-cooked egg yolk
1 egg, separated
½ cup butter, softened
½ cup powdered sugar
½ teaspoon vanilla
1¼ cups all-purpose flour
Coarse sugar crystals or crushed sugar cubes

1. Preheat oven to 350°F. Grease cookie sheets; set aside.

2. Beat cooked and raw egg yolks in medium bowl until smooth. Beat in butter, powdered sugar and vanilla. Stir in 1 cup flour. Stir in additional flour until stiff dough forms.

3. Place dough on sheet of waxed paper. Using waxed paper to hold dough, roll it back and forth to form a log; cut into 18 equal pieces. Roll each piece of dough into 8-inch rope, tapering ends.

4. Shape ropes into wreaths; overlap ends and let extend out from wreath. Place wreaths on prepared cookie sheets. Refrigerate 15 minutes or until firm.

5. Beat reserved egg white with fork until foamy. Brush wreaths with egg white; sprinkle with sugar crystals. Bake 8 to 10 minutes or until light golden brown. Remove cookies to wire racks; cool completely.

Makes about 1½ dozen cookies

Dutch Chocolate Meringues

¼ cup finely chopped pecans
2½ tablespoons unsweetened cocoa
    powder (preferably Dutch process)
3 egg whites
¼ teaspoon salt
¾ cup granulated sugar
    Powdered sugar (optional)

1. Preheat oven to 200°F. Line cookie sheets with foil; grease well. Set aside.

2. Place pecans and cocoa in medium bowl; stir to combine.

3. Beat egg whites and salt in clean large bowl with electric mixer at high speed until light and foamy. Gradually beat in granulated sugar until stiff peaks form.

4. Gently fold pecan mixture into egg white mixture with rubber spatula by gently cutting down to bottom of bowl, scraping up side of bowl, then folding over top of mixture. Repeat until pecan mixture is evenly incorporated.

5. Spoon batter into pastry bag fitted with large plain tip. Pipe 1-inch mounds 2 inches apart on prepared cookie sheets. Bake 1 hour. Turn oven off. *Do not open oven door;* let stand in oven until set, 2 hours or overnight.

6. When cookies are firm, carefully peel cookies from foil. Dust with powdered sugar, if desired. Store loosely covered at room temperature up to 2 days.

Makes about 6 dozen cookies

Dutch St. Nicolas Cookies

½ cup whole natural almonds
¾ cup butter or margarine, softened
½ cup packed brown sugar
2 tablespoons milk
1½ teaspoons ground cinnamon
¼ teaspoon ground nutmeg
¼ teaspoon ground ginger
¼ teaspoon ground cloves
2 cups sifted all-purpose flour
1½ teaspoons baking powder
½ teaspoon salt
¼ cup coarsely chopped citron

Spread almonds in single layer on baking sheet. Bake at 375°F, 10 to 12 minutes, stirring occasionally, until lightly toasted. Cool. Chop finely. In large bowl, cream butter, sugar, milk and spices. In small bowl, combine flour, baking powder and salt. Add flour mixture to creamed mixture; blend well. Stir in almonds and citron. Knead dough slightly to make ball. Cover; refrigerate until firm. Roll out dough ¼ inch thick on lightly floured surface. Cut out with cookie cutters. Place 2 inches apart on greased cookie sheets. Bake at 375°F 7 to 10 minutes, until lightly browned. Remove to wire racks to cool. *Makes about 3½ dozen cookies*

Favorite recipe from **Almond Board of California**

Dutch Chocolate Meringues

Swedish Sandwich Cookies

1 cup butter, softened
½ cup plus 2 tablespoons sugar,
   divided
1 egg yolk
1 egg, separated
2 to 2¼ cups all-purpose flour
3 tablespoons ground almonds
⅔ cup red currant or strawberry jelly

1. Grease and flour cookie sheets; set aside. Beat butter and ½ cup sugar in large bowl until light and fluffy. Beat in 2 egg yolks. Add 1½ cups flour; beat until well blended. Stir in additional flour to form stiff dough. Form dough into 2 discs; wrap in plastic wrap and refrigerate until firm, at least 2 hours.

2. Preheat oven to 375°F. Unwrap 1 disc and place on lightly floured surface. Roll out dough to ³⁄₁₆-inch thickness. Cut dough with floured 2¼-inch *round* cookie cutter. Place cutouts 1½ to 2 inches apart on prepared cookie sheets. Gently knead dough trimmings together; reroll and cut out more cookies.

3. Unwrap remaining dough disc and place on lightly floured surface. Roll out dough to ³⁄₁₆-inch thickness. Cut dough with floured 2¼-inch *scalloped* cookie cutter. Cut 1-inch centers out of scalloped cookies. Place cutouts 1½ to 2 inches apart on prepared cookie sheets. Cut equal numbers of round and scalloped cookies.

4. Beat egg white in small cup with wire whisk. Combine almonds and remaining 2 tablespoons sugar in small bowl. Brush

each scalloped cookie with egg white; sprinkle with sugar mixture. Bake all cookies 8 to 10 minutes or until firm and light golden brown. Remove cookies to wire racks; cool completely.

5. To assemble sandwich cookie, spread about ½ teaspoon currant jelly over flat side of each round cookie; top each with flat side of scalloped cookie. Repeat with remaining cookies and jelly.

6. Store tightly covered at room temperature or freeze up to 3 months.
   Makes 1½ dozen sandwich cookies

FUN FOOD FACT

Two very different fruits share the name "currant." One is a tiny, smooth berry related to the gooseberry; the other is a small dried fruit resembling a raisin. Fresh currants have shiny skins and a tart, tangy flavor. They can be red, black or white. Fresh currants are eaten out of hand, or used for jellies, syrups and liqueurs.

Swedish Sandwich Cookies

Polish Honey Bars

½ cup sugar, divided
2 tablespoons boiling water
⅓ cup honey
2 tablespoons butter
1 teaspoon ground allspice
½ teaspoon ground cinnamon
¼ teaspoon ground cloves
¼ teaspoon ground nutmeg
2 cups all-purpose flour
3 tablespoons cold water
1 egg
1 teaspoon baking soda
  Chocolate Filling (recipe follows)
1 cup semisweet chocolate chips
32 whole toasted almonds

1. Mix 2 tablespoons sugar and boiling water in saucepan over medium heat; stir until dissolved and slightly brown. Add remaining sugar, honey, butter and spices; bring to a boil over high heat, stirring constantly. Remove saucepan from heat. Place mixture in bowl; cool. Add flour, cold water, egg and baking soda to cooled sugar mixture; stir. Cover; let stand 20 minutes.

2. Preheat oven to 350°F. Grease and flour 15×10×1-inch pan; set aside. Roll dough on floured surface to almost fit size of pan. Press dough into pan to edges. Bake 10 to 13 minutes or until cookie base springs back when touched. Remove to wire rack; cool.

3. Run knife around edge of cookie base to loosen it from sides of pan. Place wire rack top side down over pan; flip rack and pan over together. Cookie base should drop out of pan onto rack. Cut cookie base in half to form two rectangles.

4. Prepare Chocolate Filling; spread over 1 rectangle. Top with other rectangle, flat side up. Wrap cookie sandwich in plastic wrap. Place baking sheet on top of cookie sandwich; place heavy cans or other weights on baking sheet to press sandwich layers together. Let sandwich stand overnight.

5. When cookie is ready to frost, melt chocolate chips in 2-cup glass measure in microwave at MEDIUM (50% power) 2 to 3 minutes, stirring occasionally. Dip wide part of each almond into chocolate; place dipped almonds on waxed paper to set.

6. Remove weights and baking sheet from cookie sandwich; unwrap. Spread remaining melted chocolate over top. Before chocolate sets, score top of cookie sandwich into 32 bars. Place 1 dipped almond on each bar. (If chocolate has set, it may be necessary to reheat almonds in microwave for a few seconds.) Let stand at room temperature until set; cut into bars.   *Makes 32 bars*

Chocolate Filling

¼ cup whipping cream
½ cup semisweet chocolate chips
1 cup natural almonds, toasted and
  ground
¾ cup powdered sugar, divided
½ teaspoon vanilla

Heat cream and chocolate chips in saucepan over medium heat until melted and smooth, stirring constantly. Remove from heat; stir in almonds, ½ cup powdered sugar and vanilla. Stir in additional powdered sugar until filling is stiff enough to spread.

Makes about 1 cup filling

Polish Honey Bars

Belgian Tuile Cookies

½ cup butter, softened
½ cup sugar
1 egg white
1 teaspoon vanilla
¼ teaspoon salt
½ cup all-purpose flour
4 ounces bittersweet chocolate,
    chopped or semisweet chocolate
    chips

1. Preheat oven to 375°F. Grease cookie sheets; set aside.

2. Beat butter and sugar in large bowl until light and fluffy. Beat in egg white, vanilla and salt. Gradually add flour. Beat until well blended. Drop rounded teaspoonfuls of batter 4 inches apart onto prepared cookie sheets. (Bake only 4 cookies per sheet.) Flatten slightly with spatula.

3. Bake 6 to 8 minutes or until cookies are deep golden brown. Let cookies stand on cookie sheet 1 minute. Working quickly, while cookies are still hot, drape cookies over rolling pin or bottle so both sides hang down and form saddle shape; cool completely.

4. Melt chocolate in small heavy saucepan over low heat, stirring constantly.

5. Tilt saucepan to pool chocolate at one end; dip edge of each cookie, turning slowly so entire edge is tinged with chocolate.

6. Transfer cookies to waxed paper; let stand at room temperature 1 hour or until set. Store tightly covered at room temperature. Do not freeze.

Makes about 2½ dozen cookies

Chocolate Madeleines

3 teaspoons butter, softened
1¼ cups cake flour or all-purpose flour
¼ cup unsweetened cocoa powder
¼ teaspoon salt
¼ teaspoon baking powder
1 cup granulated sugar
2 eggs
¾ cup butter, melted and cooled
2 tablespoons almond-flavored liqueur
    Powdered sugar

1. Preheat oven to 375°F. Using 1 teaspoon per pan, grease 3 madeleine pans with softened butter. Dust with flour; set aside.

2. Combine flour, cocoa, salt and baking powder in medium bowl. Beat sugar and eggs in large bowl 5 minutes or until mixture is light in color, thick and falls in wide ribbons from beaters. Beat in flour mixture until well blended. Beat in melted butter and liqueur until just blended.

3. Spoon level tablespoonfuls of batter into each prepared mold. Bake 12 minutes or until puffed. (If only 1 madeleine pan is available, thoroughly wash, dry, regrease and flour after baking each batch. Cover remaining dough with plastic wrap; let stand at room temperature.)

4. Let madeleines stand in pan 1 minute. Carefully loosen cookies from pan with point of small knife. Invert pan over wire rack; tap lightly to release cookies. Cool completely. (Cookies should be shell side up.) Dust with powdered sugar. Store tightly covered at room temperature up to 24 hours.

Makes 3 dozen madeleines

Belgian Tuile Cookies

Lollipop Sugar Cookies

1¼ cups granulated sugar
  1 Butter Flavor* CRISCO® Stick or
    1 cup Butter Flavor CRISCO®
    all-vegetable shortening
  2 eggs
¼ cup light corn syrup or regular
    pancake syrup
  1 tablespoon vanilla extract
  3 cups all-purpose flour
¾ teaspoon baking powder
½ teaspoon baking soda
½ teaspoon salt
    Decorative sprinkles, jimmies or
    colored sugars
20 flat ice cream sticks

*Butter Flavor Crisco is artificially flavored.

1. Combine sugar and 1 cup shortening in large bowl. Beat at medium speed of electric mixer until well blended. Add eggs, syrup and vanilla. Beat until well blended and fluffy.

2. Combine flour, baking powder, baking soda and salt. Add gradually to creamed mixture at low speed. Mix until well blended. Wrap dough in plastic wrap. Refrigerate at least 1 hour. Keep refrigerated until ready to use.

3. Heat oven to 375°F. Place sheets of foil on countertop for cooling cookies.

4. Place sprinkles, jimmies or colored sugars in shallow bowl. Shape dough into 2-inch balls. Roll ball in sprinkles, jimmies or colored sugars. Insert ice cream stick into each dough ball. Place dough balls with sticks 3 inches apart on ungreased baking sheets. Flatten dough balls slightly with spatula.

5. Bake one baking sheet at a time at 375°F for 7 to 9 minutes or until barely browned. _Do not overbake._ Cool 2 minutes on baking sheets. Remove cookies to foil to cool completely.   _**Makes about 20 cookies**_

Fruity Cookie Rings and Twists

  1 package (20 ounces) refrigerated
    sugar cookie dough
  3 cups fruit-flavored cereal, crushed
    and divided

1. Remove dough from wrapper. Combine dough and ½ cup crushed cereal in large bowl. Divide dough into 32 balls. Refrigerate 1 hour.

2. Preheat oven to 375°F. Shape dough balls into 6- to 8-inch-long ropes. Roll ropes in remaining cereal to coat; shape into rings or fold in half and twist.

3. Place cookies 2 inches apart on ungreased cookie sheets.

4. Bake 10 to 11 minutes or until lightly browned. Remove to wire racks; cool completely.   _**Makes 32 cookies**_

Lollipop Sugar Cookies

Critters-in-Holes

48 chewy caramel candies coated in
   milk chocolate
48 pieces candy corn
   Miniature candy-coated chocolate
   pieces
1 container (16 ounces) frosting, any
   flavor
1 package (20 ounces) refrigerated
   peanut butter cookie dough

1. Cut slit into side of 1 caramel candy using
sharp knife. Carefully insert 1 piece candy
corn into slit. Repeat with remaining caramel
candies and candy corn.

2. Attach miniature chocolate pieces to
caramel candies to resemble "eyes," using
frosting as glue. Decorate as desired.

3. Preheat oven to 350°F. Lightly grease
12 (1¾-inch) muffin cups.

4. Remove dough from wrapper. Cut dough
into 12 (1-inch) slices. Cut each slice into
4 equal sections. Place 1 section of dough
into each muffin cup.

5. Bake 9 minutes. Remove from oven and
immediately press 1 decorated caramel candy
into center of each cookie. Repeat with
remaining candies and cookies. Remove to
wire racks; cool completely.

Makes 4 dozen cookies

Nestlé Crunch® Pizza Cookie

1 cup plus 2 tablespoons all-purpose
   flour
¼ teaspoon baking soda
¼ teaspoon salt
½ cup (1 stick) butter or margarine,
   softened
6 tablespoons granulated sugar
6 tablespoons packed brown sugar
1 egg
½ teaspoon vanilla extract
1¾ cups (8-ounce package) NESTLÉ
   CRUNCH® Baking Pieces, divided
½ cup peanut butter

COMBINE flour, baking soda and salt in
small bowl.

BEAT butter, granulated sugar and brown
sugar in large mixer bowl. Beat in egg and
vanilla. Gradually beat in flour mixture. Stir
in ½ cup Crunch Baking Pieces. Spread or
pat dough onto bottom of greased 13×9-
inch baking pan or 12-inch pizza pan.

BAKE in preheated 350°F. oven for 14 to
18 minutes or until set and deep golden
brown. Remove from oven. Drop peanut
butter by spoonfuls onto hot crust; let stand
for 5 minutes to soften. Gently spread over
crust. Sprinkle remaining Crunch Baking
Pieces in single layer over peanut butter.
Serve warm or at room temperature.

Makes about 12 servings

Critters-in-Holes

Ice Skates

½ cup (1 stick) butter, softened
1¼ cups honey
1 cup packed brown sugar
1 egg, separated
5½ cups self-rising flour
1 teaspoon ground ginger
1 teaspoon ground cinnamon
½ cup milk
Assorted colored icings, candies and small candy canes

1. Beat butter, honey, brown sugar and egg yolk in large bowl at medium speed of electric mixer until light and fluffy.

2. Combine flour, ginger and cinnamon in small bowl. Add alternately with milk to butter mixture; beat just until combined. Cover; refrigerate 30 minutes.

3. Preheat oven to 350°F. Grease cookie sheets.

4. Roll dough on lightly floured surface to ¼-inch thickness. Cut out dough using 3½-inch boot-shaped cookie cutter. Place cutouts 2 inches apart on prepared cookie sheets.

5. Bake 8 to 10 minutes or until lightly browned. Cool 2 minutes on cookie sheets. Remove to wire racks; cool completely.

6. Decorate cookies with colored icings and candies to look like ice skates, attaching candy canes as skate blades.

Makes about 4 dozen cookies

Child's Choice

2⅓ cups all-purpose flour
1 Butter Flavor* CRISCO® Stick or 1 cup Butter Flavor CRISCO® all-vegetable shortening plus additional for greasing
1 teaspoon baking soda
½ teaspoon baking powder
1 cup granulated sugar
1 cup firmly packed brown sugar
2 eggs
1 teaspoon maple flavor
2 cups oats (quick or old-fashioned, uncooked)
¾ cup semi-sweet chocolate chips
¾ cup miniature marshmallows
¾ cup peanut butter chips

Butter Flavor Crisco is artificially flavored.

1. Heat oven to 350°F. Grease baking sheet with shortening. Place sheets of foil on countertop for cooling cookies.

2. Combine flour, 1 cup shortening, baking soda and baking powder in large bowl. Beat at low speed of electric mixer until blended. Increase speed to medium. Mix thoroughly. Beat in sugars, eggs and maple flavor. Add oats. Stir in chocolate chips, marshmallows and peanut butter chips until well blended.

3. Shape dough into 1½-inch balls. Flatten slightly. Place 2 inches apart on prepared baking sheet.

4. Bake at 350°F for 9 to 10 minutes or until light golden brown. *Do not overbake.* Cool 2 minutes on baking sheet. Remove cookies to foil to cool.　　*Makes 3½ dozen cookies*

Ice Skates

Happy Face Oatmeal Monsters

1½ cups all-purpose flour
1 teaspoon baking soda
½ teaspoon salt
1 cup butter, softened
1 cup packed brown sugar
2 eggs
1 teaspoon vanilla
2 cups uncooked quick oats
   Granulated sugar
28 chocolate-covered candies or large chocolate chips
   Cinnamon red hot candies or red licorice strings
   Colored frosting in tube and flaked coconut (optional)

1. Preheat oven to 350°F. Combine flour, baking soda and salt in small bowl; set aside. Beat butter and brown sugar in large bowl until light and fluffy. Beat in eggs, one at a time, until well blended. Beat in vanilla. Beat in flour mixture until blended. Stir in oats.

2. Drop dough by level ¼ cupfuls onto ungreased cookie sheets, spacing 3 inches apart. Flatten dough until 2 inches in diameter with bottom of glass dipped in granulated sugar. Press chocolate candies into cookies to form "eyes" and use cinnamon candies or licorice for "mouth."

3. Bake 12 to 14 minutes or until cookies are set and edges are golden. Cool cookies 2 minutes on cookie sheets; transfer to wire racks. Cool completely. If desired, decorate cookies with frosting and coconut for "hair."

Makes about 14 (4-inch) cookies

Dino-Mite Dinosaurs

1 cup (2 sticks) butter, softened
1¼ cups granulated sugar
1 large egg
2 squares (1 ounce each) semi-sweet chocolate, melted
½ teaspoon vanilla extract
2⅓ cups all-purpose flour
1 teaspoon baking powder
¼ teaspoon salt
1 cup white frosting
   Assorted food colorings
1 cup "M&M's"® Chocolate Mini Baking Bits

In large bowl cream butter and sugar until light and fluffy; beat in egg, chocolate and vanilla. In medium bowl combine flour, baking powder and salt; add to creamed mixture. Wrap and refrigerate dough 2 to 3 hours. Preheat oven to 350°F. Working with half the dough at a time on lightly floured surface, roll to ¼-inch thickness. Cut into dinosaur shapes using 4-inch cookie cutters. Place about 2 inches apart on ungreased cookie sheets. Bake 10 to 12 minutes. Cool 2 minutes on cookie sheets; cool completely on wire racks. Tint frosting desired colors. Frost cookies and decorate with "M&M's"® Chocolate Mini Baking Bits. Store in tightly covered container. *Makes 2 dozen cookies*

Cookie Canvases

**1 package (20 ounces) refrigerated
cookie dough, any flavor
All-purpose flour (optional)
Cookie Glaze (page 555)
Assorted liquid food colors**

**SUPPLIES
1 (3½-inch) square cardboard
template
1 (2½×4½-inch) rectangular
cardboard template
Small, clean craft paintbrushes**

1. Preheat oven to 350°F. Grease cookie
sheets. Remove dough from wrapper. Cut
dough in half. Wrap half of dough in plastic
wrap and refrigerate.

2. Roll remaining dough on floured surface
to ¼-inch thickness. Sprinkle with flour to
minimize sticking, if necessary. Cut out
shapes using cardboard templates as guides.
Place cookies 2 inches apart on prepared
cookie sheets. Repeat with remaining dough.

3. Bake 8 to 10 minutes or until edges are
lightly browned. Remove from oven and
straighten cookie edges with spatula. Cool
cookies completely on cookie sheets.
Prepare Cookie Glaze.

4. Place cookies on wire racks set over waxed
paper. Drizzle Cookie Glaze over cookies.
Let stand at room temperature 40 minutes
or until glaze is set. Place food colors in
small bowls. Using small, clean craft
paintbrushes, decorate cookies with food
colors by "painting" designs on cookies.

Makes 8 to 10 cookie canvases

Chocolate Pretzel Cookies

**Chocolate Cookie Dough (page 552)
White and colored rock or coarse
sugar**

1. Prepare Chocolate Cookie Dough. Cover;
refrigerate about 2 hours or until firm.

2. Preheat oven to 325°F. Grease cookie
sheets.

3. Divide dough into 4 equal sections. Reserve
1 section; refrigerate remaining 3 sections.
Divide reserved dough into 5 equal pieces.
Shape each dough piece on lightly floured
surface to 12-inch rope; sprinkle with rock
or coarse sugar.

4. Transfer 1 rope at a time to prepared
cookie sheets. Form each rope into pretzel
shape. Repeat steps with remaining dough
pieces.

5. Bake 12 to 14 minutes or until edges
begin to brown. Cool cookies on cookie
sheets 1 minute. Remove to wire racks; cool
completely. *Makes 20 cookies*

Brownie Sandwich Cookies

BROWNIE COOKIES
  1 package DUNCAN HINES®
    Chocolate Lovers Double Fudge
    Brownie Mix
  1 egg
  3 tablespoons water
    Sugar

FILLING
  1 container (16 ounces) DUNCAN
    HINES® Cream Cheese Frosting
    Red food coloring (optional)
  ½ cup semisweet mini chocolate chips

1. Preheat oven to 375°F. Grease cookie sheets.

2. For brownie cookies, combine brownie mix, fudge packet from Mix, egg and water in large bowl. Stir until well blended, about 50 strokes. Shape dough into 50 (1-inch) balls. Place 2 inches apart on prepared cookie sheets. Grease bottom of drinking glass; dip in sugar. Press gently to flatten 1 cookie to ⅜-inch thickness. Repeat with remaining cookies. Bake at 375°F for 6 to 7 minutes or until set. Cool 1 minute on cookie sheets. Remove to cooling racks. Cool completely.

3. For filling, tint frosting with red food coloring, if desired. Stir in chocolate chips.

4. To assemble, spread 1 tablespoon frosting on bottom of one cookie; top with second cookie. Press together to make sandwich cookie. Repeat with remaining cookies.

Makes 25 sandwich cookies

Peanut Butter Critter Cookies

  3 cups all-purpose flour
  1 cup peanut butter chips, melted
  ¾ cup granulated sugar
  ¼ cup packed brown sugar
  1 cup butter, softened
  1 egg
1½ teaspoons milk
  1 teaspoon vanilla
    Powdered sugar
    Prepared icing

1. Combine flour, melted peanut butter chips, granulated sugar, brown sugar, butter, egg, milk and vanilla in large bowl. Beat at low speed of electric mixer 1 to 2 minutes, scraping bowl often, until well mixed. Divide dough in half. Wrap in plastic wrap; chill 1 to 2 hours or until firm.

2. Preheat oven to 375°F. Roll out dough on well-floured surface to ⅛-inch thickness. Cut out desired shapes using 2½-inch cookie cutters. Place 1 inch apart on ungreased cookie sheets. Bake 5 to 8 minutes or until edges are lightly browned. Remove immediately to wire racks; cool completely. Sprinkle with powdered sugar or decorate with icing as desired.

Makes about 4 dozen cookies

Brownie Sandwich Cookies

Puzzle Cookie

¾ **cup shortening**
½ **cup packed light brown sugar**
6 **tablespoons dark molasses**
2 **egg whites**
¾ **teaspoon vanilla**
2¼ **cups all-purpose flour**
2 **teaspoons ground cinnamon**
¾ **teaspoon baking soda**
¾ **teaspoon salt**
¾ **teaspoon ground ginger**
¼ **teaspoon plus** ⅛ **teaspoon baking powder**
   Assorted colored frostings, colored sugars, colored decorator gels and assorted small candies

1. Beat shortening, brown sugar, molasses, egg whites and vanilla in large bowl at high speed of electric mixer until smooth.

2. Combine flour, cinnamon, baking soda, salt, ginger and baking powder in medium bowl. Add to shortening mixture; mix well. Shape dough into flat rectangle. Wrap in plastic wrap and refrigerate about 8 hours or until firm.

3. Preheat oven to 350°F. Lightly grease 15½×10½-inch jelly-roll pan.

4. Sprinkle dough with additional flour. Place dough in center of prepared pan and roll evenly to within ½ inch of edge of pan. Cut shapes into dough, using cookie cutters or free-hand, allowing at least 1 inch between each shape. Cut through dough, but do not remove cookie shapes.

5. Bake 12 minutes or until edges begin to brown lightly. Remove from oven and retrace shapes with knife. Return to oven 5 to 6 minutes. Cool in pan 5 minutes. Carefully remove shapes to wire racks; cool completely.

6. Decorate shapes with frostings, sugars, decorator gels and small candies as desired. Leave puzzle frame in pan. Decorate with frostings, colored sugars and gels to represent sky, clouds, grass and water, if desired. Return shapes to their respective openings to complete puzzle.

Makes 1 puzzle cookie

DECORATE IT!

Making this cookie is a great rainy-day activity for kids! Decorate the cookie like the one in the photo, or use different cookie cutters to create a barnyard scene, zoo scene, or even astronauts in space.

Puzzle Cookie

Peanuts

½ cup butter, softened
¼ cup shortening
¼ cup creamy peanut butter
1 cup powdered sugar, sifted
1 egg yolk
1 teaspoon vanilla
1¾ cups all-purpose flour
1 cup finely ground honey-roasted
    peanuts, divided
    Peanut Buttery Frosting (recipe
    follows)

1. Beat butter, shortening and peanut butter in large bowl at medium speed of electric mixer. Gradually add powdered sugar, beating until smooth. Add egg yolk and vanilla; beat well. Add flour; mix well. Stir in ⅓ cup ground peanuts. Cover dough; refrigerate 1 hour. Prepare Peanut Buttery Frosting.

2. Preheat oven to 350°F. Grease cookie sheets. Shape dough into 1-inch balls. Place 2 balls, side by side and slightly touching, on prepared cookie sheet. Gently flatten balls with fingertips to form into "peanut" shape. Repeat steps with remaining dough.

3. Bake 16 to 18 minutes or until edges are lightly browned. Cool on cookie sheets 5 minutes. Remove cookies to wire racks; cool completely.

4. Place remaining ⅔ cup ground peanuts in shallow dish. Spread about 2 teaspoons Peanut Buttery Frosting evenly over top of each cookie. Coat with ground peanuts.

Makes about 2 dozen cookies

Peanut Buttery Frosting

½ cup butter or margarine, softened
½ cup creamy peanut butter
2 cups powdered sugar, sifted
½ teaspoon vanilla
3 to 6 tablespoons milk

1. Beat butter and peanut butter in medium bowl at medium speed of electric mixer until smooth. Gradually add powdered sugar and vanilla until blended but crumbly.

2. Add milk, 1 tablespoon at a time, until smooth. Refrigerate until ready to use.

Makes 1⅓ cups frosting

HELPFUL HINT

Every kitchen needs a set of measuring spoons (1 tablespoon, 1 teaspoon, ½ teaspoon, ¼ teaspoon and sometimes ⅛ teaspoon). These will accurately measure small amounts of both dry and liquid ingredients.

Ultimate Rocky Road Cups

¾ cup (1½ sticks) butter or margarine
4 squares (1 ounce each) unsweetened
   baking chocolate
1½ cups granulated sugar
3 large eggs
1 cup all-purpose flour
1¾ cups "M&M's"® Chocolate Mini
   Baking Bits
¾ cup coarsely chopped peanuts
1 cup mini marshmallows

Preheat oven to 350°F. Generously grease
24 (2½-inch) muffin cups or line with foil
liners. Place butter and chocolate in large
microwave-safe bowl. Microwave on HIGH
1 minute; stir. Microwave on HIGH an
additional 30 seconds; stir until chocolate is
completely melted. Add sugar and eggs, one
at a time, beating well after each addition;

blend in flour. In separate bowl combine
"M&M's"® Chocolate Mini Baking Bits and
nuts; stir 1 cup baking bits mixture into
brownie batter. Divide batter evenly among
prepared muffin cups. Bake 20 minutes.
Combine remaining baking bits mixture
with marshmallows; divide evenly among
muffin cups, topping hot brownies. Return
to oven; bake 5 minutes longer. Cool
completely before removing from muffin
cups. Store in tightly covered container.

Makes 24 cups

Ultimate Rocky Road Squares: Prepare
recipe as directed, spreading batter into
generously greased 13×9×2-inch baking
pan. Bake 30 minutes. Sprinkle with
topping mixture; bake 5 minutes longer.
Cool completely. Cut into squares. Store in
tightly covered container. Makes 24 squares.

Ultimate Rocky Road Cups

Letters of the Alphabet

**Gingerbread Cookie Dough
(page 553)
Colored frostings and glazes, colored
sugars, sprinkles and assorted
small candies**

1. Prepare Gingerbread Cookie Dough. Cover; refrigerate about 8 hours or until firm.

2. Preheat oven to 350°F. Grease cookie sheets.

3. Divide dough into 4 equal sections. Reserve 1 section; cover and refrigerate remaining 3 sections.

4. Roll reserved dough on well-floured surface to ⅛-inch thickness. Sprinkle with flour to minimize sticking, if necessary.

5. Cut out alphabet letter shapes using 2½-inch cookie cutters. Place cutouts on prepared cookie sheets. Repeat steps with remaining dough.

6. Bake 6 to 8 minutes or until edges begin to brown. Remove cookies to wire racks; cool completely.

7. Decorate cookies with frostings, glazes, colored sugars, sprinkles and assorted small candies.   *Makes about 5 dozen cookies*

Bunch O' Balloons

**1 package (20 ounces) refrigerated
chocolate chip cookie dough
1 tub (8 ounces) COOL WHIP®
Whipped Topping, thawed
Assorted fruits and candies
Decorating gel
Red string licorice**

HEAT oven to 350°F.

SLICE cookie dough evenly into 8 slices. Pat each slice into 5-inch circle on lightly floured surface. Place 2 inches apart on ungreased cookie sheets.

BAKE 10 to 12 minutes or until lightly browned. Remove from cookie sheets. Cool completely on wire racks.

SPREAD whipped topping evenly onto each cookie. Decorate with fruit, candy and gel. Arrange decorated cookies on large serving tray to resemble a bunch of balloons. Place 1 piece of licorice at bottom edge on each cookie to resemble string. Tie strings together with additional licorice. Serve immediately.   *Makes 8 servings*

YOU'RE INVITED TO A PARTY

Under the Sea

**1 package (18 ounces) refrigerated
  sugar cookie dough
Blue liquid or paste food coloring
All-purpose flour (optional)
Royal Icing (page 556)
Assorted small decors, gummy
  candies and hard candies**

1. Preheat oven to 350°F. Grease 12-inch pizza pan.

2. Remove dough from wrapper. Combine dough and blue food coloring, a few drops at a time, in large bowl until desired color is achieved; blend until smooth. Sprinkle dough with flour to minimize sticking, if necessary.

3. Press dough into bottom of prepared pan, leaving about ¾-inch space between edge of dough and pan.

4. Bake 10 to 12 minutes or until set in center. Cool completely in pan on wire rack. Run spatula between cookie crust and pan after 10 to 15 minutes to loosen.

5. Prepare Royal Icing; tint bright blue with food coloring. Spread icing over cookie to resemble wavy sea. Once icing is set, decorate with candies as desired.

Makes 10 to 12 wedges

Domino Cookies

**1 package (20 ounces) refrigerated
  sugar cookie dough
All-purpose flour (optional)
½ cup semisweet chocolate chips**

1. Preheat oven to 350°F. Grease cookie sheets.

2. Remove dough from wrapper. Cut dough into 4 equal sections. Reserve 1 section; refrigerate remaining 3 sections.

3. Roll reserved dough to ⅛-inch thickness. Sprinkle with flour to minimize sticking, if necessary.

4. Cut out 9 (2½×1¾-inch) rectangles using sharp knife. Place 2 inches apart on prepared cookie sheets.

5. Score each cookie across middle with sharp knife.

6. Gently press chocolate chips, point side down, into dough to resemble various dominos. Repeat with remaining dough, scraps and chocolate chips.

7. Bake 8 to 10 minutes or until edges are light golden brown. Remove to wire racks; cool completely.   *Makes 3 dozen cookies*

The Thousand Legged Worm

1 package (20 ounces) refrigerated
    sugar cookie dough
2 containers (16 ounces each)
    chocolate frosting
    Black licorice strings, cut into 3-inch
    pieces
1 marshmallow and coconut covered
    chocolate snack cake
    Miniature round butter cookies and
    assorted chewy candies

1. Preheat oven to 350°F. Grease cookie sheets. Remove dough from wrapper. Cut dough into 30 (½-inch) slices. Place 2 inches apart on prepared cookie sheets.

2. Bake 8 to 10 minutes or until edges are browned. Cool completely on wire racks.

3. Spread bottom of 1 cookie with 1 tablespoon frosting. Top with another cookie, pressing gently. Set aside.

4. Spread bottom of another cookie with frosting, insert 1 piece of licorice into frosting on each side of cookie and attach to reserved sandwich cookie with frosting. Repeat until 6 cookies are sandwiched together with frosting and licorice. Place cookie stack on its side on serving platter. Repeat with remaining cookies, frosting and licorice.

5. Attach snack cake to 1 end of worm using frosting. Decorate with cookies and assorted candies to resemble face.

Makes 1 worm (3 dozen cookies)

Diamond Backs

    Gingerbread Cookie Dough
      (page 553)
2 egg yolks
½ teaspoon water
    Assorted paste food colors

1. Prepare Gingerbread Cookie Dough. Cover; refrigerate about 8 hours or until firm.

2. Combine egg yolks and water in small bowl. Divide egg mixture evenly among small custard cups. Add different food colors to each cup; blend well. Set aside. Preheat oven to 350°F. Grease cookie sheets.

3. Divide dough in half. Reserve 1 half; refrigerate remaining dough. Roll reserved dough into rectangle on floured surface to ¼-inch thickness. Cut dough into squiggly 8×1-inch strips for snake bodies, leaving one end pointed. Carefully transfer to prepared cookie sheets.

4. Reroll scraps to ¼-inch thickness; cut into 1½-inch teardrop shapes for heads.

5. Paint bodies of Diamond Backs as desired using small, clean craft paintbrushes and egg yolk paint.

6. Place teardrop heads on bodies; press gently. Decorate as desired. Repeat with remaining dough.

7. Bake 12 to 13 minutes or until set. Cool on cookie sheets 5 minutes. Remove to wire racks; cool completely.

Makes about 14 cookies

The Thousand Legged Worm

Gingerbread Farm Animals in Corral

**Gingerbread House Dough
  (page 553)**
Royal Icing (page 556)
Assorted food colors
Shredded coconut, tinted green
Assorted small hard candies

SUPPLIES
Cardboard and decorative paper

1. Preheat oven to 375°F. Prepare Gingerbread House Dough. Divide dough into 4 equal pieces. To make fence, roll 1 dough piece on large cookie sheet to ¼-inch thickness. Cut into 6 (6×2¾-inch) sections, leaving ½-inch space between sections. Bake 10 to 12 minutes or until edges are browned. Cool completely.

2. Roll second section of dough directly onto cookie sheet to ¼-inch thickness. Cut into 4 (6×2¾-inch) sections and 2 (3-inch) sections. Bake 10 to 12 minutes or until edges are browned. Cool completely on wire racks.

3. To make animals, roll remaining 2 sections of dough directly on cookie sheets to ⅛-inch thickness. Cut out animal shapes using animal-shaped cookie cutters. Bake 8 to 12 minutes or until edges are browned. Cool completely on wire racks.

4. Prepare 2 recipes Royal Icing. Tint small amounts of icing with food colors to decorate animals. Place remaining icing in small resealable plastic food storage bag. Cut off small corner of bag for piping.

5. Decorate animals and fence sections with icing and assorted candies. Cover 20-inch piece of cardboard with decorative paper and plastic wrap. Assemble fence by piping icing on bottom and side edges of fence sections. Use smaller sections to make 2 gates. Pipe icing on feet of animals; arrange so animals can be supported by fence or other animals. Sprinkle coconut around feet of animals for grass, if desired.

Makes 1 fence and 2 dozen animals

FUN FOOD FACT

Fresh coconuts are available all year, peaking in late autumn. Flaked and shredded sweetened coconut is readily available year-round in plastic bags and cans. Unsweetened dried coconut is usually available at produce markets or Asian markets.

Gingerbread Farm Animals in Corral

Hot Dog Cookies

Butter Cookie Dough (page 552)
Liquid food colors
Sesame seeds
**Shredded coconut, red and green
decorator gels, frosting and
gummy candies**

1. Prepare Butter Cookie Dough. Cover;
refrigerate 4 hours or until firm. Grease
cookie sheets.

2. Reserve ⅓ of dough to make "hot dogs."
Refrigerate remaining dough. Mix food
colors in bowl to get reddish-brown color
following chart on back of food color box.
Mix color throughout reserved dough.

3. Divide colored dough into 6 equal
sections. Roll each section into thin log
shape. Round edges; set aside.

4. To make "buns," divide remaining dough
into 6 equal sections. Roll sections into thick
logs. Make very deep indentation the length
of logs in centers; smooth edges to create
buns. Dip sides of buns in sesame seeds.
Place 3 inches apart on prepared cookie
sheets. Place hot dogs inside buns. Freeze
20 minutes.

5. Preheat oven to 350°F. Bake 17 to
20 minutes or until bun edges are light
golden. Cool completely on cookie sheets.

6. Top hot dogs with green-tinted shredded
coconut for "relish," white coconut for
"onions," red decorator gel for "ketchup"
and yellow-tinted frosting or whipped
topping for "mustard."

Makes 6 hot dog cookies

Go Fish!

½ cup (1 stick) butter, softened
¾ cup granulated sugar
¼ cup firmly packed light brown sugar
1 large egg
1 large egg white
½ teaspoon vanilla extract
2 cups all-purpose flour
1¼ teaspoons ground cinnamon
1 teaspoon baking powder
1 cup white frosting
Assorted food colorings
1 cup "M&M's"® Chocolate Mini
Baking Bits

In large bowl cream butter and sugars until
light and fluffy; beat in egg, egg white and
vanilla. In medium bowl combine flour,
cinnamon and baking powder; add to
creamed mixture. Wrap and refrigerate
dough 2 to 3 hours. Preheat oven to 325°F.
Working with half the dough at a time on
lightly floured surface, roll to ¼-inch
thickness. Cut into fish shapes using 3-inch
cookie cutters. Place about 2 inches apart
on ungreased cookie sheets. Bake 10 to
12 minutes. Cool 2 minutes on cookie
sheets; cool completely on wire racks. Tint
frosting desired colors. Frost cookies and
decorate with "M&M's"® Chocolate Mini
Baking Bits. Store in tightly covered
container. *Makes 2½ dozen cookies*

Hot Dog Cookies

Butter Pretzel Cookies

Butter Cookie Dough (page 552)
White, rainbow or colored rock or
coarse sugar

1. Prepare Butter Cookie Dough. Cover; refrigerate about 4 hours or until firm.

2. Preheat oven to 350°F. Grease cookie sheets.

3. Divide dough into 4 equal sections. Reserve 1 section; refrigerate remaining 3 sections. Divide reserved dough into 4 equal pieces. Shape each dough piece on lightly floured surface to 12-inch rope; sprinkle with rock or coarse sugar.

4. Transfer 1 rope at a time to prepared cookie sheets. Form each rope into pretzel shape. Repeat steps with remaining dough pieces.

5. Bake 14 to 18 minutes or until edges begin to brown. Cool cookies on cookie sheets 1 minute. Remove to wire racks; cool completely. *Makes 16 cookies*

Name Jewelry

Christmas Ornament Cookie Dough
(page 553)
Powdered Sugar Icing (page 556)
Colored sugars
Assorted food colors (optional)
Small candies (optional)

SUPPLIES
Plastic drinking straw
Thin ribbon or yarn

1. Prepare Christmas Ornament Cookie Dough. Divide dough in half; wrap in plastic wrap. Refrigerate 30 minutes or until firm.

2. Preheat oven to 350°F. Grease cookie sheets. Roll ½ of dough on floured surface to ¼-inch thickness. Cut out cookies using 3¾-inch cookie cutters of various shapes.

3. Place cookies on prepared cookie sheets. With plastic straw, make holes in tops of cookies, about ½ inch from top edges.

4. Bake 10 to 12 minutes or until edges begin to brown. Remove cookies to wire racks; cool completely. If necessary, push straw through warm cookies to remake holes.

5. Prepare Powdered Sugar Icing; spread over cookies. Let stand 40 minutes or until set. Spoon colored or additional icing into small resealable plastic food storage bag. Cut tiny tip from corner of bag. Pipe individual names directly onto cookies. Let stand until set. Decorate as desired.

6. Cut ribbon into 18 (32-inch) pieces. Thread ribbon through holes.
Makes about 18 cookie necklaces

Lady Bugs

¾ **cup shortening**
½ **cup sugar**
¼ **cup honey**
 1 **egg**
½ **teaspoon vanilla**
 2 **cups all-purpose flour**
⅓ **cup cornmeal**
 1 **teaspoon baking powder**
½ **teaspoon salt**
   Orange and black icing and yellow candy-coated pieces

1. Beat shortening, sugar and honey in large bowl at medium speed with electric mixer until light and fluffy. Add egg and vanilla; mix until well blended.

2. Combine flour, cornmeal, baking powder and salt in medium bowl. Add to shortening mixture; mix at low speed until blended. Cover; refrigerate several hours or overnight, if desired.

3. Preheat oven to 375°F.

4. Divide dough into 24 equal sections. Shape each section into 2×1¼-inch oval-shaped ball. Place balls 2 inches apart on ungreased cookie sheets.

5. Bake 10 to 12 minutes or until lightly browned. Cool on cookie sheets 2 minutes. Remove to wire rack; cool completely.

6. Decorate cookies with icings and candies to look like lady bugs.

Makes 2 dozen cookies

Lady Bugs

Sunshine Butter Cookies

¾ **cup butter, softened**
¾ **cup sugar**
1 **egg**
2¼ **cups all-purpose flour**
¼ **teaspoon salt**
   Grated peel of ½ lemon
1 **teaspoon frozen lemonade**
    concentrate, thawed
   Lemonade Royal Icing (page 556)
   Thin pretzel sticks
   Yellow paste food color
   Gummy fruit and black licorice
    strings

1. Beat butter and sugar in large bowl at high speed of electric mixer until fluffy. Add egg; beat well.

2. Combine flour, salt and lemon peel in medium bowl. Add to butter mixture. Stir in lemonade concentrate. Refrigerate 2 hours.

3. Prepare Lemonade Royal Icing. Cover; let stand at room temperature. Preheat oven to 350°F. Grease cookie sheets.

4. Roll dough on floured surface to ⅛-inch thickness. Cut out cookies using 3-inch round cookie cutter. Place cookies on prepared cookie sheets. Press pretzel sticks into edges of cookies to resemble sunshine rays; press gently. Bake 10 minutes or until lightly browned. Remove to wire racks; cool completely.

5. Add food color to Lemonade Royal Icing. Spoon about ½ cup icing into resealable plastic food storage bag; seal. Cut tiny tip from corner of bag. Pipe thin circle around underside of each cookie to create outline.

6. Add water, 1 tablespoon at a time, to remaining icing in bowl until thick but pourable consistency. Spoon icing in cookie centers staying within outline.

7. Decorate cookies with gummy fruit and licorice to make "sunny" faces. Let stand 1 hour or until dry.

Makes about 3 dozen cookies

HELPFUL HINT

Thaw frozen concentrate in a flash! If the can has metal ends, make sure small amounts of metal or foil may be used in your microwave. If so, remove one end from the juice can and heat at HIGH 15 to 30 seconds. Allow to stand about 1 minute. Or, remove the concentrate from the can and place in a microwavable bowl before microwaving.

Sunshine Butter Cookies

Caramel Lizard Cookies

½ cup shortening
⅓ cup packed light brown sugar
¼ cup dark molasses
 1 egg white
½ teaspoon vanilla
1½ to 2 cups all-purpose flour
 1 teaspoon ground cinnamon
½ teaspoon baking soda
½ teaspoon salt
½ teaspoon ground ginger
¼ teaspoon baking powder
 1 bag (14 ounces) caramels, unwrapped
 2 tablespoons milk
½ cup walnut chips
    Mini-chocolate chips, granola or mini chocolate candy-coated pieces, chocolate sprinkles
    Red licorice string, cut into ¾-inch pieces

SUPPLIES
  Cardboard

1. Draw pattern for lizard on cardboard, following diagram; cut out pattern.

2. Beat shortening, brown sugar, molasses, egg white and vanilla in large bowl at high speed of electric mixer until smooth.

3. Combine 1½ cups flour, cinnamon, baking soda, salt, ginger and baking powder in small bowl. Add to shortening mixture; mix well. Add additional flour, if needed. Cover; refrigerate about 8 hours or until firm.

4. Preheat oven to 350°F. Grease cookie sheets.

5. Divide dough into 4 equal sections. Reserve 1 section; cover and refrigerate remaining 3 sections. Roll reserved dough into circle on lightly floured surface to ¼-inch thickness.

6. Place sheet of waxed paper over dough. Place pattern over waxed paper. Cut dough with sharp knife; remove pattern and waxed paper. Place cutouts on prepared cookie sheets. Repeat with remaining dough.

7. Bake 9 to 11 minutes or until set. Cool on cookie sheets 5 minutes. Remove to wire racks; cool completely.

8. Melt caramels and milk in small saucepan over low heat, stirring frequently, until smooth. Keep saucepan over very low heat while decorating cookies.

9. Place cookies on sheet of waxed paper. Spread melted caramel evenly over top of lizards; sprinkle with walnuts. Decorate as desired.   *Makes about 20 cookies*

Caramel Lizard Cookies

Bird's Nest Cookies

1⅓ cups (3½ ounces) flaked coconut
1 cup (2 sticks) butter or margarine,
   softened
½ cup granulated sugar
1 large egg
½ teaspoon vanilla extract
2 cups all-purpose flour
¾ teaspoon salt
1¾ cups "M&M's"® Semi-Sweet
   Chocolate Mini Baking Bits,
   divided

Preheat oven to 300°F. Spread coconut on ungreased cookie sheet. Toast in oven, stirring until coconut just begins to turn light golden, about 25 minutes. Remove coconut from cookie sheet; set aside. Increase oven temperature to 350°F. In large bowl cream butter and sugar until light and fluffy; beat in egg and vanilla. In medium bowl combine flour and salt; blend into creamed mixture. Stir in 1 cup "M&M's"® Semi-Sweet Chocolate Mini Baking Bits. Form dough into 1¼-inch balls. Roll heavily in toasted coconut. Place 2 inches apart on lightly greased cookie sheets. Make indentation in center of each cookie with thumb. Bake 12 to 14 minutes or until coconut is golden brown. Remove cookies to wire racks; immediately fill indentations with remaining "M&M's"® Semi-Sweet Chocolate Mini Baking Bits, using scant teaspoonful for each cookie. Cool completely.

Makes about 3 dozen cookies

Baseball Caps

1 cup butter, softened
7 ounces almond paste
¾ cup sugar
1 egg
1 teaspoon vanilla
¼ teaspoon salt
3 cups all-purpose flour
   Assorted colored icings and colored
   candies

1. Preheat oven to 350°F. Grease cookie sheets. Beat butter, almond paste, sugar, egg, vanilla and salt in large bowl at high speed of electric mixer until light and fluffy. Add flour all at once; stir just to combine.

2. Roll ¼ of dough on lightly floured surface to ⅛-inch thickness. Cut out 1-inch circles. Place cutouts 2 inches apart on prepared cookie sheets.

3. Shape remaining dough into 1-inch balls.* Place one ball on top of half dough circle so about ½ inch of circle sticks out to form bill of baseball cap. Repeat with remaining dough balls and circles.

4. Bake 10 to 12 minutes or until lightly browned. If bills brown too quickly, cut small strips of foil and cover with shiny side of foil facing up. Let cool on cookie sheets 2 minutes. Remove to wire racks; cool completely. Decorate with icings and candies as desired.

Makes about 3 dozen cookies

Use a 1-tablespoon scoop to keep the baseball caps uniform in size.

Bird's Nest Cookies

Celebration COOKIES

Conversation Heart Cereal Treats

2 tablespoons margarine or butter
20 large marshmallows
3 cups frosted oat cereal with marshmallow bits
12 large conversation hearts

1. Line 8- or 9-inch square pan with aluminum foil, leaving 2-inch overhangs on 2 sides. Generously grease or spray with nonstick cooking spray.

2. Melt margarine and marshmallows in medium saucepan over medium heat 3 minutes or until melted and smooth; stir constantly. Remove from heat.

3. Add cereal; stir until completely coated. Spread in prepared pan; press evenly onto bottom using greased rubber spatula. Press heart candies into top of treats while still warm, evenly spacing to allow 1 heart per bar. Let cool 10 minutes. Using foil overhangs as handles, remove treats from pan. Cut into 12 bars.

Makes 12 bars

Prep and Cook Time: 18 minutes

Conversation Heart Cereal Treats

Strawberry Hearts

1 package (17 to 18 ounces)
    refrigerated sugar cookie dough
2 packages (8 ounces each) cream
    cheese, softened
⅔ cup powdered sugar
1 teaspoon vanilla
2 cups sliced fresh strawberries

Remove dough from wrapper. Roll out dough, cut out hearts and bake as directed on package.

Combine cream cheese, powdered sugar and vanilla; mix well.

Spread evenly onto cooled hearts; top evenly with strawberries.

Makes about 2 dozen cookies

HELPFUL HINT

When you buy fresh strawberries, choose fruit that is fresh, clean and bright red, with green caps attached. Strawberries should be stored in the refrigerator, caps attached, until ready to use. Rinse gently just before preparing, and use fresh strawberries as soon as possible for maximum freshness.

Sweets-for-the-Sweet Brownies

6 tablespoons margarine
½ cup unsweetened cocoa
¼ cup *plus* 2 tablespoons plain nonfat
    yogurt
1 cup sugar
2 egg whites *or* 1 egg
½ cup all-purpose flour
1 teaspoon vanilla extract
1 cup miniature marshmallows
1 cup "M&M's"® Milk Chocolate or
    "M&M's"® HOLIDAYS® Milk
    Chocolate Candies (Valentine's)
¼ cup unsalted dry roasted mixed nuts

Preheat oven to 350°F. Grease 8-inch square baking pan; set aside. In medium heavy-gauge saucepan over medium-low heat, melt margarine. Stir in cocoa until smooth. Remove from heat; stir in yogurt, sugar, egg whites, flour and vanilla extract until smooth.

Spread batter evenly in prepared pan. Bake 20 to 25 minutes or until center feels dry. Remove from oven. Sprinkle top with marshmallows. Return to oven 3 to 4 minutes or until marshmallows are puffed, but not brown. Remove from oven and immediately sprinkle "M&M's"® Candies and nuts over top. Press into marshmallows; cool completely before cutting. Cut into squares.

Makes about 12 brownies

Valentine's Day Cookie Cards

Butter Cookie Dough (page 552)
1 container (16 ounces) vanilla frosting
1 container (16 ounces) pink cherry-flavored frosting
Assorted candies

SUPPLIES
Pastry bags and decorating tips

1. Prepare Butter Cookie Dough.

2. Preheat oven to 350°F. Grease cookie sheets.

3. On lightly floured surface, roll out dough to ⅛-inch thickness. Cut into desired shapes with cookie cutters. Place on prepared cookie sheets.

4. Bake 8 to 10 minutes or until edges are lightly browned. Remove to wire racks; cool completely.

5. Spread cookies with desired frostings; spoon remaining frostings into pastry bags fitted with decorating tips. Decorate cookies with frostings and candies as desired to resemble Valentine's Day cards.

Makes 1 dozen cookies

Valentine's Day Cookie Cards

Cookie Decorating Party

1 can (16 ounces) strawberry frosting, at room temperature
48 vanilla wafers or sugar cookies
¼ to ½ pound assorted Valentine candies, such as cinnamon hearts, conversation hearts, chocolate candies, red hots and heart-shaped sprinkles

1. Stir frosting in can until soft and creamy. Divide frosting evenly among small paper cups to equal one paper cup per child.

2. Give each child an equal number of cookies, one paper cup of frosting and assortment of candies. Have children dip cookies into frosting or spread frosting with backs of spoons. Decorate with candies or sprinkles as desired.

Makes 4 dozen cookies

Prep and Cook Time: 10 minutes

Chocolate and Peanut Butter Hearts

Chocolate Cookie Dough (page 552)
½ cup creamy peanut butter
½ cup shortening
1 cup sugar
1 egg
3 tablespoons milk
1 teaspoon vanilla
2 cups all-purpose flour
1 teaspoon baking powder
¼ teaspoon salt

1. Prepare Chocolate Cookie Dough. Divide dough in half; wrap in plastic wrap. Chill about 2 hours or until firm. Beat peanut butter, shortening and sugar until fluffy. Add egg, milk and vanilla; mix until blended. Mix flour, baking powder and salt in bowl. Add flour mixture to peanut butter mixture until well blended. Divide dough in half; wrap in plastic wrap. Chill 1 to 2 hours or until firm.

2. Preheat oven to 350°F. Grease cookie sheets. Roll ½ of peanut butter dough on floured waxed paper to ⅛-inch thickness. Cut dough using 3-inch heart-shaped cookie cutter. Place on prepared cookie sheets.

3. Use smaller heart-shaped cookie cutter to remove small section from center of hearts; set aside. Repeat with chocolate dough.

4. Place small peanut butter hearts into large chocolate hearts; place small chocolate hearts into large peanut butter hearts. Press together lightly. Bake 12 to 14 minutes or until edges are browned. Remove to wire racks; cool.

Makes 4 dozen cookies

Cookie Decorating Party

Shamrock Ice Cream Sandwiches

Butter Cookie Dough (page 552)
3 or 4 drops green food color
1 pint ice cream or frozen yogurt, any flavor

1. Prepare Butter Cookie Dough; mix in food color. Cover; refrigerate until firm, about 4 hours or overnight.

2. Preheat oven to 350°F.

3. Roll dough on lightly floured surface to ¼-inch thickness. Cut out cookies using 3½- to 5-inch shamrock-shaped cookie cutter. Place on ungreased cookie sheets.

4. Bake 8 to 10 minutes or until cookies are lightly browned around edges. Remove cookies to wire racks; cool completely.

5. Remove ice cream from freezer; let stand at room temperature to soften slightly, about 10 minutes. Spread 4 to 5 tablespoons ice cream onto flat sides of half the cookies. Place remaining cookies, flat sides down, on ice cream; press cookies together lightly.

6. Wrap each sandwich in foil; freeze until firm, about 2 hours or overnight.

Makes 6 to 8 sandwich cookies

Valentine Ice Cream Sandwiches: Prepare and chill cookie dough as directed, substituting red food color for green food color. Cut out cookies with heart-shaped cookie cutter. Continue as directed.

Patriotic Ice Cream Sandwiches: Prepare and chill cookie dough as directed, substituting red food color for green food color. Cut out cookies with star-shaped cookie cutter. Continue as directed.

Pumpkin Ice Cream Sandwiches: Prepare and chill cookie dough as directed, substituting orange food color for green food color. Cut out cookies with pumpkin-shaped cookie cutter. Continue as directed.

Christmas Tree Ice Cream Sandwiches: Prepare, tint and chill cookie dough as directed. Cut out cookies with Christmas tree-shaped cookie cutter. Continue as directed.

Shamrock Ice Cream Sandwiches

Minty Chocolate Shamrock Cookies

¾ cup (1½ sticks) butter or margarine, softened
1 cup sugar
¼ cup light corn syrup
1 egg
1 teaspoon vanilla extract
2 HERSHEY®S Cookies 'n' Mint Chocolate Bars (7 ounces *each*), broken into pieces
2 cups all-purpose flour
¼ cup HERSHEY®S Cocoa
2 teaspoons baking soda
¼ teaspoon salt
Green decorating icing (optional)

1. Beat butter and sugar in large bowl until creamy. Add corn syrup, egg and vanilla; beat until well blended. In medium microwave-safe bowl, place chocolate bar pieces. Microwave at HIGH (100%) 1 to 1½ minutes or until chocolate is melted when stirred. Stir into butter mixture. Stir together flour, cocoa, baking soda and salt; gradually add to chocolate mixture, blending well. Cover; refrigerate dough 1 hour or until firm enough to handle.

2. Heat oven to 350°F.

3. For each shamrock cookie, shape dough into three ½-inch balls. Place in triangular position on ungreased cookie sheet with approximately ¼ inch between balls. Using slightly smaller ball, form 1½-inch stem; add to base of cookie.

4. Bake 8 to 10 minutes or until set around edges. Cool slightly; remove from cookie sheet to wire rack. Cool completely. Pipe decorating icing around edges of cookie, if desired.

Makes about 8 dozen 2-inch cookies

Minty Chocolate Slice 'n' Bake Cookies: Prepare dough as directed. Shape into two rolls, each 2 inches in diameter. Wrap both rolls in wax paper or plastic wrap; refrigerate until firm enough to slice. Cut rolls into ¼-inch-thick slices; place 2 inches apart on ungreased cookie sheet. Bake and cool as directed.

FUN FOOD FACT

Corn syrup is a thick, sweet and highly refined liquid made by treating cornstarch with acids and enzymes that cause it to liquefy. Both light and dark corn syrups are available. Light syrups are clear; whereas, dark syrups have an amber color and a subtle taste.

Frosted Easter Cut-Outs

COOKIES
1¼ cups granulated sugar
  1 Butter Flavor* CRISCO® Stick or
    1 cup Butter Flavor CRISCO®
    all-vegetable shortening
  2 eggs
¼ cup light corn syrup or regular
    pancake syrup
  1 tablespoon vanilla extract
  3 cups plus 4 tablespoons all-purpose
    flour, divided
¾ teaspoon baking powder
½ teaspoon baking soda
½ teaspoon salt

ICING
  1 cup confectioners' sugar
  2 tablespoons milk
  Food color (optional)
  Decorating icing

Butter Flavor Crisco is artificially flavored.

1. Place sugar and 1 cup shortening in large bowl. Beat at medium speed of electric mixer until well blended. Add eggs, syrup and vanilla; beat until well blended and fluffy.

2. Combine 3 cups flour, baking powder, baking soda and salt. Add gradually to shortening mixture, beating at low speed until well blended.

3. Divide dough into 4 equal pieces; shape each into disk. Wrap with plastic wrap. Refrigerate 1 hour or until firm.

4. Heat oven to 375°F. Place sheets of foil on countertop for cooling cookies.

5. Sprinkle about 1 tablespoon flour on large sheet of waxed paper. Place disk of dough on floured paper; flatten slightly with hands. Turn dough over; cover with another large sheet of waxed paper. Roll dough to ¼-inch thickness. Remove top sheet of waxed paper. Cut into desired shapes with floured cookie cutter. Place 2 inches apart on ungreased baking sheet. Repeat with remaining dough.

6. Bake one baking sheet at a time at 375°F for 5 to 7 minutes or until edges of cookies are lightly browned. *Do not overbake.* Cool 2 minutes on baking sheet. Remove cookies to foil to cool completely.

7. For icing, combine confectioners' sugar and milk; stir until smooth. Add food color, if desired. Stir until blended. Spread icing on cookies; place on foil until icing is set. Decorate as desired with decorating icing.

Makes about 3½ dozen cookies

Easter Egg Cookies

**1 package DUNCAN HINES® Golden
    Sugar Cookie Mix**
1 egg
    Assorted colored decors
    Corn syrup
    Food coloring

1. Preheat oven to 375°F.

2. Combine cookie mix, contents of buttery flavor packet from Mix and egg in large bowl. Stir with wooden spoon until thoroughly blended.

3. Place 1 level measuring teaspoonful dough on ungreased baking sheet about 2 inches apart for each cookie. Flatten dough into egg shape (an oval with one narrow end and one wide end). Decorate half the eggs with assorted decors. Press lightly into cookie dough. Bake at 375°F for 6 to 7 minutes or until cookies are light golden brown around edges. Cool 1 minute on baking sheets. Remove to cooling racks. Cool completely.

4. To decorate plain cookies, combine 1 tablespoon corn syrup and 1 or 2 drops food coloring in small bowl for each color. Stir to blend. Paint designs with tinted corn syrup using clean artist paint brushes. Sprinkle painted areas with colored decors, if desired. Store between layers of waxed paper in airtight container.

Makes 4 dozen cookies

Tip: For more even baking, keep cookie dough at an even thickness when shaping.

Festive Easter Cookies

1 cup butter, softened
2 cups powdered sugar
1 egg
2 teaspoons grated lemon peel
1 teaspoon vanilla
3 cups all-purpose flour
½ teaspoon salt
    Royal Icing (page 556)
    Assorted food colors
    Assorted sprinkles and candies

1. Beat butter and powdered sugar in large bowl at high speed of electric mixer until fluffy. Add egg, lemon peel and vanilla; mix well. Combine flour and salt in medium bowl. Add to butter mixture; mix well.

2. Divide dough in half. Wrap each half with plastic wrap. Refrigerate 3 hours or overnight.

3. Preheat oven to 375°F. Roll dough on floured surface to ⅛-inch thickness. Cut out dough using Easter cookie cutters, such as eggs, bunnies and tulips. Place cutouts on ungreased cookie sheets.

4. Bake 8 to 12 minutes or just until edges are very lightly browned. Remove to wire racks; cool completely. Prepare Royal Icing; tint with food colors as desired. Decorate with sprinkles and candies.

Makes 4 dozen cookies

Easter Egg Cookies

Giant Easter Egg Cookies

2 cups (4 sticks) butter or margarine, softened
½ cup granulated sugar
½ cup firmly packed light brown sugar
1 large egg
1 teaspoon vanilla extract
3½ cups all-purpose flour
½ teaspoon salt
1 cup chopped pecans
1¾ cups "M&M's"® Semi-Sweet Chocolate Mini Baking Bits, divided
Decorating icing in tubes

Preheat oven to 375°F. In large bowl cream butter and sugars until light and fluffy; beat in egg and vanilla. In medium bowl combine flour and salt; blend into creamed mixture. Stir in nuts and 1¼ cups "M&M's"® Semi-Sweet Chocolate Mini Baking Bits. Drop by ¼ cupfuls about 4 inches apart onto lightly greased cookie sheets; flatten each into egg shape about 4×2¾ inches. Bake 11 to 13 minutes or until lightly browned. Carefully remove to wire racks to cool completely. Decorate with icing and remaining ½ cup "M&M's"® Semi-Sweet Chocolate Mini Baking Bits. Store in tightly covered container.

Makes about 2½ dozen cookies

Grand Old Flag Cookie

1 package (18 ounces) refrigerated sugar cookie dough
1 container (16 ounces) vanilla frosting
Blue food color
50 white chocolate chips
3 red chewy fruit snack rolls, divided
2 pretzel rods

SUPPLIES
1 (15×10-inch) cake board, covered, or large platter

1. Preheat oven to 350°F. Grease 13×9-inch baking pan. Press dough evenly onto bottom of pan. Bake 15 to 18 minutes or until lightly browned. Cool in pan on wire rack 15 minutes. Remove cookie from pan to rack; cool completely.

2. Place cookie on prepared cake board. Tint ½ cup frosting blue. Spread blue frosting in 4-inch square in top left corner of cookie as background for stars. Frost remaining cookie with remaining white frosting.

3. Arrange white chocolate chips for stars, alternating 5 rows of 6 stars each with 4 rows of 5 stars each.

4. For stripes, cut fruit rolls into 3 (9-inch) strips and 4 (13-inch) strips; place on cookie. Wrap pretzel rods with remaining fruit roll lengths; place next to cookie for flag pole.

Makes 10 to 12 servings

Grand Old Flag Cookie

Pumpkin Face Surprise Cookies

⅔ cup butter or margarine, softened
¾ cup sugar
1 egg
1 teaspoon vanilla extract
2 cups all-purpose flour
⅓ cup HERSHEY'S Cocoa
1½ teaspoons baking powder
1 tablespoon milk
1 HERSHEY'S SYMPHONY® Milk
    Chocolate Bar (7 ounces)
    Orange decorating frosting

1. Beat butter, sugar, egg and vanilla in large bowl until fluffy. Stir together flour, cocoa and baking powder; add alternately with milk to butter mixture, beating well after each addition. Divide dough into quarters. Shape each quarter into ball; flatten. Wrap individually in plastic wrap. Refrigerate dough 1 to 2 hours or until firm enough to handle. Break milk chocolate bar into pieces on scored lines; cut each piece in half.

2. Heat oven to 350°F.

3. Working with one portion of dough at a time on floured surface, roll to about ⅛-inch thickness. Using 2-inch round cookie cutter, cut dough into even number of rounds. Place half the rounds on ungreased cookie sheet. Place one chocolate piece in center of each round. Place remaining rounds on top. Using tines of fork, seal edges.

4. Bake 8 minutes or until set. Remove from cookie sheet to wire rack. Cool. With frosting, decorate tops of cookies to make pumpkin faces. *Makes about 40 cookies*

Ghostly Delights

1 package (18 ounces) refrigerated
    cookie dough, any flavor
1 cup prepared vanilla frosting
¾ cup marshmallow creme
32 chocolate chips for decoration

1. Preheat oven to 350°F. Using about 1 tablespoon dough for body and about 1 teaspoon dough for head, form cookie dough into ghost shapes on greased cookie sheets. Bake 10 to 11 minutes or until browned. Cool 1 minute on cookie sheet; place warm cookies on serving plates.

2. While cookies are baking, combine frosting and marshmallow creme in small bowl until well blended.

3. Frost each ghost with frosting mixture. Press 2 chocolate chips, points up, into frosting mixture to make eyes on each ghost. Decorate with additional candy, if desired.
Makes 16 servings

Prep and Cook Time: 25 minutes

HELPFUL HINT

Make a quick and tasty fruit dip with leftover marshmallow creme. Simply mix half of a 7-ounce jar of marshmallow creme with 3 ounces of softened cream cheese. Serve with assorted fresh fruit.

Trick or Treat Ice Cream Sandwiches

½ cup margarine, softened
¾ cup granulated sugar
¾ cup packed light brown sugar
3 egg whites
1 teaspoon vanilla
2½ cups all-purpose flour
1½ teaspoons baking soda
1 teaspoon ground cinnamon
½ teaspoon salt
1 package (6 ounces) semisweet
   chocolate chips
1½ cups orange sherbet or any flavor
   nonfat frozen yogurt or ice cream,
   slightly softened

1. Preheat oven to 350°F. Grease baking sheets; set aside.

2. Beat margarine in large bowl until creamy. Add sugars; beat until fluffy. Blend in egg whites and vanilla. Combine flour, baking soda, cinnamon and salt in medium bowl. Add to margarine mixture; mix until well blended. Stir in chocolate chips.

3. Drop cookie dough by heaping teaspoonfuls onto prepared baking sheets, making 48 cookies. Bake until cookies are lightly browned, 10 to 12 minutes. Remove to wire racks to cool completely.

4. For each sandwich, place 1 tablespoon sherbet on flat side of 1 cookie; top with second cookie, flat side down. Press cookies together gently to even out sherbet layer. Repeat with remaining cookies and sherbet. Wrap tightly and store in freezer.

Makes 2 dozen sandwich cookies

Goblin Ice Cream Sandwiches: Prepare and freeze cookie sandwiches as directed. Just before serving, decorate 1 side of sandwich with Halloween candies or decorating gel to resemble goblin faces.

Colossal Cookie Sandwich: Prepare dough as directed. Substitute 2 lightly greased aluminum foil-lined 12-inch pizza pans for baking sheets. Substitute 1 quart (4 cups) frozen yogurt or ice cream for 1½ cups orange sherbet. Prepare cookie dough as directed; divide evenly in half. Spread each half evenly onto bottom of prepared pizza pan to within ½ inch of outer edge. Bake until cookies are lightly browned, 10 to 15 minutes. Cool cookies in pans just until cookies begin to firm; slide off pans onto wire racks to cool completely. Spoon yogurt onto flat side of 1 cookie. Top with remaining cookie, flat side down. Freeze until yogurt is firm, about 6 hours. Cut into wedges to serve. Makes 24 servings.

Sharing Cookies: Prepare dough as directed. Omit sherbet. Bake cookies on pizza pans as directed for Colossal Cookie Sandwich; cool completely. Serve cookies whole on large platters, allowing each person to break off their own piece. Makes 24 servings.

Pumpkin Candy Brownies

**1 package DUNCAN HINES®
Chocolate Lovers Double Fudge
Brownie Mix**
2 eggs
⅓ cup water
¼ cup vegetable oil
**1 cup DUNCAN HINES® Chocolate
Frosting**
26 pumpkin candies
**½ cup DUNCAN HINES® Vanilla
Frosting
Green food coloring**

1. Preheat oven to 350°F. Line 26 (2-inch) muffin cups with foil liners or place on baking sheets.

2. Combine brownie mix, contents of fudge packet from Mix, eggs, water and oil in large bowl. Stir until well blended, about 50 strokes. Fill each foil liner with 2 level measuring tablespoons batter. Bake 15 to 17 minutes or until firm. Cool 5 to 10 minutes in pans. Remove to wire racks.

3. Place Chocolate frosting in saucepan. Melt on low heat, stirring constantly. Frost top of 1 warm brownie with generous ½ teaspoonful melted frosting. Top with 1 pumpkin candy; push down slightly. Repeat for remaining brownies. Cool completely.

4. Tint Vanilla frosting with green food coloring. Place in decorating bag fitted with small leaf tip. Pipe 3 leaves around each pumpkin candy. Use small writing tip to pipe vines. ***Makes 26 brownies***

Spooky Ghost Cookies

Butter Cookie dough (page 552)
**Fluffy White Frosting (recipe
follows)**
**½ cup semisweet chocolate chips
(about 60 chips)**

1. Prepare Butter Cookie Dough.

2. Preheat oven to 350°F. Roll dough on floured surface to ¼-inch thickness. Cut out ghost shapes.

3. Bake on ungreased cookie sheets 10 to 12 minutes or until edges begin to brown. Remove to wire racks; cool completely.

4. Prepare Fluffy White Frosting. Spread frosting over cookies, swirling to give ghostly appearance. Position 2 chocolate chips on each cookie for eyes.
Makes about 2½ dozen cookies

Fluffy White Frosting: Mix 1 (16-ounce) container vanilla frosting and ¾ cup marshmallow creme in medium bowl; mix well. Makes about 2 cups frosting.

Pumpkin Candy Brownies

Tombstone Brownies

1 package (21.5 ounces) brownie mix
    plus ingredients to prepare mix
1 cup chocolate fudge frosting (about
    ½ of 16-ounce container)
2 milk chocolate candy bars
    (1.55 ounces each)
    Creamy Decorator's Frosting
    (page 554)
¾ cup flaked coconut, tinted green
12 pumpkin candies

1. Preheat oven to 350°F. Line 13×9-inch baking pan with foil, extending foil beyond edges of pan; grease foil.

2. Prepare brownie mix according to package directions. Spread in prepared pan. Bake 30 to 35 minutes. Do not overbake. Cool in pan on wire rack.

3. Using foil as handles, remove brownies from pan; peel off foil. Frost with chocolate frosting. Cut brownies into twelve 4×2-inch bars.

4. Break chocolate bars into pieces along scored lines. Using Creamy Decorator's Frosting, write "R.I.P." on chocolate pieces. Let stand until set.

5. Press 1 chocolate piece into end of each brownie to make tombstone.

6. Sprinkle tinted coconut on each brownie for grass. Place 1 pumpkin candy on coconut.

Makes 12 servings

Grape Jack-O'-Lantern Cookies

¾ cup dark molasses
¾ cup packed brown sugar
¼ cup water
3 tablespoons butter, softened
3 cups all-purpose flour
1 teaspoon baking soda
1 teaspoon ground ginger
½ teaspoon salt
½ teaspoon ground allspice
½ teaspoon ground cinnamon
¼ teaspoon ground cloves
    Orange Icing (recipe follows)
2 cups California seedless grapes

Mix molasses, sugar, water and butter in large bowl; mix well. Mix flour, baking soda, ginger, salt, allspice, cinnamon and cloves in medium bowl; mix well. Add to molasses mixture. Cover and refrigerate 2 hours or longer. Roll dough ⅛ to ¼ inch thick on floured surface. Cut dough into pumpkin shapes, 4½ to 5 inches in diameter. Place on lightly greased cookie sheet. Bake in preheated 350°F oven 10 to 12 minutes or until firm when lightly touched. Cool. Ice with Orange Icing and decorate with grapes.

Makes 18 to 20 large cookies

Orange Icing: Beat 6 cups powdered sugar and about ⅓ cup orange juice until smooth and of spreading consistency. Tint with 9 drops yellow food color and 10 drops red food color or to desired orange color. Makes about 1⅔ cups.

Favorite recipe from **California Table Grape Commission**

Skull & Cross Bones

1 package (21.5 ounces) brownie mix
    plus ingredients to prepare mix
1 egg white
⅛ teaspoon almond extract (optional)
¼ cup sugar
    Red and black decorator gel
1 container (16 ounces) chocolate
    frosting

SUPPLIES
    Parchment paper
    Pastry bag with medium writing tip

• Prepare and bake brownies in 13×9-inch baking pan according to package directions. Cool completely.

• Preheat oven to 250°F. Line baking sheet with parchment paper; set aside.

• Beat egg white in large bowl until foamy. Add almond extract, if desired; beat until soft peaks form. Gradually add sugar; beat until stiff peaks form.

• Fill pastry bag with egg white mixture. Pipe 24 skull and cross bones shapes onto prepared baking sheet. Bake about 12 minutes or until very lightly browned and set. Cool on pan on wire rack. Carefully remove meringues from parchment paper. Decorate with red gel for eyes and black gel for mouths.

• Frost brownies and cut into 24 rectangles. Place one meringue on each brownie.

Makes 2 dozen brownies

Skull & Cross Bones

Creepy Cookie Cauldrons

1 package (18 ounces) refrigerated chocolate cookie dough*
All-purpose flour
1 bag (14 ounces) caramels, unwrapped
2 tablespoons milk
1 cup crisp rice cereal
¼ cup mini candy-coated chocolate pieces
Black licorice whips and small gummy insects, frogs or lizards

If refrigerated chocolate cookie dough is unavailable, add ¼ cup unsweetened cocoa powder to refrigerated sugar cookie dough. Beat in large bowl until well blended.

• Grease 36 (1¾-inch) mini muffin cups. Remove dough from wrapper. Sprinkle dough with flour to minimize sticking, if necessary.

• Cut dough into 36 equal pieces; roll into balls. Place 1 ball in bottom of each muffin cup. Press dough on bottoms and up sides of muffin cups; chill 15 minutes. Preheat oven to 350°F.

• Bake 8 to 9 minutes. (Cookies will be puffy.) Remove from oven; gently press down center of each cookie. Return to oven 1 minute. Cool cookies in muffin cups 5 minutes. Remove to wire racks; cool completely.

• Melt caramels and milk in small saucepan over low heat, stirring frequently until smooth. Stir in cereal. Spoon 1 heaping teaspoon caramel mixture into each cookie cup. Immediately sprinkle with mini chocolate pieces.

• Cut licorice whips into 4½-inch lengths. For each cookie, make small slit in side; insert end of licorice strip. Repeat on other side of cookie to make cauldron handle. Decorate with gummy creatures.

Makes 3 dozen cookies

DECORATE IT!

Set a creepy table for your Halloween party! For each guest, roll up a paper napkin and use a plastic spider ring as a napkin ring.

Creepy Cookie Cauldrons

Coffin Cookies

**1 package (18 ounces) refrigerated
chocolate cookie dough***
Marshmallow Filling (recipe follows)
**Colored sprinkles and sugars,
prepared white icing and
Halloween decors**

**If refrigerated chocolate cookie dough is unavailable,
add ¼ cup unsweetened cocoa powder to refrigerated
sugar cookie dough. Beat in large bowl until well blended.*

• Draw pattern for coffin on cardboard
following diagram; cut out pattern.

• Preheat oven to 350°F. Remove dough
from wrapper. Divide dough in half. Reserve
1 half; cover and refrigerate remaining half.

• Roll reserved dough on lightly floured
surface to ⅛-inch thickness. Sprinkle with
flour to minimize sticking, if necessary. Place
pattern on cookie dough; cut dough around
pattern with sharp knife. Repeat as
necessary. Place cookies 2 inches apart on
ungreased baking sheets. Repeat with
remaining dough and scraps.

• Bake about 6 minutes or until firm but not
browned. Cool on baking sheets 2 minutes.
Remove to wire racks; cool completely.

• Prepare Marshmallow Filling. Spread half
of cookies with 2 teaspoons filling each; top
with remaining cookies. Roll cookie
sandwich edges in sprinkles. Decorate with
icing and assorted decors as desired.
Makes about 2 dozen sandwich cookies

Marshmallow Filling

1 cup prepared vanilla frosting
¾ cup marshmallow creme

• Combine frosting and marshmallow creme
in small bowl until well blended.

Coffin Cookies

Jumbo Jack-O'-Lantern Brownie

¾ cup (1½ sticks) butter or margarine, melted

1½ cups sugar

1½ teaspoons vanilla extract

3 eggs

¾ cup all-purpose flour

½ cup HERSHEY₀S Cocoa

½ teaspoon baking powder

¼ teaspoon salt

   Orange Buttercream Frosting (recipe follows)

   Decorating icing or gel and assorted candies

1. Heat oven to 350°F. Line 12-inch pizza pan with foil; grease foil.

2. Stir together butter, sugar and vanilla in medium bowl. Add eggs; with spoon, beat well. Stir together flour, cocoa, baking powder and salt; gradually add to egg mixture, stirring until well blended. Spread batter into prepared pan.

3. Bake 20 to 22 minutes or until top springs back when touched lightly in center. Cool completely in pan on wire rack.

4. Remove brownie from pan; peel off foil. Prepare Orange Buttercream Frosting; spread over top of brownie. Garnish as desired with decorating icing and candies to resemble jack-o'-lantern face.

Makes 12 to 15 servings

Orange Buttercream Frosting

3 tablespoons butter or margarine, softened

2 cups powdered sugar

2 tablespoons milk

½ teaspoon vanilla extract

   Red and yellow food colors

Beat butter in small bowl until creamy. Gradually add powdered sugar, milk and vanilla, beating until smooth and of spreading consistency. Add additional milk, 1 teaspoon at a time, if needed. Stir in food colors for desired orange color.

HELPFUL HINT

Measuring cups are specialized tools needed for accurate measuring of dry ingredients and liquid ingredients. You will need a set of four metal or plastic dry measures (1 cup, ½ cup, ⅓ cup and ¼ cup) to measure ingredients such as flour, sugar, nuts and raisins. Clear glass cups with calibrations marked on their sides are needed to measure liquids. An ideal set includes 1-cup, 2-cup and 4-cup measures.

Candy Corn Cookies

Butter Cookie Dough (page 552)
Cookie Glaze (page 555)
Yellow and orange food colors

1. Prepare Butter Cookie Dough.

2. Preheat oven to 350°F. Roll dough on floured surface to ¼-inch thickness. Cut out 3-inch candy corn shapes. Place cutouts on ungreased cookie sheets.

3. Bake 8 to 10 minutes or until edges are lightly browned. Remove to wire racks to cool completely. Prepare Cookie Glaze.

4. Place racks over waxed-paper-lined baking sheets. Divide Cookie Glaze into thirds; place in separate small bowls. Color ⅓ glaze with yellow food color and ⅓ with orange food color. Leave remaining glaze white. Spoon glazes over cookies to resemble "candy corn." Let stand until glaze is set. ***Makes about 2 dozen cookies***

Bat Cookies: Omit yellow and orange food colors. Prepare recipe as directed except use bat cookie cutter to cut out dough. Bake as directed. Tint glaze with black paste food color; spoon over cookies. Decorate with assorted candies to resemble bats.

Left to right: Candy Corn Cookies and Bat Cookie

Black Cat Cookies

**1 package (18 ounces) refrigerated
  sugar cookie dough
White Decorator Frosting (page 555)
Black paste food coloring
Assorted colored candies**

1. Preheat oven to 350°F. Remove dough from wrapper. Divide dough in half. Reserve 1 half; cover and refrigerate remaining half.

2. Roll reserved dough on lightly floured surface to ⅛-inch thickness. Sprinkle with flour to minimize sticking, if necessary.

3. Cut out dough using 3½-inch cat face cookie cutter. Place cutouts 2 inches apart on ungreased baking sheets. Repeat with remaining dough and scraps.

4. Bake 8 to 10 minutes or until firm but not browned. Cool on baking sheets 2 minutes. Remove to wire racks; cool completely.

5. Prepare White Decorator Frosting. Add desired amount of food coloring to make black. Decorate cookies with icing and assorted candies to make cat faces.

Makes about 20 cookies

Ginger Pumpkin Face Cookies

**1 cup PLANTERS® Pecan Halves,
  divided
1 cup 100% bran cereal
¼ cup light molasses
1 egg, beaten
1¼ cups all-purpose flour
1 teaspoon baking soda
1 teaspoon ground ginger
¼ teaspoon ground cloves
½ cup margarine or butter, softened
1 cup sugar, divided
  Powdered Sugar Icing, recipe follows
  Candy corn, melted chocolate,
    colored sprinkles, for garnish**

1. Set aside 36 pecan halves; finely chop remainder. Mix bran, molasses and egg in bowl; let stand 5 minutes. Mix flour, baking soda and spices in another bowl; set aside.

2. Beat margarine and ¾ cup sugar in large bowl until creamy; blend in bran mixture. Stir in flour mixture until blended. Stir in chopped pecans. Form into 1-inch balls; roll in remaining ¼ cup sugar.

3. Place 2 inches apart on greased baking sheets; flatten. Insert 1 whole pecan into top for stem. Bake at 375°F for 7 to 9 minutes. Stand 1 minute; remove to wire racks. Frost with Powdered Sugar Icing and decorate to make faces.   *Makes 3 dozen cookies*

Powdered Sugar Icing: Combine 2 cups powdered sugar and 3 to 4 tablespoons milk until smooth. Tint with red and yellow food coloring to make orange tone.

Black Cat Cookies

Boo!! Brownies

6 squares (1 ounce each) semi-sweet chocolate, coarsely chopped
¼ cup (½ stick) plus 2 tablespoons butter, softened and divided
1 tablespoon freeze dried coffee granules
1 tablespoon boiling water
½ cup granulated sugar
2 large eggs
¾ cup all-purpose flour
½ teaspoon baking powder
½ teaspoon ground cinnamon
¼ teaspoon salt
1 cup "M&M's"® Chocolate Mini Baking Bits, divided
½ cup white frosting
Assorted food colorings

Preheat oven to 350°F. Line 8×8×2-inch baking pan with aluminum foil, leaving 1½-inch overhang on two sides. Lightly grease foil; set pan aside. In small saucepan combine chocolate and 2 tablespoons butter over low heat; stir constantly until completely melted. Remove from heat; let cool slightly. In small bowl combine coffee granules and water; set aside. In large bowl beat ¼ cup butter, sugar and eggs; stir in chocolate mixture and coffee until well blended. In medium bowl combine flour, baking powder, cinnamon and salt; add to chocolate mixture. Stir in ½ cup "M&M's"® Chocolate Mini Baking Bits. Spread batter evenly in prepared pan. Bake 30 to 35 minutes or until toothpick inserted in center comes out clean. Cool completely on wire rack. Lift brownies out of pan using foil. Cut into Halloween shapes using 3-inch cookie cutters. Tint frosting desired colors. Spread frosting over each brownie shape. Decorate with remaining ½ cup "M&M's"® Chocolate Mini Baking Bits. Store in tightly covered container.

Makes 8 to 10 brownies

Give Thanks Cornucopias

8 ice cream sugar cones
3 ounces semisweet chocolate, melted
Assorted fall candies

SUPPLIES
8 (2×¾-inch) pieces lightweight cardboard (optional)

1. Dip edges of cones into melted chocolate; let stand on wire racks or waxed paper until chocolate is firm. Place each cone on its side; fill with candy.

2. To make place cards, write names on pieces of cardboard. Attach to tops of cones with melted chocolate.

Makes 8 favors or place cards

Cookie Gobblers

8 marshmallow puff cookies
4 striped shortbread ring cookies
¼ cup semisweet chocolate chips,
**   melted**
8 pieces candy corn

SUPPLIES
8 (2½×1½-inch) pieces lightweight
**   cardboard (optional)**

1. Cut down into marshmallow cookie halfway between center and edge. Starting in back, cut horizontally toward first cut. Dip knife in hot water and dry it before each cut. Discard pieces.

2. Cut striped cookies in half. Attach 1 striped cookie half with melted chocolate to cut edge of marshmallow cookie to form tail. Attach candy corn to front of turkey with melted chocolate as shown. Repeat with remaining cookies.

3. To make place cards, write names near top edges of cardboard. Place behind striped cookie half; attach with melted chocolate, if desired.   *Makes 8 place cards*

Left to right: Give Thanks Cornucopia and Cookie Gobbler

Chocolate-Flecked Pirouettes

½ cup butter, softened
½ cup sugar
2 egg whites
1 teaspoon vanilla
½ cup all-purpose flour
⅓ cup coarsely grated bittersweet or
  dark sweet chocolate bar (about
  2 ounces)

1. Preheat oven to 400°F. Grease cookie sheets well; set aside.

2. Beat butter and sugar in small bowl with electric mixer at medium speed until light and fluffy. Beat in egg whites, 1 at a time. Beat in vanilla. Add flour; beat at low speed just until blended. Gently fold in grated chocolate with rubber spatula.

3. Drop teaspoonfuls of batter 4 inches apart onto prepared cookie sheets. Spread dough into 2-inch rounds with small spatula. Make only 3 to 4 rounds per sheet.

4. Bake 1 sheet at a time 4 to 5 minutes until edges are barely golden. *Do not overbake.*

5. Remove from oven and quickly loosen edge of 1 cookie from baking sheet with thin spatula. Quickly roll cookie around clean handle of wooden spoon overlapping edges to form cigar shape. Repeat with remaining cookies. (If cookies become too firm to shape, return to oven for a few seconds to soften.) Slide cookie off handle to wire rack; cool completely. Store tightly covered at room temperature or freeze up to 3 months.

Makes about 3 dozen cookies

Crispy Chocolate Footballs

2 cups semisweet chocolate chips
½ cup light corn syrup
¼ cup butter or margarine
7 cups crisp rice cereal
  Powdered sugar
  Glaze (recipe follows)

SUPPLIES
  Pastry bag and small writing tip

1. Line baking sheets with waxed paper; set aside.

2. Combine chocolate chips, corn syrup and butter in medium saucepan. Cook and stir over low heat until chips are melted and smooth.

3. Place cereal in large bowl. Pour chocolate mixture over cereal; stir to coat evenly.

4. Lightly butter hands. Shape about ⅓ cup cereal mixture into football shapes, each about 2×1¼ inches in size. Place on prepared baking sheets.

5. Prepare Glaze. Stir in enough additional powdered sugar to glaze to make consistency suitable for piping. Using pastry bag fitted with writing tip, pipe lines and laces onto footballs.

Makes about 20 small footballs

Glaze: Combine 1 cup powdered sugar and 1 tablespoon milk in small bowl. Stir; add additional milk, ½ teaspoon at a time, to make medium-thick, pourable glaze.

Chocolate-Flecked Pirouettes

Brandy Lace Cookies

¼ cup sugar
¼ cup margarine or butter
¼ cup KARO® Light or Dark Corn
    Syrup
½ cup all-purpose flour
¼ cup very finely chopped pecans or
    walnuts
 2 tablespoons brandy
   Melted white and/or semisweet
    chocolate (optional)

1. Preheat oven to 350°F. Lightly grease and flour cookie sheets.

2. In small saucepan, combine sugar, margarine and corn syrup. Bring to a boil over medium heat, stirring constantly. Remove from heat. Stir in flour, pecans and brandy. Drop 12 half teaspoonfuls of batter 2 inches apart onto prepared cookie sheets.

3. Bake 6 minutes or until golden. Cool 1 to 2 minutes or until cookies can be lifted but are still warm and soft. Remove cookies with spatula. Curl cookies around handle of wooden spoon; slide off when crisp. If cookies harden before curling, return to oven to soften.

4. If desired, drizzle with melted chocolate.

Makes 4 to 5 dozen cookies

Prep Time: 30 minutes
Bake Time: 6 minutes, plus curling and cooling

Raspberry-Filled Chocolate Ravioli

 1 cup butter, softened
½ cup granulated sugar
 2 squares (1 ounce each) bittersweet
    or semisweet chocolate, melted
    and cooled
 1 egg
 1 teaspoon vanilla
½ teaspoon chocolate extract
¼ teaspoon baking soda
   Dash salt
2½ cups all-purpose flour
 1 cup seedless raspberry jam
   Powdered sugar

Mix butter and granulated sugar in large bowl until blended. Add melted chocolate, egg, vanilla, chocolate extract, baking soda and salt; beat until light. Blend in flour to make stiff dough. Divide dough in half. Cover; refrigerate until firm.

Preheat oven to 350°F. Lightly grease cookie sheets or line with parchment paper. Roll out dough, half at a time, ⅛ inch thick between two sheets of plastic wrap. Remove top sheet of plastic. (If dough gets too soft and sticks to plastic, refrigerate until firm.) Cut dough into 1½-inch squares. Place half the squares, 2 inches apart, on prepared cookie sheets. Place about ½ teaspoon jam on center of each square; top with another square. Using fork, press edges of squares together to seal, then pierce center of each square. Bake 10 minutes or just until edges are browned. Remove to wire racks to cool. Dust lightly with powdered sugar.

Makes about 6 dozen cookies

Chocolate-Topped Linzer Cookies

3 cups hazelnuts, toasted, skins removed and divided
1 cup unsalted butter, softened
1 cup powdered sugar, sifted
½ teaspoon grated lemon peel
¼ teaspoon salt
½ egg*
3 cups sifted all-purpose flour
½ cup nougat paste**
½ cup seedless red raspberry jam
6 squares (1 ounce each) semisweet chocolate
2 tablespoons shortening

*To measure ½ egg, lightly beat 1 egg in glass measuring cup; remove half for use in recipe.

**Nougat paste, a mixture of ground hazelnuts, sugar and semisweet chocolate is available in specialty candy and gourmet food shops. If unavailable, substitute melted semisweet chocolate to attach cookie layers.

In food processor or blender, process 1½ cups hazelnuts until finely ground. (There should be ½ cup ground nuts; if necessary, process more nuts.) Set aside remaining whole nuts for garnish.

In large bowl, beat butter, powdered sugar, lemon peel and salt until thoroughly blended; do not overmix. Add ½ egg; beat until well mixed. Stir in ground hazelnuts. Gradually stir in flour. Divide dough into quarters. Wrap each portion; refrigerate about 2 hours or until firm.

Preheat oven to 350°F. Line cookie sheets with parchment paper. Roll out dough, one quarter at a time, ⅛ to ¹⁄₁₆ inch thick on floured pastry cloth. Cut out with 1¼-inch round cookie cutter. Place ¾ inch apart on prepared cookie sheets.

Bake 7 to 8 minutes or until lightly browned. Let cookies cool completely on cookie sheets set on wire racks. Spoon nougat paste into pastry bag fitted with ¼-inch round tip. Pipe about ¼ teaspoon paste onto centers of ⅓ of cookies. Top with plain cookies; press gently.

Spoon raspberry jam into pastry bag fitted with ⅓-inch round tip. Pipe about ⅓ teaspoon jam onto centers of second cookie layers. Top with plain cookies; press gently. Let cookies stand about 1 hour.

In small heavy saucepan over low heat, melt chocolate and shortening; stir until smooth. Press cookie layers lightly together. Dip top of each cookie into chocolate mixture just to cover. Shake to remove excess chocolate. Place cookies, chocolate side up, on wire racks; press reserved whole hazelnuts into soft chocolate in centers of cookies. Let stand until chocolate is set.

Makes about 4 dozen cookies

Double-Dipped Hazelnut Crisps

¾ **cup semisweet chocolate chips**
1¼ **cups all-purpose flour**
¾ **cup powdered sugar**
⅔ **cup whole hazelnuts, toasted, hulled and finely ground***
¼ **teaspoon instant espresso powder**
   Dash salt
½ **cup butter, softened**
2 **teaspoons vanilla**
4 **squares (1 ounce each) bittersweet or semisweet chocolate**
2 **teaspoons shortening, divided**
4 **ounces white chocolate**

*To grind hazelnuts, place in food processor or blender. Process until thoroughly ground with a dry, not pasty, texture.

Preheat oven to 350°F. Lightly grease cookie sheets or line with parchment paper. Melt chocolate chips in top of double boiler over hot, not boiling, water. Remove from heat; cool. Blend flour, powdered sugar, hazelnuts, espresso powder and salt in large bowl. Blend in butter, melted chocolate and vanilla until dough is stiff but smooth. (If dough is too soft to handle, cover and refrigerate until firm.)

Roll out dough, ¼ at a time, to ⅛-inch thickness on lightly floured surface. Cut out with 2-inch scalloped round cutters. Place 2 inches apart on prepared cookie sheets. Bake 8 minutes or until not quite firm. (Cookies should not brown. They will puff up during baking and then flatten again.) Remove to wire racks to cool.

Place bittersweet chocolate and 1 teaspoon shortening in small bowl. Place bowl over hot water; stir until chocolate is melted and smooth. Dip cookies, 1 at a time, halfway into bittersweet chocolate. Place on waxed paper; refrigerate until chocolate is set. Repeat melting process with white chocolate. Dip plain halves of cookies into white chocolate; refrigerate until set. Store cookies in airtight container in cool place. (If cookies are frozen, chocolate may discolor.)

Makes about 4 dozen cookies

HELPFUL HINT

Hazelnuts, or filberts, have thin, brown skins that are often removed before eating. One way to remove the skins is to place the nuts on a baking sheet and bake them in a preheated 350°F oven for 7 to 10 minutes or until the skins begin to flake off. Remove the nuts from the oven, wrap them in a heavy towel and rub them against the towel to remove as much of the skins as possible.

Left to right: Double-Dipped Hazelnut Crisps and Pecan Florentines (page 498)

Pecan Florentines

¾ cup pecan halves, finely ground*
½ cup all-purpose flour
⅓ cup packed brown sugar
¼ cup light corn syrup
¼ cup butter
2 tablespoons milk
⅓ cup semisweet chocolate chips

To grind pecans, place in food processor or blender. Process until thoroughly ground with a dry, not pasty, texture.

Preheat oven to 350°F. Line cookie sheets with foil; lightly grease foil. Combine pecans and flour in small bowl. Combine brown sugar, syrup, butter and milk in medium saucepan. Stir over medium heat until mixture comes to a boil. Remove from heat; stir in flour mixture.

Drop by teaspoonfuls about 3 inches apart onto prepared cookie sheets. Bake 10 to 12 minutes or until lacy and golden brown. (Cookies are soft when hot, but become crisp as they cool.) Cool completely on foil.

Place chocolate chips in small resealable plastic food storage bag; seal. Microwave at HIGH 1 minute. Knead bag lightly. Repeat steps as necessary until chips are completely melted. With scissors, snip off small corner from one side of bag. Squeeze melted chocolate over cookies to decorate. Let stand until chocolate is set. Peel cookies off foil.

Makes about 3 dozen cookies

Two-Toned Spritz Cookies

1 square (1 ounce) unsweetened chocolate, coarsely chopped
1 cup (2 sticks) butter, softened
1 cup sugar
1 egg
1 teaspoon vanilla
2¼ cups all-purpose flour
¼ teaspoon salt

Melt chocolate in small heavy saucepan over low heat, stirring constantly; set aside. Beat butter and sugar in large bowl until light and fluffy. Beat in egg and vanilla. Combine flour and salt in medium bowl; gradually add to butter mixture. Reserve 2 cups dough. Beat chocolate into remaining dough until smooth. Cover both doughs and refrigerate about 20 minutes or until firm enough to handle.

Preheat oven to 400°F. Roll out vanilla dough between two sheets of waxed paper to ½-inch thickness. Cut into 5×4-inch rectangles. Place chocolate dough on sheet of waxed paper. Using waxed paper to hold dough, roll back and forth to form log, about 1 inch in diameter. Cut into 5-inch-long logs. Place chocolate log in center of vanilla rectangle. Wrap vanilla dough around log and fit into cookie press fitted with star disc. Press dough onto ungreased cookie sheets 1½ inches apart. Repeat with remaining vanilla rectangles and chocolate logs. Bake about 10 minutes or until just set. Remove cookies to wire racks; cool completely.

Makes about 4 dozen cookies

Chocolate-Gilded Danish Sugar Cones

½ cup butter, softened
½ cup sugar
½ cup all-purpose flour
2 egg whites
1 teaspoon vanilla
3 ounces bittersweet chocolate *or*
    ½ cup semisweet chocolate chips

Preheat oven to 400°F. Generously grease 4 cookie sheets. Beat butter and sugar in large bowl until light and fluffy. Blend in flour. In clean, dry bowl, beat egg whites until foamy. Blend into butter mixture. Add vanilla. Using teaspoon, place 4 mounds of dough 4 inches apart on each prepared cookie sheet. Spread mounds to 3-inch diameter with small spatula dipped in water.

Bake 1 sheet at a time, 5 to 6 minutes or until edges are just barely golden. (Do not overbake, or cookies will become crisp too quickly and will be difficult to shape.) Remove from oven and quickly loosen each cookie from cookie sheet with thin spatula. Shape each cookie into cone; cones will become firm as they cool. (If cookies become too firm to shape, return to oven for few seconds to soften.)

Melt chocolate in small bowl over hot water. Stir until smooth. When all cookies are baked and cooled, dip wide ends into melted chocolate; let stand until chocolate is set. **Makes about 16 cookies**

Chocolate-Gilded Danish Sugar Cones

Chocolate-Dipped Orange Logs

3¼ cups all-purpose flour
⅓ teaspoon salt
1 cup butter, softened
1 cup sugar
2 eggs
1½ teaspoons grated orange peel
1 teaspoon vanilla
1 package (12 ounces) semisweet
    chocolate chips
1½ cups pecan pieces, finely chopped

Combine flour and salt in medium bowl. Beat butter in large bowl with electric mixer at medium speed until smooth. Gradually beat in sugar; increase speed to high and beat until light and fluffy. Beat in eggs, 1 at a time, blending well after each addition. Beat in orange peel and vanilla until blended. Gradually stir in flour mixture until blended. (Dough will be crumbly.)

Gather dough together and press gently to form ball. Flatten into disc; wrap in plastic wrap and refrigerate 2 hours or until firm. (Dough can be prepared one day in advance and refrigerated overnight.)

Preheat oven to 350°F. Shape dough into 1-inch balls. Roll balls on flat surface to form 3-inch logs about ½ inch thick. Place logs 1 inch apart on ungreased cookie sheets.

Bake 17 minutes or until bottoms of cookies are golden brown. (Cookies will feel soft and look white on top; they will become crisp when cool.) Transfer to wire racks to cool completely.

Melt chocolate chips in top of double boiler over hot, not boiling, water. Place chopped pecans on sheet of waxed paper. Dip one end of each cookie in chocolate, shaking off excess. Roll chocolate-covered ends in pecans. Place on waxed paper-lined cookie sheets and let stand until chocolate is set, or refrigerate about 5 minutes to set chocolate. Store in airtight container.

Makes about 3 dozen cookies

FUN FOOD FACT

Probably the most popular and often-used extract is vanilla. It is derived from the long, thin pod of a tropical orchid. Through a lengthy and labor-intensive curing process, the pods are transformed into intensely-flavored, dark brown vanilla beans. Thus, pure vanilla products remain relatively expensive.

Chocolate-Dipped Orange Logs

Chocolate Tassies

PASTRY
- 2 cups all-purpose flour
- 2 packages (3 ounces each) cold cream cheese, cut into chunks
- 1 cup cold butter, cut into chunks

FILLING
- 2 tablespoons butter
- 2 squares (1 ounce each) unsweetened chocolate
- 1½ cups packed brown sugar
- 2 eggs, beaten
- 2 teaspoons vanilla
- Dash salt
- 1½ cups chopped pecans

Place flour in large bowl. Cut in cream cheese and butter. Continue to mix until dough can be shaped into ball. Wrap dough in plastic wrap; refrigerate 1 hour.

Shape dough into 1-inch balls. Press each ball into ungreased miniature (1¾-inch) muffin pan cup, covering bottom and side of cup with dough.

Preheat oven to 350°F. Melt butter and chocolate in heavy medium saucepan over low heat. Remove from heat. Blend in brown sugar, eggs, vanilla and salt; beat until thick. Stir in pecans. Spoon about 1 teaspoon filling into each unbaked pastry shell. Bake 20 to 25 minutes or until pastry is lightly browned and filling is set. Cool in pans on wire racks. Remove from pans; store in airtight containers.

Makes about 5 dozen cookies

Almond Fudge Cups

PASTRY
- ¾ cup butter, softened
- ⅓ cup sugar
- 2 cups all-purpose flour
- 1 tablespoon almond- or fruit-flavored liqueur or water
- 1 teaspoon vanilla

FILLING
- 1 cup (6 ounces) semisweet chocolate chips
- ¾ cup blanched almonds
- 2 eggs
- ½ cup sugar
- Dash salt

Lightly grease 3 dozen miniature (1¾-inch) muffin pan cups or small tart shells. Cream butter and sugar in large bowl until blended. Add flour, liqueur and vanilla; stir to make moist crumbs. Divide crumbs evenly among muffin cups; press to cover bottoms and sides of cups completely. Preheat oven to 350°F.

Place chocolate chips and almonds in food processor. Process until finely ground. Beat eggs in medium bowl until thick; stir in sugar and salt. Blend in chocolate mixture.

Spoon filling into unbaked pastry shells. Bake 20 minutes or until filling is set. Cool in pans on wire racks. Store in airtight containers.

Makes 3 dozen cookies

Double-Dipped Chocolate Peanut Butter Cookies

1¼ cups all-purpose flour
½ teaspoon baking powder
½ teaspoon baking soda
½ teaspoon salt
½ cup butter, softened
½ cup granulated sugar
½ cup packed light brown sugar
½ cup creamy or chunky peanut butter
1 egg
1 teaspoon vanilla
1½ cups semisweet chocolate chips
3 teaspoons shortening, divided
1½ cups milk chocolate chips

1. Preheat oven to 350°F. Place flour, baking powder, baking soda and salt in small bowl; stir to combine.

2. Beat butter, granulated sugar and brown sugar in large bowl until light and fluffy, scraping down side of bowl once. Beat in peanut butter, egg and vanilla, scraping down side of bowl once. Gradually stir in flour mixture, blending well.

3. Roll heaping tablespoonfuls of dough into 1½-inch balls. Place balls 2 inches apart on ungreased cookie sheets. (If dough is too soft to roll into balls, refrigerate 30 minutes.) Dip table fork into granulated sugar; press criss-cross fashion onto each ball, flattening to ½-inch thickness. Bake 12 minutes or until set. Let cookies stand on cookie sheets 2 minutes. Remove cookies to wire racks; cool completely.

4. Melt semisweet chocolate chips and 1½ teaspoons shortening in top of double boiler over hot, not boiling, water. Dip one end of each cookie one third the way up; place on waxed paper. Let stand until chocolate is set, about 30 minutes.

5. Melt milk chocolate chips with remaining 1½ teaspoons shortening in top of double boiler over hot, not boiling, water. Dip plain end of each cookie one third the way up; place on waxed paper. Let stand until chocolate is set, about 30 minutes.

6. Store cookies between sheets of waxed paper at cool room temperature.

Makes about 2 dozen (3-inch) cookies

DECORATE IT!

To add extra crunch to these delicious cookies, sprinkle them with some chopped peanuts just after dipping the cookies in the melted chocolate.

Kentucky Bourbon Pecan Tarts

Cream Cheese Pastry (recipe follows)
2 eggs
½ cup granulated sugar
½ cup KARO® Light or Dark Corn Syrup
2 tablespoons bourbon
1 tablespoon margarine or butter, melted
½ teaspoon vanilla
1 cup chopped pecans
Confectioners' sugar (optional)

1. Preheat oven to 350°F. Prepare Cream Cheese Pastry. Divide dough in half; set aside 1 half.

2. On floured surface roll out pastry to ⅛-inch thickness. If necessary, add small amount of flour to keep pastry from sticking. Cut into 12 (2¼-inch) rounds. Press evenly onto bottoms and up sides of 1¾-inch muffin pan cups. Repeat with remaining pastry. Refrigerate.

3. In medium bowl, beat eggs slightly. Stir in granulated sugar, corn syrup, bourbon, margarine and vanilla until well blended. Spoon 1 heaping teaspoon pecans into each pastry-lined cup; top with 1 tablespoon corn syrup mixture.

4. Bake 20 to 25 minutes or until lightly browned and toothpick inserted into centers comes out clean. Cool in pans 5 minutes. Remove; cool completely on wire rack. If desired, sprinkle cookies with confectioners' sugar.   *Makes about 2 dozen cookies*

Cream Cheese Pastry

1 cup all-purpose flour
¾ teaspoon baking powder
Pinch salt
½ cup margarine or butter, softened
1 package (3 ounces) cream cheese, softened
2 teaspoons sugar

1. In small bowl, combine flour, baking powder and salt.

2. In large bowl, mix margarine, cream cheese and sugar until well combined. Stir in flour mixture until well blended. Press firmly into ball with hands.

HELPFUL HINT

To make sure the oven is heated to the desired temperature, turn the oven on about 15 minutes before beginning to bake. Check the oven temperature for accuracy with an oven thermometer, and raise or lower the heat as necessary.

Top to bottom: Brandy Lace Cookies (page 494) and Kentucky Bourbon Pecan Tarts

Christmas Spritz Cookies

2¼ cups all-purpose flour
 ¼ teaspoon salt
1¼ cups powdered sugar
  1 cup butter, softened
  1 egg
  1 teaspoon almond extract
  1 teaspoon vanilla
    Green food coloring (optional)
    Candied red and green cherries and assorted decorative
      candies (optional)
    Powdered Sugar Icing (page 556, optional)

Preheat oven to 375°F. Place flour and salt in medium bowl; stir to combine. Beat powdered sugar and butter in large bowl until light and fluffy. Beat in egg, almond extract and vanilla. Gradually add flour mixture. Beat until well blended.

Divide dough in half. If desired, tint half of dough with green food coloring. Fit cookie press with desired plate (or change plates for different shapes after first batch). Fill press with dough; press dough 1 inch apart onto ungreased cookie sheets. Decorate cookies with cherries and assorted candies, if desired.

Bake 10 to 12 minutes or until just set. Remove cookies to wire racks; let cool.

Prepare Powdered Sugar Icing, if desired. Pipe or drizzle on cooled cookies. Decorate with cherries and assorted candies, if desired.

Makes about 5 dozen cookies

Christmas Spritz Cookies

Stained Glass Cookies

½ cup margarine or butter, softened
½ cup sugar
½ cup honey
¼ cup egg substitute
1 teaspoon vanilla extract
3 cups all-purpose flour
1 teaspoon DAVIS® Baking Powder
½ teaspoon baking soda
½ teaspoon salt
5 (.90-ounce) rolls Five Flavor or
    Fancy Fruits LIFE SAVERS® Candy

1. Beat together margarine, sugar, honey, egg substitute and vanilla in bowl until creamy. Mix in flour, baking powder, baking soda and salt. Cover; refrigerate at least 2 hours.

2. Roll dough on lightly floured surface to ¼-inch thickness. Cut dough into desired shapes with 2½- to 3-inch floured cookie cutters. Trace smaller version of cookie shape on dough leaving ½- to ¾-inch border of dough. Cut out and remove dough from centers of cookies; set aside. Place cut-out shapes on baking sheets lined with foil. Repeat with reserved dough, re-rolling scraps as necessary.

3. Crush each color of candy separately between two layers of wax paper. Spoon crushed candy inside centers of cut-out cookie shapes.

4. Bake in preheated 350°F oven for 6 to 8 minutes or until candy is melted and cookies are lightly browned. Cool cookies completely before removing from foil.

Makes 3½ dozen cookies

Chocolate Snowflakes

1 cup butter, softened
1 cup sugar
1 egg
1 teaspoon vanilla
2 ounces semisweet chocolate, melted
2¼ cups all-purpose flour
1 teaspoon baking powder
¼ teaspoon salt
    Powdered sugar

SUPPLIES
Parchment paper

1. Beat butter and sugar in large bowl until fluffy. Beat in egg and vanilla. Add melted chocolate; mix well. Add flour, baking powder and salt; mix well. Cover; refrigerate about 2 hours or until firm.

2. Preheat oven to 325°F. Grease cookie sheets.

3. Roll dough on floured surface to ⅛-inch thickness. Cut dough with 3-inch round cookie cutter. Place 1 inch apart on prepared cookie sheets. Bake 8 to 10 minutes or until edges begin to brown. Remove to wire racks; cool completely.

4. To make snowflakes, cut several pieces of parchment paper into 3-inch circles. Fold each in half, then into quarters. With scissors, cut small pieces from folded edges to create snowflake design. Unfold circles and place on tops of cookies. Sift powdered sugar over paper patterns. Carefully remove patterns. Repeat with remaining cookies.

Makes about 2 dozen cookies

Stained Glass Cookies

Gingerbread People

2¼ cups all-purpose flour
2 teaspoons ground cinnamon
2 teaspoons ground ginger
1 teaspoon baking powder
½ teaspoon salt
¼ teaspoon ground cloves
¼ teaspoon ground nutmeg
¾ cup butter, softened
½ cup packed light brown sugar
½ cup dark molasses
1 egg
   Powdered Sugar Icing (page 556) or prepared creamy or gel-type tube frosting (optional)
   Candies and other decorations (optional)

1. Combine flour, cinnamon, ginger, baking powder, salt, cloves and nutmeg in large bowl.

2. Beat butter and brown sugar in large bowl until light and fluffy. Beat in molasses and egg. Add flour mixture; beat until well blended. Shape dough into 3 discs. Wrap in plastic wrap; refrigerate 1 hour or until firm.

3. Preheat oven to 350°F. Working with 1 disc at a time, place on lightly floured surface. Roll out dough with lightly floured rolling pin to ³/₁₆-inch thickness. Cut out gingerbread people with floured 5-inch cookie cutters; place on ungreased cookie sheets. Press dough trimmings together gently; reroll and cut out more cookies.

4. Bake about 12 minutes or until edges are golden brown. Let cookies stand on cookie sheets 1 minute; remove to wire racks to cool completely.

5. Prepare Powdered Sugar Icing and pipe onto cooled cookies. Decorate with candies, if desired. Let stand at room temperature about 20 minutes or until set. Store tightly covered at room temperature or freeze up to 3 months.

Makes about 16 large cookies

FUN FOOD FACT

Gingerbread may refer to either one of two traditional desserts, gingerbread cake or gingerbread cookies. Gingerbread cookies date back to medieval times. They range from thin and crispy to thick and chewy. They are often cut into people shapes.

Yuletide Linzer Bars

1⅓ cups butter, softened
¾ cup sugar
1 egg
1 teaspoon grated lemon peel
2½ cups all-purpose flour
1½ cups whole almonds, ground
1 teaspoon ground cinnamon
¾ cup raspberry preserves
Powdered sugar

Preheat oven to 350°F. Grease 13×9-inch baking pan.

Beat butter and sugar in large bowl at medium speed of electric mixer until creamy. Beat in egg and lemon peel until blended. Mix in flour, almonds and cinnamon until well blended.

Press 2 cups dough into bottom of prepared pan. Spread preserves over crust. Press remaining dough, a small amount at a time, evenly over preserves.

Bake 35 to 40 minutes until golden brown. Cool in pan on wire rack. Sprinkle with powdered sugar; cut into bars.

Makes 36 bars

Yuletide Linzer Bars

Snowmen

1 package (20 ounces) refrigerated chocolate chip cookie dough
1½ cups sifted powdered sugar
2 tablespoons milk
Candy corn, gum drops, chocolate chips, licorice and other assorted small candies

1. Preheat oven to 375°F. Remove dough from wrapper. Cut dough into 12 equal sections. Divide each section into 3 balls: large, medium and small for each snowman.

2. For each snowman, place 3 balls in row, ¼ inch apart, on ungreased cookie sheet.

3. Bake 10 to 12 minutes or until edges are very lightly browned. Cool 4 minutes on cookie sheets. Remove to wire racks; cool completely.

4. Mix powdered sugar and milk in medium bowl until smooth. Pour over cookies. Let cookies stand 20 minutes or until set.

5. Decorate with assorted candies to create snowman faces, hats and arms.

Makes 1 dozen cookies

Holiday Chocolate Shortbread Cookies

1 cup (2 sticks) butter, softened
1¼ cups powdered sugar
1 teaspoon vanilla extract
½ cup HERSHEY®S Dutch Processed Cocoa or HERSHEY®S Cocoa
1¾ cups all-purpose flour
1⅔ cups (10-ounce package) HERSHEY®S Premier White Chips

1. Heat oven to 300°F. Beat butter, powdered sugar and vanilla in large bowl until creamy. Add cocoa; beat until well blended. Gradually add flour, stirring until smooth.

2. Roll or pat dough to ¼-inch thickness on lightly floured surface or between 2 pieces of wax paper. Cut into holiday shapes using star, tree, wreath or other cookie cutters. Reroll dough scraps, cutting cookies until dough is used. Place on ungreased cookie sheet.

3. Bake 15 to 20 minutes or just until firm. Immediately place white chips, flat side down, in decorative design on warm cookies. Cool slightly; remove from cookie sheet to wire rack. Cool completely. Store in airtight container.

Makes about 4½ dozen (2-inch diameter) cookies

Prep Time: 30 minutes
Bake Time: 15 minutes
Cool Time: 30 minutes

Snowmen

Candy Cane Cookies

1¼ cups granulated sugar
  1 Butter Flavor* CRISCO® Stick or
    1 cup Butter Flavor CRISCO®
    all-vegetable shortening
  2 eggs
  ¼ cup light corn syrup or regular
    pancake syrup
  1 tablespoon vanilla extract
  3 cups plus 4 tablespoons all-purpose
    flour, divided
  ¾ teaspoon baking powder
  ½ teaspoon baking soda
  ½ teaspoon salt
  ½ teaspoon red food color
  ¼ teaspoon peppermint extract

Butter Flavor Crisco is artificially flavored.

1. Combine sugar and 1 cup shortening in large bowl. Beat at medium speed of electric mixer until well blended. Add eggs, syrup and vanilla. Beat until well blended and fluffy.

2. Combine 3 cups flour, baking powder, baking soda and salt. Add gradually to creamed mixture at low speed. Mix until well blended.

3. Divide dough in half. Add red food color and peppermint extract to one half. Wrap each half in plastic wrap. Refrigerate several hours or overnight.

4. Heat oven to 375°F. Place sheets of foil on countertop for cooling cookies.

5. Roll 1 rounded teaspoonful plain dough with hands into a 6-inch rope on lightly floured surface. Repeat, using 1 teaspoonful

red dough. Place ropes side by side. Twist together gently. Pinch ends to seal. Curve one end into the "hook" of a candy cane. Transfer to ungreased baking sheet with large pancake turner. Repeat with remaining dough. Place cookies 2 inches apart.

6. Bake one baking sheet at a time at 375°F for 7 to 9 minutes, or until just lightly browned. *Do not overbake.* Cool 2 minutes on baking sheet. Remove cookies to foil to cool completely.

Makes about 4½ dozen cookies

FUN FOOD FACT

Food colors are edible dyes (usually red, green, blue and yellow) used to tint frostings and candies. The most popular type are the liquid colors available at supermarkets. When stored tightly closed in a cool, dry place, liquid colors will last up to four years.

Hanukkah Fried Cruller Bows

1¼ cups all-purpose flour
3 tablespoons powdered sugar
2 tablespoons granulated sugar
½ teaspoon salt
1 whole egg
2 egg whites
1 teaspoon vanilla
  Vegetable oil for frying
  Powdered sugar and ground
    cinnamon

SUPPLIES
Deep-frying thermometer

1. Combine flour, 3 tablespoons powdered sugar, granulated sugar and salt in small bowl. Stir in whole egg, egg whites and vanilla with fork until mixture is crumbly.

2. Form dough into ball; knead on lightly floured surface until smooth, about 5 minutes. Cover loosely; let stand about 30 minutes.

3. Heat 2 inches oil to 375°F in large heavy saucepan. Roll dough on floured surface to 12-inch square, about ⅛ inch thick. Cut into 12 (1-inch) strips; cut strips in half to form 24 (6×1-inch) strips. Tie each strip in knot.

4. Fry knots in oil, a few at a time, 3 to 4 minutes or until golden. Drain on paper towels. Sprinkle with powdered sugar and cinnamon. Serve warm.

Makes 2 dozen bows

Christmas Cookie Pops

1 package (20 ounces) refrigerated
    sugar cookie dough
  All-purpose flour (optional)
20 to 24 (4-inch) lollipop sticks
  Royal Icing (page 556)
6 ounces almond bark (any flavor)
  Shortening
  Assorted small candies

1. Preheat oven to 350°F. Grease cookie sheets; set aside. Remove dough from wrapper. Sprinkle dough with flour to minimize sticking, if necessary. Cut dough in half. Reserve 1 half; refrigerate remaining dough.

2. Roll reserved dough to ⅓-inch thickness. Cut out cookies using 3¼- or 3½-inch Christmas cookie cutters. Place lollipop sticks on cookies so that tips of sticks are imbedded in cookies. Carefully turn cookies so sticks are in back; place on prepared cookie sheets. Repeat with remaining dough.

3. Bake 7 to 11 minutes or until edges are lightly browned. Cool cookies on sheets 2 minutes. Remove cookies to wire racks; cool completely. Prepare Royal Icing.

4. Melt almond bark in microwavable bowl according to package directions. Add 1 or more tablespoons shortening if coating is too thick. Hold cookies over bowl; spoon coating over cookies. Scrape excess coating from cookie edges. Decorate with small candies and Royal Icing immediately. Place cookies on wire racks set over waxed paper; let set.

Makes 20 to 24 cookies

Yule Tree Namesakes

Butter Cookie Dough (page 552)
Cookie Glaze (page 555)
Green food coloring
Powdered sugar
Assorted candies
3 packages (12 ounces each)
semisweet chocolate chips, melted
1 cup flaked coconut, tinted green*

*To tint coconut: Dilute a few drops of food coloring with ½ teaspoon water in large plastic bag. Add 1 cup flaked coconut. Seal bag and shake until coconut is evenly tinted.

1. Prepare Butter Cookie Dough.

2. Preheat oven to 350°F. Roll dough on floured surface to ⅛-inch thickness. Cut out using 3- to 4-inch tree-shaped cookie cutter. Place 2 inches apart on ungreased cookie sheets. Bake 12 to 14 minutes until edges begin to brown. Remove to wire racks; cool.

3. Prepare Cookie Glaze; reserve ⅓ cup. Tint remaining glaze green with food coloring. Place cookies on wire rack set over waxed paper-lined cookie sheet. Spoon green glaze over cookies.

4. Add 1 to 2 tablespoons powdered sugar to reserved Cookie Glaze. Spoon into pastry bag fitted with small writing tip. Pipe names onto trees. Decorate with assorted candies. Let stand until glaze is set.

5. Spoon melted chocolate into 1¾-inch paper baking cups, filling evenly. Let stand until chocolate is very thick and partially set. Place trees upright in chocolate. Sprinkle tinted coconut over chocolate.

Makes 24 place cards

Spicy Gingerbread Cookies

COOKIES
 ¾ **cup (1½ sticks) butter, softened**
 ⅔ **cup light molasses**
 ½ **cup packed brown sugar**
 1 egg
1½ **teaspoons grated lemon peel**
2½ **cups all-purpose flour**
1¼ **teaspoons ground cinnamon**
 1 teaspoon ground allspice
 1 teaspoon vanilla
 ½ **teaspoon salt**
 ½ **teaspoon baking soda**
 ½ **teaspoon ground ginger**
 ¼ **teaspoon baking powder**

FROSTING
 4 cups powdered sugar
 ½ **cup (1 stick) butter, softened**
 4 tablespoons milk
 2 teaspoons vanilla
 Food coloring (optional)

For cookies, mix butter, molasses, brown sugar, egg and lemon peel in bowl. Beat until creamy. Add all remaining cookie ingredients; beat well. Cover; chill 2 hours. Preheat oven to 350°F. Roll dough, half at a time, on floured surface to ¼-inch thickness. (Keep remaining dough refrigerated.) Cut with 3- to 4-inch cookie cutters. Place on greased cookie sheets. Bake 6 to 8 minutes or until set. Remove from oven; let cool.

For frosting, beat powdered sugar, butter, milk and vanilla in bowl until fluffy. Tint with food coloring, if desired; spread over cookies. ***Makes about 4 dozen cookies***

Yule Tree Namesakes

Peanut Butter Cut-Outs

½ cup SKIPPY® Creamy Peanut Butter
6 tablespoons margarine, softened
½ cup packed brown sugar
⅓ cup KARO® Light or Dark Corn Syrup
1 egg
2 cups flour, divided
1½ teaspoons baking powder
1 teaspoon cinnamon (optional)
⅛ teaspoon salt

1. In large bowl with mixer at medium speed, beat peanut butter, margarine, brown sugar, corn syrup and egg until smooth. Reduce speed; beat in 1 cup flour, baking powder, cinnamon and salt. With spoon, stir in remaining 1 cup flour.

2. Divide dough in half. Between two sheets of waxed paper on large cookie sheets, roll each half of dough ¼ inch thick. Refrigerate until firm, about 1 hour.

3. Preheat oven to 350°F. Remove top piece of waxed paper. With floured cookie cutters, cut dough into shapes. Place on ungreased cookie sheets.

4. Bake 10 minutes or until lightly browned. Do not overbake. Let stand on cookie sheets 2 minutes. Remove from cookie sheets; cool completely on wire racks. Reroll dough trimmings and cut additional cookies. Decorate as desired.

Makes about 5 dozen cookies

Note: Use scraps of dough to create details on cookies.

Holiday Thumbprint Cookies

1 package (8 ounces) sugar-free low-fat yellow cake mix
3 tablespoons orange juice
2 teaspoons grated orange peel
½ teaspoon vanilla
4 teaspoons strawberry all-fruit spread
2 tablespoons pecans, chopped

Preheat oven to 350°F. Spray baking sheets with nonstick cooking spray.

Beat cake mix, orange juice, orange peel and vanilla in medium bowl with electric mixer at medium speed for 2 minutes until mixture looks crumbly. Increase speed to medium and beat 2 minutes or until smooth dough forms. *Dough will be very sticky.*

Coat hands with cooking spray. Roll dough into 1-inch balls. Place balls 2½ inches apart on prepared baking sheets. Press center of each ball with thumb. Fill each thumbprint with ¼ teaspoon fruit spread. Sprinkle with pecans.

Bake 8 to 9 minutes or until cookies are light golden brown and lose their shininess. *Do not overbake.* Remove to wire racks; cool completely. ***Makes 20 cookies***

Peanut Butter Cut-Outs

Ornament Brownies

1 tablespoon freeze dried coffee
1 tablespoon boiling water
¾ cup all-purpose flour
¾ teaspoon ground cinnamon
½ teaspoon baking powder
¼ teaspoon salt
½ cup sugar
¼ cup butter, softened
2 eggs
6 squares (1 ounce each) semisweet
   chocolate, melted
   Prepared vanilla frosting or icing
   Assorted food colors
   Small candy canes, assorted candies
   and sprinkles

1. Preheat oven to 350°F. Grease 8-inch square baking pan; set aside. Dissolve coffee in boiling water in small cup; set aside. Combine flour, cinnamon, baking powder and salt in small bowl; set aside.

2. Beat sugar and butter in large bowl until light and fluffy. Beat in eggs, 1 at a time, scraping down side of bowl after each addition. Beat in coffee mixture and melted chocolate until well combined. Add flour mixture. Beat until well blended. Spread batter evenly in prepared pan.

3. Bake 30 to 35 minutes or until center is set. Remove to wire rack; cool completely. Cut into holiday shapes using 2-inch cookie cutters.

4. Tint frosting with food colors as desired. Spread over each brownie shape. Break off top of small candy cane to create loop. Insert in top of brownie. Decorate as desired

Makes about 8 brownies

Glazed Sugar Cookies

COOKIES
1 package DUNCAN HINES® Golden
   Sugar Cookie Mix
1 egg
¼ cup vegetable oil
1 teaspoon water

GLAZE
1½ cups sifted confectioners' sugar
2 to 3 tablespoons water or milk
¾ teaspoon vanilla extract
   Food coloring (optional)
   Red and green sugar crystals,
   nonpareils or cinnamon candies

Preheat oven to 375°F.

Combine cookie mix, egg, oil and 1 teaspoon water in large bowl. Stir until thoroughly blended. Roll dough to ¼-inch thickness on lightly floured surface. Cut dough into desired shapes using floured cookie cutters. Place cookies 2 inches apart on *ungreased* baking sheets. Bake 7 to 8 minutes or until edges are light golden brown. Cool 1 minute on baking sheets. Remove to cooling racks. Cool completely.

Combine sugar, 2 to 3 tablespoons water and vanilla extract in medium bowl. Beat until smooth. Tint glaze with food coloring, if desired. Brush glaze on each cookie with clean pastry brush. Sprinkle cookies with sugar crystals, nonpareils or cinnamon candies before glaze sets. Allow glaze to set before storing between layers of waxed paper in airtight container.

Makes 4 dozen cookies

Ornament Brownies

Gingerbread Folks

Gingerbread Cookie Dough
   (page 553)
Assorted food colors
Vanilla frosting and assorted
   decorating gels
Assorted candies and decorations

SUPPLIES
   6-inch gingerbread boy and girl
   cookie cutters

1. Prepare Gingerbread Cookie Dough.

2. Preheat oven to 350°F. Grease cookie sheets.

3. Roll dough on floured surface to ⅛-inch thickness. Cut out dough with cookie cutters. Place on prepared cookie sheets. Bend arms and legs to make cookies look like they're dancing.

4. Bake 8 to 10 minutes or until edges begin to brown. Remove to wire racks; cool completely.

5. Tint frosting and decorate as desired.

Makes about 6 large cookies

Note: Gingerbread Folks can also be made into ornaments.

Holiday Sugar Cookies

1 cup butter, softened
¾ cup sugar
1 egg
2 cups all-purpose flour
1 teaspoon baking powder
¼ teaspoon salt
¼ teaspoon ground cinnamon
   Colored sprinkles or sugars
   (optional)

Beat butter and sugar in large bowl at medium speed of electric mixer until creamy. Add egg; beat until fluffy.

Stir in flour, baking powder, salt and cinnamon until well blended. Form dough into ball; wrap in plastic wrap and flatten. Refrigerate about 2 hours or until firm.

Preheat oven to 350°F. Roll out dough, small portion at a time, to ¼-inch thickness on lightly floured surface with lightly floured rolling pin. (Keep remaining dough wrapped in refrigerator.)

Cut out dough with 3-inch cookie cutters. Sprinkle with colored sprinkles or sugars, if desired. Transfer to ungreased cookie sheets.

Bake 7 to 9 minutes until edges are lightly browned. Let cookies stand on cookie sheets 1 minute; transfer to wire racks to cool completely. Store in airtight container.

Makes about 3 dozen cookies

Hanukkah Coin Cookies

1 cup (2 sticks) butter or margarine, softened
1 cup sugar
1 egg
1 teaspoon vanilla extract
1¾ cups all-purpose flour
½ cup HERSHEY®S Cocoa
1½ teaspoons baking powder
½ teaspoon salt
 Buttercream Frosting (recipe follows)

1. Beat butter, sugar, egg and vanilla in large bowl until well blended. Stir together flour, cocoa, baking powder and salt; gradually add to butter mixture, beating until well blended. Divide dough in half; place each half on separate sheet of wax paper.

2. Shape each portion into log, about 7 inches long. Wrap each log in wax paper or plastic wrap. Refrigerate until firm, at least 8 hours.

3. Heat oven to 325°F. Cut logs into ¼-inch-thick slices. Place on ungreased cookie sheet.

4. Bake 8 to 10 minutes or until set. Cool slightly; remove from cookie sheet to wire rack. Cool completely. Prepare Buttercream Frosting; spread over tops of cookies.
Makes about 4½ dozen cookies

Buttercream Frosting

¼ cup (½ stick) butter, softened
1½ cups powdered sugar
 1 to 2 tablespoons milk
½ teaspoon vanilla extract
 Yellow food color

Beat butter until creamy. Gradually add powdered sugar and milk to butter, beating to desired consistency. Stir in vanilla and food color. *Makes about 1 cup frosting*

Hanukkah Coin Cookies

Candy Cane & Wreath Ornaments

1 cup sugar
½ cup shortening
½ cup butter, softened
1 teaspoon salt
1 egg
2 teaspoons vanilla
2½ cups all-purpose flour
½ teaspoon almond extract
¼ teaspoon liquid green food coloring
¼ teaspoon peppermint extract
½ teaspoon liquid red food coloring, divided
Creamy Decorator's Frosting (page 554)
Assorted red candies

1. Beat sugar, shortening, butter and salt in large bowl with electric mixer at medium speed until light and fluffy. Beat in egg and vanilla until well blended. Beat in flour at low speed until soft dough forms. Remove half of dough from bowl; set aside. Divide remaining dough evenly between 2 medium bowls. Stir almond extract and green food coloring into one portion until well blended. Stir peppermint extract and ¼ teaspoon red food coloring into remaining portion until well blended.

2. Place level teaspoonfuls of red dough, green dough and white dough on large baking sheet. Cover; refrigerate 15 minutes or until slightly firm.

3. Preheat oven to 375°F. Place 1 teaspoon red dough, 1 teaspoon green dough and 2 teaspoons white dough on lightly floured

surface. Roll out each portion into 6- to 7-inch rope with lightly floured hands. Place 1 green rope next to 1 white rope and 1 red rope next to remaining white rope. Twist each pair of ropes together 7 or 8 times. Shape red and white rope into candy cane and green and white rope into wreath; place on ungreased baking sheet. Repeat with remaining dough.

4. Bake 7 to 9 minutes or until cookies are firm. *Do not allow to brown.* Transfer cookies to wire racks; cool completely.

5. Prepare Creamy Decorator's Frosting. Tint half of frosting with remaining ¼ teaspoon red food coloring. Spoon frostings into decorating bags fitted with writing tips. Pipe cluster of berries onto wreaths with red frosting. Glue candies onto wreaths with white frosting. Let stand 1 hour or until icing is set. Tie ribbon loops or bows onto each cookie for hanging.

Makes about 4 dozen cookies

Candy Cane & Wreath Ornaments

Star Cookie Christmas Tree

COOKIE DOUGH
2¾ cups flour
1 teaspoon ground ginger
½ teaspoon ground cinnamon
¼ teaspoon salt
⅔ cup KARO® Light Corn Syrup
½ cup packed brown sugar
6 tablespoons margarine or butter
One 10-inch wooden dowel or chopstick (about ¼-inch in diameter)
One 3- or 4-inch styrofoam ball for base

ICING
¼ cup (½ stick) margarine or butter
3 tablespoons KARO® Light Corn Syrup
1½ cups confectioners' sugar
2 teaspoons milk
1 teaspoon vanilla
Green food color
1 container (3¼ ounces) green crystal sugar
Yellow crystal sugar
Miniature colored candies or red cinnamon candies

1. FOR COOKIE DOUGH: In large bowl, stir flour, ginger, cinnamon and salt. In 1-quart saucepan, combine corn syrup, brown sugar and margarine; stir over medium heat until margarine is melted. Stir into flour mixture until well blended. On waxed paper, press dough into rectangle; divide in half.

2. Preheat oven to 350°F. On foil-lined baking sheets roll each dough half to scant ¼ inch thick.

3. With set of ten graduated star-shaped cookie cutters (or with knife), cut dough into 10 graduated stars. Using smallest cutter, cut 9 more cookies to use as spacers. Remove dough trimmings and reroll. Arrange stars on ungreased cookie sheets.

4. Bake 10 to 15 minutes or until lightly browned. While cookies are warm, use dowel to make center hole in each cookie. Cool completely on wire racks.

5. FOR ICING: In small bowl with mixer at medium speed, beat margarine, corn syrup, confectioners' sugar, milk and vanilla until smooth. Reserve about 2 tablespoons icing. Tint remaining icing with green food color.

6. FOR BASE: Cut 1-inch-thick center slice from styrofoam ball. Insert wooden dowel upright in center of slice.

7. TO ASSEMBLE TREE: Starting with largest cookie, spread stars with frosting and sprinkle with green sugar. Slide star down dowel; top with one unfrosted spacer cookie. Repeat with remaining cookies, stacking on dowel in descending size.

8. Sandwich two small stars together; spread with reserved white icing and sprinkle with yellow sugar. Place on edge to form top star. Decorate as desired with candies.

Makes one centerpiece

Prep Time: 2½ hours
Bake Time: 10 minutes, plus cooling

Star Cookie Christmas Tree

Sweet Leaf Wreath

Gingerbread Cookie Dough
   (page 553)
Chocolate Leaves (recipe follows)
1 egg white*
1 cup powdered sugar
Red cinnamon candies

SUPPLIES
   1 (8-inch) cardboard circle
   Red ribbon bow

Use only grade A clean, uncracked egg.

1. Prepare Gingerbread Cookie Dough.
Prepare Chocolate Leaves using semisweet
chocolate only.

2. Preheat oven to 350°F. Grease cookie
sheets. Roll dough on floured surface to
⅛-inch thickness. Using 3½-inch cookie
cutters, cut out 8 holly leaves and 8 rounded
leaves. Mark veins in leaves with tip of knife.
Bake 8 to 10 minutes until edges begin to
brown. Remove to wire racks; let cool.

3. Cut out center of cardboard circle, leaving
2-inch-wide ring. Cover ring with foil.
Arrange cookies on cardboard ring.

4. Beat egg white and powdered sugar in
bowl until well blended. Use frosting to
attach leaves to cardboard ring and to each
other.** Decorate wreath with candies,
Chocolate Leaves and bow, attaching with
frosting.   ***Makes 1 centerpiece***

**To prevent frosting from drying, keep bowl of frosting
covered with damp towel while working.*

Note: This wreath is designed to be used as
a centerpiece. It is not sturdy enough to hang.

Chocolate Leaves

¾ cup coarsely chopped white
   chocolate baking bars or
   confectionery coating
Red food color
Shortening
¾ cup coarsely chopped semisweet
   chocolate

SUPPLIES
   6 to 8 medium and 4 or 5 large lemon
      leaves*
   Pastry brush

These non-toxic leaves are available in florist shops.

1. Melt white chocolate in top of double
boiler over hot, not boiling water, stirring
constantly. Stir in red food color, a few drops
at a time, until desired color is reached. If
chocolate begins to thicken or loses its
shine, stir in shortening, 1 teaspoon at a
time until smooth.

2. Brush thin layer of pink chocolate on
back of each medium-sized leaf with pastry
brush. Do not spread to edge of leaf. Place
on waxed paper-lined baking sheet.
Refrigerate about 30 minutes or until firm.

3. Repeat with semisweet chocolate and
large leaves. Refrigerate about 30 minutes or
until firm.

4. Gently peel chocolate off leaves,
beginning at stem ends. Refrigerate until
ready to use.

Sweet Leaf Wreath

Holiday Peppermint Slices

**1 package (18 ounces) refrigerated
    sugar cookie dough**
**¼ teaspoon peppermint extract,
    divided**
Red food coloring
Green food coloring

1. Remove dough from wrapper. Cut dough into thirds.

2. Combine ⅓ of dough, ⅛ teaspoon peppermint extract and enough red food coloring to make dough desired shade of red. Knead dough until evenly tinted.

3. Repeat with second ⅓ of dough, remaining ⅛ teaspoon peppermint extract and green food coloring.

4. To assemble, shape each portion of dough into 8-inch roll. Place red roll beside green roll; press together slightly. Place plain roll on top. Press rolls together to form one tri-colored roll; wrap in plastic wrap. Refrigerate 2 hours or overnight.

5. Preheat oven to 350°F.

6. Cut dough into ¼-inch-thick slices. Place 2 inches apart on ungreased cookie sheets. Bake 8 to 9 minutes or until set but not browned. Cool 1 minute on cookie sheets. Cool completely on wire racks.

Makes 2½ dozen cookies

Chunky Butter Christmas Cookies

1¼ cups butter, softened
1 cup packed brown sugar
½ cup dairy sour cream
1 egg
2 teaspoons vanilla
1½ cups all-purpose flour
1 teaspoon baking soda
1 teaspoon salt
**1½ cups old-fashioned or quick oats,
    uncooked**
**1 (10-ounce) package white chocolate
    pieces**
1 cup flaked coconut
**1 (3½-ounce) jar macadamia nuts,
    coarsely chopped**

Beat butter and sugar in large bowl until light and fluffy. Blend in sour cream, egg and vanilla. Add combined flour, baking soda and salt; mix well. Stir in oats, white chocolate pieces, coconut and nuts. Drop rounded teaspoonfuls of dough, 2 inches apart, onto ungreased cookie sheet. Bake in preheated 375°F oven 10 to 12 minutes or until edges are lightly browned. Cool 1 minute; remove to cooling rack.

Makes 5 dozen cookies

Favorite recipe from **Wisconsin Milk Marketing Board**

Holiday Peppermint Slices

Santa's Chocolate Cookies

1 cup butter or margarine
⅔ cup semisweet chocolate chips
¾ cup sugar
1 egg
½ teaspoon vanilla
2 cups all-purpose flour
  Apricot jam, melted semisweet chocolate, chopped almonds, frosting, coconut or colored sprinkles (optional)

Preheat oven to 350°F. Melt butter and chocolate chips in small saucepan over low heat, or microwave at HIGH 1 minute or until completely melted. Combine chocolate mixture and sugar in large bowl. Add egg and vanilla; stir well. Add flour; stir well. Refrigerate 30 minutes or until firm.

Shape dough into 1-inch balls. Place 1 inch apart on ungreased cookie sheets. If desired, flatten balls with bottom of drinking glass, or make depression in center and fill with apricot jam.

Bake 8 to 10 minutes or until set. Remove to wire racks to cool completely. Decorate as desired with melted chocolate, almonds, frosting, coconut and colored sprinkles.

Makes about 3 dozen cookies

Festive Butter Cookies

COOKIES
1½ cups butter, softened
  ¾ cup granulated sugar
  3 egg yolks
  3 cups all-purpose flour
  1 teaspoon baking powder
  2 tablespoons orange juice
  1 teaspoon vanilla

FROSTING
  ½ cup butter, softened
  4 cups powdered sugar
  3 to 4 tablespoons milk
  2 teaspoons vanilla
    Food coloring (optional)
    Colored sugars, flaked coconut and cinnamon candies for decoration

For cookies, in large bowl, cream butter and granulated sugar. Add egg yolks; beat until light and fluffy. Add flour, baking powder, orange juice and vanilla; beat until well mixed. Cover; refrigerate 2 to 3 hours or until firm.

Preheat oven to 350°F. Roll out dough, half at a time, ¼ inch thick, on well-floured surface. Cut out with holiday cookie cutters. Place 1 inch apart on ungreased cookie sheets. Bake 6 to 10 minutes or until edges are golden brown. Remove to wire racks to cool completely.

For frosting, beat butter, powdered sugar, milk and vanilla in bowl until fluffy. If desired, divide frosting into small bowls and tint with food coloring. Frost cookies; decorate as desired. *Makes 4 dozen cookies*

Hanukkah Cookies

COOKIES
¾ cup butter or margarine, softened
2 egg yolks
2 tablespoons grated orange peel
1 package DUNCAN HINES® Moist
 Deluxe White Cake Mix

FROSTING
1 container (16 ounces) DUNCAN
 HINES® Vanilla Frosting
3 to 4 drops blue food coloring
3 to 4 drops yellow food coloring

1. For cookies, combine butter, egg yolks and orange peel in large bowl. Beat until blended. Add cake mix gradually, beating until thoroughly blended. Form dough into ball. Cover with plastic wrap and refrigerate for 1 to 2 hours or until chilled but not firm.

2. Preheat oven to 375°F.

3. Roll dough to ⅛-inch thickness on lightly floured surface. Cut with Hanukkah cookie cutters. Place 2 inches apart on ungreased cookie sheets. Bake at 375°F for 6 to 7 minutes or until edges are light golden brown. Cool 1 minute on cookie sheets. Remove to cooling racks. Cool completely.

4. For frosting, tint ½ cup Vanilla frosting with blue food coloring. Warm frosting in microwave oven at HIGH (100% power) for 5 to 10 seconds, if desired. Place writing tip in pastry bag. Fill with tinted frosting. Pipe outline pattern on cookies. Tint ½ cup frosting with yellow food coloring and leave ½ cup frosting untinted; decorate as desired.

Makes 3½ to 4 dozen cookies

Jingle Jumbles

¾ cup butter or margarine, softened
1 cup packed brown sugar
¼ cup molasses
1 egg
2¼ cups unsifted all-purpose flour
2 teaspoons baking soda
1 teaspoon ground ginger
1 teaspoon ground cinnamon
½ teaspoon salt
½ teaspoon ground cloves
1¼ cups SUN•MAID® Raisins
 Granulated sugar

In large bowl, cream butter and sugar. Add molasses and egg; beat until fluffy. In medium bowl, sift together flour, baking soda, ginger, cinnamon, salt and cloves. Stir into molasses mixture. Stir in raisins. Cover and chill about 30 minutes.

Preheat oven to 375°F. Grease cookie sheets. Form dough into 1½-inch balls; roll in granulated sugar, coating generously. Place 2 inches apart on prepared cookie sheets.

Bake 12 to 14 minutes or until edges are firm and centers are still slightly soft. Remove to wire racks to cool.

Makes about 2 dozen cookies

Fireside Cookie

**1 package (18 ounces) refrigerated
 cookie dough, any flavor
All-purpose flour (optional)
Icings, red licorice bites, black string
 licorice, gum drops and assorted
 candies**

1. Preheat oven to 350°F. Line large baking sheets with parchment paper.

2. Remove dough from wrapper. Using about ¼ of dough, roll into 12×3-inch strip. Trim to 11×2¼ inches; set aside. Roll remaining dough into 10×8-inch rectangle. Trim to 9×7¾ inches; place on prepared baking sheet. Place reserved dough strip at top of rectangle to make fireplace mantel. Roll remaining scraps and cut into stocking shapes. Place on prepared baking sheets.

3. Bake 10 minutes or until edges are lightly browned. Cool on baking sheets 5 minutes. Remove stocking cookies to wire rack. Slide large cookie and parchment paper onto wire rack; cool completely.

4. Decorate with icings and candies as shown, attaching stockings to fireplace cookie with icing.   *Makes 1 large cookie*

Holiday Wreath Cookies

**1 package (20 ounces) refrigerated
 sugar cookie dough
2 cups shredded coconut
2 to 3 drops green food color
1 container (16 ounces) French vanilla
 frosting
Green sugar or small cinnamon
 candies**

1. Preheat oven to 350°F. Remove dough from wrapper. Divide dough in half; wrap half of dough in plastic wrap and refrigerate. Roll out remaining half of dough on well-floured surface to ⅛-inch thickness. Cut with cookie cutters to resemble wreaths. Repeat with remaining half of dough.

2. Place cookies about 2 inches apart on ungreased baking sheets. Bake 7 to 9 minutes or until edges are lightly browned. Remove cookies from baking sheets to wire racks to cool completely.

3. Place coconut in resealable plastic food storage bag. Add food color; seal bag and shake until coconut is evenly tinted. Frost cookies with frosting and decorate with coconut, green sugar and cinnamon candies.
               Makes about 2 dozen cookies

Fireside Cookie

Chocolate Nut Bars

½ cup uncooked quick oats
½ cup hazelnuts, chopped
½ cup walnuts, chopped
¾ cup powdered sugar
8 ounces (1¼ cups) semisweet
   chocolate chips
1 tablespoon shortening
2 tablespoons butter
½ teaspoon salt
⅓ cup corn syrup
½ teaspoon vanilla

1. Preheat oven to 350°F. Line 8-inch square baking pan with foil, pressing foil into corners to cover completely and leaving 1-inch overhang on sides.

2. Spread oats on ungreased baking sheet. Bake 8 to 10 minutes or until light golden brown. Let cool; place in large bowl. *Reduce oven temperature to 325°F.* Spread hazelnuts and walnuts on baking sheet. Bake 9 to 11 minutes or just until cut sides begin to brown lightly. Let cool; add to toasted oats. Stir in powdered sugar; set aside.

3. Heat chocolate chips and shortening in small heavy saucepan over very low heat, stirring constantly, until melted and smooth. Remove from heat. Spread evenly on bottom of prepared 8-inch square pan. Let stand in cool place 15 to 20 minutes or until chocolate mixture begins to set, but is not firm.

4. Combine butter and salt in microwavable bowl. Microwave at HIGH 20 to 30 seconds or until butter is melted and foamy. Stir in corn syrup; let cool slightly and add vanilla. Stir corn syrup mixture into oat mixture just until moistened. Gently spoon over chocolate, spreading evenly into corners. Score lightly into 4 strips, then score each strip into 6 pieces. Cover tightly with plastic wrap and refrigerate at least 4 hours or until firm.

5. Remove bars from pan, lifting foil by edges. Place on cutting board; cut along score lines into 24 pieces. Remove foil. Store in airtight container in refrigerator.

Makes 24 bars

DECORATE IT!

Make these treats more festive by sprinkling them with red and green candy-coated chocolate pieces or sprinkles just before refrigerating.

Chocolate Nut Bars

Lollipop Cookies

Butter Cookie Dough (page 552)
1 cup semisweet chocolate chips,
 melted
½ cup finely chopped hazelnuts or
 almonds
1 cup vanilla frosting (about ½ of
 16-ounce container)
Red and green decorating gel
Colored sugars

SUPPLIES
 24 (4-inch) lollipop sticks*

*Lollipop sticks are available at stores carrying cake decorating supplies.

1. Prepare 2 recipes Butter Cookie Dough.

2. Preheat oven to 350°F. Grease cookie sheets.

3. Roll dough on floured surface to ¼-inch thickness. Cut out 48 circles using 2-inch round cookie cutter. Place 24 circles on prepared cookie sheets.

4. Combine melted chocolate and hazelnuts. Spoon rounded ½ teaspoon chocolate mixture in center of each dough circle on cookie sheet. Place lollipop sticks on circles so that tips of sticks are imbedded in filling. Top with remaining dough circles; seal edges of dough with floured fork tines.

5. Bake 10 to 12 minutes until edges begin to brown. Remove to wire racks; let cool.

6. Frost tops and sides of cookies with vanilla frosting. Decorate with decorating gel and colored sugars.

Makes 2 dozen cookies

Angels

Butter Cookie Dough (page 552)
1 egg, lightly beaten
Small pretzels, white frosting,
 toasted coconut, edible glitter dust
 and assorted small decors

1. Prepare Butter Cookie Dough.

2. Preheat oven to 350°F. Grease cookie sheets. Roll dough on floured surface to ¼-inch thickness. Cut out 12 (4-inch) triangles. Reroll scraps to ¼-inch thickness. Cut out 12 (1½-inch) circles.

3. Place triangles on prepared cookie sheets. Brush with beaten egg. Attach circle, pressing gently.

4. Bake 8 to 10 minutes or just until edges begin to brown. Remove to wire racks; cool completely.

5. Attach pretzels to back of each cookie for wings using frosting as "glue." Let dry 30 minutes. Pipe frosting around hairline of each angel; sprinkle with coconut and glitter dust.

6. Pipe frosting on body of cookie to resemble arms and gown. Decorate faces as desired. Let stand 1 hour or until dry.

Makes 1 dozen cookies

Holiday Bits Cutout Cookies

1 cup (2 sticks) butter or margarine, softened
1 cup sugar
2 eggs
2 teaspoons vanilla extract
2½ cups all-purpose flour
½ teaspoon baking powder
½ teaspoon salt
HERSHEY®S Holiday Candy Coated Bits

1. Beat butter, sugar, eggs and vanilla in large bowl on low speed of mixer just until blended. Stir together flour, baking powder and salt; add to butter mixture, stirring until well blended.

2. Divide dough in half. Cover; refrigerate 1 to 2 hours or until firm enough to handle. Heat oven to 400°F. On lightly floured surface, roll each half of the dough to about ¼ inch thick.

3. Cut into tree, wreath, star or other shapes with 2½-inch cookie cutters. Place on ungreased cookie sheet. Press candy coated bits into cutouts.

4. Bake 6 to 8 minutes or until edges are firm and bottoms are very lightly browned. Remove from cookie sheet to wire rack. Cool completely.

Makes about 3½ dozen cookies

Prep Time: 30 minutes
Chill Time: 1 hour
Bake Time: 6 minutes

Holiday Bits Cutout Cookies

Christmas Tree Cookies

1 package DUNCAN HINES® Golden
    Sugar Cookie Mix
2 eggs
⅓ cup vegetable oil
    Green food coloring
½ cup sliced natural almonds
    Pecan halves, cut in half
    Red candied cherries, cut in fourths

1. Preheat oven to 375°F. Combine cookie mix, eggs, oil and 4 to 5 drops green food coloring in large bowl. Stir until thoroughly blended. Form dough into pea-size balls. Place 15 balls with sides touching in triangle shape on ungreased baking sheet. Repeat with remaining dough balls, placing triangles 2 inches apart.

2. Insert almond slices between balls to form branches. Place 1 pecan piece in bottom of each tree to form trunk. Place 1 cherry piece on top ball of each tree. Bake at 375°F for 7 to 8 minutes or until cookies are set. Cool 1 minute on baking sheets. Remove to cooling racks. Cool completely. Store in airtight container.   *Makes 2 dozen cookies*

Note: For a delicious no-cholesterol variation, substitute 1 egg white for the whole egg.

Tip: Cookies may be stored in airtight container in freezer for up to 6 months.

Storefront Place Cards

Gingerbread Cookie Dough
   (page 553)
Powdered sugar
Cookie Glaze (page 555)
Assorted food colors
Assorted candies

SUPPLIES
   Pastry bags and small writing tips

1. Prepare Gingerbread Cookie Dough.

2. Preheat oven to 350°F. On floured surface, roll dough to about ¼-inch thickness. Cut out 16 to 20 (4×3-inch) rectangles. Place 2 inches apart on ungreased cookie sheets.

3. Bake 12 to 14 minutes or until edges begin to brown. Remove to wire racks; cool.

4. Prepare Cookie Glaze, adding 2 to 3 tablespoons additional powdered sugar to glaze; divide into separate bowl for each color of frosting desired. Tint with food colors as desired. Spoon into pastry bags fitted with writing tips. Pipe designs and names onto half of cookies. Decorate with candies to look like holiday storefronts or houses, using glaze to attach candies. Let stand until glaze is set.

5. To assemble place cards, spread some remaining glaze on top edges of undecorated cookies; press to backs of decorated cookies at top. Separate bottoms so cookies make upside-down "V," and cookies can stand without support. Let stand until glaze is set.
   Makes 8 to 10 place cards

Christmas Tree Cookies

Chocolate Reindeer

1 cup butter, softened
1 cup sugar
1 egg
1 teaspoon vanilla
2 ounces semisweet chocolate, melted
2¼ cups all-purpose flour
1 teaspoon baking powder
¼ teaspoon salt
    Royal Icing (page 556)
    Assorted food colors
    Assorted small candies

1. Beat butter and sugar in large bowl at high speed of electric mixer until fluffy. Beat in egg and vanilla. Add melted chocolate; mix well. Add flour, baking powder and salt; mix well. Divide dough in half; wrap each half in plastic wrap and refrigerate 2 hours or until firm.

2. Preheat oven to 325°F. Grease 2 cookie sheets; set aside.

3. Roll one half of dough on well-floured surface to ¼-inch thickness. Cut out with reindeer cookie cutter. Place 2 inches apart on prepared cookie sheets. Chill 10 minutes.

4. Bake 13 to 15 minutes or until set. Cool completely on cookie sheets. Repeat steps with remaining dough.

5. Prepare Royal Icing. Tint with food colors as desired. Pipe icing on reindeer and decorate with small candies. For best results, let cookies dry overnight uncovered before storing in airtight container at room temperature.   *Makes 16 (4-inch) cookies*

Pinecone Cookies

6 tablespoons butter or margarine
⅓ cup HERSHEY�ₛS Cocoa or
    HERSHEY�ₛS Dutch Processed
    Cocoa
1 cup sugar
2 eggs
1 teaspoon vanilla extract
2 cups all-purpose flour
½ teaspoon baking powder
½ teaspoon salt
¼ teaspoon baking soda
    Light corn syrup
    Sliced almonds

1. Melt butter in small saucepan; remove from heat. Add cocoa; blend well. Combine sugar, eggs, and vanilla in large bowl; blend in chocolate mixture. Stir together flour, baking powder, salt and baking soda; add to chocolate-sugar mixture, beating until smooth. Refrigerate dough about 1 hour or until firm enough to roll.

2. Heat oven to 350°F.

3. Roll small portion of dough at a time between pieces of wax paper to ⅛-inch thickness. Cut into pinecone shapes using 2- or 2½-inch oval cookie cutter. Place on lightly greased cookie sheet; lightly brush cookies with corn syrup. Arrange almonds in pinecone fashion; lightly drizzle or brush almonds with corn syrup.

4. Bake 7 to 8 minutes or until set. Cool slightly; remove from cookie sheet to wire rack. Cool completely.
    Makes about 4 dozen cookies

Chocolate Reindeer

Mini Morsel Meringue Wreaths

2 egg whites
¼ teaspoon cream of tartar
⅓ cup sugar
½ cup (¼ of 12-ounce package) NESTLÉ® TOLL HOUSE® Semi-Sweet Chocolate Mini Morsels
1 (3-ounce) package candied cherries, quartered

PREHEAT oven to 275°F. In small mixer bowl, beat egg whites and cream of tartar until soft peaks form. Gradually add sugar; beat until stiff peaks form. Fold in Nestlé® Toll House® Semi-Sweet Chocolate Mini Morsels. Spoon into pastry bag fitted with plain #7 pastry tip. Pipe 2-inch circles onto parchment paper-lined cookie sheets. Top each wreath with two candied cherry pieces. Bake 20 minutes. Turn oven off; let stand in oven 30 minutes with door ajar. Cool; peel off paper. Store in airtight container.

Makes about 2½ dozen cookies

Gingerbread People

½ cup butter, softened
½ cup packed brown sugar
⅓ cup molasses
⅓ cup water
1 egg
4 cups all-purpose flour
2 teaspoons baking soda
1 teaspoon ground ginger
½ teaspoon ground allspice
½ teaspoon ground cinnamon
½ teaspoon ground cloves
White or colored frostings

Beat butter and brown sugar in large bowl at medium speed of electric mixer until creamy. Add molasses, water and egg; beat until blended. Stir in flour, baking soda, ginger, allspice, cinnamon and cloves until well blended. Cover; refrigerate about 2 hours or until firm.

Preheat oven to 350°F. Grease cookie sheets. Roll out dough to ⅛-inch thickness on lightly floured surface with lightly floured rolling pin. Cut with cookie cutter. Place 2 inches apart on prepared cookie sheets.

Bake 12 to 15 minutes or until firm to the touch. Cool 1 minute on cookie sheets. Remove to wire racks; cool completely. Decorate with frostings. Store in airtight containers.

Makes about 4½ dozen cookies

Have-a-Heart Bear Garland

Butter Cookie Dough (page 552)
Cookie Glaze (page 555)
3 tablespoons unsweetened cocoa
powder
Powdered sugar
Yellow food color (optional)
Assorted candies

SUPPLIES
Plastic drinking straw
Pastry bags and small writing tip
Ribbon

1. Prepare Butter Cookie Dough.

2. Preheat oven to 350°F. On floured surface, roll dough to ¼-inch thickness. Cut out dough using 3½- to 4-inch bear-shaped cookie cutter. Place 2 inches apart on ungreased baking sheets. Using straw, make hole in each arm of each bear, about ¼ inch from ends; cut out heart from center of each bear using ½-inch heart-shaped cookie cutter.

3. Bake 10 to 12 minutes or until edges begin to brown. Remove to wire racks; cool completely.

4. Prepare Cookie Glaze; reserve ⅓ cup. Stir cocoa into remaining glaze. Place cookies on wire racks set over waxed-paper-lined baking sheets. Spoon cocoa glaze over cookies.

5. Add 1 to 2 tablespoons powdered sugar to reserved ⅓ cup glaze. Tint with yellow food color, if desired. Dab small dots of glaze onto heads for attaching candies for eyes and noses. Spoon remaining thickened glaze into pastry bag fitted with writing tip; use to decorate cookies as desired. Let stand until glaze is set.

6. Using ribbon, tie bears together through holes in arms. Hang on tree or drape over packages.   *Makes about 2 dozen cookies*

HELPFUL HINT

The holiday season can be so busy! For a real time-saver, prepare, bake and cool these cookies completely, but do not decorate them. Wrap the undecorated cookies airtight, and freeze them for up to 2 months. Thaw and decorate the cookies as desired when you need them.

Rugelach

1½ cups all-purpose flour
¼ teaspoon salt
¼ teaspoon baking soda
½ cup butter, softened
1 package (3 ounces) cream cheese, softened
⅓ cup plus ¼ cup granulated sugar, divided
1 teaspoon grated lemon peel, divided
1 cup ground toasted walnuts
1 teaspoon ground cinnamon
2 tablespoons honey
1 tablespoon lemon juice
Powdered sugar

Combine flour, salt and baking soda in small bowl.

Beat butter, cream cheese, ⅓ cup granulated sugar and ½ teaspoon lemon peel in large bowl with electric mixer at medium speed about 5 minutes or until light and fluffy. Gradually add flour mixture. Beat at low speed until well blended.

Form dough into three 5-inch discs; wrap in plastic wrap and refrigerate until firm, about 2 hours.

Preheat oven to 375°F. Grease cookie sheets; set aside.

Combine walnuts, remaining ¼ cup granulated sugar and cinnamon in medium bowl; set aside. Combine honey, remaining ½ teaspoon lemon peel and lemon juice in small bowl; set aside.

Working with 1 piece of dough at a time, remove plastic wrap and place dough on lightly floured surface. Roll out dough with lightly floured rolling pin to 10-inch circle. Keep remaining dough refrigerated.

Brush with ⅓ of honey mixture. Sprinkle with ⅓ cup nut mixture. Lightly press nut mixture into dough.

Cut circle into 12 triangles with pizza cutter or sharp knife. Beginning with wide end of triangle, tightly roll up, jelly-roll fashion. Place cookies 1 inch apart on prepared cookie sheet.

Repeat with 2 remaining dough pieces and filling ingredients. Bake 10 to 12 minutes or until lightly golden brown. Let cookies stand on cookie sheets 1 minute. Remove cookies to wire racks; cool completely. Sprinkle with powdered sugar. Store tightly covered.

Makes 3 dozen cookies

Note: To toast walnuts, spread them in single layer on ungreased baking sheet; bake in preheated 350°F oven 8 to 10 minutes or until golden brown, stirring frequently. Remove walnuts from baking sheet to cool. To grind walnuts, place in food processor. Process using on/off pulsing action until ground, but not pasty.

Rugelach

Buttery Almond Cutouts

1 cup butter, softened
1½ cups granulated sugar
¾ cup sour cream
2 eggs
3 teaspoons almond extract, divided
1 teaspoon vanilla
4⅓ cups all-purpose flour
1 teaspoon baking powder
1 teaspoon baking soda
½ teaspoon salt
2 cups powdered sugar
2 tablespoons milk
1 tablespoon light corn syrup
Assorted food colorings

1. Beat butter and granulated sugar in large bowl until light and fluffy. Add sour cream, eggs, 2 teaspoons almond extract and vanilla; beat until smooth. Add flour, baking powder, baking soda and salt; beat just until well blended.

2. Divide dough into 4 pieces; flatten each piece into disc. Wrap each disc tightly with plastic wrap. Refrigerate at least 3 hours or up to 3 days.

3. Combine powdered sugar, milk, corn syrup and remaining 1 teaspoon almond extract in small bowl; stir until smooth. Cover and refrigerate up to 3 days.

4. Preheat oven to 375°F. Working with 1 disc of dough at a time, roll out on floured surface to ¼-inch thickness. Cut dough into desired shapes using 2½-inch cookie cutters. Place 2 inches apart on ungreased baking sheets. Bake 7 to 8 minutes or until

edges are firm and bottoms are brown. Remove from baking sheets to wire racks to cool completely.

5. Separate powdered sugar mixture into 3 or 4 batches in small bowls; tint each batch with desired food coloring. Frost cookies. *Makes about 3 dozen cookies*

Make-Ahead Time: up to 3 days in refrigerator or up to 3 months in freezer
Final Prep Time: 30 minutes

HELPFUL HINT

Freeze this cookie dough so you'll be able to make these cookies at any time. First, prepare the dough as directed through step 2. Then place the wrapped discs in resealable plastic food storage bags and freeze for up to 3 months. Thaw the dough at room temperature before using.

Buttery Almond Cutouts

Star Christmas Tree Cookies

COOKIES
 ½ cup vegetable shortening
 ⅓ cup butter or margarine, softened
 2 egg yolks
 1 teaspoon vanilla extract
 1 package DUNCAN HINES® Moist
   Deluxe Yellow or Devil's Food
   Cake Mix
 1 tablespoon water

FROSTING
 1 container (16 ounces) DUNCAN
   HINES® Vanilla Frosting
 Green food coloring
 Red and green sugar crystals for
   garnish
 Assorted colored candies and decors
   for garnish

Preheat oven to 375°F. For cookies, combine shortening, butter, egg yolks and vanilla extract. Blend in cake mix gradually. Add 1 teaspoonful water at a time until dough is rolling consistency. Divide dough into 4 balls. Flatten one ball with hand; roll to ⅛-inch thickness on lightly floured surface. Cut with graduated star cookie cutters. Repeat using remaining dough. Bake large cookies together on *ungreased* baking sheet. Bake 6 to 8 minutes or until edges are light golden brown. Cool cookies 1 minute. Remove from baking sheet. Repeat with smaller cookies, testing for doneness at minimum baking time.

For frosting, tint Vanilla frosting with green food coloring. Frost cookies and stack,

beginning with largest cookies on bottom and ending with smallest cookies on top. Rotate cookies when stacking to alternate corners. Decorate as desired with colored sugar crystals and assorted colored candies and decors. *Makes 2 to 3 dozen cookies*

HELPFUL HINT

To separate an egg yolk from a white, gently tap the center of the egg against a hard surface, such as the side of a bowl. Gently break the egg in half over the bowl. Holding a shell half in each hand, gently transfer the yolk back and forth between the two shell halves, allowing the white to drip into the bowl. Place the yolk into another bowl.

Star Christmas Tree Cookies

Just the BASICS

Butter Cookie Dough

¾ cup butter, softened
¼ cup granulated sugar
¼ cup packed light brown sugar
1 egg yolk
1¾ cups all-purpose flour
¾ teaspoon baking powder
⅛ teaspoon salt

1. Combine butter, granulated sugar, brown sugar and egg yolk in medium bowl. Add flour, baking powder and salt; mix well.

2. Cover; refrigerate about 4 hours or until firm.

Chocolate Cookie Dough

1 cup butter, softened
1 cup sugar
1 egg
1 teaspoon vanilla
2 ounces semisweet chocolate, melted
2¼ cups all-purpose flour
1 teaspoon baking powder
¼ teaspoon salt

1. Beat butter and sugar in large bowl with electric mixer at high speed until fluffy. Beat in egg and vanilla. Add melted chocolate; mix well.

2. Add flour, baking powder and salt; mix well. Cover; refrigerate about 2 hours or until firm.

Christmas Ornament Cookie Dough

2¼ cups all-purpose flour
 ¼ teaspoon salt
 1 cup sugar
 ¾ cup butter, softened
 1 egg
 1 teaspoon vanilla
 1 teaspoon almond extract

1. Combine flour and salt in medium bowl.

2. Beat sugar and butter in large bowl with electric mixer at medium speed until fluffy. Beat in egg, vanilla and almond extract. Gradually add flour mixture. Beat at low speed until well blended.

3. Form dough into 2 discs; wrap in plastic wrap and refrigerate 30 minutes or until firm.

Gingerbread House Dough

5¼ cups all-purpose flour
 1 tablespoon ground ginger
 2 teaspoons baking soda
1½ teaspoons ground allspice
 1 teaspoon salt
 2 cups packed dark brown sugar
 1 cup butter, softened
 ¾ cup dark corn syrup
 2 eggs

1. Combine flour, ginger, baking soda, allspice and salt in medium bowl.

2. Beat brown sugar and butter in large bowl with electric mixer at medium speed until fluffy. Beat in corn syrup and eggs. Gradually add flour mixture. Beat at low speed until well blended. Cover; refrigerate about 2 hours or until firm.

Gingerbread Cookie Dough

 ½ cup shortening
 ⅓ cup packed light brown sugar
 ¼ cup dark molasses
 1 egg white
 ½ teaspoon vanilla
1½ cups all-purpose flour
 ½ teaspoon baking soda
 ¼ teaspoon baking powder
 ½ teaspoon salt
 1 teaspoon ground cinnamon
 ½ teaspoon ground ginger

1. Beat shortening, brown sugar, molasses, egg white and vanilla in large bowl with electric mixer at high speed until smooth.

2. Combine flour, baking soda, baking powder, salt and spices in small bowl. Add to shortening mixture; mix well. Cover; refrigerate until firm, about 8 hours or overnight.

Creamy Decorator's Frosting

1½ cups vegetable shortening
1½ teaspoons lemon, coconut, almond
or peppermint extract (optional)
7½ cups sifted powdered sugar
⅓ cup milk
Assorted food colorings (optional)

1. Beat shortening and extract, if desired, in large bowl with electric mixer at medium speed until fluffy.

2. Slowly add half of powdered sugar, ½ cup at a time, beating well after each addition. Beat in milk. Add remaining powdered sugar; beat 1 minute or until smooth and fluffy.

3. Tint with food colorings, if desired. Store, covered, in refrigerator. (Frosting may be used for piping decorations.)

Makes about 5 cups

Decorator Frosting

¾ cup butter, softened
4½ cups powdered sugar, sifted
3 tablespoons water
1 teaspoon vanilla
¼ teaspoon lemon extract (optional)
Assorted food colorings (optional)

1. Beat butter in medium bowl with electric mixer at medium speed until smooth. Add 2 cups powdered sugar. Beat at medium speed until light and fluffy.

2. Add water, vanilla and lemon extract, if desired. Beat at low speed until well blended, scraping down side of bowl once. Beat in remaining 2½ cups powdered sugar until mixture is creamy.

3. Tint with food colorings, if desired.

Makes about 2 cups

Ornamental Frosting

½ cup butter, softened
½ teaspoon vanilla
1 package (16 ounces) powdered
sugar, sifted
2 tablespoons milk
Assorted food colorings (optional)

1. Beat butter and vanilla in large bowl with electric mixer at medium speed until fluffy.

2. Beat in powdered sugar and enough milk at low speed until frosting is of desired spreading consistency.

3. Tint with food colorings, if desired.

Makes about 2 cups

Fudge Frosting

24 large marshmallows, halved
⅔ cup semisweet chocolate chips
½ cup vegetable shortening
½ cup water
5 cups sifted powdered sugar
3 teaspoons vanilla

1. Place marshmallows, chocolate chips, shortening and water in 1½-quart saucepan. Cook over low heat until melted and smooth, stirring constantly. Remove from heat; let stand 5 minutes.

2. Gradually beat in powdered sugar and vanilla with electric mixer at medium speed about 6 minutes or until mixture starts to lose gloss. Use frosting immediately.

White Decorator Frosting

4 cups powdered sugar
½ cup vegetable shortening or unsalted butter
1 tablespoon corn syrup
6 to 8 tablespoons milk

1. Beat powdered sugar and shortening in medium bowl with electric mixer at high speed 2 minutes.

2. Add corn syrup and milk; beat at high speed until fluffy.

Cookie Glaze

4 cups powdered sugar
4 to 6 tablespoons milk
Assorted food colorings (optional)

1. Combine powdered sugar and enough milk, 1 tablespoon at a time, to make a medium-thick pourable glaze.

2. Tint with food colorings, if desired.

Powdered Sugar Icing

2 cups powdered sugar
2 tablespoons milk or lemon juice
Assorted food colorings (optional)

1. Place powdered sugar and milk in small bowl; stir with spoon until smooth. (Icing will be very thick. If it is too thick, stir in 1 teaspoon additional milk.)

2. Tint with food colorings, if desired.

Lemonade Royal Icing

3¾ cups sifted powdered sugar
3 tablespoons meringue powder
6 tablespoons frozen lemonade
concentrate, thawed
Assorted food colorings (optional)

1. Beat all ingredients in large bowl with electric mixer at high speed until smooth.

2. Tint with food colorings, if desired.

Lemon Royal Icing

4 egg whites*
4 cups powdered sugar, sifted
1 teaspoon lemon extract or clear
vanilla extract**
Assorted food colorings (optional)

*Use only grade A clean, uncracked eggs.

**Icing remains very white when clear flavorings are used.

1. Beat egg whites in clean, large bowl with electric mixer at high speed until foamy.

2. Gradually add powdered sugar and lemon extract. Beat at high speed until thickened.

3. Tint with food colorings, if desired.

Makes 2 cups

Royal Icing

1 egg white,* at room temperature
2 to 2½ cups sifted powdered sugar
½ teaspoon almond extract
Assorted food colorings (optional)

*Use only grade A clean, uncracked egg.

1. Beat egg white in small bowl with electric mixer at high speed until foamy.

2. Gradually add 2 cups powdered sugar and almond extract. Beat at low speed until moistened. Increase mixer speed to high and beat until icing is stiff, adding additional powdered sugar if needed.

3. Tint with food colorings, if desired.

Meringue Powder Royal Icing

¼ cup meringue powder
6 tablespoons water
1 box (16 ounces) powdered sugar,
  sifted
Assorted food colorings (optional)

1. Beat meringue powder and water in medium bowl with electric mixer at low speed until well blended. Beat at high speed until stiff peaks form.

2. Beat in powdered sugar at low speed until well blended. Beat at high speed until icing is very stiff. Cover icing with damp cloth to prevent icing from drying.

3. Tint with food colorings, if desired.

Makes about 2½ cups

Note: Meringue Powder Royal Icing hardens after 5 minutes and completely dries in 20 to 30 minutes.

Egg Yolk Paint

2 egg yolks
2 teaspoons water
  Assorted liquid food colorings
  (optional)

1. Combine egg yolks and water in small bowl with fork until blended.

2. Divide paint among several bowls and tint with food coloring, if desired.

ACKNOWLEDGMENTS

The publisher would like to thank the companies and organizations listed below for the use of their recipes and photographs in this publication.

Almond Board of California

Bestfoods

Blue Diamond Growers®

Bob Evans®

California Dried Plum Board

California Table Grape Commission

California Tree Fruit Agreement

Cherry Marketing Institute

ConAgra Grocery Products Company

Cream of Wheat® Cereal

DAVIS® Baking Powder

Dole Food Company, Inc.

Domino Sugar Corporation

Duncan Hines® and Moist Deluxe® are registered trademarks of Aurora Foods Inc.

Eagle® Brand

Hershey Foods Corporation

HONEY MAID® Honey Grahams

Kellogg Company

Kraft Foods Holdings

Lipton®

©Mars, Inc. 2001

McIlhenny Company (TABASCO® brand Pepper Sauce)

Minnesota Cultivated Wild Rice Council

Mott's® is a registered trademark of Mott's, Inc.

Nabisco Biscuit Company

National Honey Board

National Sunflower Association

Nestlé USA, Inc.

Newman's Own, Inc.®

NILLA® Wafers

OREO® Chocolate Sandwich Cookies

Peanut Advisory Board

Pear Bureau Northwest

PLANTERS® Nuts

The Procter & Gamble Company

The Quaker® Oatmeal Kitchens

Reckitt Benckiser

REFINED SUGARS, INC.

ROYAL® Desserts

The J.M. Smucker Company

Sokol and Company

Sun•Maid® Growers of California

Sunkist Growers

USA Rice Federation

Washington Apple Commission

Wisconsin Milk Marketing Board

A

Absolutely Wonderful Pecan Bars, 111
Ali's Oatmeal Cookies, 349
Almond
Almond Brownies, 175
Almond Cheesecake Brownies, 153
Almond Chinese Chews, 406
Almond Cream Cheese Cookies, 200
Almond Double Chip Cookies, 49
Almond Frosting, 236
Almond Fudge Cups, 502
Almond Hearts, 230
Almond Icing, 153
Almond Rice Madeleines, 92
Almond Toffee Triangles, 106
Bolivian Almond Cookies, 388
Buttery Almond Cutouts, 548
Chocolate Almond Biscotti, 96
Chocolate Filling, 414
Cinnamon Crinkles Cookies, 73
Classic Anise Biscotti, 400
Cocoa Almond Glaze, 216
Coconut Almond Bars, 127
Double Almond Butter Cookies, 98
Double Chocolate Banana Cookies, 353
Double Chocolate Raspberry Bars, 317
Fabulous Blonde Brownies, 181
Finnish Nut Logs, 418
Glazed Oatmeal Raisin Coffee Cookies, 18
Mexican Chocolate Macaroons, 384
Norwegian Almond Squares, 409
Orange-Almond Sables, 244
Polish Honey Bars, 414
White Chocolate & Almond Brownies, 184
Yuletide Linzer Bars, 511
Almond Paste
Baseball Caps, 460
Chocolate-Dipped Almond Horns, 92
Chocolate Macaroons, 336
Double Almond Butter Cookies, 98

Angels, 538
Apples
Apple-Cranberry Crescent Cookies, 356
Apple Date Nut Blondies, 178
Autumn Apple Bars, 104
Breakfast Cookies, 352
Fruit and Nut Bars, 114
Applesauce
Apple Crumb Squares, 130
Gingerbread Apple Bars, 110
Oatmeal Raisin Cookies, 25
Wild Rice Applesauce Bars, 124
Apricot
Ali's Oatmeal Cookies, 349
Apricot Biscotti, 368
Apricot Cream Cheese Drops, 30
Apricot-Filled Pastries, 367
Apricot Filling, 367
Awesome Apricot Oatmeal Bars, 120
Cinnamon-Apricot Tart Oatmeal Cookies, 348
Easy Apricot Oatmeal Bars, 118
Peek-A-Boo Apricot Cookies, 250
White Chip Apricot Oatmeal Cookies, 350
Argentinean Caramel-Filled Crescents, 390
Autumn Apple Bars, 104
Awesome Apricot Oatmeal Bars, 120

B

Baklava, 396
Bananas
Banana Chocolate Chip Bars, 106
Banana Chocolate Chip Cookies, 367
Banana Chocolate Chip Softies, 371
Bananaramas, 358
Banana Sandies, 377
Banana Split Bars, 122
Double Chocolate Banana Cookies, 353
Elvis Would Have Loved These Peanut Butter Cookies, 382
Family Favorite Oatmeal Cookies, 346

Bananas (*continued*)
Fruit and Cookie Pizza, 376
No-Bake Banana Peanut Butter Fudge Bars, 296
Oatmeal Gorp Cookies, 350
Peanut Butter & Banana Cookies, 376
Peanut Butter Chipwiches, 293
Bar Cookie Crust, 132
Bar Cookies (*see also pages 100–141*)
Almond Chinese Chews, 406
Baklava, 396
Chocolate Cereal Bars, 275
Chocolate Nut Bars, 536
Chocolate Scotcheroos, 290
Chocolate Walnut Pie Bars, 312
Citrus Cream Bars, 288
Colossal Cookie Sandwich, 477
Conversation Heart Cereal Treats, 462
Cookie Pizza, 425
Crispy Chocolate Logs, 290
Double Chocolate Fantasy Bars, 320
Double Chocolate Raspberry Bars, 317
Double Peanut Squares, 284
Fig Bars, 380
Fireside Cookie, 534
Fruit and Cookie Pizza, 376
Fudgy Chip Bars, 317
Fudgy Chocolate Mint Oatmeal Squares, 318
Fudgy Cookie Squares, 312
Grand Old Flag Cookie, 474
Lebkuchen Jewels, 397
Nathaniel's Jumble, 292
Nestlé Crunch® Pizza Cookie, 432
No-Bake Banana Peanut Butter Fudge Bars, 296
No-Bake Chocolate Oat Bars, 294
No-Bake Pineapple Marmalade Squares, 272
Norwegian Almond Squares, 409
Original Rice Krispies Treats® Recipe, The, 292
Peanut Butter Bars, 286
Peanut Butter Chocolate No-Bake Bars, 274

Bar Cookies (*continued*)
Peanut Butter-Hop-Scotch Treats, 294
Polish Honey Bars, 414
Puzzle Cookie, 440
Rocky Road Bars, 318
Sachertorte Squares, 316
Sharing Cookies, 477
S'More Snack Treats, 268
Special Treat No-Bake Squares, 278
Spiced Chocolate Pecan Squares, 320
Tri-Layer Chocolate Oatmeal Bars, 314
Ultimate Rocky Road Squares, 443
Under the Sea, 446
Viennese Meringue Bars, 395
Yuletide Linzer Bars, 511
Baseball Caps, 460
Basic Icebox Cookie Dough, 220
Bat Cookies, 487
Belgian Tuile Cookies, 416
Berry Treasures, 226
Bird's Nest Cookies, 460
Biscochitos, 386
Bittersweet Pecan Brownies with Caramel Sauce, 144
Black and White Cut-Outs, 252
Black & White Hearts, 224
Black and White Sandwiches, 252
Black Cat Cookies, 488
Blonde Brickle Brownies, 180
"Blondie" Brownies, 182
Bolivian Almond Cookies, 388
Boo!! Brownies, 490
Brandy Lace Cookies, 494
Brandy Nut Cookies, 66
Bran Fruit and Nut Cookies, 364
Breakfast Cookies, 352
Brian's Buffalo Cookies, 14
Brownie Candy Cups, 158
Brownie Fudge, 174
Brownie Mix
Brownie Candy Cups, 158
Brownie Sandwich Cookies, 438
Brownie Sundaes For Kids, 428
Buffalo Bill Brownies, 144
Double Fudge Brownie Bars, 147
Double "Topped" Brownies, 172

Brownie Mix (*continued*)
Frosted Maraschino Brownies, 146
Oreo® Brownie Treats, 150
Pumpkin Candy Brownies, 478
Rich 'n' Creamy Brownie Bars, 164
Rocky Road Squares, 172
Scrumptious Minted Brownies, 142
Skull & Cross Bones, 481
Tombstone Brownies, 480
Brownie Pie à la Mode, 152
Brownies (*see also pages 142–187*)
Boo!! Brownies, 490
Brownie Sundaes For Kids, 428
Jumbo Jack-O'-Lantern Brownie, 486
No-Bake Fudgy Brownies, 280
Ornament Brownies, 520
Pumpkin Candy Brownies, 478
Quick No-Bake Brownies, 278
Skull & Cross Bones, 481
Sweets-for-the-Sweet Brownies, 464
Tombstone Brownies, 480
Brownie Sandwich Cookies, 438
Brownie Sundaes For Kids, 428
Brown Sugar Granola Cookies, 55
Brown Sugar Icing, 370
Buffalo Bill Brownies, 144
Bunch O' Balloons, 444
Butter Cookie Dough, 552
Butter Cookies, 232
Buttercream Frosting, 523
Butterfly Cookies, 236
Butter Pecan Crisps, 91
Butter Pretzel Cookies, 454
Butterscotch and Chocolate Bars, 126
Butterscotch Brownies, 176, 184
Butterscotch Chewy Cookies, 83
Butterscotch Chips
Butterscotch and Chocolate Bars, 126
Butterscotch Brownies, 176
Butterscotch Chewy Cookies, 83
Butterscotch Chip Drizzle, 83
Butterscotch Fruit Drops, 372
Butterscotch Walnut Crisps, 24
Cherry Butterscotch Bars, 112
Chewy Rocky Road Bars, 114
Chocolate Scotcheroos, 290

Butterscotch Chips (*continued*)
Choco-Scutterbotch, 324
No-Bake Butterscotch Haystacks, 282
Peanut Butter-Hop-Scotch Treats, 294
S'More Cookie Bars, 104
Butterscotch Fruit Drops, 372
Butterscotch Walnut Crisps, 24
Butter Toffee Chocolate Chip Crunch, 303
Buttery Almond Cutouts, 548

C
Cake Mix
Chocolate Candy Cookies, 304
Chocolate Caramel Pecan Squares, 161
Choco-Scutterbotch, 324
Cinnamon Crinkles Cookies, 73
Hanukkah Cookies, 533
Holiday Thumbprint Cookies, 518
Lemon Cookies, 38, 80
Orange Chess Bars, 140
Orange Pecan Gems, 34
Pinwheel Cookies, 188
Star Christmas Tree Cookies, 550
Candy
Argentinean Caramel-Filled Crescents, 390
Brownie Candy Cups, 158
Brown Sugar Granola Cookies, 55
Butter Toffee Chocolate Chip Crunch, 303
Canned Peanut Butter Candy Cookies, 80
Caramel Lizard Cookies, 458
Checkerboard Bars, 214
Chewy Fingers, 336
Chocolate Candy Cookies, 304
Chocolate Caramel Pecan Squares, 161
Chocolate-Dipped Cinnamon Thins, 208
Chocolate Mint Ravioli Cookies, 249
Chocolate Orange Macadamia Cookies, 377
Chocolate Peanutty Crumble Bars, 120

Candy (*continued*)
Chocolate Pinwheels, 250
Conversation Heart Cereal Treats, 462
Cookie Decorating Party, 466
Cookie Pizza, 425
Creepy Cookie Cauldrons, 482
Critters-in-Holes, 432
Dandy Candy Oatmeal Cookies, 58
Dark Chocolate Dreams, 304
Fudgy Raisin Pixies, 330
Happy Face Oatmeal Monsters, 436
Holiday Bits Cutout Cookies, 539
Luscious Cookie Drops made with Milky Way® Bars, 40
Minty Chocolate Shamrock Cookies, 470
Minty Chocolate Slice 'n' Bake Cookies, 470
Mrs. J's Chip Cookies, 72
Nestlé Crunch® Pizza Cookie, 432
Peanut Butter Jumbos, 36
Peanut Butter Jumbo Sandwiches, 36
Peanut Butter S'Mores, 424
Peanut Butter Surprise Cookies, 28
Peanut Pillows, 341
Peek-A-Boo Apricot Cookies, 250
Pumpkin Candy Brownies, 478
Pumpkin Face Surprise Cookies, 476
Scrumptious Minted Brownies, 142
Stained Glass Cookies, 508
Super Chocolate Cookies, 308
Sweets-for-the-Sweet Brownies, 464
Toffee Chunk Brownie Cookies, 298
Tombstone Brownies, 480
Candy Cane & Wreath Ornaments, 524
Candy Cane Cookies, 514
Candy Corn Cookies, 487
Canned Peanut Butter Candy Cookies, 80
Cappuccino Cookies, 207

Caramel Fudge Brownies, 156
Caramel Lace Chocolate Chip Cookies, 50
Caramel Lizard Cookies, 458
Caramel Oatmeal Chewies, 124
Cardamom-Chocolate Sandwiches, 221
Carrot & Spice Bars, 123
Carrot Oatmeal Cookies, 16
Cereal
Bran Fruit and Nut Cookies, 364
Brian's Buffalo Cookies, 14
Carrot & Spice Bars, 123
Chocolate Cereal Bars, 275
Chocolate Fruit Crispies, 280
Chocolate Orange Granola Cookies, 49
Chocolate Scotcheroos, 290
Choco-Scutterbotch, 324
Conversation Heart Cereal Treats, 462
Corn Flake Macaroons, 28
Creepy Cookie Cauldrons, 482
Crispy Chocolate Footballs, 492
Crispy Chocolate Logs, 290
Fruity Cookie Rings and Twists, 430
Ginger Pumpkin Face Cookies, 488
Mrs. J's Chip Cookies, 72
Monkey Bars, 284
No-Bake Cherry Crisps, 290
Original Rice Krispies Treats® Recipe, The, 292
Peanut Butter and Jelly Crispies, 108
Peanut Butter Crispy Treats, 281
Peanut Butter-Hop-Scotch Treats, 294
Prized Peanut Butter Crunch Cookie, 22
Championship Chocolate Chip Bars, 110
Checkerboard Bars, 214
Cheery Chocolate Animal Cookies, 296
Cheesecake Marble Brownies, 160
Cherries
Cherry Butterscotch Bars, 112
Cherry Cashew Cookies, 368
Cherry Thumbprint Cookies, 380

Cherries (*continued*)
Cherry White Chip Brownies, 166
Chewy Cherry Chocolate Chip Cookies, 360
Choco-Cherry Cookies Supreme, 310
Chocolate-Cherry Slice 'n' Bake Cookies, 216
Chocolate Covered Cherry Cookies, 341
Danish Cookie Rings, 406
Double Chocolate Cherry Cookies, 326
Frosted Maraschino Brownies, 146
Maraschino Cherry Cookies, 220
Maraschino Date Pinwheels, 220
Maraschino Thumbprint Cookies, 220
No-Bake Cherry Crisps, 290
Oatmeal Chocolate Cherry Bars, 134
Chewy Cherry Chocolate Chip Cookies, 360
Chewy Chocolate No-Bakes, 285
Chewy Choco-Peanut Pudgies, 68
Chewy Fingers, 336
Chewy Hazelnut Bars, 123
Chewy Rocky Road Bars, 114
Child's Choice, 434
Chippy Cheeseys, 138
Chipwiches, 293
Choco-Cherry Cookies Supreme, 310
Choco-Coco Pecan Crisps, 200
Chocolate, Bittersweet
Belgian Tuile Cookies, 416
Bittersweet Pecan Brownies with Caramel Sauce, 144
Chocolate-Flecked Pirouettes, 492
Chocolate-Gilded Danish Sugar Cones, 499
Chocolate Macadamia Bars, 128
Double-Dipped Hazelnut Crisps, 496
Raspberry-Filled Chocolate Ravioli, 494

Chocolate, German Sweet
Dreamy Chocolate Chip
Cookies, 310
German Chocolate Oatmeal
Cookies, 300

Chocolate, Semisweet
Almond Cheesecake Brownies,
153
Boo!! Brownies, 490
Butter Pecan Crisps, 91
Cheesecake Marble Brownies,
160
Chocolate and Peanut Butter
Hearts, 466
Chocolate Cookie Dough,
552
Chocolate Cookies, 254
Chocolate-Dipped Almond
Horns, 92
Chocolate Glaze, 160
Chocolate Leaves, 528
Chocolate Macaroons, 336
Chocolate Pinwheels, 250
Chocolate Pretzel Cookies,
437
Chocolate-Raspberry Kolacky,
328
Chocolate Reindeer, 542
Chocolate Snowflakes, 508
Chocolate-Topped Linzer
Cookies, 495
Coconutty "M&M's"® Brownies,
150
Danish Orange Cookies,
405
Divine Double Dark Brownies,
160
Double Chocolate Raspberry
Bars, 317
Florentine Cookies, 402
Irish Brownies, 154
Mexican Chocolate Macaroons,
384
Nathaniel's Jumble, 292
Orange Cappuccino Brownies,
167
Ornament Brownies, 520
Peanut Butter-Hop-Scotch
Treats, 294
Spiced Chocolate Pecan
Squares, 320
Sweet Leaf Wreath, 528
Tic-Tac-Toe Cookies, 204

Chocolate, Unsweetened
Brownie Fudge, 174
Caramel Fudge Brownies,
156
Chocolate-Coconut Cookies,
366
Chocolate Fudge Cookie
Cakes, 342
Chocolate Mint Sandwiches,
217
Chocolate-Orange Chip
Cookies, 308
Chocolate Pistachio Cookies,
306
Chocolate Spritz, 326
Chocolate Tassies, 502
Chocolate Thumbprints, 333
Cinnamon-Chocolate Cutouts,
254
Cream Cheese Swirled
Brownies, 148
Easy Chocolate Icing, 307
German Chocolate Brownies,
170
Nutty Clusters, 307
Toffee Chunk Brownie Cookies,
298
Triple Chocolate Pretzels, 340
Ultimate Rocky Road Cups,
443
Chocolate Candy Cookies, 304
Chocolate-Cherry Slice 'n' Bake
Cookies, 216

Chocolate Chips, Milk
Banana Chocolate Chip Softies,
371
Bananaramas, 358
Brownie Fudge, 174
Butter Toffee Chocolate Chip
Crunch, 303
Cardamom-Chocolate
Sandwiches, 221
Chocolate Chip Pecan Squares,
122
Chocolate Orange Macadamia
Cookies, 377
Choco-Scutterbotch, 324
Dandy Candy Oatmeal
Cookies, 58
Double-Dipped Chocolate
Peanut Butter Cookies, 503
Dreamy Chocolate Chip
Cookies, 310

Chocolate Chips, Milk (continued)
Elvis Would Have Loved These
Peanut Butter Cookies, 382
Fudge Topping, 174
Island Cookies, 48
Mocha Chips 'n' Bits, 46
Peanut Butter Cocoa Cookies,
302
Peanut Butter Crispy Treats,
281
Raspberry Fudge Brownies, 168
S'Mores on a Stick, 272

Chocolate Chips, Mint
Chocolate Mint Snow-Top
Cookies, 76
Chocolate Mint Sugar Cookie
Drops, 74
Double Chocolate Mint Chip
Cookies, 307
Fudgy Chocolate Mint Oatmeal
Squares, 318
Hershey®s Mint Chocolate
Cookies, 52
Mint Chocolate Pinwheels, 210
Moist and Minty Brownies, 170

Chocolate Chips, Semisweet
Almond Brownies, 175
Almond Double Chip Cookies,
49
Almond Fudge Cups, 502
Banana Chocolate Chip Bars,
106
Bird's Nest Cookies, 460
Black and White Cut-Outs,
252
Black & White Hearts, 224
Black and White Sandwiches,
252
Boo!! Brownies, 490
Brian's Buffalo Cookies, 14
Brownie Fudge, 174
Brownie Pie à la Mode, 152
Brown Sugar Granola Cookies,
55
Butterscotch and Chocolate
Bars, 126
Butterscotch Brownies, 176
Butter Toffee Chocolate Chip
Crunch, 303
Caramel Fudge Brownies, 156
Caramel Lace Chocolate Chip
Cookies, 50
Caramel Oatmeal Chewies, 124

Chocolate Chips, Semisweet
(*continued*)

Championship Chocolate Chip Bars, 110
Cheery Chocolate Animal Cookies, 296
Chewy Cherry Chocolate Chip Cookies, 360
Chewy Chocolate No-Bakes, 285
Chewy Choco-Peanut Pudgies, 68
Chewy Fingers, 336
Chewy Hazelnut Bars, 123
Chewy Rocky Road Bars, 114
Child's Choice, 434
Chippy Cheeseys, 138
Chocolate Almond Biscotti, 96
Chocolate & Peanut Butter Tweed Cookies, 208
Chocolate Biscotti Nuggets, 374
Chocolate Caramel Pecan Squares, 161
Chocolate Cereal Bars, 275
Chocolate Chip Cinnamon Crinkles, 78
Chocolate Chip Glaze, 258
Chocolate Chip Peanut Butter Swirl Cookies, 322
Chocolate Chip Walnut Bars, 132
Chocolate Chocolate Cookies, 44
Chocolate Chunk Cookies, 63
Chocolate Coating, 96
Chocolate-Coconut Toffee Delights, 300
Chocolate Covered Cherry Cookies, 341
Chocolate-Dipped Orange Logs, 500
Chocolate Filling, 414
Chocolate Fruit Crispies, 280
Chocolate Ganache, 162
Chocolate Gingerbread Boys and Girls, 264
Chocolate Haystacks, 282
Chocolate Hazelnut Cookie Drops, 46
Chocolate Marbled Blondies, 186
Chocolate Molasses Gems, 73
Chocolate Nut Bars, 536

Chocolate Chips, Semisweet
(*continued*)

Chocolate-Orange Chip Cookies, 308
Chocolate Orange Dreams, 52
Chocolate Orange Gems, 117
Chocolate Orange Granola Cookies, 49
Chocolate Pecan Pie Bars, 112
Chocolate Raspberry Streusel Squares, 111
Chocolate Scotcheroos, 290
Chocolate Thumbprints, 333
Chocolate Walnut Pie Bars, 312
Choco-Scutterbotch, 324
Cinnamon Nut Chocolate Spirals, 206
Coconutty "M&M's"® Brownies, 150
Colorful Blondies, 186
Colossal Cookie Sandwich, 477
Cookie Pizza, 425
Cranberry Cheese Bars, 107
Crayon Cookies, 428
Crispy Chocolate Footballs, 492
Crispy Chocolate Logs, 290
Date Fudge Cookies, 370
Decadent Blonde Brownies, 178
Dino-Mite Dinosaurs, 436
Double Chocolate Banana Cookies, 353
Double Chocolate Cherry Cookies, 326
Double Chocolate Chunk Cookies, 330
Double Chocolate Cranberry Chunkies, 356
Double Chocolate Fantasy Bars, 320
Double-Decker Confetti Brownies, 182
Double-Dipped Chocolate Peanut Butter Cookies, 503
Double-Dipped Hazelnut Crisps, 496
Double Fudge Brownie Bars, 147
Double Peanut Butter Supremes, 90
Dreamy Chocolate Chip Cookies, 310

Chocolate Chips, Semisweet
(*continued*)

Eggnog Crisps, 56
Festive Rugelach, 238
First Family's Chocolate Chip Oatmeal Cookies, The, 24
Fudge Sauce, 152
Fudge Topping, 174
Fudgy Chip Bars, 317
Fudgy Cookie Squares, 312
Ghostly Delights, 476
Giant Easter Egg Cookies, 474
Goblin Ice Cream Sandwiches, 477
Go Fish!, 452
Gold Mine Nuggets, 348
Hawaiian Drops, 17
Hershey's Soft & Chewy Cookies, 44
Honey Brownies, 156
Honey Chocolate Chippers, 48
Inside-Out Peanut Butter Cups, 94
Kickin' Brownies, 162
Lollipop Cookies, 538
Malted Dream Drops, 44
Marbled Mocha Drops, 54
Mini Chip Slice and Bake Cookies, 190
Mini Morsel Meringue Wreaths, 544
Minty Shortbread Squares, 102
Mrs. J's Chip Cookies, 72
Mocha Glaze, 340
Monster Cookies, 10
No-Bake Banana Peanut Butter Fudge Bars, 296
No-Bake Chocolate & Peanut Butter Cookies, 276
No-Bake Chocolate Oat Bars, 294
Nutty Chocolate Chunk Bars, 116
Oasis Date Bars, 128
Oatmeal Chocolate Cherry Bars, 134
Oatmeal Coconut Chocolate Chip Cookies, 20
Oatmeal Gorp Cookies, 350
Orange Cappuccino Brownies, 167
Patchwork Cream Cheese Cookies, 60

Chocolate Chips, Semisweet
(*continued*)
P.B. Swirls, 222
Peanut Butter and Chocolate Bars, 126
Peanut Butter and Chocolate Spirals, 212
Peanut Butter Bars, 286
Peanut Butter Chocolate Chip Cookies, 82
Peanut Butter Chocolate No-Bake Bars, 274
Peanut Butter Cut-Out Cookies, 258
Peanut Butter-Hop-Scotch Treats, 294
Peanut Butter Jumbos, 36
Peanut Butter Jumbo Sandwiches, 36
Peanut Chip Cookies, 14
Polish Honey Bars, 414
Polka Dot Macaroons, 50
Pumpkin & Chocolate Chip Cookies, 358
Rocky Road Bars, 318
Rocky Road Brownies, 168
Rocky Road Squares, 172
Santa's Chocolate Cookies, 532
Sharing Cookies, 477
S'More Cookie Bars, 104
S'More Snack Treats, 268
Spicy Rum Corn Crisps, 262
Super-Duper Chocolate Pecan Cookies, 66
Trick or Treat Ice Cream Sandwiches, 477
Triple Chipper Monsters, 54
Triple Chocolate Pretzels, 340
Ultimate Chippers, 302
Ultimate Rocky Road Cups, 443
Ultimate Rocky Road Squares, 443
Viennese Hazelnut Butter Thins, 394
Viennese Meringue Bars, 395
White Chocolate Brownies, 176
Whole Grain Chippers, 74
Yule Tree Namesakes, 516
Ultimate Rocky Road Squares, 443

Chocolate Crackles, 62
Chocolate-Dipped Cinnamon Thins, 208
Chocolate Filled Sandwich Cookies, 206
Chocolate Glaze, 175
Chocolate Madeleines, 416
Chocolate Mint Ravioli Cookies, 249
Chocolate Peanutty Crumble Bars, 120
Choco-Scutterbotch, 324
Christmas Cookie Pops, 515
Christmas Ornament Cookie Dough, 553
Christmas Spritz Cookies, 506
Christmas Tree Cookies, 540
Christmas Tree Ice Cream Sandwiches, 468
Chunky Butter Christmas Cookies, 530
Cinnamon-Apricot Tart Oatmeal Cookies, 348
Cinnamon-Chocolate Cutouts, 254
Cinnamon Crinkles Cookies, 73
Cinnamon Nut Chocolate Spirals, 206
Citrus Cream Bars, 288
Classic Anise Biscotti, 400
Classic Refrigerator Sugar Cookies, 218
Cocoa Almond Glaze, 216
Cocoa Brownie Cookie Bars, 118
Cocoa Crinkle Sandwiches, 327
Cocoa Fruit Balls, 270
Cocoa Gingerbread Cookies, 265
Coconut
Almond Rice Madeleines, 92
Bird's Nest Cookies, 460
Chewy Rocky Road Bars, 114
Choco-Coco Pecan Crisps, 200
Chocolate-Coconut Cookies, 366
Chocolate-Coconut Toffee Delights, 300
Chunky Butter Christmas Cookies, 530
Cocoa Fruit Balls, 270
Coconut Almond Bars, 127
Coconut Topping, 150
Coconutty "M&M's"® Brownies, 150

Coconut (*continued*)
Corn Flake Macaroons, 28
Date-Nut Macaroons, 378
Double Chocolate Fantasy Bars, 320
Double Fudge Brownie Bars, 147
Fruitcake Slices, 212
Fudgy Chip Bars, 317
German Chocolate Brownies, 170
German Chocolate Oatmeal Cookies, 300
Hawaiian Drops, 17
Holiday Wreath Cookies, 534
Homemade Coconut Macaroons, 37
Island Cookies, 48
Marvelous Macaroons, 381
Mocha Chips 'n' Bits, 46
No-Bake Cherry Crisps, 290
Oat & Dried Fruit Balls, 274
Oatmeal Coconut Chocolate Chip Cookies, 20
Orange Drop Cookies, 31
Pineapple Coconut Snowballs, 354
Polka Dot Macaroons, 50
Prized Peanut Butter Crunch Cookie, 22
Special Treat No-Bake Squares, 278
Sunflower Cookies, 22
Sunflower Cookies in Flowerpots, 242
Thumbprint Cookies, 84
Tombstone Brownies, 480
Tropical Coconut Squares, 140
Yule Tree Namesakes, 516
Coffin Cookies, 484
Colorful Blondies, 186
Colorful Sugar Cutouts, 234
Colossal Cookie Sandwich, 477
Conversation Heart Cereal Treats, 462
Cookie Bowl and Cookie Fruit, 228
Cookie Canvases, 437
Cookie Cups, 422
Cookie Decorating Party, 466
Cookie Filling, 97
Cookie Glaze, 555
Cookie Gobblers, 491

Cookie Mix
Almond Hearts, 230
Banana Chocolate Chip
Cookies, 367
Christmas Tree Cookies, 540
Easter Egg Cookies, 472
Fudgy Cookie Squares, 312
Glazed Sugar Cookies, 520
Orange Drop Cookies, 31
Peanut Butter Handprints,
426
Peanut Butter Jewels, 84
Special Chocolate Chip
Sandwiches, 42
Cookie Pizza, 425
Cookie Pops, 420
Cool Cookie-wiches, 270
Corn Flake Macaroons, 28
Cranberry
Apple-Cranberry Crescent
Cookies, 356
Cranberry Cheese Bars, 107
Double Chocolate Cranberry
Chunkies, 356
Fruit & Nut Biscotti Toasts,
362
Lemon-Cranberry Bars, 100
Crayon Cookies, 428
Cream Cheese
Almond Cream Cheese
Cookies, 200
Apricot Cream Cheese Drops,
30
Cheesecake Marble Brownies,
160
Chippy Cheeseys, 138
Chocolate Macadamia Bars,
128
Chocolate Tassies, 502
Cranberry Cheese Bars, 107
Cream Cheese Cutout Cookies,
236
Cream Cheese Pastry, 504
Cream Cheese Swirled
Brownies, 148
Double Peanut Butter
Supremes, 90
Double Peanut Squares, 284
Festive Rugelach, 238
Fruit and Cookie Pizza, 376
Orange Chess Bars, 140
Patchwork Cream Cheese
Cookies, 60

Cream Cheese (*continued*)
Rich 'n' Creamy Brownie Bars,
164
Strawberry Hearts, 464
Creamy Cocoa Icing, 146
Creamy Decorator's Frosting,
554
Creamy Mint Filling, 217
Creamy Vanilla Frosting, 122
Creepy Cookie Cauldrons, 482
Crispy Chocolate Footballs, 492
Crispy Chocolate Logs, 290
Critters-in-Holes, 432
Cut-Out Sugar Cookies, 240
Czech Bear Paws, 392

D
Dandy Candy Oatmeal Cookies,
58
Danish Cookie Rings, 406
Danish Lemon-Filled Spice
Cookies, 404
Danish Orange Cookies, 405
Dark Chocolate Dreams, 304
Dates
Apple Date Nut Blondies, 178
Chocolate Biscotti Nuggets,
374
Date Fudge Cookies, 370
Date-Nut Cookies, 372
Date Nut Macaroons, 378
Date Pinwheel Cookies, 222
Maraschino Date Pinwheels,
220
Oasis Date Bars, 128
Oatmeal-Date Cookies, 344
Decadent Blonde Brownies, 178
Decorator Frosting, 554
Delightful Peanut Butter
Marshmallow Cookie Bars,
136
Diamond Backs, 448
Dino-Mite Dinosaurs, 436
Divine Double Dark Brownies,
160
Domino Cookies, 446
Domino® Sugar Cookies, 199
Double Almond Butter Cookies,
98
Double Chocolate Banana
Cookies, 353
Double Chocolate Cherry
Cookies, 326

Double Chocolate Chunk
Cookies, 330
Double Chocolate Cranberry
Chunkies, 356
Double Chocolate Fantasy Bars,
320
Double Chocolate Mint Chip
Cookies, 307
Double Chocolate Raspberry Bars,
317
Double-Decker Confetti Brownies,
182
Double-Dipped Chocolate Peanut
Butter Cookies, 503
Double-Dipped Hazelnut Crisps,
496
Double Drizzle, 126
Double Fudge Brownie Bars, 147
Double Lemon Delights, 26
Double Peanut Butter Supremes,
90
Double Peanut Squares, 284
Double "Topped" Brownies, 172
Dreamy Chocolate Chip Cookies,
310
Dried Plum Purée, 24, 60, 63,
342
Drop Cookies (*see also pages
10–57*)
Banana Chocolate Chip
Cookies, 367
Banana Chocolate Chip Softies,
371
Bananaramas, 358
Bolivian Almond Cookies, 388
Bran Fruit and Nut Cookies,
364
Breakfast Cookies, 352
Butterscotch Fruit Drops, 372
Butter Toffee Chocolate Chip
Crunch, 303
Cherry Cashew Cookies, 368
Chewy Cherry Chocolate Chip
Cookies, 360
Chewy Chocolate No-Bakes,
285
Choco-Cherry Cookies
Supreme, 310
Chocolate Candy Cookies, 304
Chocolate-Coconut Cookies,
366
Chocolate-Coconut Toffee
Delights, 300

Drop Cookies (*continued*)
Chocolate Haystacks, 282
Chocolate-Orange Chip Cookies, 308
Chocolate Pistachio Cookies, 306
Chunky Butter Christmas Cookies, 530
Cinnamon-Apricot Tart Oatmeal Cookies, 348
Dark Chocolate Dreams, 304
Date Fudge Cookies, 370
Date-Nut Cookies, 372
Date-Nut Macaroons, 378
Double Chocolate Banana Cookies, 353
Double Chocolate Cranberry Chunkies, 356
Double Chocolate Mint Chip Cookies, 307
Dreamy Chocolate Chip Cookies, 310
Elvis Would Have Loved These Peanut Butter Cookies, 382
Family Favorite Oatmeal Cookies, 346
Florentine Cookies, 402
Fruitcake Cookies, 366
Fruity Crunchy Sunflower Cookies, 353
Fudgey Cocoa No-Bake Treats, 275
German Chocolate Oatmeal Cookies, 300
Goblin Ice Cream Sandwiches, 477
Gold Mine Nuggets, 348
Harvest Pumpkin Cookies, 362
Marvelous Macaroons, 381
No-Bake Butterscotch Haystacks, 282
No-Bake Chocolate & Peanut Butter Cookies, 276
No-Bake Peanutty Chocolate Drops, 288
Nutty Clusters, 307
Oatmeal-Date Cookies, 344
Peach Oatmeal Cookies, 352
Peanut Butter & Banana Cookies, 376
Peanut Butter Chip Pineapple Drops, 359

Drop Cookies (*continued*)
Peanut Butter Cocoa Cookies, 302
Pecan Florentines, 498
Pineapple Coconut Snowballs, 354
Pumpkin & Chocolate Chip Cookies, 358
Pumpkin White Chocolate Drops, 364
Rum Fruitcake Cookies, 354
Super Chocolate Cookies, 308
Toffee Chunk Brownie Cookies, 298
Trick or Treat Ice Cream Sandwiches, 477
Ultimate Chippers, 302
Dutch Chocolate Meringues, 410
Dutch St. Nicolas Cookies, 410

E
Easter Egg Cookies, 472
Easy Apricot Oatmeal Bars, 118
Easy Chocolate Icing, 307
Easy Linzer Bars, 392
Easy Microwave Brownies, 154
Eggnog Crisps, 56
Egg Yolk Paint, 557
Elvis Would Have Loved These Peanut Butter Cookies, 382
English Thumbprint Cookies, 398

F
Fabulous Blonde Brownies, 181
Fabulous Fruit Bars, 137
Family Favorite Oatmeal Cookies, 346
Festive Butter Cookies, 532
Festive Easter Cookies, 472
Festive Lebkuchen, 265
Festive Rugelach, 238
Fig Bars, 380
Fillings
Apricot Filling, 367
Chocolate Filling, 414
Cookie Filling, 97
Creamy Mint Filling, 217
Lemon Filling, 404
Marshmallow Filling, 484
Finnish Nut Logs, 418
Finnish Spice Cookies, 418
Fireside Cookie, 534

First Family's Chocolate Chip Oatmeal Cookies, The, 24
Florentine Cookies, 402
Fluffy White Frosting, 478
Frosted Easter Cut-Outs, 471
Frosted Maraschino Brownies, 146
Frosted Sugar Cookies, 231
Frostings, Glazes & Icings
Almond Frosting, 236
Almond Icing, 153
Brown Sugar Icing, 370
Buttercream Frosting, 523
Chocolate Chip Glaze, 258
Chocolate Coating, 96
Chocolate Glaze, 160, 175
Cocoa Almond Glaze, 216
Cookie Glaze, 555
Creamy Cocoa Icing, 146
Creamy Decorator's Frosting, 554
Creamy Vanilla Frosting, 122
Decorator Frosting, 554
Double Drizzle, 126
Easy Chocolate Icing, 307
Egg Yolk Paint, 557
Fluffy White Frosting, 478
Fudge Frosting, 555
Glaze, 492
Irish Cream Frosting, 154
Lemonade Royal Icing, 556
Lemon Glaze, 128, 397, 408
Lemon Royal Icing, 556
Meringue Powder Royal Icing, 557
Mocha Glaze, 340
Orange Buttercream Frosting, 486
Orange Icing, 480
Ornamental Frosting, 554
Peanut Buttery Frosting, 442
Powdered Sugar Glaze, 37
Powdered Sugar Icing, 488, 556
Royal Icing, 556
Satiny Chocolate Glaze, 316
Vanilla Frosting, 231
Vanilla Glaze, 117
Vanilla Icing, 234
White Chip Drizzle, 166
White Decorator Frosting, 555
Fruit and Cookie Pizza, 376
Fruit and Nut Bars, 114
Fruit & Nut Biscotti Toasts, 362

Fruitcake Cookies, 366
Fruitcake Slices, 212
Fruited Oat Thumbprints, 86
Fruity Cookie Rings and Twists, 430
Fruity Crunchy Sunflower Cookies, 353
Fudge Frosting, 555
Fudge Sauce, 152
Fudge Topping, 174
Fudgey Cocoa No-Bake Treats, 275
Fudgy Chip Bars, 317
Fudgy Chocolate Mint Oatmeal Squares, 318
Fudgy Cookie Squares, 312
Fudgy Peanut Butter Jiffy Cookies, 25
Fudgy Raisin Pixies, 330
Funny Face Cookies, 293

G
Gaiety Pastel Cookies, 64
German Chocolate Brownies, 170
German Chocolate Oatmeal Cookies, 300
Ghostly Delights, 476
Giant Easter Egg Cookies, 474
Gingerbread Apple Bars, 110
Gingerbread Bears, 266
Gingerbread Cookie Dough, 553
Gingerbread Cookies, 260, 262
Gingerbread Farm Animals in Corral, 450
Gingerbread Folks, 522
Gingerbread House Dough, 553
Gingerbread People, 510, 544
Gingerbread Teddies, 91
Ginger Pumpkin Face Cookies, 488
Ginger Snap Oats, 26
Gingersnaps, 12
Give Thanks Cornucopias, 490
Glaze, 492
Glazed Oatmeal Raisin Coffee Cookies, 18
Glazed Sugar Cookies, 520
Goblin Ice Cream Sandwiches, 477
Go Fish!, 452
Gold Mine Nuggets, 348

Grand Old Flag Cookie, 474
Grape-Filled Cookies, 378
Grape Jack-O'-Lantern Cookies, 480

H
Hanukkah Coin Cookies, 523
Hanukkah Cookies, 533
Hanukkah Fried Cruller Bows, 515
Happy Face Oatmeal Monsters, 436
Harvest Pumpkin Cookies, 362
Have-a-Heart Bear Garland, 545
Hawaiian Drops, 17
Hazelnuts
    Ali's Oatmeal Cookies, 349
    Chewy Hazelnut Bars, 123
    Chocolate Hazelnut Cookie Drops, 46
    Chocolate Nut Bars, 536
    Chocolate-Topped Linzer Cookies, 495
    Czech Bear Paws, 392
    Double-Dipped Hazelnut Crisps, 496
    Hazelnut Biscotti, 404
    Viennese Hazelnut Butter Thins, 394
Heavenly Hash Brownies, 146
Hermits, 34
Hershey's Mint Chocolate Cookies, 52
Hershey's Soft & Chewy Cookies, 44
Holiday Bits Cutout Cookies, 539
Holiday Chocolate Shortbread Cookies, 512
Holiday Peppermint Slices, 530
Holiday Sugar Cookies, 522
Holiday Thumbprint Cookies, 518
Holiday Wreath Cookies, 534
Homemade Coconut Macaroons, 37
Honey Brownies, 156
Honey Carrot Cookies, 67
Honey Chocolate Chippers, 48
Honey Ginger Snaps, 70
Hot 'n' Nutty Cookies, 62
Hot Dog Cookies, 452

I
Ice Cream
    Brownie Pie à la Mode, 152
    Brownie Sundaes For Kids, 428
    Chipwiches, 293
    Christmas Tree Ice Cream Sandwiches, 468
    Colossal Cookie Sandwich, 477
    Goblin Ice Cream Sandwiches, 477
    Ice Cream Cookie Sandwiches, 194
    Old-Fashioned Ice Cream Sandwiches, 334
    Oreo® Brownie Treats, 150
    Patriotic Ice Cream Sandwiches, 468
    Peanut Butter Ice Cream Triangles, 256
    Pumpkin Ice Cream Sandwiches, 468
    Shamrock Ice Cream Sandwiches, 468
    Sunflower Cookies in Flowerpots, 242
    Trick or Treat Ice Cream Sandwiches, 477
    Valentine Ice Cream Sandwiches, 468
Ice Cream Cookies, 194
Ice Skates, 434
Inside-Out Peanut Butter Cups, 94
Irish Brownies, 154
Irish Cream Frosting, 154
Irresistible Peanut Butter Cookies, 32
Island Cookies, 48

J
Jam Thumbprint Gems, 86
Jingle Jumbles, 533
Jumbo Jack-O'-Lantern Brownie, 486

K
Kaleidoscope Cookies, 199
Kentucky Bourbon Pecan Tarts, 504
Kickin' Brownies, 162
Kitty Cookies, 426
Kolacky, 248

L

Lady Bugs, 455
Layered Chocolate Cheesecake
   Squares, 108
Lebkuchen Jewels, 397
Lemon
   Danish Lemon-Filled Spice
      Cookies, 404
   Double Lemon Delights, 26
   Lemonade Royal Icing, 556
   Lemon Bars, 134
   Lemon Cookies, 38, 80
   Lemon-Cranberry Bars, 100
   Lemon Filling, 404
   Lemon Glaze, 128, 397, 408
   Lemon Royal Icing, 556
   Lemony Butter Cookies, 226
   Lip-Smacking Lemon Cookies,
      190
   Luscious Lemon Bars, 116
   Mini Lemon Sandwich
      Cookies, 248
Letters of the Alphabet, 444
Linzer Cookies, 97
Linzer Sandwich Cookies, 232
Lip-Smacking Lemon Cookies,
   190
Lollipop Cookies, 538
Lollipop Sugar Cookies, 430
Low Fat Molasses Jumbles, 60
Luscious Cookie Drops made with
   Milky Way® Bars, 40
Luscious Lemon Bars, 116

M

Macadamia Nuts
   Chocolate Macadamia Bars, 128
   Chocolate Orange Macadamia
      Cookies, 377
   Chunky Butter Christmas
      Cookies, 530
   Decadent Blonde Brownies,
      178
   Dreamy Chocolate Chip
      Cookies, 310
   Hawaiian Drops, 17
   Island Cookies, 48
   Tropical Coconut Squares, 140
Malted Dream Drops, 44
Maraschino Cherry Cookies, 220
Maraschino Date Pinwheels, 220
Maraschino Thumbprint Cookies,
   220

Marble Brownies, 158
Marbled Mocha Drops, 54
Marbled Peanut Butter Brownies,
   167
Marshmallow Creme
   Brownie Fudge, 174
   Chocolate Cereal Bars, 275
   Coffin Cookies, 484
   Fluffy White Frosting, 478
   Fudge Topping, 174
   Ghostly Delights, 476
   Marshmallow Filling, 484
   Spooky Ghost Cookies,
      478
   Toffee Creme Sandwich
      Cookies, 282
Marshmallows
   Chewy Chocolate No-Bakes,
      285
   Chewy Rocky Road Bars, 114
   Child's Choice, 434
   Chocolate Fruit Crispies, 280
   Conversation Heart Cereal
      Treats, 462
   Crispy Chocolate Logs, 290
   Delightful Peanut Butter
      Marshmallow Cookie Bars,
      136
   Elvis Would Have Loved These
      Peanut Butter Cookies, 382
   Fudge Frosting, 555
   Heavenly Hash Brownies, 146
   Marshmallow Sandwich
      Cookies, 324
   Monkey Bars, 284
   Oreo® Decadence Bars, 136
   Original Rice Krispies Treats®
      Recipe, The, 292
   Peanut Butter Crispy Treats,
      281
   Peanut Butter S'Mores, 424
   Rocky Road Bars, 318
   Rocky Road Brownies, 168
   Rocky Road Squares, 172
   S'More Cookie Bars, 104
   S'More Snack Treats, 268
   S'Mores on a Stick, 272
   Sweets-for-the-Sweet Brownies,
      464
   Ultimate Rocky Road Cups,
      443
   Ultimate Rocky Road Squares,
      443

Marvelous Macaroons, 381
Meringue Powder Royal Icing,
   557
Mexican Chocolate Macaroons,
   384
Mincemeat Pastries, 360
Mini Chip Slice and Bake
   Cookies, 190
Mini Lemon Sandwich Cookies,
   248
Mini Morsel Meringue Wreaths,
   544
Mint
   Chocolate Mint Ravioli
      Cookies, 249
   Chocolate Mint Sandwiches,
      217
   Chocolate Mint Snow-Top
      Cookies, 76
   Chocolate Mint Sugar Cookie
      Drops, 74
   Creamy Mint Filling, 217
   Double Chocolate Mint Chip
      Cookies, 307
   Fudgy Chocolate Mint Oatmeal
      Squares, 318
   Hershey®s Mint Chocolate
      Cookies, 52
   Holiday Peppermint Slices, 530
   Mint Chocolate Pinwheels, 210
   Minty Chocolate Shamrock
      Cookies, 470
   Minty Chocolate Slice 'n' Bake
      Cookies, 470
   Minty Shortbread Squares, 102
   Mocha Mint Crisps, 70
   Mocha Mint Sugar, 70
   Moist and Minty Brownies, 170
   Scrumptious Minted Brownies,
      142
Mrs. J's Chip Cookies, 72
Mocha Chips 'n' Bits, 46
Mocha Glaze, 340
Mocha Mint Crisps, 70
Mocha Mint Sugar, 70
Mocha Pecan Pinwheels, 194
Moist and Minty Brownies, 170
Moist Pumpkin Cookies, 37
Molded Scotch Shortbread, 388
Monkey Bars, 284
Monster Cookies, 10
Moons and Stars, 230
Moravian Spice Crisps, 391

N

Name Jewelry, 454
Nathaniel's Jumble, 292
Nestlé Crunch® Pizza Cookie, 432
No-Bake Banana Peanut Butter
  Fudge Bars, 296
No-Bake Butterscotch Haystacks,
  282
No-Bake Cherry Crisps, 290
No-Bake Chocolate & Peanut
  Butter Cookies, 276
No-Bake Chocolate Oat Bars, 294
No-Bake Cookies (*see also pages*
  268–297)
  Conversation Heart Cereal
    Treats, 462
  Cookie Decorating Party, 466
  Cookie Gobblers, 491
  Crispy Chocolate Footballs, 492
  Give Thanks Cornucopias, 490
  Layered Chocolate Cheesecake
    Squares, 108
No-Bake Fudgy Brownies, 280
No-Bake Gingersnap Balls, 270
No-Bake Peanutty Chocolate
  Drops, 288
No-Bake Pineapple Marmalade
  Squares, 272
Norwegian Almond Squares, 409
Norwegian Pepper Cookies, 408
Norwegian Wreaths, 409
Nuts (*see also* **Almond**;
  **Hazelnuts; Macadamia
  Nuts; Peanuts; Pecans;
  Walnuts**)
  Butterscotch Chewy Cookies,
    83
  Caramel Oatmeal Chewies, 124
  Championship Chocolate Chip
    Bars, 110
  Cherry Cashew Cookies, 368
  Chewy Rocky Road Bars, 114
  Chocolate Pistachio Cookies,
    306
  Fruit and Nut Bars, 114
  Fudgy Chocolate Mint Oatmeal
    Squares, 318
  Lemon Cookies, 80
  Marbled Mocha Drops, 54
  Nutty Clusters, 307
  Quick No-Bake Brownies, 278
  Rocky Road Brownies, 168
  Rum Fruitcake Cookies, 354

Nuts (*continued*)
  Sour Cream Brownies, 174
  White Chip Meringue Dessert
    Bars, 130
  Wild Rice Applesauce Bars,
    124
Nutty Chocolate Chunk Bars, 116
Nutty Clusters, 307
Nutty Spice Cookies, 260
Nutty Sunflower Cookies, 98

O

Oasis Date Bars, 128
Oats
  Absolutely Wonderful Pecan
    Bars, 111
  Ali's Oatmeal Cookies, 349
  Apple Crumb Squares, 130
  Awesome Apricot Oatmeal
    Bars, 120
  Banana Chocolate Chip Bars,
    106
  Breakfast Cookies, 352
  Brian's Buffalo Cookies, 14
  Butterscotch Walnut Crisps, 24
  Caramel Oatmeal Chewies, 124
  Carrot Oatmeal Cookies, 16
  Chewy Chocolate No-Bakes,
    285
  Chewy Fingers, 336
  Child's Choice, 434
  Choco-Cherry Cookies
    Supreme, 310
  Chocolate Biscotti Nuggets, 374
  Chocolate Peanutty Crumble
    Bars, 120
  Chocolate Raspberry Streusel
    Squares, 111
  Chunky Butter Christmas
    Cookies, 530
  Cinnamon-Apricot Tart
    Oatmeal Cookies, 348
  Cranberry Cheese Bars, 107
  Dandy Candy Oatmeal
    Cookies, 58
  Double Chocolate Banana
    Cookies, 353
  Easy Apricot Oatmeal Bars, 118
  Family Favorite Oatmeal
    Cookies, 346
  First Family's Chocolate Chip
    Oatmeal Cookies, The, 24
  Fruit and Nut Bars, 114

Oats (*continued*)
  Fruited Oat Thumbprints,
    86
  Fruity Crunchy Sunflower
    Cookies, 353
  Fudgey Cocoa No-Bake Treats,
    275
  Fudgy Chocolate Mint Oatmeal
    Squares, 318
  Fudgy Peanut Butter Jiffy
    Cookies, 25
  German Chocolate Oatmeal
    Cookies, 300
  Ginger Snap Oats, 26
  Glazed Oatmeal Raisin Coffee
    Cookies, 18
  Gold Mine Nuggets, 348
  Happy Face Oatmeal Monsters,
    436
  Hawaiian Drops, 17
  Honey Chocolate Chippers,
    48
  Mint Chocolate Pinwheels,
    210
  Monkey Bars, 284
  Monster Cookies, 10
  No Bake Banana Peanut Butter
    Fudge Bars, 296
  No-Bake Chocolate Oat Bars,
    294
  No-Bake Peanutty Chocolate
    Drops, 288
  Nutty Chocolate Chunk Bars,
    116
  Oat & Dried Fruit Balls, 274
  Oatmeal Brownies, 164
  Oatmeal Chocolate Cherry
    Bars, 134
  Oatmeal Coconut Chocolate
    Chip Cookies, 20
  Oatmeal Cookies, 12
  Oatmeal-Date Cookies, 344
  Oatmeal Gorp Cookies, 350
  Oatmeal Raisin Cookies, 25
  Oatmeal Snowballs, 76
  Outlandish Oatmeal Bars, 102
  Peach Oatmeal Cookies, 352
  Peanut Butter Chocolate
    No-Bake Bars, 274
  Peanut Butter Jumbos, 36
  Peanut Butter Jumbo
    Sandwiches, 36
  Peanut Chip Cookies, 14

Oats *(continued)*
    Prized Peanut Butter Crunch Cookie, 22
    Raisin Spice Drops, 18
    Roasted Honey Nut Sandwich Cookies, 97
    Sunflower Cookies, 22
    Thumbprint Cookies, 84
    Tri-Layer Chocolate Oatmeal Bars, 314
    White Chip Apricot Oatmeal Cookies, 350
    Whole Grain Chippers, 74
Old-Fashioned Ice Cream Sandwiches, 334
Old World Pfeffernüsse Cookies, 397
Orange
    Chocolate-Dipped Orange Logs, 500
    Chocolate Filled Sandwich Cookies, 206
    Chocolate-Orange Chip Cookies, 308
    Chocolate Orange Dreams, 52
    Chocolate Orange Gems, 117
    Chocolate Orange Granola Cookies, 49
    Chocolate Orange Macadamia Cookies, 377
    Danish Orange Cookies, 405
    Orange-Almond Sables, 244
    Orange Cappuccino Brownies, 167
    Orange Chess Bars, 140
    Orange Drop Cookies, 31
    Orange Icing, 480
    Orange Marmalade Cookies, 40
    Orange Pecan Gems, 34
    Orange Pecan Refrigerator Cookies, 206
    Peanut Butter Orange Blossoms, 64
Orange Buttercream Frosting, 486
Oreo® Brownie Treats, 150
Oreo® Decadence Bars, 136
Original Rice Krispies Treats® Recipe, The, 292
Ornamental Frosting, 554
Ornament Brownies, 520
Outlandish Oatmeal Bars, 102

P
Party Peanut Butter Cookies, 192
Patchwork Cream Cheese Cookies, 60
Patriotic Ice Cream Sandwiches, 468
P. B. Graham Snackers, 285
P.B. Swirls, 222
Peach Oatmeal Cookies, 352
Peanut Butter *(see also* **Peanut Butter Chips**)
    Bananaramas, 358
    Breakfast Cookies, 352
    Canned Peanut Butter Candy Cookies, 80
    Chewy Choco-Peanut Pudgies, 68
    Chocolate and Peanut Butter Hearts, 466
    Chocolate Chip Peanut Butter Swirl Cookies, 322
    Chocolate Scotcheroos, 290
    Cookie Filling, 97
    Dandy Candy Oatmeal Cookies, 58
    Delightful Peanut Butter Marshmallow Cookie Bars, 136
    Double-Dipped Chocolate Peanut Butter Cookies, 503
    Double Peanut Butter Supremes, 90
    Double Peanut Squares, 284
    Elvis Would Have Loved These Peanut Butter Cookies, 382
    Fudgy Peanut Butter Jiffy Cookies, 25
    Hot 'n' Nutty Cookies, 62
    Inside-Out Peanut Butter Cups, 94
    Irresistible Peanut Butter Cookies, 32
    Marbled Peanut Butter Brownies, 167
    Monster Cookies, 10
    Nathaniel's Jumble, 292
    No-Bake Banana Peanut Butter Fudge Bars, 296
    No-Bake Cherry Crisps, 290
    No-Bake Peanutty Chocolate Drops, 288
    Nutty Chocolate Chunk Bars, 116

Peanut Butter *(continued)*
    Party Peanut Butter Cookies, 192
    P. B. Graham Snackers, 285
    P.B. Swirls, 222
    Peanut Butter & Banana Cookies, 376
    Peanut Butter and Jelly Crispies, 108
    Peanut Butter and Jelly Sandwich Cookies, 202
    Peanut Butter and Jelly Sandwich Surprises, 259
    Peanut Butter and Jelly Thumbprints, 88
    Peanut Butter Bars, 286
    Peanut Butter Chipwiches, 293
    Peanut Butter Chocolate Chip Cookies, 82
    Peanut Butter Chocolate No-Bake Bars, 274
    Peanut Butter Cocoa Cookies, 302
    Peanut Butter Cookies, 63
    Peanut Butter Crunchies, 78
    Peanut Butter Cut-Outs, 518
    Peanut Butter Handprints, 426
    Peanut Butter-Hop-Scotch Treats, 294
    Peanut Butter Ice Cream Triangles, 256
    Peanut Butter Jewels, 84
    Peanut Butter Jumbos, 36
    Peanut Butter Jumbo Sandwiches, 36
    Peanut Butter Orange Blossoms, 64
    Peanut Butter S'Mores, 424
    Peanut Butter Sugar Cookies, 255
    Peanut Butter Surprise Cookies, 28
    Peanut Butter Thumbprints, 87
    Peanut Buttery Frosting, 442
    Peanut Chip Cookies, 14
    Peanut Pillows, 341
    Peanuts, 442
    Prized Peanut Butter Crunch Cookie, 22
    Roasted Honey Nut Sandwich Cookies, 97

Peanut Butter Chips
Cheery Chocolate Animal Cookies, 296
Child's Choice, 434
Chocolate & Peanut Butter Tweed Cookies, 208
Double Fudge Brownie Bars, 147
Elvis Would Have Loved These Peanut Butter Cookies, 382
No-Bake Chocolate & Peanut Butter Cookies, 276
Peanut Butter and Chocolate Bars, 126
Peanut Butter and Chocolate Spirals, 212
Peanut Butter Bars, 286
Peanut Butter Chip Pineapple Drops, 359
Peanut Butter Critter Cookies, 438
Peanut Butter Crunchies, 78
Peanut Butter Cut-Out Cookies, 258
Reese's® Cookies, 42
Peanut Chip Cookies, 14
Peanuts
Bananaramas, 358
Chewy Choco-Peanut Pudgies, 68
Double Peanut Squares, 284
No-Bake Peanutty Chocolate Drops, 288
Nutty Chocolate Chunk Bars, 116
Peanut Butter Bars, 286
Peanuts, 442
Prized Peanut Butter Crunch Cookie, 22
Super Chocolate Cookies, 308
Ultimate Rocky Road Cups, 443
Ultimate Rocky Road Squares, 443
Pear Blondies, 180
Pecans
Absolutely Wonderful Pecan Bars, 111
Apple Date Nut Blondies, 178
Bittersweet Pecan Brownies with Caramel Sauce, 144
Butter Pecan Crisps, 91
Butter Toffee Chocolate Chip Crunch, 303

Pecans *(continued)*
Caramel Fudge Brownies, 156
Choco-Coco Pecan Crisps, 200
Chocolate Caramel Pecan Squares, 161
Chocolate Chip Pecan Squares, 122
Chocolate-Coconut Cookies, 366
Chocolate-Dipped Orange Logs, 500
Chocolate Filled Sandwich Cookies, 206
Chocolate Orange Gems, 117
Chocolate Pecan Pie Bars, 112
Chocolate Tassies, 502
Coconut Topping, 150
Coconutty "M&M's"® Brownies, 150
Corn Flake Macaroons, 28
Dark Chocolate Dreams, 304
Date-Nut Macaroons, 378
Eggnog Crisps, 56
Elvis Would Have Loved These Peanut Butter Cookies, 382
English Thumbprint Cookies, 398
Fruited Oat Thumbprints, 86
German Chocolate Brownies, 170
German Chocolate Oatmeal Cookies, 300
Giant Easter Egg Cookies, 474
Ginger Pumpkin Face Cookies, 488
Harvest Pumpkin Cookies, 362
Honey Chocolate Chippers, 48
Kentucky Bourbon Pecan Tarts, 504
Mocha Chips 'n' Bits, 46
Mocha Pecan Pinwheels, 194
Orange Pecan Gems, 34
Orange Pecan Refrigerator Cookies, 206
Pecan Florentines, 498
Pecan Pie Bars, 112
Pecan Praline Cookies, 72
Pecan Toffee Filled Ravioli Cookies, 234
Raspberry Pecan Thumbprints, 88
Raspberry Vanilla Nut Bars, 126
Snowball Cookies, 82

Pecans *(continued)*
Spiced Chocolate Pecan Squares, 320
Strawberry Pecan Jumbles, 132
Super-Duper Chocolate Pecan Cookies, 66
White Chocolate Biggies, 32
Peek-A-Boo Apricot Cookies, 250
Peppersass Cookies, 192
Pineapple
Banana Split Bars, 122
Fruit and Cookie Pizza, 376
Gold Mine Nuggets, 348
Marvelous Macaroons, 381
No-Bake Pineapple Marmalade Squares, 272
Peanut Butter Chip Pineapple Drops, 359
Pineapple Coconut Snowballs, 354
Pinecone Cookies, 542
Pinwheel Cookies, 188
Playing Card Cookies, 241
Polish Honey Bars, 414
Polka Dot Macaroons, 50
Powdered Sugar Cookies, 36
Powdered Sugar Glaze, 37
Powdered Sugar Icing, 488, 556
Prized Peanut Butter Crunch Cookie, 22
Pudding Drop Cookies, 56
Pumpkin
Harvest Pumpkin Cookies, 362
Moist Pumpkin Cookies, 37
Pumpkin & Chocolate Chip Cookies, 358
Pumpkin White Chocolate Drops, 364
Pumpkin Candy Brownies, 478
Pumpkin Face Surprise Cookies, 476
Pumpkin Ice Cream Sandwiches, 468
Purchased Cookie Dough
Black Cat Cookies, 488
Bunch O' Balloons, 444
Christmas Cookie Pops, 515
Coffin Cookies, 484
Cookie Canvases, 437
Cookie Cups, 422
Cookie Pizza, 425
Cookie Pops, 420
Creepy Cookie Cauldrons, 482

Purchased Cookie Dough
(continued)
Critters-in-Holes, 432
Domino Cookies, 446
Fireside Cookie, 534
Fruit and Cookie Pizza, 376
Fruity Cookie Rings and Twists, 430
Ghostly Delights, 476
Grand Old Flag Cookie, 474
Holiday Peppermint Slices, 530
Holiday Wreath Cookies, 534
Kaleidoscope Cookies, 199
Kitty Cookies, 426
Nutty Sunflower Cookies, 98
Peanut Butter and Chocolate Spirals, 212
Peanut Butter and Jelly Sandwich Cookies, 202
Playing Card Cookies, 241
Sandwich Cookies, 235
Shapers, 196
Smushy Cookies, 422
Snowmen, 512
Strawberry Hearts, 464
Thousand Legged Worm, The, 448
Under the Sea, 446
Puzzle Cookie, 440

Q
Quick No-Bake Brownies, 278

R
Rainbows, 198
Raisins
Breakfast Cookies, 352
Chewy Chocolate No-Bakes, 285
Fudgy Raisin Pixies, 330
Ginger Snap Oats, 26
Glazed Oatmeal Raisin Coffee Cookies, 18
Hermits, 34
Jingle Jumbles, 533
Lebkuchen Jewels, 397
Mocha Chips 'n' Bits, 46
Moist Pumpkin Cookies, 37
Oatmeal Gorp Cookies, 350
Oatmeal Raisin Cookies, 25
Peach Oatmeal Cookies, 352

Raisins *(continued)*
Raisin Spice Drops, 18
Rum Fruitcake Cookies, 354
Super Chocolate Cookies, 308
Raspberry
Chocolate-Raspberry Kolacky, 328
Chocolate Raspberry Streusel Squares, 111
Double Chocolate Raspberry Bars, 317
Kickin' Brownies, 162
Linzer Cookies, 97
Outlandish Oatmeal Bars, 102
Raspberry-Filled Chocolate Ravioli, 494
Raspberry Fudge Brownies, 168
Raspberry Pecan Thumbprints, 88
Raspberry Pyramids, 241
Raspberry Vanilla Nut Bars, 126
Thumbprint Cookies, 84
Viennese Meringue Bars, 395
Yuletide Linzer Bars, 511
Reese's® Cookies, 42
Refrigerator Cookies *(see also pages 188–223)*
Hanukkah Coin Cookies, 523
Holiday Peppermint Slices, 530
Minty Chocolate Slice 'n' Bake Cookies, 470
Refrigerator Cookies, 193
Thousand Legged Worm, The, 448
Viennese Hazelnut Butter Thins, 394
Rich 'n' Creamy Brownie Bars, 164
Roasted Honey Nut Sandwich Cookies, 97
Rocky Road Bars, 318
Rocky Road Brownies, 168
Rocky Road Squares, 172
Rolled Cookies *(see also pages 224–267)*
Angels, 538
Apple-Cranberry Crescent Cookies, 356
Apricot-Filled Pastries, 367
Argentinean Caramel-Filled Crescents, 390

Rolled Cookies *(continued)*
Bat Cookies, 487
Biscochitos, 386
Black Cat Cookies, 488
Buttery Almond Cutouts, 548
Candy Corn Cookies, 487
Caramel Lizard Cookies, 458
Chocolate and Peanut Butter Hearts, 466
Chocolate-Raspberry Kolacky, 328
Chocolate Reindeer, 542
Chocolate Snowflakes, 508
Chocolate-Topped Linzer Cookies, 495
Christmas Cookie Pops, 515
Christmas Tree Ice Cream Sandwiches, 468
Coffin Cookies, 484
Cookie Canvases, 437
Cookie Pops, 420
Danish Orange Cookies, 405
Diamond Backs, 448
Dino-Mite Dinosaurs, 436
Domino Cookies, 446
Double-Dipped Hazelnut Crisps, 496
Dutch St. Nicolas Cookies, 410
Festive Butter Cookies, 532
Festive Easter Cookies, 472
Finnish Spice Cookies, 418
Frosted Easter Cut-Outs, 471
Gingerbread Farm Animals in Corral, 450
Gingerbread Folks, 522
Gingerbread People, 510, 544
Glazed Sugar Cookies, 520
Go Fish!, 452
Grape-Filled Cookies, 378
Grape Jack-O'-Lantern Cookies, 480
Hanukkah Cookies, 533
Have-a-Heart Bear Garland, 545
Holiday Bits Cutout Cookies, 539
Holiday Chocolate Shortbread Cookies, 512
Holiday Sugar Cookies, 522
Holiday Wreath Cookies, 534
Ice Skates, 434

Rolled Cookies (*continued*)
Kitty Cookies, 426
Letters of the Alphabet, 444
Lollipop Cookies, 538
Mincemeat Pastries, 360
Moravian Spice Crisps, 391
Name Jewelry, 454
Old-Fashioned Ice Cream
  Sandwiches, 334
Patriotic Ice Cream
  Sandwiches, 468
Peanut Butter Critter Cookies,
  438
Peanut Butter Cut-Outs,
  518
Peanut Butter Handprints,
  426
Pinecone Cookies, 542
Pumpkin Face Surprise
  Cookies, 476
Pumpkin Ice Cream
  Sandwiches, 468
Raspberry-Filled Chocolate
  Ravioli, 494
Rugelach, 546
Shamrock Ice Cream
  Sandwiches, 468
Smushy Cookies, 422
Spicy Gingerbread Cookies,
  516
Spooky Ghost Cookies, 478
Stained Glass Cookies, 508
Star Christmas Tree Cookies,
  550
Star Cookie Christmas Tree,
  526
Storefront Place Cards,
  540
Strawberry Hearts, 464
Sunshine Butter Cookies,
  456
Swedish Sandwich Cookies,
  412
Sweet Leaf Wreath, 528
Valentine Ice Cream
  Sandwiches, 468
Valentine's Day Cookie Cards,
  465
Yule Tree Namesakes, 516
Royal Icing, 556
Rugelach, 546
Rum Fruitcake Cookies,
  354

S
Sachertorte Squares, 316
Sandwich Cookies
Berry Treasures, 226
Black and White Sandwiches,
  252
Brownie Sandwich Cookies,
  438
Cardamom-Chocolate
  Sandwiches, 221
Chipwiches, 293
Chocolate Filled Sandwich
  Cookies, 206
Chocolate Mint Sandwiches,
  217
Chocolate-Topped Linzer
  Cookies, 495
Christmas Tree Ice Cream
  Sandwiches, 468
Cocoa Crinkle Sandwiches,
  327
Coffin Cookies, 484
Colossal Cookie Sandwich,
  477
Cool Cookie-wiches, 270
Danish Lemon-Filled Spice
  Cookies, 404
Goblin Ice Cream Sandwiches,
  477
Ice Cream Cookie Sandwiches,
  194
Linzer Cookies, 97
Linzer Sandwich Cookies,
  232
Marshmallow Sandwich
  Cookies, 324
Mini Lemon Sandwich
  Cookies, 248
Old-Fashioned Ice Cream
  Sandwiches, 334
Patriotic Ice Cream
  Sandwiches, 468
Peanut Butter and Jelly
  Sandwich Cookies, 202
Peanut Butter and Jelly
  Sandwich Surprises, 259
Peanut Butter Chipwiches,
  293
Peanut Butter Ice Cream
  Triangles, 256
Peanut Butter Jumbo
  Sandwiches, 36
Peanut Butter S'Mores, 424

Sandwich Cookies (*continued*)
Pumpkin Ice Cream
  Sandwiches, 468
Roasted Honey Nut Sandwich
  Cookies, 97
Sandwich Cookies, 235
Shamrock Ice Cream
  Sandwiches, 468
S'Mores on a Stick, 272
Smushy Cookies, 422
Special Chocolate Chip
  Sandwiches, 42
Swedish Sandwich Cookies,
  412
Thousand Legged Worm, The,
  448
Toffee Creme Sandwich
  Cookies, 282
Trick or Treat Ice Cream
  Sandwiches, 477
Valentine Ice Cream
  Sandwiches, 468
Santa's Chocolate Cookies, 532
Satiny Chocolate Glaze, 316
Scrumptious Minted Brownies,
  142
Shamrock Ice Cream Sandwiches,
  468
Shaped Cookies (*see also pages*
  58–99)
Ali's Oatmeal Cookies, 349
Almond Fudge Cups, 502
Apricot Biscotti, 368
Banana Sandies, 377
Baseball Caps, 460
Belgian Tuile Cookies, 416
Bird's Nest Cookies, 460
Brandy Lace Cookies, 494
Brownie Sandwich Cookies,
  438
Bunch O' Balloons, 444
Butter Pretzel Cookies, 454
Candy Cane & Wreath
  Ornaments, 524
Candy Cane Cookies, 514
Cherry Thumbprint Cookies,
  380
Chewy Fingers, 336
Child's Choice, 434
Chocolate Biscotti Nuggets,
  374
Chocolate Chip Peanut Butter
  Swirl Cookies, 322

Shaped Cookies (*continued*)
Chocolate Covered Cherry Cookies, 341
Chocolate-Dipped Orange Logs, 500
Chocolate-Flecked Pirouettes, 492
Chocolate Fudge Cookie Cakes, 342
Chocolate-Gilded Danish Sugar Cones, 499
Chocolate Macaroons, 336
Chocolate Madeleines, 416
Chocolate Orange Macadamia Cookies, 377
Chocolate Pretzel Cookies, 437
Chocolate Spritz, 326
Chocolate Tassies, 502
Chocolate Thumbprints, 333
Choco-Scutterbotch, 324
Christmas Spritz Cookies, 506
Christmas Tree Cookies, 540
Classic Anise Biscotti, 400
Cocoa Crinkle Sandwiches, 327
Cocoa Fruit Balls, 270
Cookie Cups, 422
Crayon Cookies, 428
Creepy Cookie Cauldrons, 482
Crispy Chocolate Footballs, 492
Critters-in-Holes, 432
Czech Bear Paws, 392
Danish Cookie Rings, 406
Danish Lemon-Filled Spice Cookies, 404
Double Chocolate Cherry Cookies, 326
Double Chocolate Chunk Cookies, 330
Double-Dipped Chocolate Peanut Butter Cookies, 503
Dutch Chocolate Meringues, 410
Easter Egg Cookies, 472
Easy Linzer Bars, 392
English Thumbprint Cookies, 398
Finnish Nut Logs, 418
Fruit & Nut Biscotti Toasts, 362
Fruity Cookie Rings and Twists, 430

Shaped Cookies (*continued*)
Fudgy Raisin Pixies, 330
Ghostly Delights, 476
Giant Easter Egg Cookies, 474
Ginger Pumpkin Face Cookies, 488
Hanukkah Fried Cruller Bows, 515
Happy Face Oatmeal Monsters, 436
Hazelnut Biscotti, 404
Holiday Thumbprint Cookies, 518
Hot Dog Cookies, 452
Jingle Jumbles, 533
Kentucky Bourbon Pecan Tarts, 504
Lady Bugs, 455
Lollipop Sugar Cookies, 430
Maraschino Thumbprint Cookies, 220
Mexican Chocolate Macaroons, 384
Mini Morsel Meringue Wreaths, 544
Minty Chocolate Shamrock Cookies, 470
Molded Scotch Shortbread, 388
No-Bake Cherry Crisps, 290
No-Bake Gingersnap Balls, 270
Norwegian Pepper Cookies, 408
Norwegian Wreaths, 409
Oat & Dried Fruit Balls, 274
Oatmeal Gorp Cookies, 350
Old World Pfeffernüsse Cookies, 397
P. B. Graham Snackers, 285
Peanut Butter Crispy Treats, 281
Peanut Butter S'Mores, 424
Peanut Pillows, 341
Peanuts, 442
Santa's Chocolate Cookies, 532
Snowmen, 512
Spanish Churros, 386
Surprise Cookies, 338
Swiss Mocha Treats, 332
Triple Chocolate Pretzels, 340
Two-Toned Spritz Cookies, 498
Ultimate Rocky Road Cups, 443

Shaped Cookies (*continued*)
Welsh Tea Cakes, 398
White Chip Apricot Oatmeal Cookies, 350
White Chocolate Chunk Cookies, 330
Shapers, 196
Sharing Cookies, 477
Skull & Cross Bones, 481
Slice 'n' Bake Ginger Wafers, 196
S'More Cookie Bars, 104
S'More Snack Treats, 268
S'Mores on a Stick, 272
Smushy Cookies, 422
Snowball Cookies, 82
Snowmen, 512
Soft Molasses Spice Cookies, 38
Soft Spicy Molasses Cookies, 77
Sour Cream Brownies, 174
Spanish Churros, 386
Special Chocolate Chip Sandwiches, 42
Special Treat No-Bake Squares, 278
Spiced Chocolate Pecan Squares, 320
Spiced Wafers, 211
Spicy Gingerbread Cookies, 516
Spicy Ginger Molasses Cookies, 41
Spicy Rum Corn Crisps, 262
Spooky Ghost Cookies, 478
Stained Glass Cookies, 508
Star Christmas Tree Cookies, 550
Star Cookie Christmas Tree, 526
Storefront Place Cards, 540
Strawberry Hearts, 464
Strawberry Pecan Jumbles, 132
Sugar Cookie Dough, 378
Sugar Cookies, 246
Sunflower Cookies in Flowerpots, 242
Sunflower Seeds
Fruity Crunchy Sunflower Cookies, 353
Nutty Sunflower Cookies, 98
Sunflower Cookies, 22
Whole Grain Chippers, 74
Sunshine Butter Cookies, 456
Super Chocolate Cookies, 308
Super-Duper Chocolate Pecan Cookies, 66
Surprise Cookies, 338

Swedish Sandwich Cookies, 412
Sweet Leaf Wreath, 528
Sweets-for-the-Sweet Brownies, 464
Swiss Mocha Treats, 332

T
Thousand Legged Worm, The, 448
Thumbprint Cookies, 84
Tic-Tac-Toe Cookies, 204
Toffee Bits
  Blonde Brickle Brownies, 180
  Chocolate-Coconut Toffee Delights, 300
  Fabulous Blonde Brownies, 181
  Toffee Creme Sandwich Cookies, 282
Toffee Chunk Brownie Cookies, 298
Toffee Creme Sandwich Cookies, 282
Tombstone Brownies, 480
Toppings
  Coconut Topping, 150
  Fudge Topping, 174
Trick or Treat Ice Cream Sandwiches, 477
Tri-Layer Chocolate Oatmeal Bars, 314
Triple Chipper Monsters, 54
Triple Chocolate Pretzels, 340
Tropical Coconut Squares, 140
Two-Toned Spritz Cookies, 498

U
Ultimate Chippers, 302
Ultimate Rocky Road Cups, 443
Ultimate Rocky Road Squares, 443
Under the Sea, 446

V
Valentine Ice Cream Sandwiches, 468
Valentine's Day Cookie Cards, 465
Vanilla Frosting, 231
Vanilla Glaze, 117
Vanilla Icing, 234
Viennese Hazelnut Butter Thins, 394
Viennese Meringue Bars, 395

W
Walnuts
  Baklava, 396
  Brandy Nut Cookies, 66
  Bran Fruit and Nut Cookies, 364
  Brownie Fudge, 174
  Butterscotch Brownies, 184
  Butterscotch Walnut Crisps, 24
  Caramel Lizard Cookies, 458
  Cherry Thumbprint Cookies, 380
  Chippy Cheeseys, 138
  Chocolate Chip Walnut Bars, 132
  Chocolate Nut Bars, 536
  Chocolate Walnut Pie Bars, 312
  Cinnamon Nut Chocolate Spirals, 206
  Colorful Blondies, 186
  Date-Nut Cookies, 372
  Divine Double Dark Brownies, 160
  Double Chocolate Fantasy Bars, 320
  Fruit & Nut Biscotti Toasts, 362
  Fudge Topping, 174
  Fudgy Cookie Squares, 312
  Heavenly Hash Brownies, 146
  Hermits, 34
  Honey Brownies, 156
  Lebkuchen Jewels, 397
  Malted Dream Drops, 44
  Mrs. J's Chip Cookies, 72
  Nutty Spice Cookies, 260
  Oatmeal Gorp Cookies, 350
  Oreo® Decadence Bars, 136
  Powdered Sugar Cookies, 36
  Rocky Road Bars, 318
  Rocky Road Squares, 172
  Rugelach, 546
  Walnut Meringues, 30
Welsh Tea Cakes, 398
White Chip Apricot Oatmeal Cookies, 350
White Chip Drizzle, 166
White Chip Meringue Dessert Bars, 130
White Chocolate (*see also* **White Chocolate Chips**)
  Black and White Cut-Outs, 252
  Black and White Sandwiches, 252

White Chocolate (*continued*)
  Chocolate Leaves, 528
  Double-Dipped Hazelnut Crisps, 496
  Peanut Butter Sugar Cookies, 255
  Sweet Leaf Wreath, 528
  Triple Chocolate Pretzels, 340
  White Chocolate & Almond Brownies, 184
  White Chocolate Brownies, 176
White Chocolate Chips
  Ali's Oatmeal Cookies, 349
  Almond Double Chip Cookies, 49
  Cherry Cashew Cookies, 368
  Cherry White Chip Brownies, 166
  Chunky Butter Christmas Cookies, 530
  Dark Chocolate Dreams, 304
  Fabulous Blonde Brownies, 181
  Grand Old Flag Cookie, 474
  Holiday Chocolate Shortbread Cookies, 512
  Kickin' Brownies, 162
  Oreo® Decadence Bars, 136
  Outlandish Oatmeal Bars, 102
  Pumpkin White Chocolate Drops, 364
  Raspberry Vanilla Nut Bars, 126
  Ultimate Chippers, 302
  White Chip Apricot Oatmeal Cookies, 350
  White Chip Drizzle, 166
  White Chip Meringue Dessert Bars, 130
  White Chocolate Biggies, 32
  White Chocolate Chunk Cookies, 330
  White Ganache, 162
White Decorator Frosting, 555
White Ganache, 162
Whole Grain Chippers, 74
Wild Rice Applesauce Bars, 124

Y
Yuletide Linzer Bars, 511
Yule Tree Namesakes, 516

METRIC CONVERSION CHART

VOLUME MEASUREMENTS (dry)

1/8 teaspoon = 0.5 mL
1/4 teaspoon = 1 mL
1/2 teaspoon = 2 mL
3/4 teaspoon = 4 mL
1 teaspoon = 5 mL
1 tablespoon = 15 mL
2 tablespoons = 30 mL
1/4 cup = 60 mL
1/3 cup = 75 mL
1/2 cup = 125 mL
2/3 cup = 150 mL
3/4 cup = 175 mL
1 cup = 250 mL
2 cups = 1 pint = 500 mL
3 cups = 750 mL
4 cups = 1 quart = 1 L

VOLUME MEASUREMENTS (fluid)

1 fluid ounce (2 tablespoons) = 30 mL
4 fluid ounces (1/2 cup) = 125 mL
8 fluid ounces (1 cup) = 250 mL
12 fluid ounces (1 1/2 cups) = 375 mL
16 fluid ounces (2 cups) = 500 mL

WEIGHTS (mass)

1/2 ounce = 15 g
1 ounce = 30 g
3 ounces = 90 g
4 ounces = 120 g
8 ounces = 225 g
10 ounces = 285 g
12 ounces = 360 g
16 ounces = 1 pound = 450 g

DIMENSIONS

1/16 inch = 2 mm
1/8 inch = 3 mm
1/4 inch = 6 mm
1/2 inch = 1.5 cm
3/4 inch = 2 cm
1 inch = 2.5 cm

OVEN TEMPERATURES

250°F = 120°C
275°F = 140°C
300°F = 150°C
325°F = 160°C
350°F = 180°C
375°F = 190°C
400°F = 200°C
425°F = 220°C
450°F = 230°C

BAKING PAN SIZES

Utensil	Size in Inches/Quarts	Metric Volume	Size in Centimeters
Baking or Cake Pan (square or rectangular)	8 × 8 × 2	2 L	20 × 20 × 5
	9 × 9 × 2	2.5 L	23 × 23 × 5
	12 × 8 × 2	3 L	30 × 20 × 5
	13 × 9 × 2	3.5 L	33 × 23 × 5
Loaf Pan	8 × 4 × 3	1.5 L	20 × 10 × 7
	9 × 5 × 3	2 L	23 × 13 × 7
Round Layer Cake Pan	8 × 1½	1.2 L	20 × 4
	9 × 1½	1.5 L	23 × 4
Pie Plate	8 × 1¼	750 mL	20 × 3
	9 × 1¼	1 L	23 × 3
Baking Dish or Casserole	1 quart	1 L	—
	1½ quart	1.5 L	—
	2 quart	2 L	—